YOUR

ASTROLOGY

GUIDE

2007

YOUR ASTROLOGY GUIDE

2007

RICK LEVINE & JEFF JAWER

STERLING PUBLISHING CO., INC.
NEW YORK

Library of Congress Cataloging-in-Publication Data Available

2 4 6 8 10 9 7 5 3 1

Published by Sterling Publishing Co., Inc.
387 Park Avenue South, New York, NY 10016

Distributed in Canada by Sterling Publishing
c/o Canadian Manda Group, 165 Dufferin Street
Toronto, Ontario, Canada M6K 3H6
Distributed in the United Kingdom by GMC Distribution Services
Castle Place, 166 High Street, Lewes, East Sussex, England BN7 1XU
Distributed in Australia by Capricorn Link (Australia) Pty. Ltd.
P.O. Box 704, Windsor, NSW 2756, Australia

Sterling ISBN-13: 978-1-4027-4162-3
        ISBN-10: 1-4027-4162-6

For information about custom editions, special sales, premium and
corporate purchases, please contact Sterling Special Sales
Department at 800-805-5489 or specialsales@sterlingpub.com.

Jacket and interior design by 3+Co., New York

TABLE OF CONTENTS

ACKNOWLEDGMENTS

This book has two writers and many midwives. Paul O'Brien, our agent, our friend, and the creative genius behind Tarot.com, is first among them. His vision opened the way. Gail Goldberg has tirelessly worked as our in-house editor, clarifying concepts, untangling sentences, and sharpening words. She has performed this and many other invaluable services since the three of us started StarIQ.com in 1999. We are grateful to Michael Fragnito, editorial director at Sterling Publishing, for his vision of what this book could be, his tireless support for the project, and his trust in our work. Barbara Berger, Sterling's supervising editor on this book, has guided the project with Taurean persistence and good humor under the pressure of a very tight deadline. We thank Loretta Mowat for her careful reading and refinement of the text. We are thankful to Charles Nurnberg, Jeremy Nurnberg, Jason Prince, Karen Nelson, Elizabeth Mihaltse, Rena Kornbluth, Kelly Galvin, and Chantal Flavien at Sterling. Thanks go to Bob Wietrak and Jules Herbert at Barnes & Noble, and whoever said yes in the beginning. For the wonderful design, we offer thanks to 3+Co and Asami Matsushima; and thanks for the art and ideas from Jessica Abel and the rest of the Tarot.com team. Thanks, as well, to Tara Gimmer and company for the cover photo.

Rick: Thank you, Jeff, for being such a great writing partner. I appreciate how you combine your talents with such a commitment to excellence. And a personal thanks to Gail for her unwavering vision of what this book could be, for participating with fiery compassion, and for believing that we can make a difference.

Jeff: Danick, Laura and Lyana, you are the people I love living with every day. Thanks for being so creative. Thank you so much, Rick. You showed up with wit and wisdom, and love. The love of astrology that we share and the love of humanity that we also share. We are brothers in astrology. Hey, I love ya man.

INTRODUCTION

YOU ARE THE STAR OF YOUR LIFE

The more you learn about yourself, the better able you are to wisely use the energies in your life. For more than 3,000 years, astrology has been the sharpest tool in the box for describing the human condition. Used by virtually every culture on the planet, astrology continues to illuminate the link between individual lives and planetary energies and cycles.

The purpose of this book is to help you take a more active role in creating your present and, by extension, your future by showing you how to apply astrology's ancient wisdom to today's world. Our aim is to facilitate your day-to-day journey by revealing the turns in the road of life and describing the best ways for you to navigate them.

Astrology's highest use is to enable you to gain knowledge of yourself and perspective of your surroundings. It is common to go through life feeling blown about by forces beyond your control. Astrology can help you see the changing tides within and outside you. By allowing you to recognize the shifting patterns of mood and circumstance at work in your life, it helps you to stay centered and empowered. As you follow along in this book, you will grow to better understand your own needs as well as the challenges and opportunities you encounter.

In *Your Astrology Guide: 2007*, we describe the patterns of your life as they are reflected in the great cycles of the sky above. We do not simply predict events, although we give examples of them throughout the book. Rather, we are reporting the planetary energies—the cosmic weather in which you are living—so that you understand these conditions and know how to use them effectively. The power, though, is not in the stars, of course, but in your mind, your heart, and the choices that you make every day. Regardless of how strongly you are buffeted by the winds of change or bored by stagnation, your mind has many ways to see any situation. Learning about the energies of the Sun, Moon, and planets will both sharpen and widen your perspective. Thousands of years of human experience have proven astrology's value; our purpose is to show you how to enrich your life with it.

The language of astrology gives the gift of awareness, not a rigid set of rules. It works best when blended with common sense, intuition, and self-trust. This is your life, and no one knows how to live it as well as you. Take what you need from this book and leave the rest. Think of the planets as setting the stage for the year ahead, but it is you who are the writer, director, and star of your life.

ABOUT US

We were practicing astrology independently when we joined forces in 1999 to launch StarIQ.com. Our shared interest in making intelligent astrology available to as wide an audience as possible led to StarIQ, as well as a relationship with Tarot.com and the creation of this book. While we have continued to work independently as well, our collaboration has been a success and a joy as we've made our shared goals a reality, and we plan for it to continue long into the future.

RICK LEVINE

I've always wanted to know the answer to unanswerable questions. As a youth, I studied science and mathematics because I believed that they offered concrete answers to complex questions. I learned about the amazing conceptual breakthroughs made by modern man due to the developing technologies that allowed us to peer into the deep reaches of outer space and also into the tiniest subatomic realms. But as I encountered imaginary numbers in higher mathematics, along with the uncertainty of quantum physics, I began to realize that our modern sciences, as advanced as they are, would never satisfy my longing to understand my own individual life or the world around me. I learned that our basic assumptions of time and space fall apart at both ends of the spectrum—the very big and the very small. I became obsessed with solving the puzzle of the cosmos and discovering its hidden secrets.

As a college student at the State University of New York at Stony Brook in the late sixties, I studied psychology and philosophy, and participated in those times as a student of the universe. I read voraciously and found myself more interested in the unexplainable than in what was already known. As a psychology student, I was less concerned with running rats through mazes than with understanding how the human mind worked. I naturally gravitated to the depth psychologies of Sigmund

Freud and Carl Jung. Additionally, the life-altering information coming from the humanistic psychology movement presented me with an academic framework with which to better understand how human potential could be further developed. I knew then and there that human consciousness was expanding and that I wanted to be a part of this evolutionary process. In this environment, I first encountered the writings of R. Buckminster Fuller. He appealed to my scientific mind-set, but blessed me with new ways to view my world. In the early 20th century, Albert Einstein had clearly demonstrated that energy is simply the transformation of light into mass and mass into light—but that was just an intellectual concept to me.

Bucky Fuller, however, went on to establish a scientific language to describe the relationships between mass and light, particles and waves. His incredible geodesic domes are merely representations of what he discovered. I began to understand that what we can see is but a faint shadow of the knowable universe. I learned that everything vibrates. There are no things out there, just different frequencies of vibration—many of which are so fast that they give us the illusion of a solid world. Even something as basic as the color green or red is merely a label for certain frequencies of light vibration.

This was my world when I first discovered that astrology was more than just a parlor game. Already acquainted with the signs of the zodiac, I knew that I was an impulsive Aries, a pioneer, and an independent thinker. I noticed how my friends and professors fit their sun signs. Then, I was astounded to learn that Jung's *Analytical Psychology of Four Types* was based upon the astrological elements of fire, earth, air, and water. And I was amazed to discover that great scientists, such as Johannes Kepler—the Father of Modern Astronomy—was himself a renowned astrologer. The more I read, the more I realized that I had to become an astrologer myself. I needed to know more about astrology and how it works. Now, nearly 40 years later, I know more about astrology—a lot more—with still so much to learn.

Astronomers have their telescopes, enabling them to see things *tele*, or far away. Biologists have microscopes to see what is *micro*, or small. We astrologers have the horoscope, extending our view of the *horo*, or hour. For more than three decades, I have calculated horoscopes—first by hand, later with computer—and have observed the movement of time in its relationship to the heavenly bodies. I have watched the timing of the transitions in my own life and in the lives of my family, friends, and clients. I have been privileged to see, again and again, the unquestionable harmony between the planetary cycles and our individual lives.

I am proud to be a part of an astrological renaissance. Astrology has become increasingly popular because it fulfills our need to know that we are a part of the cosmos, even though modern culture has separated us from nature. It is not man versus nature. We are nature—and our survival as a species may depend on humanity relearning this concept. I take my role as an astrologer very seriously as I use what I have learned to help people expand their awareness, offer them choices, and educate them on how to cooperate with the cosmos instead of fighting against it. I contributed to reestablishing astrology in academia as a founding trustee of the Kepler College of Astrological Arts and Science (Lynnwood, Washington). I maintain an active role in the international community of astrologers as a member of the International Society for Astrological Research (ISAR), the National Council for Geocosmic Research (NCGR), the Association for Astrological Networking (AFAN), and the Organization for Professional Astrology (OPA).

In 1999, I partnered with Jeff Jawer to create StarIQ.com, an innovative astrology Web site. Since then Jeff and I have been working together to raise the quality of astrology available to the public, first through StarIQ.com and, later, through our partnership with Tarot.com. It continues to be a real privilege and thrill to work with Jeff and to now offer the fruits of our labors to you.

JEFF JAWER

I've been a professional astrologer for more than 30 years. Astrology is my career, my art, and my passion. The excitement that I felt when I first began is still with me today. My first encounter with real astrology was in 1973 when I was going through a painful marriage breakup. All I knew about astrology at the time was that I was a Taurus, which didn't sound very exciting to me. "The reliable Bull is steadfast and consistent," I read. "Not given to risk taking or dramatic self-expression, Taurus prefers peace and comfort above all." Boring. Fortunately, I quickly discovered that there was more to astrology—much more.

An amateur astrologer read my chart for me on my 27th birthday, and I was hooked. I bought the biggest astrology book I could find, began intensive study, found a teacher, and started reading charts for people. Within a few months, I changed my major at the University of Massachusetts at Amherst from communications to astrology under the Bachelor's Degree with Individual Concentration program. There were no astrology classes at the university, but I was able to combine courses in astronomy, mythology, and psychology, with two special seminars on the history of astrology to graduate in 1975 with a B.A. in the history and science of astrology. In 1976, I moved to Atlanta, Georgia, the only city in the United States with a mandatory examination for professional astrologers. I passed it, as well as the American Federation of Astrologers' professional exam, and served twice as president of the Metro Atlanta Astrological Society and as chairman of the City of Atlanta Board of Astrology Examiners.

For several years, I was the corporate astrologer for International Horizons, Inc., a company that sold courses on English as a second language in Japan. The owner had me research the founding dates of banks he was interested in acquiring so that I could advise him based on their charts. Later, he and I created Astro, the world's first electronic astrology calculator. In 1982, I was one of the founding members of the Association for Astrological Networking (AFAN), an organization that plays a major role in defending the legal rights of astrologers. AFAN joined with two other organizations, the International Society for Astrological Research (ISAR) and the National Council for Geocosmic Research (NCGR), to present the first United Astrology Congress (UAC) in 1986. UAC conferences were the largest astrology events in North America for more than a decade. I served on the UAC board for four years.

I began teaching at astrology conferences in the late 1970s, and there I met many of the world's leading astrologers, many of whom are my friends to this day. I have taught at dozens of conferences and local astrology groups around the United States. I have lectured at the World Astrology Congress in Switzerland four times, as well as in Holland, France, England, Belgium, Spain, Germany, Canada, Brazil, and Australia. However, the most important time for me personally was the two years I spent teaching for the Network of Humanistic Astrologers based in France. There I met my wife Danick in 1988. Her double-Pisces sensitivity has added to my work and my life immeasurably.

Counseling individual clients is the core of my professional life, as it is for most astrologers, but writing about astrology has always been important to me. I've written hundreds of articles for journals, magazines, books, Web sites, and newspapers ranging from the monthly calendar for *The Mountain Astrologer* to sun sign forecasts for *CosmoGIRL!* magazine. Currently, I write "LoveScopes" (a weekly sun-sign romance horoscope), the "New Moon Report," and other specialized material for Tarot.com, AOL, and StarIQ.com. I've also been employed in the astrology industry as director of public relations for Matrix Software and vice president of Astro Communication Services, two of the field's oldest companies. Rick and I founded StarIQ in 1999, the beginning of our professional collaboration. We produce a daily audio forecast called *Planet Pulse*, and *StarTalkers*, a weekly radio broadcast. Early in my career, I contributed to pioneering the field of experiential astrology, also called astrodrama. It's been a great adventure to combine theater games, psychodrama, Gestalt techniques, visualization, movement, art, and sound to bring astrology to life in workshops around the world. To experience astrology through emotions and in the body, rather than by the intellect alone, can ground one's understanding of the planets and signs in a very useful way.

Think about Venus, for example. She's the goddess of love, the planet of beauty and attraction. What if you need more sweetness in your life? Imagine how Venus walks. Now, get up and do your own Venus walk to the kitchen. Feel in balance and graceful as your feet embrace the floor and as your hips sway. Be Venus; invite her presence to you. Glide, slide, and be suave; you're so beautiful. Remember this walk if you're feeling unloved and, the next thing you know, Venus will arrive. Each planet is different, of course, according to its unique character. You'll learn another dance from responsible Saturn—a slower march across the floor, head upright, shoulders back—steady and straight, but not too stiff. Try that one for self-discipline.

Astrology describes the energy of time, how the quality of Tuesday afternoon is different than Wednesday morning. Seeing when and where patterns arise in your life gives you clearer vision and a better understanding of the choices that are open to you. The rich language of astrology makes a cosmic connection that empowers you and rewards the rest of us as you fulfill more and more of your potential.

ASTROLOGY'S ORIGINS

Astrology is as old as time. It began when events in the sky were first observed to affect events here on earth. The turning of day into night, the rising and falling of the tides with the Moon's cycles, and the changing seasons were watched by humanity long before written history, even at the very dawn of human civilization. Ancient Egyptians tracked the star Sirius to predict the flooding of the Nile River, which was essential to their agriculture. Babylonians, Mayans, Hindus, Chinese, and virtually every other group of people on the planet have practiced a form of astrology. Part science, part religion, calendar, mythology, and almanac, astrology remains the most comprehensive and coherent system for understanding life on this planet.

In the 2nd century AD, Claudius Ptolemy codified astrology, based on its origins in Mesopotamia and development in classical Greece. Astrology was an essential part of the scientific and philosophical evolution that gave birth to Western civilization. Another major path of development occurred in India, where Vedic astrology remains an integral part of the culture. Astrology was originally used to address collective concerns such as climate and warfare. It was rarely applied to the lives of individuals, except for rulers whose fates were considered tied to those of the nation. Astrology is still applied to public concerns, especially in the burgeoning field of financial astrology, which is used for stock-market forecasting. Today, however, the vast majority of astrology is applied to the lives of individuals through personal consultations, computer-generated reports, horoscope columns, books, and the Internet.

The importance of astrology has risen, fallen, and risen again in the Western world. Through the Renaissance and the Elizabethan period, astrology was part and parcel of daily life. Shakespeare's numerous references to it are just one indicator of its wide acceptance and popularity in his time. However, the rationalism of René Descartes and his followers took hold in philosophical circles and demanded that modern science exclude anything that cannot be proven according to its methods. Astrology was banished from academia in 1666, and it remained outside the intellectual mainstream for almost 300 years. Modern astrology began its rebirth in the early part of the 20th century largely due to the work of Alan Leo, the father of sun-sign astrology. A second, and larger, wave of interest grew out of the counterculture movement of the 1960s when interest in metaphysics and Eastern religions also gained momentum. The brilliant works of the Swiss psychologist Carl Jung and French-American astrologer Dane Rudhyar inspired a new generation of astrologers, including the authors of this book.

ASTROLOGY TODAY: EMPOWERMENT

Thanks to Jung, Rudhyar, and many other brilliant minds, modern astrology has largely separated itself from the fatalism of the past when, for example, the sighting of an approaching comet meant the king would die and nothing more. Today's astrology is, as Rudhyar wrote, "person-centered," with the focus on individual choice and personal growth rather than the simple prediction of events. In fact, while we do write about events in this book, we spend more time describing energy patterns and emotions for several reasons.

First, you're a unique individual. You may share characteristics and tendencies with fellow members of your sun sign, but you will experience them in your own way. In addition, you have a personal birth chart in which the positions of the Moon, planets, and other factors distinguish you from the other members of your sun-sign clan. Analyzing how all the planets and signs interact in a person's chart is the foundation of a personal consultation with a professional astrologer or a detailed custom report like those available at http://www.tarot.com/astrology/astroprofile.

ENERGY, EVENTS, AND EMOTION

At its essence, astrology describes energy. Energy can take many forms; it can be an event, emotion, or attitude. We suggest the possible outcomes of astrological events in this book, but they are examples or models of how the planetary energies might be expressed. Each person is going to experience these patterns in his or her own unique way. We have learned that it is more helpful to understand the underlying energy patterns of events than it is to describe them. You may not be able to change the world outside you, but you have an enormous range of choice when it comes to your thoughts and attitudes.

We are here to assist you with ideas and information rooted in history and woven into the cloth of our culture. We recognize and honor you as the center of your life. This book is not a collection of ideas that are foreign to your nature, but a recollection of human experiences that exist within all of us. Whether you know their meanings or not, all the signs and planets live within you. They are part of your human heritage, a gift of awareness, a language not meant to label you and stick you in a box, but a treasure map to yourself and the cosmos beyond. It is a glorious journey we all share. May your way be filled with light this year and in the years to come.

♈ ♉ ♊ ♋ ♌ ♍ ♎ ♏ ♐ ♑ ♒ ♓

2007

PART 1

ASTROLOGY & YOU

HOW TO USE THIS BOOK

ASTROLOGY BASICS

WHAT'S YOUR SIGN?

In this book, we present a view of the year ahead for each sun sign. Your sign is based on the Sun's position at the moment of your birth. As most people know, the Sun travels through the twelve signs of the zodiac over the course of a year. However, the Sun doesn't change signs at the exact moment on the same date every year. If you were born within two days of the cusp (the end or beginning) of a sign, a more exact calculation may be required to determine your sun sign. So, if you are uncertain about your sign, consult an astrologer or get a free copy of your birth chart from http://www.tarot.com/astrology/astroprofile to determine the correct one. In addition to giving you the exact position of the Sun at the moment of your birth, an individual birth or natal chart includes the positions of the Moon and planets as well, which provides a much more detailed astrological view of your life. This information is used in private consultations and computer-generated astrology reports. The sun sign does not tell your entire astrological story. But it is powerful enough to light up your consciousness with ideas that can change your life.

For those of you who have your astrology chart, in addition to reading the chapter in this book on your sun sign, you will also want to read about your moon and rising signs as well. Your intuition will guide you as you integrate the information.

TRANSITS

The information presented in this book is based on the relationship of the planets, including the Sun and the Moon, to the twelve signs of the zodiac in 2007. The movement of the planets in their cycles and their geometric relationship to one another as they interact are called **transits**; they are the primary forecasting tool for astrologers.

As planets enter into specific relationships with one another, astrologers consider the astrological events that occur. For example, when the Sun and the Moon align in a certain way, an event called an **eclipse** occurs. As you read this book, many of you will study more than one sign, whether you are checking up on someone you know or on your own moon or rising sign. You will notice that certain dates are often mentioned repeatedly from sign to sign. This is because major planetary events affect everyone, but some more than others, and in different ways.

For example, in 2007, there is a New Moon Eclipse in Pisces on March 18. Everyone will feel the power of the eclipse, but their reactions will differ. It will be felt most immediately by Pisces and its opposite sign, Virgo. Since this particular eclipse is stressed by Pluto, it will also be challenging for Scorpios, the sign ruled by this planet. The cosmic weather rains on all of us; the water can be parted in twelve ways, each a door to a sign, a Self, another aspect of being human.

RULING OR KEY PLANETS

Every sign is associated with a key or ruling planet. There is an affinity between signs and their planetary rulers—a common purpose that connects them, like lungs with breathing or feet with walking. In astrology's early days, the Sun (Leo) and the Moon (Cancer) ruled one sign each, and the rest of the known planets— Mercury, Venus, Mars, Jupiter, and Saturn—ruled two. However, in the modern era, new planets have been discovered and astrology has evolved to reflect this. The discovery of Uranus in the late eighteenth century coincided with revolutions in the United States and France, triggered a technological revolution that's still going on today, and transformed astrology's traditional rulership system. Radical Uranus was assigned to rule inventive Aquarius, while its old ruler, Saturn, took a step back. Neptune, discovered with photography sixty-five years later, became the ruler of Pisces, nudging Jupiter into the background. And if Pluto hasn't purged Mars from Scorpio, it's certainly taken the dominant role in expressing this sign's energy.

We mention ruling planets quite a bit in the book as we track the cycles of a given sign. The sign Aries, named for the Greek god of war, is ruled by Mars, the Roman name for the same god. Transits of Mars, then, play a leading role in the forecasts for Aries. Venus is used in the same way in the forecasts for Taurus. For double-ruled Scorpio, Aquarius, and Pisces, we take the traditional and modern planetary rulers into account. The planets and the signs they rule are further discussed later in this section.

ELEMENTS

The four astrological elements are fire, earth, air, and water. The action-oriented fire signs—Aries, Leo, and Sagittarius—are warm and dynamic. The sense-oriented earth signs—Taurus, Virgo, and Capricorn—are practical and realistic. The thought-oriented air signs—Gemini, Libra, and Aquarius—are logical and sociable. The emotion-oriented water signs—Cancer, Scorpio, and Pisces—are intuitive and instinctual. Signs of the same element work harmoniously together. In addition, fire and air signs work well together, as do earth and water.

INGRESSES

An **ingress** is the entry of a planet into a new sign. The activities and concerns of the planet will be colored by that sign's energy. For example, when the communication planet Mercury enters Leo, the expressive qualities of that sign tend to make for more dramatic speech than in the previous sign, self-protective Cancer. When Mercury leaves Leo for detail-oriented Virgo, thoughts and words become more precise. Each planet has its own unique rhythm and cycle in terms of how long it takes that planet to move through all the signs. This determines how long it stays in one sign. The Moon, for example, flies through a sign in two and a half days, while Uranus takes seven years.

HOUSES

Your natal chart is divided into twelve astrological houses that correspond to different areas of your life. This book uses solar houses that place your sun sign in the 1st House. In this system, when a planet enters a new sign, it also enters a new house. Thus, the effect of a planet's ingress into a particular sign depends also on which house of the sign in question it's entering. For example, for a Gemini sun sign, Gemini is its own 1st House, followed by Cancer for the 2nd, Leo for the 3rd House, and so on. If you are a Taurus, your 4th House is Leo. As a Scorpio, your 8th House is Gemini. If this is confusing, don't worry about counting houses; we do it for you. The influence of an astrological event differs considerably based on which house of a sign it falls in.

You'll notice that there are many different, but related, terms used to describe each house, sign, and planet. For example, Mars is called feisty, assertive, impatient, or aggressive at different times throughout the book. Also, we use different house names depending on the emphasis we perceive. You'll find the 4th House described as the 4th House of Home and Family, the 4th House of Security, and the 4th House of Roots—all are valid. We change the descriptions to broaden your understanding, rather than repeat the same limited interpretation over and over. Later in this section is a brief description of all the houses.

ASPECTS

Aspects are geometrically significant angles between planets and a key feature of any astrological forecast. A fast-moving body like the Moon will form every possible aspect to every degree of the zodiac during its monthly orbit around the Earth. The Sun will do the same in a year, Mars in two years, Jupiter in twelve. The slower a planet moves, the less common its aspects, which makes them more significant because their effect is longer. A lunar aspect lasts only a few hours, and one from Mercury a day or two, but a transit like the Jupiter-Neptune square that occurs three times this year can last for a week or two or more.

The qualities of the two planets involved in an aspect are important to its meaning, but so is the angle between them. Soft aspects like **sextiles** and **trines** grease the cosmic wheels, while hard ones like squares and oppositions often reflect bumps in the road. **Conjunctions**, when two planets are conjoined, are arguably the most powerful aspect and can be easy or difficult according to the nature of the planets involved. To learn more about the nature of the aspects, turn to the next chapter.

The effect of an aspect on each sun sign is modified according to the houses of that sign where the planets fall. A Venus-Mars trine from Cancer to Scorpio is the harmonious expression of Venus's desire for security with Mars's instinct to protect. They are both in water signs, thus compatible. And if you are a Pisces, Venus in Cancer is in your 5th House and Mars in Scorpio is in your 9th, stirring romance and adventure. Alternatively, if you are a Gemini, Venus in Cancer is in your 2nd House and Mars in Scorpio is in the 6th. Applying the cozy relationship of a trine to Gemini's chart gives the interpretation that there will be a comfortable flow in the practical realms of money and work.

RETROGRADES

All true planets (i.e., excluding the Sun and Moon) turn **retrograde** from time to time. This means that the planet appears to go backward in the zodiac, revisiting recently traveled territory. As with other planetary phenomena, astrologers have observed specific effects from retrogrades. The days when planets turn from direct, or forward, motion to retrograde and back again are called **stations** (because the planet appears to be stationary). These are significant periods that emphasize the energy of the stationing planet.

A retrograde station, when backward motion begins, indicates the beginning of a relatively introspective cycle for that planet's energy. At a direct station, the energy that has been turned inward during the retrograde period begins to express itself more overtly in the outer world once again. Retrogrades can cause certain aspects to occur three times—first forward, then retrograde, then forward again. These triple events can be like a play that unfolds in three acts. The first aspect often raises an issue that's reconsidered or adjusted during the second transit and completed during the third.

LUNATIONS AND ECLIPSES

New Moons, Full Moons, and eclipses are important astrological events. These aspects involving the Moon are called **lunations**. Every month the Sun and Moon join together at the New Moon, seeding a fresh lunar cycle that affects us each in a personal way. The New Moon in the partnership sign of Libra sparks relationships, while the New Moon in the resource sign of Taurus brings attention to money. Two weeks later, the Moon opposes the Sun at the Full Moon. This is often an intense time due to the pull of the Moon in one direction and the Sun in another.

The Full Moon in Cancer, for example, pits the need (Moon) for inner security (Cancer) against the Sun in Capricorn's urge for worldly recognition. The Full Moon can be stressful, but it is also a time of illumination that can give rise to greater consciousness. At the Full Moon, instead of seeing yourself pulled apart by opposing forces, it helps to imagine that you're the meeting point where the opposition is resolved by a breakthrough in awareness.

Planets that form significant aspects with the New or Full Moon play a key role in shaping their character. A New Moon square Jupiter is challenged by a tendency to be overexpansive, a negative quality of that planet. A Full Moon conjunct Saturn is bound in seriousness, duty, or doubt symbolized by this planet of necessity.

Eclipses are a special class of New and Full Moons where the Sun and Moon are so close to their line of intersection with the Earth that the light of one of them is darkened. The shadow of the Moon on the Sun at a Solar Eclipse (New Moon) or of the Earth on the Moon at a Lunar Eclipse (Full Moon) makes them memorable. They work, in effect, like super New or Full Moons, extending the normal two- to four-week period of these lunations to an influence up to six months before or after the eclipse. An eclipse will affect each person differently, depending on where it falls in a chart. But they can be unsettling because they usually mark the end of chapters in one's life.

HOW THIS BOOK IS ORGANIZED

In this book, we take a look at what 2007 holds in store for each of the twelve signs. We evaluate each sign according to the transits to it, its ruler, and its solar houses. The chapter on each sign begins with an overview of the year for the sign. Here we suggest some of the key themes that the sign will encounter in 2007 in general as well as in specific areas of life: love, career, money, health, home, travel, and spirituality. Each of these areas is identified with an icon, as shown at the top of the next page, for easy reference.

The overview is followed by a month-by-month analysis of all of the most important astrological events for that sign. This will enable you to look at where you are as well as what may be coming up for you, so that you can best make choices about how you'd like to deal with the planetary energies at work.

KEY TO ICONS IN OVERVIEW SECTIONS FOR EACH SIGN

LOVE AND RELATIONSHIPS

CAREER AND PUBLIC LIFE

MONEY AND FINANCES

HEALTH AND VITALITY

HOME AND FAMILY

TRAVEL AND HIGHER EDUCATION

SPIRITUALITY AND PERSONAL GROWTH

TIMING, KEY DATES, AND SUPER NOVA DAYS

The monthly forecast for each sign includes a description of several Key Dates that month. (Eastern time is used throughout the book.) We provide some likely scenarios of what may happen or how someone born under the sign might experience the planetary effects at the time of the Key Dates. It is wise to pay closer attention to your own thoughts, feelings, and actions during these times. Certain Key Dates are called Super Nova Days because they are the most intense energetic periods, positive or negative, of the month.

Note that the exact timing of events, and your awareness of their effects, can vary from person to person, sometimes coming a day or two earlier or arriving a day or two later than the Key Dates given.

The period of influence of a transit from the Sun, Mercury, or Venus is a day before and a day after the exact aspect. A transit of Mars is in effect for about two days coming and going; Jupiter and Saturn lasts for a week or more; and Uranus, Neptune, and Pluto can be two weeks.

Although the Key Dates are the days when a particular alignment is exact, some people are so ready for an event that they'll act on a transit a day or two before. And some of us are so entrenched in the status quo or unwilling to change that it may take a day or two for the effect to manifest. Give yourself an extra day around each Key Date to utilize the energy, maximize the potential, and feel the impact of the event. If you find astrological events consistently unfold in your life earlier or later than predicted, adjust the dates accordingly.

Our goal is to help you understand what is operating within you, below the surface, rather than simply to tell you what's going to happen. This is where you have control so that, to a large degree, what happens is up to you. We describe which buttons are being pushed so that you can see your own patterns and have greater power to change them if you want. Every astrological event has a potential for gain or loss. Fat, juicy, easy ones can make us lazy, while tough ones can temper the will and make us stronger. It usually takes time and hindsight to measure the true value of an experience.

THE PLANETS, HOUSES
& ASPECTS

THE PLANETS

The planets are the basic building blocks of astrology. As our ancestors observed the cycles of these wandering stars, they attributed characteristics to them. Each of these richly symbolic archetypes represents a particular spectrum of meaning. Their intimate relationship to the Greek and Roman myths helps us tell stories about them that are still relevant to our lives today. No matter what your sun sign is, every planet impacts your life according to its symbolism and its placement.

THE SUN

Rules Leo
Keywords: *Consciousness, Will, Vitality*
The Sun is our home star, the glowing filament in the center of our local system, and is associated with the sign Leo. Our ancestors equated it with God, for it is the source of energy and is what animates us. In fact, we base our entire calendar system on the Earth's relationship to the Sun. It represents the core of individual identity and consciousness. The masculine Sun has dignity, courage, and willpower. We feel the Sun's role as our main purpose in life; it fuels our furnace to fulfill our mission. We recognize its brightness in anyone who has a "sunny" personality. It is charismatic, creative, and generous of heart. But it can also be proud, have too much pride, and turn arrogant or self-centered. When the Sun is shining, we can see the world around us; it gives us a world of "things" that we can name and describe. It could be said that the Sun symbolizes objective reality.

THE MOON

Rules Cancer
Keywords: *Subconscious, Emotions, Habits*

We've all seen how the Moon goes through its phases, reflecting the light of the Sun, and have felt the power of the Full Moon. Lunations are important astrological markers. The Moon changes signs every two and a half days and reflects the mood of the public in general. Although our year calendar is based upon the Sun, each month (comes from "moon"—*moonth*) closely approximates the cycle of the Moon. The Moon is closer to Earth than anything else in the heavens. Astrologically, it represents how we reflect the world around us through our feelings. The Moon symbolizes emotions, instincts, habits, and routine. It describes how we nurture others and need to be cared for ourselves. The feminine power of the Moon is also connected with the fertility cycle of women. Because it is the source of security and familial intimacy, our Moon sign is where we feel at home. The Moon is associated with the sign Cancer and with concerns about our home and family.

MERCURY

Rules Gemini and Virgo
Keywords: *Communication, Thoughts, Transportation*

Mercury, the Heavenly Messenger, races around the Sun four times each year. Its nearly ninety-day cycle corresponds with the seasons of the calendar. Mercury, our intellectual antenna, is the planet of perception, communication, rational thought, mobility, and commerce. It is the mental traveler, able to move effortlessly through the realms of thought and imagination. Mercury organizes language, allows us to grasp ideas, enables us to analyze and integrate data, and assists us in all forms of communication. Cars, bicycles, telephones, delivery services, paperwork, and the mind itself are all manifestations of quicksilver Mercury, the fastest of the true planets. However, Mercury also has a trickster side and can cleverly con us into believing something that just isn't true. Mercury is associated with curious Gemini in its information-gathering mode, and with discerning Virgo when it's analytically sorting through the data.

VENUS

Rules Taurus and Libra

Keywords: *Desire, Love, Money, Values*

Venus is the goddess of love, our relationship antenna, associated with the spectrum of how we experience what is beautiful and pleasurable to us. With Venus, we attach desire to our perceptions. On one end, Venus can indicate romantic and sensual love. On the other end, Venus is about money and all things of value—financial and emotional. This manifests as our attraction to art, music, and even good food. Every beautiful flower and every act of love contains the essence of sweet Venus. We look to Venus to describe what we like—an important key to understanding partnerships, particularly personal ones. To a certain extent, our chemistry with other people is affected by Venus. Although Venus is traditionally associated with femininity, both women and men are impacted by its rhythms. A morning star, Venus rules Taurus and is associated with the simple and sensual side of physical reality. As an evening star, it rules Libra, where it represents the more intellectual side of love and harmony.

 MARS

Rules Aries, co-rules Scorpio

Keywords: *Action, Physical Energy, Drive*

Mars, the god of war, is the planet of action, physical energy, initiative, and aggression. It is the first planet beyond Earth's orbit, and its role is to take what we have and extend it to the outer world. Mars represents the masculine force of individuality that helps define the ego and our sense of unique identity. It represents how we move forward in life and propels us toward new experiences and into the future. Mars drives us to assert ourselves in healthy ways, but the angry red planet can also be impatient and insensitive, engendering violence and destruction. When insecure, it turns offensive and can attack others. Mars can also express erotic passion, the male counterpart of the female Venus; together they are the cosmic lovers. As the pioneering risk taker, Mars rules fiery Aries. As a volcanic force of power, it is the traditional ruler of Scorpio.

♃ JUPITER

Rules Sagittarius, co-rules Pisces
Keywords: *Expansion, Growth, Optimism*
Jupiter is the largest of the true planets. It represents expansion, growth, and optimism. It was called the Greater Benefic by ancient astrologers due to its association with good fortune. Today, modern astrologers understand that too much of a good thing is not necessarily beneficial. Jupiter rules the excesses of life; undoubtedly, it's the planet of bigger, better, and more. Wherever there's too much, you're apt to find Jupiter. Often called the lucky planet, Jupiter symbolizes where opportunity knocks. Yet it is still up to us to open the door and walk through. Jupiterian people are jovial, but this gassy giant is also associated with humor, philosophy, enthusiasm, and enterprise. In its adventurous mode, Jupiter rules globetrotting Sagittarius, but as the planet of religion and belief systems, it has a traditional connection to Pisces.

♄ SATURN

Rules Capricorn, co-rules Aquarius
Keywords: *Contraction, Maturity, Responsibility*
Saturn is the outermost planet visible to the naked eye, and as such represented the end of the road for our sky-watching ancestors. In premodern times, Saturn was the limit of our human awareness; beyond it were only the fixed stars. Now, even with our telescopic capability to peer farther into the vastness of space and time, Saturn still symbolizes the limits of perception. It is about structure, order, necessity, commitment, and hard-earned accomplishments. It's the stabilizing voice of reality and governs rules, regulations, discipline, and patience. Saturn is Father Time, and represents the ultimate judgment that you get what you deserve. But Saturn isn't only stern or rigid; it is also the teacher and the wise old sage. When we embrace Saturn's discipline, we mature and learn from our experiences. As the serious taskmaster, Saturn is the ruler of ambitious Capricorn. As the co-ruler of Aquarius, Saturn reminds us that rigid rules may need to be broken in order to express our individuality.

CHIRON

(Does not rule a sign)

Keywords: *Healing, Pain, Subversion*

Chiron is the mythological Wounded Healer, and although not a true planet in the traditional sense, it has become a useful tool for modern astrologers. Chiron is a relative newcomer to the planetary lineup and was discovered in 1977 between the orbits of Saturn and Uranus. It describes where we can turn our wounds into wisdom to assist others. It is associated with the story of the wounded Fisher King, who, in medieval tales about the Holy Grail, fished (for souls) in order to salve his incurable suffering. Chiron not only symbolizes where and how we hurt, but also how our words and actions can soothe the pain of others. It doesn't, however, always play by the rules and can work against the status quo. Its rhythms can stir up old memories of emotional discomfort that can lead to increased understanding, vulnerability, and the transformation of heartache and grief into the gifts of love and forgiveness.

 ## URANUS

Rules Aquarius

Keywords: *Awakening, Unpredictable, Inventive*

Uranus is the first planet discovered with technology (the telescope). Its discovery broke through the limitations imposed by our five senses. It symbolizes innovation, originality, revolution, and delighting in unexpected surprises. Uranus operates suddenly, often to release tensions, no matter how hidden. Its action is like lightning—instantaneous and exciting, upsetting and exhilarating. Uranus provokes and instigates change; its restless and rebellious energy hungers for freedom. Its high frequency and electrical nature stimulate the nervous system. This highly original planet abhors the status quo and is known to turn normal things upside down and inside out. As the patron planet of the strange and unusual, it is the ruler of eccentric Aquarius.

NEPTUNE

Rules Pisces
Keywords: *Imagination, Intuition, Spirituality*
Neptune is god of the seas, from which all life arises and is eventually returned. Imaginative Neptune lures us into the foggy mists where reality becomes so hazy that we can lose our way. It is the planet of dreams, illusions, and spirituality. It dissolves boundaries and barriers, leading us into higher awareness, compassion, confusion, or escapism. Grasping the meaning of Neptune is like trying to hold water in our hands. No matter how hard we try, it slips through our fingers—for Neptune is ultimately elusive and unknowable. It rules all things related to fantasy and delusion. A highly spiritual energy, the magic of Neptune encourages artistic vision, intuitive insight, compassion, and the tendency to idealize. Neptune governs the mystic's urge to merge with the divine and is associated with the spiritual sign Pisces.

PLUTO

Rules Scorpio
Keywords: *Passion, Intensity, Regeneration*
Pluto, lord of the underworld, is the planet of death, rebirth, and transformation. As the most distant of the planets, Pluto moves us inexorably toward a deeper understanding of life's cycles. Under Pluto's influence, it often seems as though the apparently solid ground has disintegrated, forcing us to morph in ways we cannot intellectually understand. Pluto is the mythological phoenix, a magical bird that rises from the ashes of its own destruction by fire. It contains the shadow parts of ourselves that we would prefer to keep hidden, but healing and empowerment come from facing the unfathomable darkness and turning it into light. Manipulation and control are often issues with Pluto. A healthy relationship with Pluto adds psychological understanding and clarity about our motivations. As the ruler of magnetic Scorpio, it is associated with power and emotional intensity.

☊ ☋ NODES OF THE MOON

(Do not rule a sign)
Keywords: *Karma, Soul, Past Lives*
The Nodes of the Moon are opposing points where the Moon's orbit around the Earth intersects the Earth's orbit around the Sun. Although not real planets, these powerful points have an astrological influence in that they describe the ways we connect with others. They are useful in understanding the challenges and opportunities we face in our soul's journey through its lifetime here on Earth. For many astrologers, the Lunar Nodes are symbolic of past lives and future existences. The South Node, at one end of the nodal axis, represents the past—the unconscious patterns of our ancestral heritage or those brought into this life from previous incarnations. These are often talents that can easily be overused and become a no-growth path of least resistance. At the other end, the North Node represents the future—a new direction for growth, development, and integration.

THE HOUSES

Every astrology chart is divided into twelve houses, each ruling different areas of life and colored by a different sign. Just as planets move through the zodiac signs, they also move through the houses in an individual chart. The twelve houses have a correspondence to the twelve signs, but in an individualized chart, the signs in each house will vary based on the sign on the cusp of the 1st House, called a rising sign or ascendant. The rising sign is determined by the exact time of your birth. We use solar houses, which place the sun sign as your 1st House, or rising sign.

1ST HOUSE

Corresponding Sign: Aries
Keywords: *Self, Appearance, Personality*
A primary point of self-identification: When planets move through this sector, the emphasis is on your individuality and surface appearances. It is often associated with how we interact with others when we first meet them. Planets here tend to take on great importance and become more integrated into your personality.

2ND HOUSE

Corresponding Sign: Taurus
Keywords: *Possessions, Values, Self-Worth*
Associated with values, resources, income, and self-esteem: When planets move through the 2nd House, they can modify your attitudes about money and earning. This is a concrete and practical area of the chart, and although it is linked to possessions, the 2nd House typically does not include things you cannot easily move, such as real estate or what you share with someone else.

3RD HOUSE

Corresponding Sign: Gemini
Keywords: *Communication, Siblings, Short Trips*
Relates to how you gather information from your immediate environment: It's associated with the day-to-day comings and goings of your life. Siblings can be found here, for this is where we first learn to build intimacy when we're young. Planets moving through this house can affect the pace and quality of your day and how you communicate with those around you.

4TH HOUSE

Corresponding Sign: Cancer
Keywords: *Home, Family, Roots*
Associated with the earliest imprints of childhood, your family roots, and how you're connected to your own feelings: This is your emotional foundation and describes what you need to feel at home. This is where you are nurtured, so when planets travel through this sector, they stir up issues of security and safety. As the deepest place in your chart, it is sometimes only you who knows about it.

5TH HOUSE

Corresponding Sign: Leo
Keywords: *Love, Romance, Children, Play*
Associated with fun, but also represents self-expression, creativity, love affairs, and children: The 5th House is about the discovery of self through play, and includes sports, games, and gambling. When planets move through your 5th House, they can excite you to take risks and connect with the innocence of your inner child.

6TH HOUSE

Corresponding Sign: Virgo
Keywords: *Work, Health, Daily Routines*
Related to service and working conditions: Like the 3rd House, it describes your daily life, but the consistency of it rather than the noisy distractions—it's where you strive for efficiency and effectiveness. Planets here modify your habits, diet, and exercise. Although considered the house of health and hygiene, transits here don't always indicate illness; they can also increase our concern for healthier lifestyles.

7TH HOUSE

Corresponding Sign: Libra
Keywords: *Marriage, Relationships, Business Partners*
Encompasses one-to-one relationships: Its cusp is called the descendant and is the western end of the horizon. It's where and how we meet other people, both personally and professionally. In a larger sense, this is how you project who you are onto others. Planets moving through here can stimulate intimate relationships, but can also increase the intensity of all of your interactions with the outside world.

8TH HOUSE

Corresponding Sign: Scorpio
Keywords: *Intimacy, Transformation, Shared Resources*
A mysterious and powerful place, associated with shared experiences, including the most intimate: Traditionally the house of sex, death, and taxes, it's the place where you gain the deepest levels of relationship, personally and professionally. When planets move through your 8th House, perspectives can intensify, intimacy issues are stimulated, and compelling transformations are undertaken.

9TH HOUSE

Corresponding Sign: Sagittarius
Keywords: *Travel, Higher Education, Philosophy*
Associated with philosophy, religion, higher education of all kinds, and long-distance travel: It's where you seek knowledge and truth—both within and without. Planets moving through this house open portals to inner journeys and outer adventures, stretching your mind in ways that expand your perspectives about the world.

10TH HOUSE

Corresponding Sign: Capricorn
Keywords: *Career, Community, Ambition*
The most elevated sector of your chart; its cusp is called the midheaven: This is the career house, opposite to the home-based 4th House. When planets move through your 10th House, they activate your ambition, drive you to achieve professional excellence, and push you up the ladder of success. This is where your public reputation is important and hard work is acknowledged.

11TH HOUSE

Corresponding Sign: Aquarius
Keywords: *Friends, Groups, Associations, Social Ideals*
Traditionally called the house of friends, hopes, and wishes: It's where you go to be with like-minded people. The 11th House draws you out of your individual career aspirations and into the ideals of humanity. Planets traveling here can activate dreams of the future, so spending time with friends is a natural theme.

12TH HOUSE

Corresponding Sign: Pisces
Keywords: *Imagination, Spirituality, Secret Activities*
Complex, representing the ending of one cycle and the beginning of the next: It is connected with mysteries and places outside ordinary reality. When planets move through this house, they stimulate your deepest subconscious feelings and activate fantasies. It's a private space that can seem like a prison or a sanctuary.

ASPECTS

As the planets move through the sky in their various cycles, they form ever-changing angles with one another. Certain angles create significant geometric shapes. For example, when two planets are 90 degrees apart, they conform to a square. A sextile, or 60 degrees of separation, conforms to a six-pointed star. Planets create aspects to one another when they are at these special angles. All aspects are divisions of the 360-degree circle. Aspects explain how the individual symbolism of a pair of planets combines into an energetic pattern.

CONJUNCTION

0 degrees ★ **Keywords:** *Compression, Blending, Focus*
A conjunction is a blending of the separate planetary energies involved. When two planets conjoin, your job is to integrate the different influences—which in some cases is easier than others. For example, a conjunction of the Moon and Venus is likely to be a smooth blending of energy because of the similarity of the planets. But a conjunction between the Moon and Uranus is likely to be challenging because the Moon needs security, while Uranus prefers risk.

SEMISQUARE AND SESQUISQUARE

45 and 135 degrees ★ **Keywords:** *Annoyance, Mild Resistance*
Semisquares and sesquisquares are minor aspects that act like milder squares. They're one-eighth and three-eighths of a circle, respectively. Like the other hard aspects (conjunctions, oppositions, and squares) they can create dynamic situations that require immediate attention and resolution. Although they are not usually as severe as the other hard aspects, they remind us that healthy stress is important for the process of growth.

SEXTILE

60 degrees ★ **Keywords:** *Supportive, Intelligent, Activating*
Sextiles are supportive and intelligent, combining complementary signs—fire and air, earth and water. There's an even energetic distribution between the planets involved. Sextiles often indicate opportunities based on our willingness to take action in smart ways. Like trines, sextiles are considered easy: the good fortune they offer can pass unless you consciously take an active interest in making something positive happen.

QUINTILE

72 and 144 degrees ★ **Keywords:** *Creativity, Metaphysics, Magic*
Quintiles are powerful nontraditional aspects based on dividing the zodiac circle into five, resulting in a five-pointed star. Related to ancient goddess-based religious traditions, quintiles activate the imagination, intuition, and latent artistic talents. They're clever, intelligent, and even brilliant as they stimulate humor to relieve repressed tensions.

SQUARE

90 degrees ★ **Keywords:** *Resistance, Stress, Dynamic Conflict*
A square is an aspect of resistance, signifying energies at odds. Traditionally, they were considered negative, but their dynamic instability demands attention, so they're often catalysts for change. When differences in two planetary perspectives are integrated, squares can build enduring structures. Harnessing a square's power by managing contradictions creates opportunities for personal growth.

TRINE

120 degrees ★ **Keywords:** *Harmony, Free-Flowing, Ease*
A trine is the most harmonious of aspects because it connects signs of the same element. In the past, trines were considered positive, but modern astrologers realize they are so easy that they can create a rut that is difficult to break out of. When two planets are one-third of a circle apart, they won't necessarily stimulate change, but they can often help build on the status quo. With trines, you must stay alert, for complacency can weaken your chances for success.

QUINCUNX

150 degrees ★ **Keywords:** *Irritation, Adjustment*
A quincunx is almost like a nonaspect, for the two planets involved have a difficult time staying aware of each other. As such, this aspect often acts as an irritant, requiring that you make constant adjustments without actually resolving the underlying problem. This is a challenging aspect because it can be more annoying than a full-fledged crisis. Quincunxes are a bit like oil and water—the planets are not in direct conflict, but they have difficulty mixing with each another.

OPPOSITION

180 degrees ★ **Keywords:** *Tension, Awareness, Balance*
When two planets are in opposition, they are like two forces pulling at either end of a rope. The tension is irresolvable, unless you are willing to hold both divergent perspectives without suppressing one or the other. More often than not, we favor one side of the opposition over the other and, in doing so, project the unexpressed side onto others or situations. For this reason, oppositions usually manifest as relationship issues.

ASTROLOGY

WORLD REPORT 2007

Astrology works for individuals, groups, and even humanity as a whole. You will have your own story in 2007, but it will unfold among six billion other tales of human experience in the year ahead. We are each unique, yet our lives touch one another; our destinies are woven together by weather and war, by economy, science, politics, religion, and all of the other threads of life on this planet. We make personal choices every day, yet there are great events beyond the control of any one individual. When the power goes out in a neighborhood, individual astrology patterns will describe the response of each person, yet everyone will be without electricity. We are living at a time when the tools of self-awareness fill bookshelves and broadcasts, and we benefit greatly from them. Yet in spite of all of this wisdom, conflicts between groups cause enormous suffering every day. Understanding personal issues is a powerful means for increasing happiness, but knowledge of our collective issues is equally important for our safety, sanity, and well-being. This astrological look at the major trends and planetary patterns for 2007 provides a framework of understanding the potentials and challenges we face together so that we can advance with tolerance and respect as a community and fulfill our potential as individuals.

The astrological events used for this forecast are the transits of the outer planets, Chiron, and the Moon's Nodes, as well as the retrograde cycles of Mercury and eclipses of the Sun and the Moon.

MAJOR PLANETARY EVENTS

JUPITER IN SAGITTARIUS: AIMING HIGH IN THE SKY

November 23, 2006–December 18, 2007

Optimistic Jupiter is back in its enthusiastic home sign, where shooting arrows of hope into the sky is a favorite pastime. Taking risks is what life is about—going all out in the pursuit of adventures both material and spiritual. Expect a paradoxical opening of minds and an increase in orthodoxy due to Jupiter in Sagittarius's combination of broad vision and self-righteousness. The planet of truth becomes more zealous in the sign of religion and philosophy. Hunger for ultimate answers may begin with an open mind, but once we have found what we are seeking, it's tempting to assume that the next step is to convince everyone else that our way is the only way to salvation. The satisfaction that comes from gaining wisdom can fade quickly as we're bound by these new laws. However, greater fulfillment comes from continuing to learn and explore, from being a seeker, a lover of the never-ending journey of the mind. The full potential for learning inherent in Jupiter in Sagittarius is fulfilled when we remember that there is no absolute end to which all paths must lead, but a multitude of ways to explore the human experience.

Jupiter in Sagittarius inspires new political or religious movements. It's a time of prophets and leaders whose lofty aspirations motivate groups of people who are seeking direction in these rapidly changing times. But this engenders gullibility, as our desire to put to rest the complexity of competing ideas and eliminate the gray areas of uncertainty can reduce our critical faculties. Discerning minds ask questions and expect detailed answers, not slogans, to counter the polemical excesses of otherwise generous Jupiter in Sagittarius.

The wilder side of Jupiter appears during its three tense squares with eccentric Uranus on January 22, May 10, and October 9. Going to extremes can feel as natural then as going out for a cup of coffee. These are times for breakdowns of old expectations and breakthroughs to new beliefs and aspirations. Shocking news related to travel, the law, and religious issues can be expected, although voyages for educational purposes are generally favored throughout the year. A more sober side of Jupiter appears on March 16 and May 5 when stabilizing trines are formed with responsible Saturn. This harmonious alignment of the planets of expansion and contraction widens possibilities while showing concrete ways to make them real. These are excellent periods for connecting a futuristic vision with current reality to establish an effective strategy for reaching your goals. This solid contact in creative fire signs between Jupiter in Sagittarius and Saturn in Leo can produce positive change when a bold idea is matched with a well-designed plan. On December 11, a conjunction between Jupiter and Pluto intensifies differences of opinion, philosophy, and religious beliefs. Extreme statements provoke even more extreme responses unless cooler heads prevail. The discovery of ancient relics or documents, though, can reconnect modern thought to its traditional origins.

SATURN IN LEO: TAMING THE HEART

July 16, 2005–September 2, 2007

Saturn, the planet of hard, cold reality, takes twenty-nine years to orbit the Sun and pass through all twelve signs of the zodiac. Saturn is the planet that defines limits and responsibilities, showing where work is needed to overcome old limits and build new structures in our lives. Saturn thrives on patience and commitment, rewarding persistent effort but punishing carelessness.

Saturn's passage through Leo, the sign of individual will, ego, and identity, is a period during which excessive self-importance and immature need for attention will not be rewarded. Where arrogance runs amuck, Saturn sets boundaries and demands accountability. If ego has pushed you out on a limb, Saturn will saw it off. The fall can be a painful comedown, an embarrassing loss of status. We can expect overblown heroes to have a tough time of it this year, especially Leos like Barry Bonds and Jerry Falwell.

On the other hand, Saturn in Leo is a time to become your own hero, to follow the flame of your heart's desire with the conviction to turn it into reality. It's a chance for each individual to tap into his or her piece of human potential and apply it in a direct and meaningful way. Personality is the vehicle: a means for expression and service to humanity that is not to be rejected as a less than perfect expression of the ideal, but something to be expressed with as much courage and nobility as possible. The great resource needed to save the planet is in the heart of every person. Saturn in Leo reminds us to harness our individual power, making each of us a star in our own way. This isn't, however, a competition; there are no Oscars or gold medals given to the winners because everyone can win. One small step forward in the face of fear in your life adds to our collective courage. Pride, which is associated with Leo, is an asset when it motivates creative action. But when it primarily serves to bolster an insecure image, the consequences are not likely to be pleasant. Saturn in Leo does not indulge show-offs, bullies, or preening peacocks, but it does reward the courageous individual who does the work to earn his or her place in the sun.

On August 31, 2006, serious Saturn opposed Neptune, planet of dreams and fantasies, a pattern that repeats on February 28 and June 25, 2007. These are the most powerful astrological aspects of the year. The opposition between the planets of form and faith marks a time of spiritual passage. Beliefs will be tested against the pressures of reality. Frauds will be exposed, especially in the entertainment industry and the field of religion. Yet practical breakthroughs in psychic awareness and electronic imagery are likely as well.

This Saturn-Neptune opposition is a halfway mark in a longer cycle that began during their conjunction in 1989, when the Exxon Valdez ran aground, creating one of the worst environmental disasters in history. Oil is associated with Neptune, so the opposition from restrictive Saturn can create even higher levels of pressure about fuel supplies as we face the harsh realities of limited natural resources. Prices at the gas pumps have already risen to record highs and will continue to push upward, but it's not just oil that is scarce; so are consumer dollars to pay for it. We may see changes in driving habits as big cars become unaffordable luxuries. As the planet of necessity, though, Saturn's aspect to Neptune can also correspond with a new commitment to alternative energy sources. So, in typical Saturn fash-ion, a problem can be defined more clearly, which then leads to a solution. This will not happen overnight, however, so gas rationing is a strong possibility. Just as the 1989 oil spill helped raise consumer consciousness about recycling and environ-mental issues in general, the opposition is again bringing awareness to these unsolved problems by presenting us with discouraging news. We could even see innovative solutions in response to the crisis offered by the large oil companies as they continue to get more involved with alternative sources of energy.

Neptune is a planet of compassion that connects us to all humans, including the weakest among us, whether at home in New Orleans or overseas in Darfur. The tragic story of mass starvation continues in spite of sufficient provisions to feed the world. This has largely been ignored by the media, except for occasional news reports that are so painful that most of us want to forget what we've seen as quickly as possible. Saturn's opposition to Neptune, though, is a challenge to put compassion into action, even addressing the seemingly overwhelming problem of world hunger. Inspiring leaders may draw attention to this and other problems among the poor and disadvantaged. A commitment to act on compassion, rather than just feeling it, requires individual heroics that personify Saturn in Leo. We saw examples of this kind of heroism during the Hurricane Katrina disaster when the government was so slow to respond. Surprisingly, the deep financial and spiritual commitment of entertainers including Angelina Jolie, Bono, Robert Redford, and George Clooney shows our political leaders what's truly important. Celebrities, such as Oprah Winfrey, are as much of a moral compass these days as our religious leaders. Whenever and wherever that soft feeling of caring arises, there is an opportunity this year to make the hard choice of doing something about it. A billion tiny acts of kindness add up to a universe of healing for humanity.

Leo is a fire sign, so Saturn's presence may continue to turn up the heat on global warming. This unfortunate trend is unlikely to be stopped in a single year, but expect awareness of the problem to grow throughout 2007.

On the religious front, the Saturn-Neptune opposition can be a test to see whether we are more interested in the spiritual principles of our faith than in making one religion the leading brand in the marketplace. The core truths of all religions— sometimes referred to as "the Perennial Philosophy"—are essentially the same, yet the divisions we make among religions overshadow these common elements. Unforgiving Saturn can reveal the shadowy flaws of moral leaders in its opposition to deceptive Neptune, but may also signal a courageous commitment to finding peace among the competing ideologies. This may be the year when visionary individuals whose faith in any unifying higher power, no matter the name, come together and create a balance to the extremism that has been increasing in recent years. We may be reaching a point when the survival of humanity requires us to learn that we can remain loyal to a single religion while we acknowledge the freedom of choice for others.

SATURN IN VIRGO: CORRECTIVE ACTION

September 2, 2007–October 29, 2009

Saturn's passage through detail-oriented Virgo is a time to perfect skills, cut waste, and develop healthier habits. Saturn and Virgo are both practical, which is excellent for improving the quality of material life. Organizational upgrades and maintenance projects increase efficiency for individuals and groups. Education and training become more valuable than ever. Carelessness grows quite costly as minor errors can escalate into major problems. Systems break down easily, requiring closer attention than usual. Problems like bird flu and mad cow disease will remain newsworthy. Bodies can be more susceptible to illnesses caused by impure food or water, making this an ideal time to improve your diet.

Virgo is the sign of the worker, putting labor issues and employee rights in the spotlight. When fearful, Virgo can be overly discriminating, so we can expect that immigration issues will continue to polarize people everywhere. A new era of relatively modest consumption can shift the economy away from purchases of more cars, bigger homes, and disposable goods. Do-it-yourself classes and products, personal services, pets, and outdoor activities are likely to be even more popular.

Saturn in Virgo will highlight flaws and make it easier to be critical of oneself and others. Yet its purpose is to solve problems, not simply complain about them. Taking responsibility and constructive action is the solution.

URANUS IN PISCES: BREAKTHROUGH TO A NEW DIMENSION

March 3, 2003–May 27, 2010

Uranus takes eighty-four years to orbit the Sun and spends about seven years in each sign. This long transit's influence tends to be less obvious in daily life than those of faster-moving Saturn and Jupiter. Nevertheless, Uranus's impact can be even greater. This planet of liberation in Pisces, the last sign of the zodiac, is about breaking down the barriers of faith, fantasy, and illusions that subtly shape our lives. The most powerful beliefs lie just beyond the border of consciousness yet hold our minds in a universe of assumptions that are almost never questioned. Uranus's presence in Pisces, though, tears down these invisible walls and awakens us from sweet dreams and nightmares alike.

We've already experienced the destructive power of water with the December 2004 tsunami and Hurricane Katrina in August 2005 both occurring when a Jupiter-Neptune trine was in effect. With shocking Uranus remaining in this water sign, we may experience more hurricanes and floods than predicted. But waves of religious thought can also wash away intellectual progress. The resurgence of biblical authority versus accepted science is present in the United States with attempts to put "intelligent design" on an equal academic footing as the theory of evolution. However, this is shown not just by Uranus's presence in Neptune's sign, Pisces, but also by Neptune's presence in Uranus's sign, Aquarius. This exchange of ruling planets is called "mutual reception" and indicates a closer connection between the planets and signs involved. Uranus is scientific, the first planet discovered by telescope. Neptune is spiritual, so we can expect continuing debate over stem-cell research, cloning, abortion, in vitro fertilization, and assisted suicide issues.

Uranus is a planet of individuality, the unique, original, and singular force that steps outside the norm to revolutionize the world. Small radical groups or even one person can make powerful changes with influence that ripples around the globe. Expansive Jupiter's tense squares to Uranus on January 22, May 10, and October 9 multiply these radicalizing forces. They may arise as explosive social or political events, but the potential for breakthroughs in consciousness is just as high for individuals. The challenge, both collectively and personally, is to maintain a calm center in the middle of the storm. The solid values of a person or nation applied in a flexible and up-to-date manner permit intelligent responses as opposed to dangerous, knee-jerk reactions.

NEPTUNE IN AQUARIUS: SPIRIT INTO SCIENCE

January 28, 1998–April 4, 2011

Aquarius is a sign of intellect, and Neptune is a planet of faith. This unusual combination inspires minds at its best but makes for fuzzy arguments at its worst. The oppositions from solid Saturn on February 28 and June 25, though, demand accountability from this vaguest of planets. Its spiritual ideals and promises for a better tomorrow are boldly challenged by the urgency of needs today. A tug-of-war between the perfect and the practical may have one side leaping to unprecedented acts of charity while the other's insistence on religious purity resists.

As mentioned, Neptune is associated with oil, so Saturn's oppositions to this planet will continue to force issues based on limited supplies, environmental damage, and high prices. Oil spills and accidents involving chemicals may be more frequent. However, technological breakthroughs, perhaps involving biological agents, may reduce potentially devastating effects. Water, our most precious liquid, is slated to become a more newsworthy subject, with tainted supplies and privatization triggering headlines.

Imaginary Neptune is also considered the planet of film, and Aquarius represents futuristic ideas, so we will, no doubt, continue our love affair with science fiction movies. But watch for a blockbuster that changes the genre, such as *Star Wars* did in 1977. As mentioned with respect to Uranus in Pisces, the mixing of faith and science is a gift and a curse of Neptune in Aquarius. Intellectual deception and willful denial of logic are expected. But for the metaphysically oriented, Neptune in Aquarius is likely to continue the popularization of quantum physics–inspired ideas presented in the movie *What the Bleep Do We Know!?* and the controversial spiritual issues raised by *The Da Vinci Code*, among others. The boundaries between fact and fiction are blurred, and our belief systems are challenged and inspired by art.

On an individual level, Neptune in Aquarius is part of a process for connecting feelings with intellect by recognizing the link between emotions and thoughts. Although we might not be able to realize it from watching television, the mind is not simply a mechanical system that operates separately from the rest of the body. The media are flooded with quick solutions to physical problems that disregard the body/mind connection. Pharmaceutical drugs permeate the mainstream and are now accepted by the masses. Prescription pills are easier to find than holistic help for emotional, spiritual, or nervous conditions. Instead of running to the drugstore to alleviate anxiety, insomnia, or sexual dysfunction, accentuate the positive side of Neptune by adding herbal remedies, acupuncture, or activities like meditation, yoga, and tai chi to calm jangled nervous systems.

PLUTO IN SAGITTARIUS: PHILOSOPHICAL EXTREMES

January 17, 1995–January 25, 2008

Pluto, the most recently discovered and slowest-moving planet, represents transformation, a process that takes us from the depths to the heights before finding a new point of balance. This powerful planet's long transit through Sagittarius, the sign of religion, was expressed most painfully by the September 11, 2001 attacks in the United States. Pluto represents death; Sagittarius is about not only religion but also faraway places and long-distance travel, as in airplanes. Saturn, the planet of structure, was in Gemini, the Twins (as in Twin Towers), and opposed by Pluto that day. While that transit recedes, it is succeeded by an easier Saturn-Pluto trine on August 6. This harmony presents the possibility of putting fear into a rational container. Rather than allowing ourselves and our leaders to surrender reason in the name of security, we are likely to realize that reason is our security.

Pluto's penchant for intolerance in religious Sagittarius will be with us throughout the year. Still, 2007 may present some opportunities to evolve past the cultural schisms of the past with pragmatic Saturn's help. But some true believers tend to go to extremes, because they fear that if they don't dominate, they will be defeated. Armageddon consciousness arises when organizations and individuals do not see ways of adapting to change they cannot control. The imagined destruction of their world produces the panic of absolutism and the end of dialogue.

CHIRON IN AQUARIUS: HEALING THE WOUNDED COMMUNITY

February 21, 2005–April 19, 2010

Chiron, discovered in 1977 between the orbits of Saturn and Uranus, was named after a mythological centaur known for its healing powers. Astrologers studying the new member of the solar system have found it to be a meaningful point that most have added to their charts. Chiron in Aquarius represents wounds in communities and the ideals that bind people together. This can lead to a shift away from traditional group identification to allow new alignments less rooted in old national, regional, or racial differences.

THE MOON'S NODES

MOON'S NORTH NODE IN PISCES, SOUTH NODE IN VIRGO: INTENT COUNTS MORE THAN CONTENT

June 21, 2006–December 18, 2007

The North and South Nodes are opposing points: the Dragon's Head and Tail that connect the orbits of the Moon around the Earth and the Earth around the Sun. Habit pulls us toward the South Node, but it is the North Node that points in a direction of growth and integration. The North Node in Pisces marks a period in which feelings count more than facts. The South Node sign of Virgo is concerned with details and data, which are normally important matters. However, at this time, too much concern with these topics leads to a focus that becomes so narrow that judgment suffers. Pisces is a sign with a wide view, one that doesn't analyze but dives in, even if there's no sense of how deep the water is. This transit reminds us that compassion is more valuable than intellectual understanding and that intent counts more than content. Individuals and organizations that put the spirit of the law before the letter of the law are stronger candidates for success now.

MERCURY RETROGRADES

All true planets appear to move retrograde from time to time as a result of viewing them from the moving platform of Earth. The most significant retrograde periods are those of Mercury, the communication planet. These occur three times a year for roughly three weeks at a time and are periods when difficulties with details, information flow, and technical matters are likely. Be aware that occasionally during the retrograde period, Mercury will temporarily back into the previous sign.

Extra attention should be paid to all of your communication exchanges to avoid misunderstandings and omissions. Retrograde Mercury requires us to clean up unfinished business as we review, redo, reconsider, and, in general, revisit the past. This year these three retrogrades all start in emotional water signs (Pisces, Cancer, and Scorpio), which can be very useful for introspection and therapies that help you reevaluate your personal history.

Because of retrograde Mercury's emphasis on water signs this year—when the planet of intellect is already less inclined to objectivity—information will be highly subjective at these times. No matter how analytical our thinking is, the filter of feelings tends to bend reality in a way that's harder for others to understand. Using images and symbols as well as being more sensitive to the tone and rhythm of your voice can open channels of intuitive connection where ordinary reason may fail.

FEBRUARY 13–MARCH 7 IN PISCES: REMEMBER YOUR DREAMS

Mercury turns retrograde in Pisces just short of a conjunction with electric Uranus and a square with opportunistic Jupiter. We can feel like we're on the brink of a breakthrough or the edge of a breakdown, but the messenger planet's reverse shift pulls us back from a mental leap and gives us several more weeks to reconsider matters before taking the plunge. On February 22, Mercury conjuncts the Sun, aligning the "eye" of perception with the "I" of identity that offers a deep insight into one's life purpose. Late on February 26, Mercury backs into Aquarius, an intellectual air sign offering a bit of cool detachment that calms thinking and opens up communication. Direct Mercury will finally join Uranus on April 1—a day not for fools, but of sudden awakening that may shock the world and rocket individuals to a higher level of consciousness.

JUNE 15–JULY 9 IN CANCER: REVISIT YOUR PAST

Mercury retrograde in the nostalgic sign of Cancer stirs childhood memories and, perhaps, a yearning for the past. Whether the old days were good ones or not, looking back in time is unavoidable during this period. Opportunities to reconnect with estranged family members or close friends arise. However, the wounds of painful relationships are likely to return to consciousness as well. Regrets, revenge, and remorse may surface in emotionally upsetting ways, but the great healing potential of this time comes from allowing all feelings without becoming overly attached to them. Imagine that you're watching the river of your life, with its previous disappointments floating by one last time before you let go forever. Mercury conjuncts the Sun while forming a harmonious trine to the Moon's helpful North Node on June 28, a day when especially intense emotions can be released.

OCTOBER 11–NOVEMBER 1 IN SCORPIO: DISCOVER YOUR MYSTERY

Mercury's retrograde turn in Scorpio when the Moon is in the same probing sign is, perhaps, the deepest emotional dive. A tense square with wounded Chiron could start another round of picking over the past. However, the complexity of issues regarding power, control, and sharing could be more than words can describe. Scorpio is the sign of mysteries, so Mercury's U-turn there might lead us to such deep and dark places that discussion with others about what's been found can be too mortifying to bear. We have the right to privacy, and as long as we're not hiding the truth from ourselves, there's no urgency to talk yet. Mercury meets the Sun on October 23 just before the communication planet retreats into reasonable Libra. A threshold of awareness may be crossed then that will enable feelings to form into words so that meaningful conversations can recommence.

ECLIPSES

Solar and Lunar Eclipses are special New and Full Moons that indicate meaningful changes for individuals and groups. They are powerful markers of events with influences that can appear up to three months in advance of and last up to six months after the eclipse. Eclipses occur when the New or Full Moon is conjunct one of the Moon's Nodes, usually in pairs twice a year. Solar Eclipses occur at the New Moon and are visible in unique paths, not everywhere that the Sun appears. Locations where an eclipse is visible are more strongly influenced by it. Lunar Eclipses occur during Full Moons and are visible wherever the Moon can be seen.

MARCH 3, LUNAR ECLIPSE IN VIRGO: CHALLENGE THE STATUS QUO

An opposition from electric Uranus and a tough square from expansive Jupiter to the eclipse can shake the planet. Earthquakes and social upheaval rock the globe with unexpected power. A sudden reorientation of politics is also possible with revolutionary Uranus pushing philosophical Jupiter to make radical changes. Demagogues might stir up the masses with outrageous statements, adding more confusion to a disoriented world. However, this eclipse could mark the emergence of a new kind of leader, one whose fresh vision and charisma are matched with compassion and pragmatism. Virgo is a sign of systems, health, and sanitation, all of which may be in some peril at this time. Wide-angle Jupiter square the eclipse point may exaggerate the dangers, but alarm can be a sure way to turn attention to hidden problems. Fear of foreigners and untraditional ideas can lead to a reactive backlash. Resist the impulse to cling to previously solid but currently outmoded ideas. Flexibility on mental, physical, and emotional levels is the most effective way to absorb the shock of unexpected events. Work changes may be common when new fields suddenly open as old ones fall away. Whether you are changing jobs, careers, or duties, an attitude of discovery, rather than one of control, makes adjusting to rapidly moving conditions easier and could transform a potentially dangerous situation into a rewarding opportunity.

MARCH 18, SOLAR ECLIPSE IN PISCES: REALIGNMENT OF POWER

Potent Pluto's tight square to the eclipse stirs feelings from the deep. Long-repressed memories can rise to the surface and upset the balance in current relationships. Power struggles grow from distrust, especially of those in positions of authority. Heads of state may fall, captains of industry could tumble, and the president of the PTA or local scout leader may resign. Illusions crumble, and we must reorder our priorities in light of emerging revelations about what we most desire and what we can no longer endure. Pluto is astrology's bogeyman, scaring us with threats of loss or taking us on terrifying journeys to parts unknown. Yet this planet of purging doesn't destroy essence; it simply peels away the dead layers of skin that no longer serve a purpose. Pisces is a sign of spirituality, so an eclipse here can turn atheists toward God and push religious individuals to extremes. Doubting one's faith is natural, an appropriate test of one's beliefs that will only strengthen core convictions if they remain valid. Still, the fear of loss of any kind may lead us to dig in our heels and resist change. Pushing back against those who lovingly encourage forward movement is not a sign of confidence, but evidence of uncertainty. Hold your ground where you wish to stand rather than simply to avoid going to an unfamiliar place.

AUGUST 28, LUNAR ECLIPSE IN PISCES: FOLLOW ONE DREAM

This Pisces Full Moon is a reservoir of dreams. The Earth's shadow crossing its face is a reminder to stop floating on the surface of possibilities and select one inspiring project on which to act. Cut out the distraction of fantasies that can never come true. Discard impractical theory to roll up your sleeves and take hold of your future with a firmer hand. Plant a seed of commitment for your future. Then do whatever it takes to nurture the garden by learning, growing, and changing in whatever ways you can give life to your dream. Avoid so-called experts whose only advice is to abandon hope or adjust your course so radically that it no longer feels like your journey. And if you don't have that grain of inspiration within you, feed yourself with regular helpings of healthy habits for your body and spirit that will certainly yield the vision you are seeking.

SEPTEMBER 11, SOLAR ECLIPSE IN VIRGO: TIME TO CLEAN HOUSE

Revolutionary Uranus returns in a key role for the last eclipse of the year with a close opposition to the Sun and Moon in Virgo. This is more than enough to shake the face of power and shuffle the chairs of authority almost overnight. Those low on the totem pole can suddenly find themselves at the top. Individuals wielding great power could find themselves wielding brooms. These blustery conditions, though, are being blown not only by eccentric Uranus; stormy Jupiter and assertive

Mars are also whipping up winds of change. These two planets form a 90-degree square to the eclipse point that is bound to heat the air with outlandish statements and even threats of aggression. Climatic conditions could take a sudden turn with unprecedented events scattered around the globe. Worldwide communications might even be interrupted by solar activity, natural disaster, technical failure, or sabotage. Individually, we may feel overwhelmed by pressures coming from a variety of directions. The sheer flow of data is, in fact, too much to be processed logically. Instead of thinking your way through the situation, rely on feelings as a guide. Let go and let intuition lead the way, even when the precise direction seems unclear. Virgo's practical principles are being challenged, and existing systems may be failing. Methods that have worked in the past may not be expansive enough to adapt to current demands. Deconditioning and letting go of old habits may feel like giving up hope, but this eclipse is about letting go of old tools and picking up new ones to ride the rising tides of change.

THE BOTTOM LINE

Saturn is generally the clearest marker of the tasks that lie ahead for you. Its presence in Leo through September 2 points to the wisdom of the heart as a guide for successfully managing our lives. Normally, its passage into Virgo refines creative impulses through systematic learning and skillful application. However, the stormy September 11 eclipse in Virgo washes away familiar tools and methods, which delays the implementation of this practical sign's capacity to organize and manage even the most chaotic conditions. Try to flow with the changes this autumn, rather than following the normal seasonal return to order. The North Node in Pisces, too, is a reminder that feelings can guide us through places where intellect alone will fail. Compassion is essential when uncertainty becomes the collective norm.

Contraction under pressure is a natural reaction, but tightness of judgment, especially about oneself, squeezes out the juice of caring that is so vital during these times. Jupiter's extreme sense of right and wrong condemns innocents when, in fact, we are all simply learning what it means to be human. Kindness softens the punishing voices and condemning attitudes so that questions can be heard within the din of imposing rules and regulations. Surprise yourself again and again to catch the wild Jupiter-square-Uranus wave of brilliance, and ride it into a revitalized future of undiscovered promise.

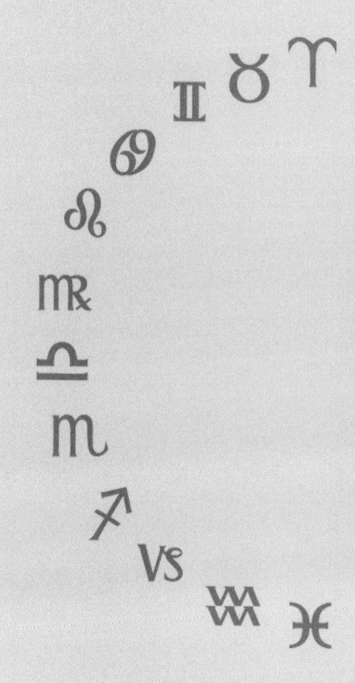

2007

PART 2

ASTROLOGICAL

FORECASTS

ARIES

MARCH 21–APRIL 19

ARIES OVERVIEW

Last year was one of hard work and steady progress. There were also many useful lessons to be learned, even if you faced obstacles or disappointment in love. **This year, as serious Saturn continues moving through your 5th House of Love and Creativity, you will be required to finish what you have already started.** This won't be easy, for the validity of your dreams will be tested as Saturn's tense opposition to nebulous Neptune persists throughout much of 2007. Issues that surfaced in your life during the first opposition last summer will return to the front burner this year, coming back into focus in late winter and then to culmination by early summer. Although this Saturn-Neptune opposition affects everyone, it can work wonders for you Rams if you are willing to face the very issues you would rather avoid.

Your greatest challenge this year may be about seeking balance between expressing what's in your heart and building foundations that have long-term stability. Since Saturn entered fiery Leo in the summer of 2003, you have been attempting to express yourself with integrity—not always a simple matter. You struggle with self-expression because of the price you pay when you walk your talk. Now, however, you learn how to constrain your impulses in a healthy way, leading to increased stability in all of your relationships. **This is no time to be lazy even if you can get by with little effort,** for when Saturn leaves Aries-friendly Leo in early September, additional work responsibilities will increase.

Expansive Jupiter is your ally this year as it travels through adventurous Sagittarius. Its harmonious trine with Saturn offers you specific opportunities to achieve your goals. Make concrete plans for mid-March and early May, when this aspect is exact, to ride this constructive wave to maximum success. Minimally, this is about optimism that has immediate impact; your positive attitude can make big things happen, so don't be afraid to reach out in your personal and professional worlds. **Broaden your horizons in ways that have practical application.** It's a great year to further your education or to travel for work or pleasure.

Your key planet, Mars, is moving at warp speed for the first half of the year, adding excitement to all aspects of your life and kicking you into high gear. By

August, however, assertive Mars gradually slows down as it moves toward a retrograde phase beginning in mid-November. **Initiate new plans and projects early on, for getting started will become more difficult as the year progresses.**

No matter what challenges you face throughout the year, you have an inner strength that will serve you well. Ultimately, your own assessment of life is more important now than what others may say. Listen to the advice given to you by your peers, but don't let their negativity take the wind out of your sails. Be willing to stare discouragement in the face without blinking. Have faith in your own judgments, and you'll be able to move along your path with the confidence and integrity needed.

TRUST IN THE WISDOM OF YOUR FEELINGS

Sweet rewards may be restricted, but your perseverance will pay off. Somber Saturn is in your 5th House of Heart until September 2, forcing you to view love through a realistic filter. Romance is not easy now. Still, with dreamy Neptune tugging at your heartstrings, you can fool others into believing that everything is lovely. The real question for you this year is "What do you want?" You may not be ready to give up hope, but might also be reluctant to share your heart's desire for fear of rejection. If you are in an intimate relationship, work on the foundation while you can still impact the outcome. If you are single, stand up for your ideals without making premature sacrifices for the sake of emotional gratification.

CREATIVE EXPRESSION WORKS

Your career goals are important to you this year, but you may have a difficult time channeling your energy in ways that bring you quick returns. Patience is the key that can unlock the doors to success. The more persistently you tap into your creativity, the greater the rewards. But sometimes it's difficult to express your most inspired ideas in the narrow confines of the work world. Don't give up; even if your best idea falls short, show up with another. Saturn's restraint on your imagination will ease throughout the summer as your efforts are compensated.

SPEND WISELY

Self-restraint may earn you more money this year than anything else. In other words, your indulgences can get you into financial trouble. Although your chart is wired for travel this year, this can be an expensive proposition. Additionally, tuition may be a factor if you are considering going back to school. Don't be afraid to spend money as an investment in yourself. If, however, you are planning a vacation, keep in mind that you can enjoy yourself just as much by traveling inexpensively. Every dollar you save really is another dollar earned.

PREVENTION VERSUS REACTION

Four eclipses activate your 6th House of Health this year, indicating a need to pay special attention to physical symptoms before they become chronic. By focusing your attention on improving your daily habits, including exercise and diet, you can avert the problems that may otherwise surface. The Full Moon Eclipse on March 3 involves Uranus, the planet of sudden changes. You will need to decide if you want to be the cause or the effect of these changes. The New Moon Eclipse on March 18 involves powerful Pluto and is a great time to strengthen your new health routines, such as enrolling in a yoga class. The eclipses of August 28 and September 11 again have electric Uranus playing an important role. Alternative solutions to unsolved complaints can bear fruit. Be experimental this year in how you take responsibility for your well-being.

PLAY IT SAFE

You may be unwilling to fully accept the obligations that home and family now place upon you. You are quite intent on freeing yourself from the burdens of your past. Tread carefully here, Aries, for you have been known to make impulsive decisions that you later regret. Keep in mind that your vision is somewhat clouded through the first part of the year. It may be better to hold off on long-term decisions about moving or refinancing your home until the effects of the Saturn-Neptune opposition begin to wane through the summer. In fact, if you are planning to renovate or remodel, it may be best to start the project at the beginning of August so that you can pick up on the structural integrity of the harmonious Saturn-Pluto trine.

TRAVEL WITH PURPOSE

This could be a year of globe-trotting for you Rams, but you might have to assume additional duties as you travel. For example, if you are going somewhere with a partner or your family, the planning and execution may fall on your shoulders. Or perhaps you'll find yourself in airports and hotels because of business obligations. Boundless Jupiter spends most of the year in your 9th House of Travel and Higher Education, so even if you don't succumb to your wanderlust, you may find yourself enrolled in a course of study that expands your philosophical, spiritual, or political horizons. Additionally, with Jupiter's tense squares to erratic Uranus on January 22, May 10, and October 9, sudden changes in your itinerary could have you running in circles. Keep your goals in sight instead of being distracted by turmoil. Remember that there are many roads that lead to Rome.

TRANSFORM DISAPPOINTMENT INTO MAGIC

Be prepared for major breakthroughs in your understanding of the cosmos. These awakenings will not happen, however, without hard work along the way. There are two processes interweaving in your life now. With Saturn, the planet of hard, cold reality, opposing Neptune, the planet of spiritual vision, your wildest dreams may come crashing down to earth. This not only affects your self-esteem; it impacts your relationships to your family and your community. With Uranus the Awakener receiving a boost from wise Jupiter, you have the ongoing opportunity this year to learn from disappointment and to turn it into metaphysical magic.

RICK & JEFF'S TIP FOR THE YEAR:
Do Not Take No for an Answer

Above everything else, your relentless persistence can set the stage for your greatest successes. Make the most of your more serious approach to life while it lasts. Build your foundations early in the year, but prepare to go on a journey to reach them. Flexibility will help, but that doesn't mean sacrificing what's important. By the time autumn rolls around, your work may become more about details than general planning. Accomplishments will not come without effort this year, for you must earn what you receive.

JANUARY

CLIMB THE MOUNTAIN

This year begins with your mind aiming into the distance. Your goals are lofty, maybe even beyond reach. And you want to reach them now. Patience may not be your strongest suit, but you have lessons to learn and can increase your chances for success by slowing down now and being methodical in your planning. Your key planet, Mars, is quite content in adventurous Sagittarius through **January 16**, encouraging you to just say yes. But there is also a cautious undertone coming from several planets in conservative Capricorn. The Full Moon on **January 3** widens the gulf between your willingness to sacrifice for long-term career ambitions and your need for emotional security in the present moment. As tempted as you might be to do something unexpected to add excitement to your life, you can choose to act maturely if needed. Mars is receiving powerful support from stabilizing Saturn, helping you plan and organize effectively. Their exact trine on **January 8** is a great time to make final travel arrangements for an upcoming trip.

The energy shifts mid-month as pushy Mars passes by passionate Pluto on **January 13**, stirring up deeply rooted emotional issues. Then, on **January 16**, Mars enters earthy Capricorn; you are now ready to dig in your heels and take on whatever additional hard work must be done so that you can complete the tasks you've previously started. The New Moon on **January 18** confirms what you already know, but the future is arriving quickly. You must be ready to make a decision and set out on a new course. This desire for immediate change comes to a peak around **January 22**, when expansive Jupiter squares electric Uranus, setting a unconventional background theme for the entire year.

> **KEEP IN MIND THIS MONTH**
>
> *As much as you desire excitement in your life now, the work you do must also set the stage for the future.*

KEY DATES

JANUARY 3 ★ *unexpected solutions*

Today's Full Moon in moody Cancer can be stressful, yet your reactions to a current situation can tilt events in your favor. You may feel as if there is no easy way to meet obligations while being true to yourself. Instead of shooting from the hip—which often works well for you—engage in constructive dialogue. A quantum leap can occur from finding common ground instead of attacking what may be the source of the problem.

JANUARY 18 ★ *imagination overcomes resistance*
Today's New Moon in reliable Capricorn blends with dreamy Neptune. You have
focused much of your attention on duties and obligations; now it's time to change
your direction. This isn't about walking away from responsibility. Rather, it's about
allowing your fantasies to trickle out into your everyday life.

JANUARY 20–22 ★ *the future is bright*
You could write your own script now, starring in your version of "The Comeback
Kid." Whatever hardships you have recently endured no longer seem to stand in
your way. Or, if they do, you have a plan or two to overcome these persistent
obstacles. An exciting square between unpredictable Uranus and buoyant Jupiter
has hope springing forth from the deepest wells, teasing you with endless
possibilities. Which path do you take? There are so many options, but you may not
be able to take off on your next adventure just yet. Sweet Venus is temporarily
thwarted by immovable Saturn. Take your time; your need for unrestrained
freedom will not wane.

JANUARY 28 ★ *back to the drawing board*
An oppressive opposition between mental Mercury and authoritative Saturn can
throw intellectual roadblocks into your path. This isn't about failure; it's reality's
way of asking you to do even better. Reconsider your plans. Tighten up your
thinking. Make progress with determination.

ARIES

FEBRUARY

FAITH AND PATIENCE FACILITATE ADVANCEMENT

February is a significant month for you Rams—one filled with challenges, excitement, disappointments, and recognition. Stern Saturn in your 5th House of Creativity continues to restrain self-expression with diffusive Neptune in your 11th House of Dreams opposing it. This long-term transit began last summer, when you may have experienced despair. If you have been rebuilding a vision for your future, a second encounter between these powerful planets on **February 28** could present a series of situations that distort your view of reality. You may question your previous choices while seeking unobtainable concrete answers to your spiritual malaise. On the other hand, this can be your time to overcome hopelessness by relinquishing control and trusting the process you began last year. How you respond to the planetary pressures will set larger waves in motion that reach fruition by the end of June. The Sun accentuates the Saturn-Neptune conjunction from **February 8 to 10**, possibly highlighting personal issues regarding children, friends, or lovers that need your attention.

Mercury the Messenger spends most of the month in compassionate Pisces, softening your typically blunt approach. Mercury turns retrograde on **February 13**, encouraging you to reconsider decisions you may have made hastily earlier in the month. The Sun, too, enters emotional Pisces on **February 18**, reminding you to pay attention to your intuition and dreams before initiating action. This may be somewhat difficult, for lovely Venus pushes ahead of the Sun into impulsive Aries on **February 21** as you aim your sights at the objects of your desires. Then, starting on **February 25**, your inbox fills with intelligent input from your friends and associates as your key planet, Mars, rushes into social Aquarius.

> **KEEP IN MIND THIS MONTH**
>
> *Don't let frustration get the best of you; remember that your attitude now will impact the coming events in ways that you cannot yet understand.*

KEY DATES

FEBRUARY 1–3 ★ *somewhere over the rainbow*
The enthusiastic Leo Full Moon on **February 1** sets the tone for your month by demonstrating the positive things that can happen when you are willing to go the extra distance. With benevolent Jupiter supporting the Sun, it feels as if your pot of

gold is just over the next hill. And as your key planet, Mars, forms a cooperative sextile with surprising Uranus on **February 3**, the results of your efforts might just pay off much more quickly than you expect.

SUPER NOVA DAYS
FEBRUARY 7-10 ★ *imagination takes you on a wild goose chase*
An unexpected outpouring of fantasy may catch you off guard, even if you are doing most of the talking. The Sun's alignment with spiritual Neptune fuzzes your boundaries, making you more susceptible to whatever is shared, especially in a romantic situation. But this can also affect your pocketbook; you may become suddenly attached to an object of great beauty, whether or not it's worth the asking price. On **February 10**, the Sun makes its annual opposition to stern Saturn, pulling your head out of the clouds and teaching you exactly what you need to learn. You can make it easier on yourself with a little restraint and self-discipline sooner rather than later.

FEBRUARY 13-17 ★ *can't get no satisfaction*
The days leading up to Saturday's Aquarian New Moon are fraught with delays and minor problems. You might think the culprit is chatty Mercury, who turned retrograde on **February 13**, but that's just part of the story. A rare double quincunx on **February 14** from authoritative Saturn to the lovers, Venus and Mars, tends to keep satisfaction out of reach. The more you try to make everything mellow, the less cozy it gets—right up to the unpredictable New Moon, which changes the dynamics. Your difficulties will not suddenly disappear, but at least your path will be illuminated.

FEBRUARY 21 ★ *awakening desires*
Today, as sensual Venus enters your sign, you can feel adrenaline rush throughout your body. Every desire can produce an immediate scenario, and whether or not you act on any one feeling, this can be a great time to be alive. Breathe deeply and smile. Outside it may still be cold winter, but emotionally spring is in your heart.

FEBRUARY 28 ★ *acknowledge life's limitations*
When an enduring transit is exact, like today's Saturn-Neptune opposition, it's important to stand back from the immediate situation and try to create a wider perspective. You are aware of the gulf between your fantasy and the current reality. Your foundations are in flux; accept your limitations and move on to what's next.

MARCH

STEADY PROGRESS

You move forward this month, Aries—not by huge leaps and bounds, but by the consistent efforts you make day by day. Communicative Mercury ends its retrograde phase on **March 7**, so tie up as many loose ends as you can right away. Two eclipses this month can be the source of unexpected behind-the-scenes pressure that requires you to make significant changes. The Virgo Full Moon Eclipse on **March 3** activates your 6th House of Work, so you can expect volatile dynamics on the job, especially with erratic Uranus also in the picture. The Pisces New Moon Eclipse on **March 18** indicates a shift in an ongoing power struggle. A tense square from the Sun and Moon to powerful Pluto is the culprit, and you'll need to tread lightly in social situations lest you stir up a hornet's nest that is not easily put back to rest.

    The first of two harmonious trines this year between gigantic Jupiter and titanic Saturn occurs on **March 16** and offers you as much potential for good fortune as you are willing to take. Saturn's presence makes you work for what you want, but Jupiter all but guarantees success if you are sincere and ambitious. You can quickly see relationships between your goals and what you must do to achieve them. The second beneficial Jupiter-Saturn trine is on **May 5**, so it's critical to take carefully considered actions until then. Attractive Venus can bring beauty and money into your life as she moves through fiery Aries. On **March 8**, Venus mutually trines the applying Jupiter-Saturn trine, creating a magical and stabilizing moment in your life.

> **KEEP IN MIND THIS MONTH**
>
> *Don't let this moment or this month slip by without taking a risk and making the most of the opportunities that come your way.*

KEY DATES

MARCH 3 ★ *lightning strikes*

Today's Full Moon Eclipse is opposite freedom-loving Uranus. Buried tensions, deep secrets, and hidden agendas are suddenly out in the open. You might feel like a victim of circumstance because you are not in control of these current revelations. On the other hand, you could take the lightning into your own hands by stepping into the open and exposing the truth yourself.

SUPER NOVA DAYS
MARCH 8-9 ★ *enjoy success with a smile*
You are even more impulsive these days than usual, but as Venus in direct Aries hooks up with both expansive Jupiter and contractive Saturn, you receive a powerful cosmic blessing. Jupiter encourages you by making everything appear even better than it is, while Saturn makes you quite the realist. Jupiter gives you the gift of heightened charm as Saturn tempers your appeal with deliberate thought. No question about it: you are a force to be reckoned with in business or in love. The problem, however, could be lack of motivation. Don't let your present comfort and ease lull you into laziness.

MARCH 15-16 ★ *accomplishing the impossible*
A rare conjunction of the Moon with assertive Mars and painful Chiron on **March 15** can stop you in your tracks as you consider a current situation in light of a previous failure. You can think of countless reasons why your present path won't lead you to success and are in no mood to repeat the past. Thankfully, the steady hand of Saturn now supports the distant vision of Jupiter. You feel closer to your goals, and your confidence returns quickly. The pieces are all in place; it's now up to you.

MARCH 20-22 ★ *no shortcuts allowed*
The Sun enters courageous Aries on **March 20**, marking the first day of spring. You can feel the fiery energy now from the Sun in your own sign, but you immediately face a roadblock. Your key planet, Mars, tensely opposes authoritative Saturn on **March 22**, forcing you to slam on the brakes. You cannot just ram your way through this one. Slow down, listen to what reality is telling you, and alter your plans as needed before pushing ahead.

MARCH 23-25 ★ *proceed with cautious confidence*
Mars in your 10th House of Career is giving the go-ahead, signaling that your path is now clear. Your confidence has returned; you may even feel unbeatable. Be careful at work; with Neptune involved, you may be missing something important. Your imagination can inspire you to great heights or it can lead you astray. Think twice before going too far too quickly.

APRIL

The Full Moon in relationship-oriented Libra on **April 2** jump-starts the month with irresolvable contradictions. You may experience sudden mood swings, alternating your innate need for independence with a strong desire for intimate companionship. Even with the support you receive all month from the continuing trine between expansive Jupiter and contractive Saturn, the cosmic regulators cannot make your interpersonal problems disappear. You have much to learn, and you won't get the full impact of these lessons if you hurry through the rough roads you now must travel. It might even seem like opportunities are slipping away as beneficent Jupiter slows to a halt, turning retrograde on **April 5**. It may take longer for you to reach your objectives than you wish, especially as your key planet, Mars, slips into dreamy Pisces on **April 6**. But this is not a negative time, for you can lay the groundwork to turn your fantasies into reality. Stoke the fires of enthusiasm by focusing on your personal growth. Unless you take care of your spiritual needs, you can deplete your energy helping others.

The self-directed New Moon in Aries on **April 17** confirms your direction in life, but it can also remind you how far off course you veered. Since the New Moon is in your 1st House of Personality, this is your chance to make a statement about your true identity. Don't let this opportunity pass you by without making mid-course corrections, if needed. Your primary concern is exploring new avenues for self-expression until **April 20**, when the Sun enters sensible Taurus. No longer can you get away with simply having another good idea. Focus on building financial security as you take what you've started and create something substantial.

> ### KEEP IN MIND THIS MONTH
>
> *You have immense power to create your future. Begin this next phase of your journey with purpose and determination as you move toward your destination.*

KEY DATES

APRIL 1-3 ★ *relationship discomfort*

Difficult aspects to unsettling Uranus and Taskmaster Saturn on **April 1** have you wondering if it might be easier to just withdraw and not worry about what others think. But this is not going to happen, as the Full Moon on **April 2** in ambivalent Libra in your 7th House of Partnerships focuses your attention on the very relationship issues you want to avoid. If you can accept the instability of these days without overreacting, it will be easier to move graciously through your own feelings of insecurity.

APRIL 8-10 ★ *confidence breeds success*
Your confidence is your best weapon now to combat any covert resistance. The Sun in Aries forms mutual trines with both broad-minded Jupiter and cautious Saturn, giving you the perfect balance between optimism and realism and emphasizing an ongoing theme that endures through May. Invest your energy wisely so that you can use it for anything you wish over the weeks ahead.

SUPER NOVA DAY
APRIL 17 ★ *claim your power*
Forceful Pluto harmoniously trines the Aries New Moon, reminding you to acknowledge your feelings in everything you do. There isn't much room today for compromise; you are required to stand up for your beliefs, regardless of the consequences. If your life is on track, this will give you the chance to demonstrate your honesty and integrity. If not, you'll be facing your worst fears. Either way, the power of resilience is on your side. It's time to be courageous and let the world know the real you.

APRIL 20-21 ★ *stand up for your beliefs*
As the Sun enters determined Taurus on **April 20**, you can feel the force of your willpower working to your advantage. Your mind is like a steel trap now; whatever you think can become real. Mental Mercury picks up on the harmonious trines to both Jupiter and Saturn; this ongoing pattern reinforces the fair and balanced information you previously received. If you are working on a long-term project, now is the time to share your thoughts with others. You have a rare ability these days to take grandiose philosophical ideas and bring them down to earth.

APRIL 27-30 ★ *at the edge*
Assertive Mars conjuncts brilliant Uranus, flooding you with a desire to break free of constraints. However, it's not wise to recklessly shatter the stability you've worked so hard to create. Keep in mind that your judgment may be clouded by your own illusions. Go ahead and express yourself, but do it in a thoughtful manner that doesn't destroy what's important.

ARIES

MAY

AN ACT OF BALANCE

May is action-packed with planetary drama, but when all is said and done, there might be more bark than bite. The fixed Scorpio Full Moon on **May 2** involves wordy Mercury, stirring a need to communicate your deepest passions. Your mind cannot easily find a place to rest amid the intensity of your feelings. But behind lots of surface noise, optimistic Jupiter and realistic Saturn revisit a harmonious linkage on **May 5** that began in March and culminates in January 2008. This lets you perform an exquisite balancing act between your long-term educational objectives and your current interests. However, Jupiter's expansive nature runs into the erratic individuality of Uranus by **May 10**, when boredom can lead to unproductive yet thrilling risk-taking.

The pace of life picks up even more on **May 11**, when chatty Mercury skips into its home sign of curious Gemini. And when your key planet, Mars, rushes into its own sign of independent Aries on **May 15**, you turn your energy directly toward anything or anyone standing in your way. But the New Moon in stable Taurus on **May 16** can ground you just enough to prevent you from taking foolish action that you might later regret.

The second part of the month is not quite as busy as the first, but you still may be running in circles. An unexpected emotional encounter or a change in your primary relationship status gives you good reason to refocus your energy on personal matters. But the Sun's entrance into flighty Gemini on **May 21** doesn't promote the needed follow-through. Meanwhile, emotions continue to apply an uncomfortable pressure as the Moon waxes to a rare second Full Moon on **May 31**.

> **KEEP IN MIND THIS MONTH**
>
> *Loosen your control; something has to give, as much as you try to hold your life together in anticipation of the larger changes coming.*

KEY DATES

SUPER NOVA DAYS
MAY 5–7 ★ *grab the bull by its horns*
Energized Mercury, coupled with a harmonious Jupiter-Saturn trine, stimulates your nervous system while stabilizing your world. There are powerful changes afoot, but it may not be your place to decide exactly how

and when they take shape. Harnessing energies much greater than yours can be tricky, yet you're up for this Herculean task. Trust your survival instincts, for you have the right combination of serious thinking, the willingness to do inner work, and the ability to grow from your experience. Remember that your creativity can bring rich satisfaction, but an innovative road can feel a bit bumpy now. Slow down and brace yourself for the transformation.

MAY 9-10 ★ *change of plans*
No matter how tight your plan, you must make radical adjustments to your schedule. Your best efforts could backfire if you try to force others to do your bidding. If you struggle to have your way, you will exhaust yourself before you are finished. If, however, you are able to temporarily set aside your own agenda, you may be surprised with the gift of appreciation and support.

MAY 13-16 ★ *know when to let go*
In order to initiate a new cycle of action, you first must complete unfinished business. But you may have run into an insurmountable problem that will prevent you from reaching your destination. Aggressive Mars crosses swords with powerful Pluto on **May 13**, but the angry red planet cannot sustain the intensity. It may be better to call for a truce than to lose a battle defending your personal, political, or religious values in a situation you cannot win. Anyway, you have more pressing projects to launch as your key planet, Mars, enters self-directed Aries on **May 14**. Use the New Moon on **May 16** to separate yourself from the past as you move assertively toward your next venture.

MAY 20 ★ *think faster; act slower*
A fast-moving square between curious Mercury and innovative Uranus can excite your mind, bringing original thoughts to the surface faster than you can integrate them. You cannot act on every new idea, or you'll scatter your energy and may not have anything to show for your mental brilliance.

MAY 27-28 ★ *beware of the blame game*
Eloquent Mercury is activated by dark Pluto, and your words hurt more than you intend. Conversations escalate into adversarial encounters. On **May 28**, Mercury dons an invisibility cloak as it enters emotionally passive Cancer. Don't overreact to a harsh encounter by shutting down. Find supportive ways to make your point without playing the role of victim or villain.

JUNE

THE WHOLE TRUTH AND NOTHING BUT THE TRUTH

There is no room for self-deception this month as dreamy Neptune aligns opposite realistic Saturn. This slow-moving transit started impacting your life last summer as you faced disenchantment in love, possibly even with life. Perhaps you thought you could maintain your sense of individuality as you merged your life or goals with someone else's. Maybe you have had to take on additional responsibilities, especially with children. Or maybe an investment isn't bringing you the expected returns. No matter how your emotional or financial fortunes have changed, **June 25** marks the culmination of this process. Authenticity is more important than anything else. Stay on guard, but don't let paranoia rule your life.

Luckily, energetic Mars in proactive Aries until **June 24** sparks the very enthusiasm you need to combat any irrational suspicions. Additionally, loving Venus enters expressive Leo in your 5th House of Fun on **June 5**, lifting your spirits even more. Many excellent opportunities for learning, especially through travel, knock on your door throughout the first half of the month, but it's up to you to make something happen. **June 4, 11, and 13** are the best days for initiating action. On **June 9**, however, you may have to respond to unexpected developments, especially if you have overextended your commitments.

The Gemini New Moon in your 3rd House of Siblings on **June 14** may indicate increased family interactions, possibly with too much talking and planning for your tastes. Remain flexible, as Mercury turns retrograde on **June 15** and even best-laid plans can fall apart. The Capricorn Full Moon in your 10th House of Career on **June 30** may have you working harder without additional pay. You have plenty to do, so don't let negative attitudes get in the way of production.

> **KEEP IN MIND THIS MONTH**
>
> *Act from your heart with the wisdom of your experience combined with compassion. Don't let fear stand in your way of loving others.*

KEY DATES

JUNE 4–5 ★ *contagious positivity*

It might feel as if you can do no wrong now and this is, to some extent, true. After being less sure of yourself, your confidence returns. Turn your positive thinking into clear action while you can. Just remember that as the enthusiasm boils over from red-hot Mars harmonizing with fortunate Jupiter, there is also the possibility of taking on too much too quickly. A trip or an intellectual journey will be successful as long as you don't overwhelm others with all that you do.

SUPER NOVA DAYS
JUNE 11-14 ★ *sustain excitement*
As you get closer to the New Moon on **June 14,** your eagerness and joy become colored by the hard, cold reality of Saturn. But this won't stop you from expressing your heart; it just cools you down enough to sustain your emotions over a longer period of time. Assertive Mars harmonizes with constraining Saturn on **June 11,** giving you an ideal balance between acceleration and caution. Your organizational skills can effectively be put to use now for work or for play. Remember that it's not about what you accomplish today; it's about applying your energy toward your long-term aspirations.

JUNE 18-21 ★ *assume power with grace*

Your survival instincts are quite strong now and could even stir up resistance from others who are threatened by your force and power. Others may shrink in fear from engaging with serious opponents, but you are even more courageous than usual as Mars, the god of war, harmonizes with Pluto, the lord of the underworld. This is an amazing partnership, however temporary, so take advantage of it while you can. Remember, though, that normally fast-footed Mercury turned retrograde on **June 15,** so you may have to put some of your efforts toward reworking what you thought was already finished. In fact, as you get closer to your destination, it may morph into something else. Take your time as reality continues to change; you don't need to be in a hurry anymore.

JUNE 30 ★ *not as bad as it seems*

The Full Moon in somber Capricorn issues you a reality check today, and you might not like the report card you receive. You might be told to cool your heels or may even get tossed into a cold emotional shower as warm Venus runs into stern Saturn. Relationships might not offer you much-needed support, and financial difficulties, too, could be exacerbated. But be careful; you might have an overly pessimistic appraisal of the situation or yourself. Don't make any long-term decisions now; wait until you're feeling a bit more positive.

ARIES

JULY

SLOW DOWN; YOU'RE MOVING TOO FAST

Your key planet, Mars, receives its marching orders this month from sensible Taurus, requiring you to plod through your chores in a practical and determined manner. Normally, you Aries like to rush ahead of the pack, but this type of impulsive behavior will not be supported at this time. If you feel as if you are in a race, you still must ease your foot off the accelerator to gain mastery and maintain control of your life. Resistance to fiscal responsibilities and rebellion against emotional obligations will prove futile. You can increase your sense of security now by working carefully toward increased material success.

The month opens with a cautionary conjunction between sensual Venus and restrictive Saturn, restraining romantic desires and discouraging self-indulgent behavior. You receive encouraging words from a loved one as protective Mercury in Cancer ends its retrograde phase on **July 9**. On **July 14**, the Cancer New Moon in your 4th House of Family reminds you once again of the cozy benefits of accepting where you are rather than hurrying off somewhere else. You gain more now through fostering emotional connections with loved ones than through advancing your social status.

Your judgment could be a little off as optimism leads you to overestimate the potential return on an investment of time or money. Although you may feel a creative rush as the Sun enters playful Leo on **July 22**, contrary signals around **July 27** tell you to play it cool with your money and in love as Venus begins its retrograde cycle, which lasts through **September 8**. Remember, however, that staying open to these conflicting ideas can ultimately make you stronger.

> **KEEP IN MIND THIS MONTH**
>
> *Take it easy; if you don't slow yourself down, reality may have to do it for you.*

KEY DATES

JULY 1 ★ *overcome inhibitions*

Share your feelings today, even if it's not easy for you. Your emotional vulnerability could contribute to your silence, but self-isolation is not the cure. Expressive Mercury, now in nurturing Cancer, is supporting your key action planet, Mars. Move delicately as you start to talk about sensitive topics, but forge ahead firmly as you confront your fears.

JULY 9-10 ★ *cautious optimism*

You may have taken a walk down memory lane as old issues about your home and family resurfaced over the last few weeks. Now, although your feelings deepen, it's time to let go of the past and move on. Mentally active Mercury, though remaining in emotional Cancer all month, encourages this forward thinking as it begins moving direct again on **July 9**. Be careful, however, for you may be so jazzed about the possibilities ahead that you jump into the pool before checking to see that it's filled with water.

JULY 14 ★ *find comfort at home*

Today's powerful New Moon in fearful Cancer galvanizes your awareness about what you want to do and why you cannot do it your way. Consider how your actions affect loved ones as assertive Mars crosses paths with wounded Chiron, activating fears of inadequacy. Uncharacteristic passivity increases your impatience; you boil over with displeasure. Additionally, attractive Venus becomes fussier as she steps into fault-finding Virgo. Don't waste energy being hypercritical. Accept the present as it is; you will have opportunities for change soon enough.

JULY 24 ★ *lost at sea*

Mars in steady Taurus makes you determined to succeed, but as it tensely squares murky Neptune, you may feel as if you are lost at sea with no direction home. Avoid temptations to escape from your discouraging situation, especially with drugs or alcohol. Turn your malaise into something beautiful by heading toward your feelings, not away from them. Writing in a journal, listening to music, or dancing your sorrows away can help you move through this disorienting phase.

SUPER NOVA DAYS
JULY 29-31 ★ *don't give up*

You might think that you have failed, but you just have one more hurdle before you get a clear path to your destination. The Full Moon in airy Aquarius on **July 29** can bring a love-related issue to a head as you attempt to detach from a difficult situation. You may feel stifled, but as forceful Mars squares tough Saturn on **July 31**, you realize that hard work and brutal honesty will show you a way out. Stand up to harsh pressures as best you can. A very slow-moving trine between heavyweights Saturn and Pluto will grant you a hard-earned victory in the days ahead.

AUGUST

CONCENTRATE ON THE POWER OF LOVE

August offers you abundant energy, yet you must use it wisely or you could be left with little to show for it. Starting on **August 6**, you are up for nearly anything with action-oriented Mars moving through interactive Gemini. However, you won't want to scatter your intentions as austere Saturn and powerful Pluto—both in Aries-friendly fire signs—harmonize throughout the first half of the month, giving you much-needed self-control. You can positively transform a current relationship simply by taking responsibility for your actions. In love, you can be more serious without losing the ability to have fun. In dealing with children, you may have to play the role of stern parent, yet your high spirits remain intact.

An influential gathering of five planets in dramatic Leo culminates at the New Moon in your 5th House of Self-Expression on **August 12**. Retrograde Venus backing into restrictive Saturn at this time may feel like water thrown onto your fire of spontaneity. Cooling down your desires now can help to make love endure the metamorphosis you may be experiencing. Although the theme of restraint and self-discipline continues to be emphasized as mental Mercury conjuncts Saturn on **August 18**, followed by the Sun on **August 21**, fantasy also enters the picture.

> **KEEP IN MIND THIS MONTH**
>
> *Managing your schedule as effectively as possible allows you to accomplish plenty and still have time to indulge in your dreams.*

Otherworldly Neptune is tensely activated on **August 13** by the Sun, on **August 14** by Mercury, and on **August 25** by beautiful Venus, followed by a Full Moon Eclipse on **August 28** in Neptune's sign, Pisces. Unforeseen changes in your schedule can force you to loosen your grip on your calendar. Don't be afraid to seek solace in your dreams, but be careful not to confuse them with your mundane obligations.

KEY DATES

AUGUST 1–3 ★ *more isn't always best*

August is kick-started with a lucky trine between the Sun and joyful Jupiter, encouraging you to take risks. Your optimism pushes you forward, but assertive Mars is irritated now by Pluto's quest for power. Dark secrets and hidden agendas can distort an otherwise great situation—so much so that you may misjudge and overshoot your mark. Although you may be tempted to act first and think later, it's much healthier now to talk about your intended moves before you make them.

SUPER NOVA DAYS
AUGUST 6-9 ★ *create your future*
Forceful Mars enters versatile Gemini on **August 6**, and as long as you don't try to do too much or move too quickly, these can be highly productive days. There's a creative buzz as artistic Venus squares Mars on **August 7** just prior to Venus's retrograde back into playful Leo on **August 8**. However, slow-moving transits have long-lasting ramifications, and now persistent Saturn harmoniously trines evolutionary Pluto. Although there's a lot of surface noise, current choices about your daily routines are quite important. This dynamic is amplified by beneficent Jupiter now turning direct, making this a perfect time to set your plans in motion.

AUGUST 12-16 ★ *small steps to success*
For all its apparent simplicity, the showy Leo New Moon on **August 12** is rich with intricate complexity, receiving exceptional support from transformational Pluto, lack of certainty from illusory Neptune, contradictory information from revolutionary Uranus, and delayed gratification from austere Saturn. You feel as if this may be your big chance, but be prepared for the changes to unfold slowly over the days ahead. Nothing is going to reach fruition as quickly as you wish, yet these days are too critical to waste. Your success may depend upon being patient and knowing your limits.

AUGUST 23-25 ★ *you think; therefore, you stress*
Although you are feeling rather focused with the Sun in picky Virgo, an exuberant opposition between assertive Mars and expansive Jupiter could trick you into believing that you can reach any height. The power of positive thought really does work, but you can set yourself up for failure if you don't correctly assess the size of the job. This opposition is further stressed by tense squares to analytical Mercury now in practical Virgo. You may vacillate between unrealistic optimism and defeatist pessimism. Then, on **August 25**, when Venus, the planet of personal love, opposes Neptune, the planet of spiritual love, you are caught in a fantasy of your own making. It's best to check out any assumptions you make about your partner before you set yourself up for disillusionment.

SEPTEMBER

MAKING HEALTHY CHOICES

When slow-moving planets, such as Saturn, change signs, they signal deep shifts in the focus of our lives. September begins with stern Saturn entering analytical Virgo in your 6th House of Health and Work. These two apparently separate areas of your life both involve your habits, good and bad. Good health is not achieved all at once; it comes from establishing beneficial daily routines, including sensible choices in diet, physical activity, and lifestyle. Saturn is not very forgiving; you must attend to your body and mind with steadfast devotion. Work, too, requires that you show up and deliver with similar clockwork dependability. You may face longer hours or additional burdens from your job, but Saturn appreciates sincere effort and faithfulness. The 6th House loves rhythmic stability, and with Saturn as a long-term visitor, you can expect to get what you truly deserve. This phase lasts until the autumn of 2009, giving you plenty of time to develop healthier habits, but don't wait to make positive changes; the sooner you start, the greater the benefits.

On **September 8**, loving Venus in your 5th House of Children and Romance turns direct, allowing you to be more spontaneous and playful. On **September 11**, a Virgo New Moon Eclipse in your 6th House can focus your attention to sudden changes at work. Issues that arise now should not be avoided or suppressed, or they will cause trouble later. The Aries Full Moon on **September 26** may create tension between your drive for independence and the stability of a current relationship. With mental Mercury harmonized to emphatic Mars now, you can state your needs without seeming too rude or forceful. Just remember that asking for what you want doesn't guarantee that you will get it.

> **KEEP IN MIND THIS MONTH**
>
> *Moderation is essential, even when making healthy changes. Small improvements have a better chance of enduring than the over-the-top ones.*

KEY DATES

SEPTEMBER 2–3 ★ *temper impulses with diplomacy*

You may not be willing to hand over your independence without a fight, and if you feel threatened, you could blow your top at the slightest provocation. Your key planet, Mars, now in flighty Gemini, forms a harsh square with jolting Uranus, setting your nerves on edge. Luckily, Mars is receiving soothing signals from charming Venus to keep you from going too far. Pretending everything is okay won't work. You can, however, ameliorate ill will by looking at your situation from another person's point of view.

SEPTEMBER 8-9 ★ *the high price of love*
Your desires are heightened; however, all is not well in the land of gratification. Freedom-loving Uranus won't let you settle into a comfortable place. No matter how much you want the sweet satisfaction of love, you cannot pay the required price. Forceful Mars is energetically merging into soothing Neptune, pacifying the fires of your passions as you escape into your favorite fantasies. Although this can temporarily calm you, it doesn't solve the underlying problems. Face your dilemma creatively; don't sidestep it by slipping out of reality and into illusion.

SUPER NOVA DAYS
SEPTEMBER 17-21 ★ *ambitions stir up anger*
The days leading up to a volcanic opposition between compulsive Pluto and red-hot Mars on **September 21** can set the stage for intense power struggles. Whatever tensions have been eased by your goodwill and diplomacy are now back, perhaps stronger than ever. And you aren't as eager to accommodate the needs of others this time. Your patience has worn thin; your resolve is firm. Anyone who stands in your way can feel the brunt of your temper. But direct conflict will only stir up deeper issues and make matters worse. How you handle this dynamic period is entirely within your command. Stay present with your feelings. Don't bury them; express them in a careful and controlled manner without giving others a reason to work against you. Channeling this turbulent energy toward positive transformation isn't easy but is exactly what's required now.

SEPTEMBER 26 ★ *carpe diem*
The emotionally expressive Aries Full Moon belongs to you, flooding your consciousness with dreams that you would usually forget during the day. Now, however, you cannot put them out of your mind. Also, talkative Mercury harmonizes with assertive Mars. You can say what's on your mind in a straightforward, no-nonsense manner. Your words carry the sense of your self-assurance. Do whatever is needed to seize this moment, for both Mercury and Mars change signs in the next couple of days, rapidly dissolving this great opportunity.

OCTOBER

SLOWING DOWN GRACEFULLY

October is a month of emotional growth. The pace of your life isn't as fast as usual, and if you are in a hurry, you might feel somewhat frustrated. The primary culprit is your key planet, Mars. Normally energetic Mars rushes through a sign in about six weeks, but it just entered emotionally passive Cancer on **September 28**, and due to its biannual retrograde cycle, it's stuck here for most of the next six months. Mars doesn't turn retrograde until mid-November, but its motion has already slowed to a snail's pace. Additionally, impulsive Mars isn't particularly thrilled to be stagnating in timid Cancer. But there's a dominant nesting theme as Mars carefully makes its way through your 4th House of Home and Family. It's not time to conquer the world; now you must pay extra attention to personal matters. Retreating into more intimate spaces, taking care of loved ones, and even initiating projects at home are all likely.

The other contributor to your energetic disengagement is normally talkative Mercury, which turns retrograde on **October 11** and stays in reverse for the rest of the month. Mercury retrograde is less physical than Mars; this is about mental refuge. As always during Mercury's backward cycle, you should revisit recent decisions, reconsider your plans, and in general be willing to retrace your past.

The gracious Libra New Moon on **October 11** is in your 7th House of Partnerships. A harmonious trine to imaginative Neptune inspires your closest relationships with visions of the future. The materialistic Taurus Full Moon on **October 26** is in your 2nd House of Possessions, emphasizing creature comforts. A trine to hardworking Saturn is best utilized by applying efforts to stabilize your finances and resources.

> **KEEP IN MIND THIS MONTH**
>
> *Gather your forces by revitalizing your emotional life. Spend time nurturing those you love and accepting emotional support.*

KEY DATES

OCTOBER 1–3 ★ *going the extra mile*

Your thoughts are clear and your words concise as Mercury sextiles dutiful Saturn. People listen as you speak with authority. You are decisive, with good reason for your no-nonsense approach. Perhaps you have been given new responsibilities at work and must motivate others to do their part. Or maybe a loved one needs your financial assistance. Either way, your current actions can appear effortless as you take care of your obligations. Just because your thoughts and feelings align with each other, don't become lackadaisical and fall asleep at the wheel. What makes you so productive these days is your willingness to put in the extra effort.

SUPER NOVA DAYS
OCTOBER 8-11 ★ *create harmony*
A cooperative sextile between forceful Mars and authoritative Saturn on **October 8** makes you more effective in any task you do. And although there may be chores that you need to do both at work and at home, the friendly Libra New Moon on **October 11** emphasizes your relationship to others. Decide what you can do to make your spouse, coworker, or friend more content. The long-term square between broad-minded Jupiter and brilliant Uranus gives you the ability to see things from a unique perspective and formulate an unorthodox plan. You can accomplish great things now if you don't take on more than you can handle. Thorough forethought will prevent you from having to head back to the drawing board when Mercury turns retrograde on **October 11**.

OCTOBER 16-20 ★ *controlled expression*
Retrograde Mercury backs into a synergistic trine with not-so-assertive Mars in emotional Cancer. Communicating indirectly in a nonconfrontational manner plays out to your advantage. Another restraining signal comes from socially active Venus and calculating Saturn, adding tact and maturity to your words. You are quite clear about your feelings, and expressing them in a controlled way works in your favor, even if you are raising delicate issues.

OCTOBER 26 ★ *keep it simple*
A Full Moon in simplistic Taurus reminds you to take care of basics as you look ahead to the winter months. You may be somewhat self-indulgent, though, for even as restrictive Saturn plays strongly at this lunation, beautiful Venus is heading toward a duel with opulent Jupiter. Additionally, a potentially reckless opposition from Venus to unconventional Uranus excites you with possibilities of immediate gratification; however, you may not want to sacrifice your freedom in order to be loved. Don't fall victim to unproductive impulses. Set your priorities on increasing your financial security and being more responsible at work.

NOVEMBER

PROGRESS GRINDS TO A HALT

You Rams are known for your impatient, spontaneous style of living. You can be headstrong when charged with enthusiasm. Your key planet, Mars, usually drives you into new situations, but this month is a different story, as the assertive planet turns retrograde on **November 15**. Typically, Mars races through the zodiac, but this month, the "get there faster" planet moves only one degree. Start cooling your heels sooner rather than later, or you could become quite disgruntled by the lack of progress, especially regarding emotional issues with family members. This is not a hopeless time, though; you receive sustenance from the Sun in passionate Scorpio and unpredictable Uranus in psychically sensitive Pisces. Rather than competing with someone, your battles are within your own heart. Be courageous by staying true to yourself while remaining sensitive to the needs of others.

The powerful Scorpio New Moon on **November 9** is in your 8th House of Shared Resources, initiating a new cycle relating to joint property or financial issues. Examine your current holdings so that you can creatively manage what you have. Since intimate relationships are also a shared resource, involve your partner in any fiscal decisions you must make. Your desire for emotional excitement is sustained by a harmonious trine between ardent Mars and inventive Uranus. You stand to get what you want, but you'll need to break through your insecurities to succeed. The busy Gemini Full Moon on **November 24** in your 3rd House of Immediate Environment stirs up a festive holiday party, but this might only distract you from the real work at hand. Passive resistance isn't a healthy substitute for compassionate engagement.

> **KEEP IN MIND THIS MONTH**
>
> *Finding comfort within the shell of your private world is a good start yet not enough. Expressing emotional vulnerability widens the path toward trust and intimacy.*

KEY DATES

NOVEMBER 1–4 ★ *magic in the air*

Talkative Mercury in socially aware Libra turns direct on **November 1** as your thoughts happily turn to relationships. You are more eager than ever to make others feel at ease. Dynamic Mars receives an energetic boost from the Sun on **November 4**, making it possible to enroll others in your plan for happiness.

Additionally, a series of magical quintiles with the lovers, Venus and Mars, and spiritual Neptune gives you the juice to create an extraordinary experience.

NOVEMBER 8-11 ★ *sweet fantasy*
Romantic Venus enters your 7th House of Partnerships on **November 8**, indicating your need for peaceful interactions. The New Moon in emotionally intense Scorpio on **November 9**, coupled with a dynamic square to elusive Neptune, can introduce uncertainty as your imagination overtakes the real world. Increase your spiritual awareness and undertake artistic endeavors instead of escaping into fantasy.

SUPER NOVA DAY
NOVEMBER 19 ★ *gentle persuasion*
Several planets form aspects with retrograde Mars, creating relationship tension that is resolvable through active discussion. A square to sensual Venus may mean that you don't get your needs met without having to stand up for yourself. Unfortunately, this act of assertion may appear aggressive and could alienate the same love you seek. A tense sesquisquare to the Sun throws additional emotional roadblocks in your path. Luckily, a harmonious trine to thoughtful Mercury shows a way through this rough spot. Communication is your saving grace. Direct and concise statements are only half the solution; you must also remain receptive to what others say to you.

NOVEMBER 24-26 ★ *miraculous thoughts*
The Full Moon in changeable Gemini on **November 24** incites you to jump ahead in your thoughts, even if your situation is stagnant. Focused Mercury dynamically squares blurry Neptune, making it hard to stay on task. Even a fleeting daydream can absorb your attention for hours. Also, Mercury's creative quintile to stabilizing Saturn can save the day, but will require clever thinking. Your thoughts will either limit your choices or show you options you hadn't even dreamed of.

NOVEMBER 28-30 ★ *apply the brakes*
You may not be able to shut off your brain from attempting to ram your way through a series of obstacles. But your thinking isn't as effective as you wish, and you can't use logic to solve problems. The best strategy may be to apply the brakes, or you will likely run into a wall. The world isn't working against you; it's simply reminding you that there are other ways to reach your destination besides brute force.

DECEMBER

INNER ANGST YIELDS OUTER SUCCESS

Ongoing pressure from forceful Mars retrograding in self-protective Cancer has you on emotional yellow alert. Be cautious about letting down your guard, for your vulnerabilities are close to the surface. Find socially acceptable ways to express your feelings, including the difficult ones, for suppressed anger in particular can tint your world with negativity and even be converted to unpleasant physical symptoms. You receive strong assistance from a gathering of planets in Aries-friendly Sagittarius throughout most of the month, reaching a culmination around the New Moon on **December 9**, when the Sun, the Moon, Mercury, Jupiter, and Pluto all encourage you to move beyond the edges of your comfort zone and travel to distant lands. If possible, plan an adventurous vacation for the holidays; if you're homebound, throw a huge bash. Additionally, start a course of study that allows you to travel in your mind.

Fortuitous Jupiter in inspirational Sagittarius has been opening doors of opportunity for you all year and on **December 11** conjoins with transformational Pluto, giving you a sense of urgency with respect to your goals. You might become a bit fanatic and fight for a cause, whether or not it's a sensible one. You feel that time is running out—and it is. Jupiter leaves Sagittarius on **December 18** and enters more realistic Capricorn, where it remains throughout 2008. You become more serious as studious Mercury chases Jupiter into Capricorn on **December 20**, followed by the Sun on **December 21**, the Winter Solstice. The Cancer Full Moon on **December 23** brings your month to a crescendo, with jolly Jupiter and fiery Mars ensuring you a grand finish to the year.

> **KEEP IN MIND THIS MONTH**
>
> *Resist your tendency to be silent about important issues. Although you may face opposition, it's more productive to face it head on than to postpone confrontation.*

KEY DATES

DECEMBER 1-3 ★ *into the great beyond*

Mental Mercury enters philosophical Sagittarius on **December 1**, where it remains until **December 20**, stretching your thoughts farther away from practical reality and into more metaphysical realms. A supportive aspect between pleasant Venus and extravagant Jupiter adds to your current state of optimism. By **December 3**, however, Venus shifts alliance to intense Pluto, deepening your desires. Some discomfort could arise as you attempt to balance your need for simple pleasures with more powerful passions.

SUPER NOVA DAYS
DECEMBER 7-11 ★ *anything can happen*

Erratic energy can turn your life upside down as dynamic squares to electric Uranus pepper these days with excitement. However, a stabilizing aspect from constraining Saturn to your key planet, Mars, on **December 8** gives you the self-discipline needed to turn upset into victory. The Sagittarius New Moon on **December 9** activates a short-term cycle of growth, but you must act quickly to capture this moment. On **December 11**, optimistic Jupiter meets transformational Pluto, as it does every thirteen years, punctuating this phase of your life. You have intense work to do now and, fortunately, the fortitude to do it. Make use of the lovely trine between the lovers, Venus and Mars, also on **December 11**. In all aspects of romance and creativity, calculated risks can pay off, provided you are willing to give it everything you have while remaining open to a surprise or two.

DECEMBER 22-26 ★ *expansion and contraction*

You are more reserved and serious now that the Sun, Mercury, and successful Jupiter are all in conservative Capricorn, yet the emotional Cancer Full Moon conjunct Mars on **December 23** overwhelms your system, encouraging you to make commitments you may not keep. Fiery Mars opposes expansive Jupiter on **December 26**, taking your buoyant feelings past your own resistance into the open, so others enjoy your company even more than usual. Thankfully, a harmonious trine between logical Mercury and stable Saturn adds caution. Balance your "I can do anything" attitude with common sense so that you don't promise the impossible.

DECEMBER 30-31 ★ *consider all invitations*

The possibilities for love are enticing as vixen Venus jumps into adventurous Sagittarius, providing you with a great reason to end the year at a big party. But once again, a counterbalance comes from constrictive Saturn as it receives a fortunate trine from the Sun in ambitious Capricorn. Assure yourself that social activities meet your criteria before accepting any invitations. An irritating quincunx between sensual Venus and assertive Mars will likely make you grumpy if you find yourself in an environment that isn't up to your standards.

TAURUS

APRIL 20–MAY 20

TAURUS OVERVIEW

You know what you like and tend to like what you know, Taurus, but **the big rewards this year come from tasting unfamiliar flavors and discovering their strange delights.** It's Jupiter, the planet of expansion and opportunity, that places the goodies outside your usual comfort zone and encourages you to stretch your boundaries to reach them. Sure, you can play it safe and stick to the people, activities, pleasures, and places that have always rung your bell. But the old, familiar tunes are likely to be less exciting than in the past. "Been there, done that" isn't generally a turnoff to you, yet it almost certainly will be in 2007, when variety will add more spice to your life.

Lucky Jupiter in Sagittarius reminds you to shoot your arrows at faraway targets, reaching farther to find the happiness you seek. **Take risks not only in what you do, but in what you say as well.** You can be lucky in relationships even if you are swimming in uncharted waters, so maybe it's safe to talk to strangers this year. Instead of kicking the ground with your head down and that "aw shucks" attitude that makes you so likable, don't be afraid to sell your wares with passion. Muted messages are not likely to be heard, and even when they are, they probably won't get the responses that you want. **An outgoing, adventurous attitude this year will attract more of what you want in your life.**

Like last year, serious Saturn in Leo is challenging your earthy Taurus Sun to stop grazing and start growling. This planet of necessity demands a better show than usual, even if you must practice in front of the mirror to get a look of confidence that you don't quite feel inside. It's not dishonest to want to upgrade your image in the world. Leo, like Sagittarius, is fire, the element of creation. **Instead of simply building on your current foundation, let your imagination paint a picture of a brighter future.** Once you've found an inspiration, take the practical steps required to make it real. When you have the fever, you can find the force to push forward. Your juices flow, your energy rises, and you might be able to advance yourself faster and further than ever before. Bold moves can shake your world and upset some people, especially those closest to you, but standing still is far from the best option now.

Expansive Jupiter and practical Saturn form harmonious trines with each other on March 16 and May 5, making these exceptionally constructive periods for committing to a long-term plan. The balance between optimism and reality is excellent, giving you good judgment and a strategic vision to light your way. Another key time is the Venus retrograde cycle from July 27 to September 8. This is generally when relationships take a U-turn, as you double back to deal with unfinished personal business. With resourceful Venus as your ruling planet, it's an especially powerful time to review your finances, reclaim your self-worth, and recharge your batteries.

BEING HONEST CREATES OPPORTUNITIES FOR LOVE

Jupiter in your house of intimacy ups the ante in relationships. Just trying to maintain the status quo will probably push you backward. If you're in an ongoing partnership, it may take some extra effort to sustain your interest. Being totally honest with yourself and your partner is essential to reopening the wings of love. If you're single, this is a great year to widen your perspective and reach out to someone who is not your usual type. Movement and growth are the keys to emotional fulfillment, which means opening your mind and heart to reconsider some of the beliefs that have been anchoring you in place. The Venus retrograde period of July 27 to September 8 marks a turning point in matters of intimacy. Thoughts of an ex-partner or forgotten memories of romance can resurface to stir your emotional waters. Don't hide from your feelings, especially the uncomfortable ones. Discontent might not be fun, but could provide the impetus needed to grow closer with someone special this year.

TURNING DREAMS INTO REALITY

Idealistic Neptune continues its long journey through your 10th House of Career this year. This imaginative planet sometimes leads to fantasies and sacrifices that can hinder your professional success. Yet on February 28 and June 25, serious Saturn opposes dreamy Neptune, adding a much-needed dose of reality. These are times when you're best able to make a practical assessment of your situation so that you can stop wasting your time and energy by giving selflessly and getting little in return. Additionally, these are periods when you can build a workable path to achieve your professional dreams by combining inspiration with the focus, patience, and commitment required for success.

PARTNER UP TO MAKE EXTRA CASH

Hard work always helps, but it is imagination and, perhaps, a bold partner that can bring in the big bucks this year. Generous Jupiter is in your 8th House of Shared Resources, which is why hooking up with an outgoing, sales-oriented individual might juice the numbers in your savings account. You have to spend money to make money now, so show willingness to gamble to cash in on these opportunities. You shouldn't bet your kid's college fund or drain your retirement nest egg, but tightening up on expenses to free up a bit of investment capital could create a rare business opportunity for you.

EVERY BREATH YOU TAKE

Breathe deeply. Getting fresh air into your lungs is every bit as important as healthy eating and exercising this year. Clear your head and stretch your muscles by trading in the gym for a long walk outside. Reap the mental as well as the physical benefits from discovering what nature has to offer. If you're in a big city, visit the parks as frequently as you can. It also helps to get out of town and escape from the traffic and noise once in a while. Organize and clean up your home environment to keep things fresh. Open your windows as much as you can to help energy flow freely throughout the year.

BE A CREATIVE AUTHORITY FIGURE

Stern Saturn in your 4th House of Home and Family can make power and control issues more common on the home front this year. When faced with pressure, you're likely to dig in your heels to show that you can't be pushed around. Being stubborn may only worsen the situation by undermining trust. Instead, be creative in how you set boundaries so that everyone feels appreci-ated and respected. The key to making this happen is self-confidence, so take care of your needs first. Then you'll have the strength, patience, and flexibility needed to maintain a sense of control without being heavy-handed.

ARGUE TO LEARN, NOT TO WIN

You have the most to learn from people whose ideas might rub you the wrong way at first. This isn't about fighting, but it is meant to expand your thinking. Let go of having to stand on the solid ground of certainty before you accept new ideas. Your willingness to explore unknown territory, both mentally and physically, can teach you more about life than you previously imagined. Conflicting opinions don't have to put an end to conversations if you're able to accept them as a natural part of learning. The goal isn't to pin the other person to the mat; it's to stretch your mind so that it can encompass a broader view of reality.

LAUGH YOUR WAY TO HIGHER CONSCIOUSNESS

Spiritual growth and personal awareness come through the give and take of relationships this year. You may embarrass yourself or go overboard with someone in ways that could make you want to hide in shame (or attack with blame), but don't do it. You'll go further in your self-understanding if you're able to overcome caution. You can laugh your way to higher wisdom and expanded consciousness if you simply allow yourself to be a student of life, instead of thinking that you can't make any mistakes. The little tussles that seem so dramatic in the moment are just those events that awaken you with awareness and a giggle about how silly life can be at times.

RICK & JEFF'S TIP FOR THE YEAR:
Expand Your Boundaries

It's the nature of your sign to value steadiness over speed, Taurus. But this year, with planetary biggies Jupiter and Saturn in fire signs, success comes from stepping on the hot coals and moving quickly. Try to minimize your need for control so that you can free yourself to explore and expand in the areas of life that are most important to you. This is not a year for standing still; allow ambition to broaden your horizons, raise your thoughts to higher possibilities, and then challenge yourself to leap over any barriers that stand in your way.

TAURUS

JANUARY

INNOVATIVE IDEAS MOVE YOU INTO NEW TERRITORY

Your year gets off to a fast start thanks to bright ideas that open up a new world of options in your professional life or with friends and groups. Your ruling planet, Venus, enters experimental Aquarius on **January 3**, the same day as the Full Moon that's full of surprises. But the excitement of a fresh vision can also shake your foundation, Taurus, since moving from concept to reality involves a destabilizing shift of values. Giving up beliefs and behaviors that anchor you isn't necessarily easy; you could have the sensation that your life is floating off somewhere beyond your control. The challenge is to stretch yourself enough to keep your feet on the ground while your head leads you to unique people, unknown places, and unusual experiences. Be patient and give yourself time to learn the ropes before regaining the familiarity that you find so comforting.

The Sun enters forward-thinking Aquarius on **January 20**, shining the bright light of future possibilities into the routine of your daily life. If you're alarmed at how quickly things are moving, seek out the emotional security of old friends and favorite foods to give you the support you need. Then take this valuable fuel and invest it in unconventional and innovative behavior that will get you noticed. Tell your boss the "crazy" idea you have about making the business more efficient or creating a new product. Ask a friend to attend a lecture on UFOs or to take a dance class with you. Sure, this is out-of-the-box thinking, Taurus, but when you're the one who comes up with the surprises, the ride can be much more exhilarating now.

> **KEEP IN MIND THIS MONTH**
>
> *Set higher goals in your relationships: you may be aiming for something that's out of reach, but at least you will be making progress.*

KEY DATES

JANUARY 3 ★ *be a team leader*
A Full Moon in Cancer usually inspires you to turn off your alarm and put your head under the pillow. But today's lunar event brings the gift of brilliance that might launch you out of bed and into action among friends or at work. With Venus entering group-oriented Aquarius, you have an instinctive sense of how to sell your ideas without appearing too pushy. Knowing what's best for everyone and presenting it in a nonthreatening way makes you a powerful player on any team now.

JANUARY 12-14 ★ *adding spice to your social life*
Your social life should be cooking this weekend with a sweet sextile between
pleasure-seeking Venus and no-limits Jupiter as the Moon rolls into your 7th
House of Partnerships. The teasing side of your personality can be especially
alluring, but be aware of whom you're attracting with your charms. An intense
conjunction of combative Mars and Pluto can provoke unexpectedly strong
reactions. What feels like a game to you can be deadly serious to someone else,
so choose your playmates carefully. Good judgment about the company you keep
makes it safe to be sexy and sassy without inviting negative feedback.

JANUARY 18 ★ *a loving heart lifts your spirits*
This is a day of romantic dreams and creative imagination. Venus, the planet of
love, joins boundless Neptune, planetary headquarters for both enlightenment
and illusion. It is a time of inspiration, faith, and forgiveness, when bending rules
makes you free of their usual restraints. This can open your heart, allowing
differences that have kept you apart from someone to melt away. Still, it's
important to use common sense to avoid wasting time or money on a person
or activity that may not be as wonderful as it appears.

SUPER NOVA DAYS
JANUARY 22-23 ★ *slow down to make it last*
Reality returns with a vengeance, demanding accountability for any recent
lack of discipline in financial or emotional matters. This clarification of values, thanks to a Venus-Saturn opposition, brings trust that encourages frank
communication. Brilliant ideas are spawned like seeds in the wind; slow down
to capture the best ones to turn them into reality. Shift from talk to action to
create something lasting out of this wealth of information.

JANUARY 26-27 ★ *avoid pressure; seek pleasure*
Don't confuse tough behavior with clear thinking. A bully doesn't necessarily know
any more than you do, especially now when facts—no matter how solid they look—
tend to be slippery. Avoid major decision-making under pressure. Venus enters
dreamy Pisces on **January 27**, which is better suited for love and pleasure than
serious negotiations.

FEBRUARY

THE BIGGER THE PLAN, THE SLOWER THE MOVEMENT

The month starts with a boisterous Full Moon in Leo that falls in your 4th House of Home and Family on **February 1**. A little drama around the old hacienda is likely to be more noise than nuisance. With expansive Jupiter harmoniously aspecting the Full Moon, it's just another chance to grow beyond your emotional safety zone, so don't take the commotion too seriously. Going over the top is sometimes necessary to see past your current limits. In any case, communicative Mercury turning retrograde on **February 13** may force you to slam on the brakes with a project involving a friend or colleague. If you're in a hurry, taking the time to deal with every little mishap and misunderstanding can be exhausting. Set your priorities and focus on the most important ones.

Your moods may shift easily, especially after the Sun enters sensitive Pisces on **February 18** and Venus moves into go-getter Aries three days later. The sense that opportunity must be grabbed right now or be lost forever is keen but may not reflect the true story. It's the slower-moving outer planets, Saturn and Neptune, that really tell the tale of dreams and reality this month. Their opposition on **February 28** is the second of a series that began late last August and finishes this year in late June. This major aspect between the planets of form and fantasy can squeeze the life out of old illusions to make way for new forms of inspiration. This process can't be hurried, even if you're anxious to make big changes now. Snap judgments are fine in your personal life, so let love or shopping impulses take you, if they must. But treat your biggest dreams with the care of a papa penguin holding his baby's egg on a long, cold Antarctic night.

> **KEEP IN MIND THIS MONTH**
>
> *Develop confidence in yourself. You can act the part even if you don't feel it just yet. Have faith in your vision, and stay with it in spite of your doubts.*

KEY DATES

FEBRUARY 7-9 ★ *new tastes challenge old values*
A Venus-Uranus conjunction on **February 7**, along with a Venus-Jupiter square on **February 9**, makes for a restless relationship life. Old sources of pleasure seem stale, while attractions to new people, unusual appearances, and unconventional activities grab your attention. You're in the pleasure lab, trying out some unique flavors. Just don't sign up for any long-term commitments. This is only a test of

your capacity to broaden your tastes; individuals and objects of interest may appear to be more desirable than they actually are.

FEBRUARY 13-14 ★ *lust, loss, and readjustment*
It's difficult today to know whether to share your desires or to keep them to yourself. Lovely Venus hooks up with hunky Mars on **February 13**, heating up the mood for Valentine's Day delights. Yet at the same time, Mercury the Messenger stands still in diffusive Pisces, muddling communication and spreading confusion. A simple statement can be misinterpreted, wounding feelings and taking the air out of a romantic balloon. On **February 14**, Saturn, the enforcer of law and order, rudely pulls Venus aside with a quizzical quincunx that forces adjustments in tastes and relationships that may eliminate an opportunity for fun. Be prepared to change your expectations to fit these more sober circumstances.

SUPER NOVA DAYS
FEBRUARY 19-21 ★ *examine desires and explore pleasures*
A tense square between Venus and Pluto on **February 19** can complicate relationships with mistrust, self-doubt, or jealousy. The point, though, is simply to take a deeper look at your desires and motivations to make sure that what you're after is really what you want. On **February 21**, Venus leaves behind Pluto's shadow land of suspicion and moves into insouciant Aries, where love can make a fresh start. Innocence and impulsiveness open doors to enjoyment in new ways that seem to appear out of the blue. Give yourself permission to explore these pleasures without being too concerned about what they might lead to in the long term.

FEBRUARY 25 ★ *safeguard your dreams*
Tough aspects from Venus to Saturn and Neptune heighten sensitivity that can instill feelings of uncertainty and fear of rejection. High hopes may slide into the depths of despair when imagination overcomes objectivity. You can tame the wild ride by matching dreams with concrete actions, turning clouds of fantasy into enduring images of inspiration that keep you on track to reaching your goals. Seek out the company of supportive individuals, and avoid serial doubters, skeptics, and put-down artists. Your cause is worthy and merits wisdom, not wisecracks.

MARCH

CREATIVE BREAKTHROUGHS

Two eventful eclipses, mental Mercury turning direct, and romantic Venus entering your sign make for a very busy month. The total Lunar Eclipse on **March 3** is especially volatile, with explosive Uranus and expansive Jupiter pushing your emotions to extremes. This can shake your romantic life, bring surprises with children, or rattle a friendship. But this is also about significant breakthroughs in self-expression. Creative skills that have been difficult to master can pop open like piñatas, releasing your ability to paint, dance, cook, love, and play like never before. On **March 7**, Mercury starts moving forward, which can release information that you've been waiting to receive, especially related to your professional life.

Your key planet, Venus, enters sensual Taurus on **March 17**, a shift that is quite likely to bring more joy and pleasure into your life. An increased sense of self-worth is one of the benefits, along with a greater appreciation for the sensual delights of touch, sound, scent, and taste. During almost four weeks of Venus in her home sign, your special charms receive more attention and admiration from others. Still, all is not perfect in your personal Garden of Eden, as the New Moon in sensitive Pisces on **March 18** is a Solar Eclipse squared by Pluto. This most distant planet, the mythological lord of the underworld, puts the squeeze on overextended egos and any inflated sense of self-importance. The eclipsed Sun-Moon conjunction falls in your 11th House of Friends and Associates, so power struggles are a distinct possibility. If you find yourself battling to maintain harmonious relationships with a pal or within a group, consider reducing your commitment. You may even need to walk away if the price of compromise is too high.

> **KEEP IN MIND THIS MONTH**
>
> *Use chaos creatively. If your world is rocky, you may need to reconsider your goals and, perhaps, set your course in a radical new direction.*

KEY DATES

MARCH 2-3 ★ *the truth incites powerful emotions*

Expect an edgy undercurrent with the Lunar Eclipse and a tense aspect between communicative Mercury and sweet Venus. With erratic Uranus conjunct the Sun, it will be difficult not to speak the truth. It's easy for a simple remark to provoke an over-the-top reaction. Choose words wisely and listen with an easygoing attitude to avoid turning an intimate conversation into an exhausting argument.

MARCH 8-9 ★ *sparks ignite a lasting fire*

Venus in adventurous Aries forms harmonious aspects with Jupiter, Saturn, and Neptune, providing a constructive framework in which to bring visionary ideas to life. Your social skills are especially strong, and your ability to approach relationships with both vitality and responsibility enhances your personal life. Impulses to create art, establish a new enterprise, or organize a social event can fill you with an enduring passion. Whatever attracts you now can become a steadfast inspiration that not only brings you lasting pleasure but also earns you well-deserved respect.

SUPER NOVA DAYS
MARCH 16-18 ★ *tie up loose ends*

A healthy Venus-Pluto trine combined with a stabilizing Jupiter-Saturn trine encourages you to set priorities that are vital for making smart choices leading up to Sunday's powerful Solar Eclipse. Venus entering Taurus on **March 17** presents more appetizing alternatives than those presently on your plate, so finish off old projects and clear the decks to make room for new delights. You may be tempted to hold on to people, practices, and possibilities that cost too much for what they give you in return—but let go to receive more rewarding pleasures.

MARCH 20-21 ★ *stretch, but don't overreach*

The Sun's entry into risk-taking Aries kicks off the astrological year, bringing a fresh taste for adventure. But a bumpy Venus-Jupiter aspect can promote excess. Overestimating someone's commitment or spending too much money can lead to disappointment. It's great to be enthusiastic—and expanding your social horizons is healthy—but a dose of common sense can prevent costly mistakes.

MARCH 29-31 ★ *integrity comes from within*

A tough Venus-Pluto connection may undermine trust in relationships or, worse, your trust in yourself. If you're unhappy with a situation, don't rationalize away those feelings. Be honest with yourself about your desires without worrying about what others will think. When you feel the truth within, you're well on your way to figuring out what changes, if any, are needed. Besides, a clever Venus-Uranus sextile on **March 31** reveals alternative paths to satisfaction that should give you an unexpected solution to your problem.

APRIL

A CAUTIOUS BEGINNING, AN EXPLOSIVE ENDING

The big event of the month is the annual movement of the Sun from the fiery impatience of Aries to the comfortable earth of Taurus. This occurs on **April 20**, marking a shift from you playing a behind-the-scenes role to taking center stage. However, contrasting transits earlier in the month send mixed signals. Assertive Mars enters gentle Pisces on **April 6**, which tends to make you hypersensitive about your effect on people and less direct in your actions. On the other hand, Mercury, the communication planet, enters impatient Aries on **April 10**, which tends to provoke impulsive and aggressive speech. Fortunately, Venus can help you navigate between these two extremes when it enters adaptable Gemini on **April 11**. Your ruling planet in the mobile sign of the Twins makes it easy to maneuver quickly between meandering Mars in Pisces and Mercury in to-the-point Aries. A skillful shifting of gears enables you to blend the gifts of fresh thought and subtle movement to drive your ideas forward in a nonthreatening manner.

No matter how cool and collected you remain, you can expect the lid to blow toward the end of the month. The key elements are high-intensity aspects from Mars to both shocking Uranus and over-the-top Jupiter on **April 28 and 30**. Sedated as Mars might be in spiritual Pisces, it's still the warrior planet and will not fail to produce lightning bolts when conjunct electric Uranus. Mars's stressful square to expansive Jupiter two days later magnifies the powerful release of energy that may shake the world. Avoid getting dragged into others' disputes; taking sides under such conditions can be dangerous. Your key to applying these potent forces is to change your own behavior, rather than trying to alter anyone else's. Be flexible and realistic, as sudden surprises are nearly inevitable.

> **KEEP IN MIND THIS MONTH**
>
> *Step into your future; traveling into the unknown can feel dangerous, but is actually safer and less stressful than holding on to the past.*

KEY DATES

APRIL 1–4 ★ *reality shifts*

You're no fool on **April 1** with serious Saturn square sweet Venus. This may be a less than playful time, but you can become clearer about relationships and values. The mood shifts quickly, then, with the lovely Libra Full Moon on **April 2** and

Venus's aspects to expansive Jupiter and idealistic Neptune on **April 3 and 4**. Times go from tight to loose, so much so that common sense could be lost along the way. Try to keep at least one foot on the ground at all times.

APRIL 10–11 ★ *love comes to play*
A grumpy moment on **April 10** may be the result of jealousy and feelings of insufficiency that expose your distrust of others. But then Venus glides into giddy Gemini on **April 11**, providing a breath of fresh air for relationships that can soften your patterns of fear and rigidity. Your flirtatious side is likely to emerge now as the game of love begins to feel more like play than work.

SUPER NOVA DAYS
APRIL 20–22 ★ *the fascination of flirtation*
The Sun enters your sign one day after form-building Saturn turns direct. This is your time to make it real, Taurus, as you gain traction in moving toward your goals. **April 22** is an especially spicy day, with Venus and Mars squaring in a seductive tango. Your magnetic allure is hard to resist, even if you aren't the flirtatious type. If you don't like being teased, though, this can be slightly uncomfortable. Yet if you're willing to take the initiative and maintain a playful attitude, this should be an especially entertaining weekend.

APRIL 26 ★ *make friends with the unexpected*
A challenging right-angle square between peace-loving Venus and unpredictable Uranus can throw you off balance today. Plans change; tried-and-true formulas don't work; hair won't stay in place. You can resist the surprises, but it's less stressful and more enjoyable to go with the unexpected flow of events and feelings, no matter how sudden and strange.

APRIL 28–30 ★ *stay cool in an overheated environment*
The eruptive forces of Mars, Uranus, and Jupiter can keep you jumping with sudden outbreaks of emotion that defy reason. Venus opposing Jupiter on **April 28** adds to the environment of excess. Ideally, it can lead you to a leap of faith that carries you into exciting but uncharted territory. A healing trine between gracious Venus and compassionate Neptune on **April 30** brings much-needed faith, forgiveness, and a large enough perspective to avoid any potential crisis.

TAURUS

MAY

BE A FORCE FOR CHANGE

This is a stressful month when you are more than likely to dig in your heels and resist any external pressures, real or imagined. Taskmaster Saturn hooks up with the Full Moon in penetrating Scorpio on **May 2** and the New Moon in your sign on **May 16**, which doesn't leave you much breathing room. Stubbornly holding your ground, though, is a sure way to go nowhere. Instead, Saturn trining confident Jupiter—exact on **May 5**—motivates you to build new foundations rather than retreat behind existing walls. Energetic Mars may be somewhat muddled in sensitive Pisces through the first half of the month, so ask friends or colleagues for assistance in getting a project off the ground. But on **May 15**, the action planet fires into its home sign of Aries, adding high-octane fuel to your tank. The impulse to act, both creatively and aggressively, can just flow through you, as if you're being directed by some unknown force. As long as it's taking you in a positive direction, ride it for all it's worth.

Dreamy Neptune shows up for the New Moon with a tense square to the Sun-Moon conjunction in fixed Taurus. While this can blur focus and confuse purpose, it's also a time for softening around the edges and dissolving entrenched values or beliefs. Being right is less important than being adaptable, because by pruning what is no longer useful, you're not giving up on principle; you are opening up to more creativity in your life. You might not know your next destination, but think of wandering as exploring alternative possibilities rather than being lost. With the Sun's entry into dualistic Gemini on **May 21**, the message is that there are many possible roads leading to your goals.

> **KEEP IN MIND THIS MONTH**
>
> *It's better to move forward with uncertainty than to stand still now. Remain flexible; you can always make adjustments as you go along.*

KEY DATES

SUPER NOVA DAYS
MAY 6-7 ★ *cleaning out the emotional closet*
Buried feelings surface with a Venus-Pluto opposition on **May 6**. Unaddressed issues can explode with an intensity that seems out of proportion to your

current situation. Resentment, distrust, and dissatisfaction are signs that dramatic changes in relationships are necessary. If you feel underappreciated, demanding more from others might not do the trick. The key is to dig deeply to reclaim lost talents and revive faded dreams of love. Venus's entry into nurturing Cancer on **May 7** is a perfect balm for sharing your vulnerability as a first step toward healing. Your willingness to face the complicated questions of self-worth can be rewarded with a fresh start that brings more hope than ever for pleasure, partnership, and creative fulfillment.

MAY 11-13 ★ *express your desires*
Be clear and precise about what you want on **May 11,** rather than following the crowd and hoping that somehow you'll get your needs met without saying anything. Responsible Saturn is rubbing against charming Venus, which can constrict your social life and reduce enjoyment unless you know exactly what you crave and have put in the necessary effort to deserve it. This is a complicated weekend, with both escapism and aggression in the air. It's tempting to duck a confrontation that is bound to ruffle feathers, but what's left unsaid can wind up costing more in the long run. Fortunately, information-rich Mercury is now in its airy home sign of Gemini, so a variety of ideas and multiple ways to communicate can help you tailor your message to your audience, reducing the likelihood of confusion and hurt feelings.

MAY 23-24 ★ *unconventional play*
You may toss caution to the wind, spending more and speaking more openly than usual now. It's healthy to stretch your budget a little to gift yourself with clothes or creative tools that increase your self-confidence. A positive Venus-Uranus trine broadens your perspective on love, pleasure, and beauty, showing you fresh ways to play that are bound to make life more fun. Barriers to joy are broken, and limits on relationships are relaxed by a new attitude or a new playmate.

MAY 28-30 ★ *fairness in relationships*
It may not take much to provoke strong feelings now, especially when it comes to pride and recognition from others. Venus, your key planet, is sensitized by vulnerable Neptune, which usually makes for thin skin, and even more so while Venus is also clashing with the Sun, principal of ego and identity. The upside, though, is in recognizing where you give more than you get at work or at home so that you can start to bring more balance into those relationships.

TAURUS

JUNE

SEEK NEW SOURCES OF INCOME

The Full Moon in fiery Sagittarius on **May 31** shines brightly for the first half of June, rousing a spirit of adventure and making even comfortable Taurus itchy for new experiences. Uncharacteristic restlessness can distract your attention from your usual routines, so regular tasks will require more concentration to handle them competently. Passion will likely overtake logic this month as romantic Venus enters outgoing and demonstrative Leo on **June 5**, a shift that provokes greater self-expression and generosity. Mercury, the planet associated with objective thought, turns retrograde on **June 15**, beginning a three-week period during which feelings tend to overcome intellect. However, this doesn't mean that you're necessarily going to act foolishly. It's simply that truth comes from within and at this time expresses more through heartfelt actions than mere words.

The New Moon in ever-curious Gemini on **June 14** is a powerful event that might shake up your 2nd House of Finances and could even lead to a new source of income. The intensely transformative pair of Pluto and Uranus opposes and squares this monthly Sun-Moon conjunction, a combination that sometimes leads to emotional anxiety or even panic—so stay as calm as possible as you respond to necessary of change. Ideally, this influence can lead you to a reassessment of priorities when it comes to cash. If you're interested in finding a different way to pay the bills, then support, energy, and encouragement will arrive with active Mars's entrance into your sign on **June 24**. Your ambitious side is showing, so taking on additional responsibilities in your current position or seeking training for a totally different career fits in the picture perfectly well.

> **KEEP IN MIND THIS MONTH**
>
> *The highest intelligence is found in your heart, not your head. Don't overly complicate issues when simple answers can arise spontaneously.*

KEY DATES

JUNE 3–5 ★ *a narrow passage into a wider world*

An edgy Venus-Pluto quincunx on **June 3** dredges up issues of insecurity in relationships. Sunday's emotional squeeze may be a final reckoning before you open your heart and wallet wide in days to come. The forces of doubt won't linger long with an energetic Mars-Jupiter trine buoying your spirits on **June 4**, followed by Venus's entrance into extravagant Leo on **June 5** while the Sun opposes Jupiter.

JUNE 11-13 ★ *spend energy to get energy*

A series of helpful trines and sextiles connects the Sun, Mars, Saturn, and Neptune while the Moon is passing through your sign. These transits allow you to overcome self-imposed limits as you focus your considerable will with purpose (Saturn) and inspiration (Neptune). Taking action now rewards you with more resources, rather than exhausting your current ones. The more you give personally or professionally, the more you will receive in return.

JUNE 19 ★ *love without keeping score*

A free-flowing trine between loving Venus and joyous Jupiter blesses you with an abundance of what you love. You may even feel more accepted and appreciated than perhaps you think you deserve. Don't allow a little snag to ruin the party. This is a day when the spirit of generosity is strong, so try to overlook a small disappointment that casts a meaningless cloud on this otherwise glorious day.

JUNE 24-26 ★ *strong but flexible*

This is a period of twists and turns as you head off with clear purpose and direction when forceful Mars enters determined Taurus on **June 24**. Yet the slow Saturn-Neptune opposition is exact on **June 25**, which can muddle even the best-laid plans. Combining the focus of Mars and Saturn in the murky world of Neptune's fog is tricky business that can leave you feeling like you're faking it, even if you know exactly what you are doing. A flaky Venus-Uranus quincunx on **June 26** brings surprises from others that can throw you off course. Stay open to the unexpected changes instead of resisting them.

SUPER NOVA DAY

JUNE 30 ★ *from dream to reality*

The Capricorn Full Moon lights up your 9th House of Travel and Higher Education, inspiring you to plan a trip abroad or head back to school. The adventurous emotions of this Sun-Moon opposition broaden your horizons, yet the practical nature of Capricorn can fill you with doubts about the feasibility of such ideas. The contrast between the ideal and the real is repeated with a romantic Venus-Neptune opposition today, followed by a super-serious Venus-Saturn conjunction tomorrow. Honor your dreams by doing the hard work to make them come true.

TAURUS

JULY

REVIEW, REEVALUATE, AND REVISE

This is a pivotal time of the year as your ruling planet, Venus, turns retrograde on **July 27**, staying in reverse gear until **September 8**. Relationships, self-worth, pleasure, beauty, and income are all associated with this planet, so expect to make adjustments in some or all of these areas. The retrograde cycle starts with Venus in your 5th House of Romance, which could throw a monkey wrench into your love life, maybe even bringing back an ex-partner to complicate matters. On **August 8**, the planet backs into your 4th House of Home and Family, beginning a good period for redecorating your house or revisiting childhood memories that have shaped your sense of self-worth and ideas about pleasure. Digging through past disappointments can be painful, yet could be a powerful step toward healing old wounds and unlocking a greater potential for joy in your life.

Mercury turns direct on **July 9**, which shifts your mental energy into forward gear. The communication planet has been retrograde since **June 15** in the 3rd House of your chart, an area associated with information flow and local travel. If the same stories and lessons have been replaying in your life, you're finally about to be released from this endless loop. Messages that were delayed by clerical errors, postal snafus, or e-mail glitches may now resurface. Mechanical errors and travel mix-ups are less likely to occur. Still, with the more dramatic Venus retrograde just over the horizon, managing the free-flowing data is just a first step to a deeper reevaluation of relationships and rewards. You will need emotional digestion before you can apply the best information in lasting and practical ways.

> **KEEP IN MIND THIS MONTH**
>
> *Patience gives you the time to let ideas simmer long enough to bring out the full flavor of their meaning.*

KEY DATES

JULY 1 ★ *make a choice that will last*

Value-conscious Venus conjuncts super-real Saturn, adding weight to any romantic or financial decisions made today. There's a serious undertone, even in the most playful situations. Teasing and joking can be the nervous appetizer for a much more substantial main course of conversation. Letting others know exactly where you stand, even if they don't want to hear it, is a mark of integrity that earns you trust and respect.

SUPER NOVA DAYS

JULY 8-9 ★ *irresistible allure*

There's an emotional warm front heading your way on **July 8** that's fueled by a passionate Venus-Pluto trine and the allure of the Moon in your sensual sign. Now is the time to express your most intimate desires, since your judgment about what to say and how to say it is excellent. Between your captivating conversation and your penetrating gaze, someone who said no in the past might not be able to resist you now.

JULY 14 ★ *appearances count*

Venus, the planet of beauty, enters your 5th House of Romance—a signal that you are going to be noticed and admired. You don't have to be perfect to be appreciated, but any polishing of your appearance with a stylish haircut or a newly purchased outfit will upgrade your self-confidence and get heads turning your way. Whether you're trying to impress a potential partner, boss, or client, the sharper your image, the more attention you'll receive.

JULY 24 ★ *intuition trumps force*

Mars in your usually solid sign crosses paths today with Neptune, the cosmic eraser, making it easy to lose your way and waste your time and energy. Act with intuition and sensitivity so that you can readjust your course, rather than plowing forward with your head down and missing your target entirely. It's tempting to lash out in all directions, which is a real sign of frustration and fatigue. Stop what you're doing if you're feeling wobbly or out of sorts. Recharge your batteries and recheck your internal compass before moving on.

JULY 27-29 ★ *stay within your budget*

Retrograde Venus on **July 27** sets you up for an emotionally charged weekend. A tense Mercury-Venus semisquare gives the mildest criticism the weight of a sledgehammer. Add the high energy of an Aquarius Full Moon on **July 29**, and feelings might soar to the heights of hope or plunge to the depths of despair. This is not an ideal environment for making important decisions, especially related to love and money. Keep a firm grip on your heart and your ATM card before spending on anything that might bust your emotional or financial budget. Play if you can afford to lose, but stay out of the game if you can't.

AUGUST

OLD LOVES, NEW MONEY

Your ruling planet, Venus, continues its retrograde motion this month, keeping relationship, money, and self-worth issues under review and reconstruction. But life is not simply seen through the rearview mirror as two planetary events nudge you forward early in the month. Expansive Jupiter turns direct and active Mars enters mobile Gemini on **August 6**. The former pushes the frontiers of intimacy in your 8th House, offering opportunities to broaden and deepen emotional and financial partnerships. The latter puts a charge in your 2nd House of Money that can motivate you to diversify your marketable skills and discover additional sources of revenue. The extroverted Leo New Moon on **August 12** sows seeds of creativity, awakening your potentials for performing and self-promotion. A little drama on the home front can turn a minor matter into an operatic event. Don't make more of an issue out of it just to get attention.

The energy is big and loud later this month, with a high-energy Mars-Jupiter opposition on **August 23** that is followed by stressful squares to both planets from Mercury the Communicator. Conflicts over money and other resources may produce heated discussions. The more agitated you get, the more essential it is for you to cool down and search for solutions, rather than simply rehashing problems. Relationships, too, may boil over with accusations that can damage goodwill. Avoid acting like a victim even if you feel wronged. This is a time when bold but well-planned initiatives can resolve the most complex dilemmas. The Full Moon in compassionate Pisces on **August 28** is a total Lunar Eclipse that falls in your 11th House of Groups and Friends. If you're being emotionally drained by a pal or are underappreciated as a member of a team, it may be time to make significant changes.

> **KEEP IN MIND THIS MONTH**
>
> *There is more than one way to solve any problem. When you feel stuck, seek alternative solutions instead of maintaining the status quo.*

KEY DATES

AUGUST 7–8 ★ *a question of taste*
A Venus-Mars square puts an edge on relationships with rapid responses of attraction and repulsion. The line between sensuality and aggression is easily crossed as matters of appropriate behavior and good taste are brought into

question. Venus backs into ego-driven Leo on **August 8**, reminding you of the importance of self-respect but also making pride a delicate matter.

AUGUST 13 ★ *reconsider your desires*

Recognition for your accomplishments is crucial, as the day's Venus-Saturn conjunction too often is a time of feeling undervalued. Commitment to your goals, as well as to a lover or friend, may be tested. Are you willing to pay the price to achieve your ends? If not, it's appropriate to reexamine your desires more deeply and then decide to invest more or put an end to an unsatisfying adventure.

> **SUPER NOVA DAYS**
> **AUGUST 15-17** ★ *be kind to yourself*
> This is an intense period of supersensitivity, with retrograde Venus passing between the Sun and the Earth. You can feel like you're in the spotlight even when there's no one else around. Any comments made about you take on a greater importance than usual, but you're the only judge whose opinion counts. Focus on your gifts, your grace, and your beauty. When you start with the premise that you are worthy of love and adoration, creativity and joy are bound to follow.

AUGUST 22-23 ★ *share with caution*

Brilliant solutions to complicated relationship issues may come easily on **August 22** with a clever Venus-Mars quintile. The Sun enters your 5th House of Romance and Self-Expression on **August 23**, encouraging you to show your feelings openly. Still, discretion is key, as the enthusiastic Mars-Jupiter opposition squared by Mercury can provoke reactions that are stronger than expected. It just takes a little push to produce an avalanche of response, so be gentle when taking the initiative.

AUGUST 25 ★ *enjoy the magic while it lasts*

An opposition between attractive Venus and imaginative Neptune is likely to bring on a romantic mood. However, logic and good judgment are often sacrificed in the pursuit of ideal love. If you're falling for someone, enjoy the feeling, but let some time pass so that your mind can clear before making any serious long-range plans together. The magic is in the moment with no guarantee that it will last. The same goes for objects of desire that entice you to break your budget. Beware of buyer's remorse; spend prudently to avoid disappointment.

TAURUS

SEPTEMBER

Summer is ending in the Northern Hemisphere, but the planets continue to heat up your life this month. The most welcome news is that sweet Venus turns direct on **September 8**. Love, pleasure, and self-worth—the principles of your ruling planet—have been going through the wash of reconsideration since late July. Take what you have learned and begin to put it into action. This is not a one-day event, but an ongoing process of taking your inner image of joy and turning it into reality. A dramatic Solar Eclipse in your 5th House of Love and Creativity on **September 11** will loosen up old patterns of playing it safe in these areas. Inventive Uranus is in the middle of the picture, which can rattle friendships but is there to shake you free of outmoded social habits. Taking more risks in self-expression can be very rewarding for you now.

Surprises can be expected as rising pressures may force you to express those thoughts that you've been keeping to yourself. There's little safety in suppressing yourself when you sense the urge to say things or act out in ways that make others uncomfortable. Be flexible; release yourself from promises to never behave with haste, aggression, or impulsiveness. It's healthier to give in a little to these rising forces than to try to repress them. The Aries Full Moon on **September 26** falls in your 12th House of Secrets, provoking you to reveal a hidden side. There's no shame in self-discovery, even if newly awakened desires threaten current relationships or your image as a well-mannered individual. The reward for bold action is a feeling of freedom that allows you to tear down barriers and overcome old fears.

> **KEEP IN MIND THIS MONTH**
>
> *Don't hold back when it comes to showing your feelings. Upsets are possible, but the truth can set you free.*

KEY DATES

SEPTEMBER 3 ★ *stay cool in a volatile situation*
A socially skillful Venus-Mars sextile can help you keep a potentially explosive situation from getting out of hand. People are touchy now, so even an act of kindness or an innocent remark can backfire when someone misinterprets it. Retreat from overheated tensions if you can, since emotional recovery can take longer than expected. Allow for differences of opinion to be expressed passionately, rather than pushing for agreement now.

SEPTEMBER 6-8 ★ *too early to decide*

Anything less than total approval could shake your confidence now. You may feel like you're suspended in air without any support under you. It's beautiful Venus standing still just before turning direct on **September 8** that tends to make every choice weigh so heavily. Powerful Pluto turns direct as well on **September 7**, bringing old issues up for another round of discussion. Be patient; there's no need to reach a final judgment quite yet.

SUPER NOVA DAYS

SEPTEMBER 17-19 ★ *gifts within the gloom*

The Sun in your 5th House of Love crosses swords with assertive Mars and passionate Pluto, which are opposing each other. These are intense times for everyone, but your challenges are most likely to be about romance, creativity, and the recognition you receive from others. You may be tempted to burn everything down and walk away from it all. But don't discount your previous good work, even if you're discouraged now. There are nuggets of gold to be extracted from the ashes and applied to rebuilding so that you don't have to start all over from scratch.

SEPTEMBER 21 ★ *keep your eyes wide open*

The more certain someone acts now, the more suspicious you should be about his or her motives. Idealistic Venus opposite nebulous Neptune loves the fantasy of perfection. Your desire for total sensual satisfaction makes it easy to be fooled. Moments of delight are possible, but full awareness of what you're doing and with whom you're doing it is required to receive this pleasure at a fair price.

SEPTEMBER 27-28 ★ *dive into feelings*

Mercury, the communication planet, enters penetrating Scorpio on **September 27**. This is the door to your 7th House of Partnerships and Public Life, making this a good time to reach out and connect with others. Deep conversations can strengthen personal relationships and take a business project to a higher level. Your intuition is keen, with bright ideas popping into your head without warning. Active Mars enters reflective Cancer on **September 28**, beginning a long stay in your 3rd House of Information and stirring interest in subjects from your past.

OCTOBER

RENEGOTIATE RELATIONSHIPS

Further backtracking in your relationships is likely this month, Taurus. It's true that once you're heading in one direction, you like to keep moving on the same track, but there's a great deal to be gained by altering that pattern. Communicative Mercury turns retrograde in your 7th House of Relationships on **October 11**, opening a three-week window for renegotiating with others. Any partnerships or agreements may be adjusted during this period. A romantic partner, close friend, or colleague may want to change the nature of your association, or if you are not happy, you may wish to revise the arrangement. Look into your heart of hearts and decide what you really want, rather than yielding to your desire to keep things simple. You usually dislike complications, but they're worth the extra effort if they are needed to rebuild trust and deepen your degree of satisfaction.

On **October 23**, Mercury backs into diplomatic Libra while the Sun enters possessive Scorpio. The former suggests that you can find a more objective stance on relationships or even change a strong opinion about someone. The latter, though, signals a deepening passion about partnership that is anything but logical. This complex combination, then, suggests an internal inconsistency that is not ideal for decision-making. You may be able to see and feel all sides of a situation, but don't let confusion force your hand. There's no need to advance or retreat with a person or a project right now. A subtle but powerful Jupiter-Neptune sextile is bringing a wave of intuition later this month that can place these matters on more solid emotional and perhaps even spiritual ground.

> **KEEP IN MIND THIS MONTH**
>
> *The message from Mercury retrograde is to think twice, then twice more before making any serious statements, commitments, or purchases.*

KEY DATES

OCTOBER 3 ★ *focused intention gets results*
A wise Venus-Pluto trine can help you work through a complex situation with calm, confidence, and emotional self-control. You can focus on exactly what you need from someone and are able to express it safely. This allows you to broach a delicate subject without offending others. You can touch and be touched deeply without making a big fuss about it.

OCTOBER 10-13 ★ *reality rules relationships*
A sticky Sun-Venus semisquare on **October 10** has the ability to undermine self-confidence, but with Mercury turning retrograde on **October 11**, misinterpretations are quite possible. Get the facts, no matter how difficult to discern or to hear, because loving Venus conjuncts no-nonsense Saturn on **October 13**. Being real is the only way to get a handle on your life now. Even disappointing news can be useful if it clarifies where you stand with someone or helps you define your desires more precisely.

OCTOBER 16 ★ *make time for pleasure*
This should be a day of delight, a time perhaps to linger over lunch with a good book or a chatty friend or lover. Social Venus aligns sweetly with assertive Mars and talkative Mercury, a combination that's bound to bring some spice into your life, but not enough to burn your tongue. Witty conversation about art, movies, music, clothes, or even love should fit your agenda nicely. Be playful in how you dress and act to turn an ordinary time into a mini-celebration of life.

OCTOBER 24-25 ★ *originality saves the day*
The only tense aspect possible between Venus and Mercury occurs on **October 24**, increasing the likelihood for misunderstandings, especially while the messenger planet is still moving retrograde. On **October 25**, a shocking opposition between Venus and Uranus can lead to an unusual turn of events, an unexpected shift in your finances or values, or a relationship surprise. Be adaptable and turn this potential for chaos into an exciting time for breakthroughs in creativity or romance.

OCTOBER 29 ★ *indulge in moderation*
A tough square between charming Venus and expansive Jupiter can lead to excessive spending or overestimating someone's potential. At the same time, a wobbly quincunx between Venus and foggy Neptune can be like looking through someone else's glasses, making it difficult for you to see clearly. Perceptions and values are skewed, leading to questionable judgment about people, pleasure, and money. Yet the message is to broaden your tastes and reach out even when you're unsure of where that might lead. Rather than going overboard or blocking new experiences, this is a time to peek around the corner of possibilities and take a small dose of adventurous delight.

NOVEMBER

INVEST MORE IN RELATIONSHIPS

Relationships continue to be a key theme for you this month. Communicative Mercury turns forward on **November 1**, freeing your mind to pick up the thread of conversations suspended for the last three weeks. Your ruling planet, Venus, changes signs on **November 8**, leaving hardworking Virgo for socially skillful Libra. Diplomacy at your job can be a key to success, as navigating through the complexities of office politics becomes vital to maintaining harmony in the workplace. The intense Scorpio Sun shines in your 7th House of Partnerships until moving on to adventurous Sagittarius in your 8th House of Intimacy on **November 22**.

The New Moon in transformative Scorpio on **November 9** is followed by Mercury's entry into the same sign on **October 10**. Deep conversations concerning jealousy and commitment can grow more passionate with new pressure for satisfaction or change. The stakes in the game of partnership are increasing. It's time to ante up by making a choice; invest either more or less of yourself, but don't keep things the same. If you care about a lover, friend, or colleague, leaving your emotional comfort zone is the price to pay to meet the current challenge. The only sure way to resolve these issues is to bravely dive in with total honesty about your feelings and intentions.

On **November 15**, Mars, the planet of initiative, turns retrograde in sensitive Cancer, continuing to move backward until early next March. Life does advance during Mars retrograde, but at a slower pace and with more reflection about the consequences of our actions. Simple statements of fact can rouse uncomfortable memories that provoke anger or defensive behavior. But what's being stirred are old wounds whose exposure—uncomfortable as it might be—is a first step toward healing.

> **KEEP IN MIND THIS MONTH**
>
> *Face your feelings wherever they may take you, for they have their own complicated logic that can lead you to happiness.*

KEY DATES

NOVEMBER 4–5 ★ *dig deep to the bottom of desire*

A sensual Sun-Mars trine on **November 4** can put you physically at ease with someone, drawing the two of you closer together. Working or playing with a lover, friend, or relative flows with little need for words of explanation. On **November 5**, however, a Venus-Pluto square rears its jealous head, perhaps even undermining trust or self-confidence. Doubts get dredged up from the basement of uncertainty, and small requests can feel like impossible demands. Yet this is also a time to reconnect with an ex-partner, recover lost creative interests, or reexamine your desires. Just keep digging through the dark parts and you'll find the light you crave.

NOVEMBER 11-12 ★ *fabulous fantasies*

Two challenging aspects from hazy Neptune to the Sun and lovely Venus take a bite out of reality. It's natural to want to escape the usual routine, so allow some time to explore your fantasies. Dreams of perfect love or a spiritually impeccable life are meant to inspire you rather than bring you down. Falling short of your ideals is natural when you aim so high. Be gentle with yourself to encourage your heart's growth, and try not to allow others' lack of sensitivity to reflect on your own self-worth. Vulnerability is a sign not of weakness but of awakening. Treating others with compassion, and doing the same for yourself, can add a touch of the divine to all of your activities.

SUPER NOVA DAYS
NOVEMBER 19-21 ★ *an unexpected change of tastes*

An intense square between Venus and hot Mars on **November 19** can set off a chain of reactions that will either propel a relationship forward or knock it completely off track. Your responses can quickly bounce from strong attraction to repulsion with little room for compromise. A difficult aspect between the Sun and Venus occurs on **November 20**, stretching tight with social tension that can keep you walking on eggshells. On **November 21**, an annoying Venus-Uranus quincunx further destabilizes relationships with unexpected fluctuations of desires and expectations. Flexibility during this period, however, can help you shake out old habits that stand in the way of new forms of partnership and pleasure.

NOVEMBER 29-30 ★ *clarity builds trust*

Discussions about what you're willing to give for what you want in return are likely now. Serious Saturn aspects both the Sun and Venus—a signal to be precise about what you wish to accomplish with others. It may not feel romantic or generous to be so definitive, but this kind of clarity builds a solid foundation that will ensure trust and intimacy in the long run.

DECEMBER

LIFE IS TOO SERIOUS TO TAKE YOURSELF SO SERIOUSLY

The planetary fireworks are extensive this month as vivacious Venus slinks into Scorpio in your 7th House of Partnerships on **December 5**, raising the temperature in all of your relationships. The New Moon in friendly Sagittarius square wild and crazy Uranus lands in your 8th House of Intimacy on **December 9**, bringing shocks, unexpected delights, and breakthroughs in your connections with others. Old rules may linger, but you're in a new arena that's likely to shake your values and stir up personal and professional partnerships. Opinionated Jupiter makes a once-every-thirteen-years conjunction with impassioned Pluto in Sagittarius on **December 11**, a long-wave influence that can provoke religious, moral, and political extremism. Absolute certainty is often a sign of insecurity, so if you feel yourself puffing up with self-righteousness, have a giggle at your own expense.

Jupiter then moves into ambitious Capricorn on **December 18**, framing a new set of principles to guide plans for the next year or so. Still, with Mercury and the Sun transiting from intense Pluto to larger-than-life Jupiter from **December 19 to 22**, the noise level is high with opinion and argument. The best answers will come from further study with four planets gathering in your 9th House of Higher Education, helping you to temper emotions with facts and reason. Developing your mind through disciplined practice provides major benefits in the year ahead.

Intensity continues through the end of the month with a Cancer Full Moon in your 3rd House of Immediate Environment on **December 23** aligned with a fiery Mars-Jupiter opposition that's exact on **December 26**. Old grievances served up with a big holiday meal may upset your stomach. If you start feeling queasy in the midst of a highly charged conversation, give yourself some emotional distance so that you can regain your sense of balance.

> **KEEP IN MIND THIS MONTH**
>
> *Maintaining a sense of humor allows you to engage in serious differences of opinion without degenerating into arguments.*

KEY DATES

DECEMBER 1–3 ★ *give a little; receive a lot in return*

A harmonious sextile between lucky Jupiter and Venus on **December 1** makes it easy for you to be generous and gracious, even with someone who lacks those qualities. The same aspect between Venus and Pluto on **December 3** enables you to maximize your return of investment without appearing pushy or greedy. A little well-placed pressure from you should produce bountiful results.

SUPER NOVA DAYS
DECEMBER 11-12 ★ *looking hot and making it last*
A sexy Venus-Mars trine on **December 11** can make you frisky and playful while maintaining total control over your emotions. This is a very attractive quality that should get you attention effortlessly. You can take the initiative or follow someone else's lead with equal skill. A constructive Venus-Saturn sextile on **December 12** suggests that recent social gains and creative activities will have a lasting, positive effect.

DECEMBER 15-17 ★ *creating new rules*
Don't let insecurities lead to overcompensation by giving more than you should or trying too hard to impress others on **December 15 and 16**. It is worthwhile to express yourself frankly on matters of money, power, or sex, but what someone else does with that information is his or her own responsibility—so be honest but kind. Fortunately, a Venus-Uranus trine on **December 17** stimulates exciting new ideas about how to be happy in relationships. Realizing that there are many ways to enjoy time with someone special reduces pressure to make the "right" move.

DECEMBER 21-22 ★ *respect your feelings*
Your ruling planet, Venus, forms challenging aspects with aggressive Mars on **December 21** and then with dreamy Neptune on **December 22** that can make you extra sensitive with others. It's possible that you will overreact to statements that are not meant to be as harsh as you think. The more you expect harmony at this time, the harder it can be to accept dissension with those who know you best. If you are feeling vulnerable, don't fight; it only adds fuel to the fire. Respect your emotions, whatever they are, rather than trying to justify yourself to others.

DECEMBER 30 ★ *quiet strength*
Your feet are solidly planted on the ground now, thanks to the stabilizing influence of a Sun-Saturn trine. As a result, you trust yourself, and others are likely to trust you more. A quiet sense of confidence allows you to compromise—if that's what it takes to get a job done peacefully—without feeling like you must give up any of your authority or power.

GEMINI

MAY 21–JUNE 20

GEMINI OVERVIEW

This is your year to make lasting choices and stick to them. Instead of fluttering from one project to another, establishing priorities will be your biggest challenge but can also lead to your greatest rewards. Deep, dark Pluto, the no-nonsense planet of transformation, has been opposite your sign since 1996, so you've already learned a great deal about cutting through the clutter of possibilities to get down to what's most important, especially in relationships. Yet with many new opportunities coming your way, it may take a sharper knife than usual to cut through all of the distractions and home in on the exact target you want to hit. But the potential payoff is worth the sacrifice. Playing for the big jackpot is more likely to deliver the prize than accepting crumbs. **Expect abundance this year, and you just might get it.**

Bountiful Jupiter is in its expansive home sign of Sagittarius almost all year. This can be very lucky. Sagittarius is in your 7th House of Relationships, casting you in a better light with other people. **Your ability to come across as more confident and successful is quite likely to get you the attention and support that you want.** Be open to prosperity, and your life may be blessed with many gifts. Deeper friendships, expanded professional opportunities, and loads of fun in relationships could be presents from Santa Jupiter's bag. **Your own generosity is the best guarantee that you'll be well rewarded in return.** Be temperate in how you express your opinions, for this is one place where less will get you more. The power of your words is forceful, so a few carefully chosen ones will make your point more effectively than a philosophical rant.

Saturn, the planet of hard, cold reality, is in Leo this year, bringing maturity to your thinking and communication. Its passage through your 3rd House of Information makes this a great time to study, write, or teach. Your integrity will be important, as you may be held to a higher standard of accuracy. You'll earn respect and reduce the chances for embarrassment when you check facts carefully before presenting them. Gossip is fun, but be selective about when you engage in this activity. **Speaking with authority is more valuable to you than engaging in idle chatter,** even if it seems that you're taking yourself more seriously than usual. Creative trines connecting Jupiter and Saturn in March and May should be helpful when you're trying to make a good impression, especially when it comes to your professional life. **Combining the visionary principles of Jupiter with the tested reliability of Saturn enables you to see the big picture and to develop a successful plan for achieving your goals.** These important planets are in energetic fire signs, so harness your enthusiasm and apply it with concentration to reach your highest potential.

THE DOOR TO LOVE IS WIDE OPEN

Jupiter, the planet of opportunity, in your 7th House of Partnerships makes this a year of satisfying growth in relationships. If you have a significant other, learning and traveling together are good ways to deepen your love. It's risky to tolerate a stagnant situation where habit, rather than inspiration, keeps you together. Pushing forward is needed to maintain a healthy bond, and having a shared vision of the future is essential to advance as a couple. Dramatically different goals or philosophies can weaken your ties. If you're single, generous Jupiter can open doors to new and interesting people. Join organizations, take classes, and attend a wide range of cultural and educational events to attract potential mates into your life. Raise your public profile by standing up for what you believe or speaking for a cause, as this can also be a bridge to a personal connection. Whether you're unattached or have a partner, do not lower your standards this year, and let the truth in your heart speak loudly.

A GREAT LEAP FORWARD

A sudden event can radically change the direction of your professional life this year. An opportunity can pop out of the blue that will require a quick decision on your part. Spontaneous Uranus in your 10th House of Career forms power-packed squares with boundless Jupiter in January, May, and October—months when a radical turn of events is most likely. Stepping out of your field may be the best way to advance in work. It can feel risky to leave behind a familiar situation, but holding tightly to what you have may only make the inner drum-beat of restlessness beat louder. Be ready to jump ship before you're tossed overboard. In this volatile environment, you've got a better chance to wind up in a happy place if you make the first move.

CONVICTION SELLS

There may be good money for you in sales this year, even if you've got a full-time job already. Chances to pick up some cash on the side are possible if you're willing to step forward and be more assertive. When you believe in the product or service, your enthusiasm will motivate you to find receptive customers. Mercury's retrograde from June 15 to July 9 is a critical period when financial carelessness can prove costly. Cleaning up loose ends and catching up on paperwork during this time, however, can put you on a more solid fiscal foundation for the rest of the year.

REDUCE THE BUZZ

A key to maintaining good health and vitality this year is to keep your nervous system in top shape. You tend to be wired by nature, but even more surges of electricity may pass through your body now. Be moderate in your intake of stimulants like caffeine and sugar. Techniques that calm the mind such as yoga or meditation are major stress relievers. Low-impact physical activities also help slow down the busyness in your head. Spend as much relaxing time outdoors in nature as you can for deeper healing of both body and mind.

A SPIRIT OF TOLERANCE

Harmony on the home front can be disturbed by both extreme beliefs and uncompromising attitudes. The need to be right can be excessive and is a sure source of friction when everyone's not on the same philosophical, political, or religious page. A spirit of tolerance will go a long way toward keeping a friendly discussion from exploding into a major war of words. On a physical level, this is a good year to alter the way you use your living space. Rearranging furniture, changing the functions of rooms, or even moving to a new place are all reasonable possibilities.

A NEW WORLD OF AWARENESS

You may be ready to separate yourself from long-standing traditions or values that no longer address your intellectual needs. Old beliefs are shaken by new experiences and a desire to find truth in your own way. Rebelling against teachers or religious authorities is to be expected. Rather than fighting over the past, however, consider yourself an explorer who doesn't need external approval to validate your experiences. Courses outside your usual areas of interest and travel to exotic places are good ways to feed your need for novel ideas. But just because you've made a major breakthrough, don't expect what you've learned to be easily assimilated by others. You may be impatient to bring them on board, but if resistance is strong, back up rather than forcing your opinions on anyone else.

 ## EVER-CHANGING TRUTH

A spiritual teacher may enter your life this year, and answers that you are seeking can come in a flash. You don't need devotional practice to take you farther along on the path of enlightenment. Gifts of instantaneous knowing can come when you least expect them. Yet these experiences will be surprising, rather than seeming like a logical extension of what you've been learning all of these years. Truth might appear like a joker who shows you that everything you thought was true is false. But take time to assimilate such radical ideas, because the awareness game can be very tricky now. What appears to be so accurate one day can prove to be false the next. Every answer will just spur you on to ask another question.

RICK & JEFF'S TIP FOR THE YEAR:
Speak the Truth Boldly

You can radically change the way that others see you this year. Use this skill to advance your position in different kinds of relationships. Personally and professionally, this is a time when it's possible to increase the respect and recognition you get from others. It will take some boldness to make this happen, so don't be shy about coming on too strong, as long as you know what you're talking about. People will listen, but make sure that your material is worthy of their attention. When you feel the truth inside yourself, that message will come across loud and clear.

JANUARY

SO MANY CHOICES

This month begins with an emotional Cancer Full Moon in your 2nd House of Possessions on **January 3** that activates your ruling planet, Mercury. Your thoughts turn inward as probing Mercury—now in your 8th House of Shared Resources— sheds light on your dependency on others and urges you to be more self-sufficient. Although you may have enjoyed indulging those you love during the holidays, now it's time to put your finances in order—especially concerning jointly held property—by taking advantage of money-oriented Venus in realistic Capricorn. Although there are other factors contributing to your current practicality, such as a calming trine between insistent Mars and dependable Saturn on **January 8**, there are still complications. A misjudgment on **January 11** might provoke a display of emotions from a partner that could take a few days to settle down.

A steady flow of planets from conservative Capricorn into quirky Aquarius in your 9th House of Journeys helps you to look ahead with an open-minded perspective. Sweet Venus leads the parade on **January 3**, followed by mental Mercury on **January 15** and the Sun on **January 20**—setting the stage for a rare six-planet pileup in your 9th House just a couple of days after the ambitious Capricorn New Moon on **January 18**. There isn't much that can restrain you these days from reaching for the stars; your heart and mind are not in the present moment. Instead, you are fascinated by the future, dreaming about making an innovative statement, and planning to undertake a truly great adventure. The end of the month, though, is dominated by a long-lasting square between fortunate Jupiter and freedom-loving Uranus on **January 22**. Whether you are considering travel, an educational path, or a change in career, find your bearings and get ready to fly.

> **KEEP IN MIND THIS MONTH**
>
> *You are enticed by unusual possibilities, yet you can't follow every dream. Let the fantasies play out in your mind, but prepare to make choices when necessary.*

KEY DATES

SUPER NOVA DAY
JANUARY 3 ★ *no time for distractions*
An extraordinary Full Moon in Cancer has you worrying about debt—related to your credit cards or possibly regarding an unfulfilled emotional commitment.

Mercury is futilely attempting to be logical in serious Capricorn, yet you are totally turned on by an electric sextile from Uranus. With stylish Venus now moving into futuristic Aquarius, you are on the edge of a new form of love or pleasure. Your good intentions are tested as responsibilities call loudly. Sudden distractions are all alluring, but you cannot sidestep your obligations. Focus on your priorities and get down to business, as there is plenty to do.

JANUARY 11–13 ★ *stay cool*

These are uncomfortable days as Mercury is agitated first by restrictive Saturn on **January 11** and then by explosive Uranus on **January 13**, creating a sense of instability. Your fear of being proven wrong has you obsessing over something until it's blown out of proportion. With fiery Mars joining passionate Pluto—also on **January 13**—you might even feel like someone at work is threatening you, but you are probably reacting to the intensity of the situation. Establish your necessary boundaries without becoming overly defensive.

JANUARY 18 ★ *first the old, then the new*

A conjunction in progressive Aquarius between loving Venus and spiritual Neptune has you daydreaming of other times and places. Your imagination takes you on exotic adventures into the future. Your sense of romantic love reaches new heights, but it's difficult to separate your ideal of beauty from the reality of the current situation. Today, you can easily make it up as you go along, so be careful what you conjure up. It could become real! However, the New Moon in reliable Capricorn restrains you till the last possible moment, forcing you to fulfill your previous promises before initiating anything new. Take care of unfinished business first and then you can revel in your sweet fantasies.

JANUARY 26–28 ★ *get real*

Conceptual Mercury makes an unusual transition from soft Neptune on **January 26** to stern Saturn on **January 28**. At first, your thoughts are fuzzy, with Neptune shrouding you in the mists of illusion. Even if you are overwhelmed by the details you must now face, you have no desire to put a stop to your fantasies. But just as you arrive in nirvana, the boss appears, and he's not happy with your attempted escape. Often, you can talk your way out of just about anything. Now, however, Saturn is in control, jamming the emergency brake on until you take responsibility for what you think, say, and do.

FEBRUARY

FIGHTING THE FOG OF FANTASY

Last month's easygoing energy dissipates throughout this month, starting on **February 1** with the relentless Leo Full Moon in your 3rd House of Short Trips. Even something as simple as a run to the store can interrupt your concentration and disrupt your schedule. On **February 2**, your ruling planet, Mercury, enters the world of emotional Pisces. As an airy Gemini, you play comfortably in Mercury's mental realm, yet you will be required to feel your way through unfamiliar territory. It is more difficult to remain objective these days, as your moods will color your thoughts more than usual. But it's not entirely disagreeable; gentle Venus, in Pisces until **February 20**, draws you into a colorful world of imagination. One minute you are fighting your own personal demons; the next, you're a successful executive. And just one day after the emotionally detached Aquarius New Moon on **February 17**, the Sun enters spiritual Pisces. Other worlds loom larger than the real one for a couple of days as five planets congregate in the sign of the Fish. You might resist trusting your intuition, but it is unusually reliable now.

Mercury turns retrograde on **February 13**, further confusing your normally quick mind. It's frustrating to redo work you thought was already completed, but you are also struggling to concentrate on specific tasks. Behind all of this surface malaise lies the growing energy of the opposition between the giants, austere Saturn and nebulous Neptune. It's a challenge to know what's real as your ability to communicate effectively is tested. You may get discouraged as you encounter misunderstandings with close friends or siblings. Use this time to reconnect and reconfirm your affection for them.

> **KEEP IN MIND THIS MONTH**
>
> *Finding a place to stand is nearly impossible. Your best strategy might be to sink deep into your imagination and trust your intuition.*

KEY DATES

FEBRUARY 1 ★ *the waiting game*

The Full Moon in fiery Leo dramatizes how your perceptions of a situation will impact your immediate environment. Trying to put your ideas into action, however, creates unexpected undercurrents as your efforts are blocked by the resistance of others. Stay focused on long-term goals so that you might reduce your anxiety over short-term difficulties.

SUPER NOVA DAYS
FEBRUARY 7-10 ★ *connect to the artist within*
A hectic turn of events impacts your work environment as Venus conjuncts
unpredictable Uranus in your 10th House of Public Status on **February 7**.
Monitor your own reactions; with overbearing Jupiter involved, you can get
yourself in over your head unless you consciously avoid conflict. Additionally,
the Sun conjuncts slippery Neptune, making you believe that everything will
turn out rosy, but this may just be a trick. Don't swallow the bait unless you
are really ready to engage. On the positive side, you can also use these days
to get in touch with your inner visionary artist, poet, writer, or musician. As
you soar above it all, make sure you don't lose sight of the ground, or you may
crash as the Sun opposes unforgiving Saturn on **February 10**.

FEBRUARY 13 ★ *rethink plans*
Messenger Mercury turns retrograde in your 10th House of Career, marking the
beginning of a three-week period when your key planet activates a variety of
communication issues relating to your work. Although you are meeting former
colleagues for lunch, you must also patch up current relationships on the job.
However, don't fall into the trap of thinking you must take dramatic action of any
kind. Reconsidering your options, tying up loose ends, returning e-mail, and
cleaning up your résumé are tasks more important than doing anything new.

FEBRUARY 17 ★ *commit to your dreams*
The Aquarius New Moon in your 9th House of Higher Education is a harbinger of
change in your professional life. These transitions may be the result of studies
that you now undertake to sharpen your technical skills and to solidify your
qualifications. Support from a sextile to Pluto in your 7th House of Partnerships
indicates the possibility of assistance from a powerful ally. Show your appreciation
to someone special by making a serious commitment to realize your most
important dreams.

FEBRUARY 27-28 ★ *move beyond doubt*
At the height of the long-term Saturn-Neptune opposition that began last summer,
you begin to doubt the decisions you made over the past year. Although familiar
routines in your daily life are changing, draw comfort from the knowledge that
ultimately you will find a way to live a more authentic life in the months ahead.

★ GEMINI

MARCH

BALANCE RISK WITH REWARD

Two eclipses focus planetary attention on your 10th House of Career this month, turning your life topsy-turvy with surprises—some quite pleasant, others more troublesome. The first, a Full Moon Eclipse in Virgo on **March 3**, falls in your 4th House of Home and Family, opposite the 10th House, making it difficult to find balance between your domestic needs and the instability at work. Erratic Uranus is aligned with the Sun, shading your life with a high-frequency hum that puts you on edge while seeking additional freedom, perhaps stressing your family situation.

Your ruling planet, Mercury, is retrograde in intelligent Aquarius until **March 7**, requiring you to finish old business prior to moving on to new projects. Your mind is occupied more with potential, not actualities, until Mercury swims into intuitive Pisces in your 10th House of Career on **March 17**. Although you still may struggle for focus, the emphasis shifts to getting ahead at work or improving your standing within the community. The New Moon Eclipse in Pisces on **March 18** may be a turning point in your desire for a new direction in your professional life. First, however, you must overcome resistance from someone who feels threatened by your ambitions.

A deep undercurrent of planetary stability supports you throughout the month. Amid these changes, optimistic Jupiter in your 7th House of Partnerships harmoniously trines pessimistic Saturn in your 3rd House of Communication. This creates a rather perfect balance that allows you to see the best in others without placing unrealistic expectations on them. You can clearly see the relationships between the present situation and what you must do to attain your goals.

> **KEEP IN MIND THIS MONTH**
>
> *Set long-term goals, make well-defined plans, and commit to them. The results will be worth the wait, even if current circumstances throw you off course.*

KEY DATES

MARCH 3–5 ★ *brilliant thoughts rattle your cage*

The Lunar Eclipse on **March 3** is opposite the conjunction between freedom-loving Uranus and the Sun in your 10th House of Public Status. A surprise at work could increase your personal autonomy or hand you an unexpected promotion. However, instability may come along with the deal. You are on a mental high, and your thoughts run so fast that it's not easy to bring them down to earth. It's hard to focus your attention, so try to create a protective space around you. Keep down the extraneous noise by closing your office door or even just saying less when you have to be around others.

MARCH 8-9 ★ *time to indulge*

Charming Venus stimulates the stabilizing trine between powerhouses Jupiter and Saturn now, allowing you to make long-lasting impressions on others in ways that enhance your status. You feel as lucky as a leprechaun, and you won't even have to wave a magic wand to make your wishes come true. It's time to move the energy out of your head and into your body by treating yourself to sensual experiences such as an evening of art or music, a gourmet meal, or a relaxing massage.

SUPER NOVA DAYS
MARCH 16-18 ★ *up for the challenge*

You are well equipped to overcome any obstacles that appear in your life, for you have the vision of Jupiter along with the support of Saturn working in your favor. Although the Jupiter-Saturn trine is exact on **March 16**, this long-lasting transit resurfaces on **May 5** and lingers throughout the entire year. You are more capable now of accepting assistance from others and integrating their efforts with your own work. Additionally, both verbal Mercury and stylish Venus are harmonizing with powerful Pluto. Your words align with your intent, making you more attractive and compelling than ever.

MARCH 22-25 ★ *control your enthusiasm*

Recent developments may have opened new avenues of expression in relationships and career, but now you may have to tap on the brakes to negotiate the curves. Self-directed Mars is resisted by stern Saturn on **March 22**, demanding that you curb travel plans, cut back on your course load, or deemphasize your spiritual quest. Your best strategy is persistence, so don't give up, even if you feel that unseen forces are conspiring against you. By **March 25**, Mars catches up to illusory Neptune, so don't bend the truth. Your actions can inspire others, so there is no need for embellishment. Even if it isn't glamorous, it's better to be honest.

GEMINI

APRIL

STABILITY AMID THE NOISE

Illuminating flashes of intuition jump-start the month as quicksilver Mercury contacts unpredictable Uranus in the compassionate seas of watery Pisces. Your thinking is nimble now, perhaps moving so rapidly that you cannot make practical use of the brilliant ideas. And although you can see your place in the outer world quite clearly as the mental lightning strikes, just moments later you are lost again in the murky depths of your subconscious mind. On **April 2**, a diplomatic Libra Full Moon in your 5th House of Romance and Children can encourage you to be fair-minded and kind as you fulfill your parental obligations or in a lover's quarrel.

The pace of your social life picks up a notch when your ruling planet, Mercury, enters speedy Aries in the 11th House of Groups and Friends on **April 10**, where it remains until **April 26**. Additionally, sensual Venus dances her way into your sign and into your life on **April 11**. While visiting curious Gemini, the planet of love attracts you to a variety of new experiences. Your accentuated charm and light-hearted style make you more popular than ever. The impulsive Aries New Moon on **April 17** in your 11th House punctuates an already exciting time with a series of exclamation points prior to your life settling down in the days ahead.

Even though this month's calendar is bustling with social engagements, your busy lifestyle won't necessarily interfere with your productivity. The residual effects of March's trine between powerhouses Jupiter and Saturn are recharged by trines from the Sun on **April 8 to 9** and from Mercury on **April 20 to 21**. Consolidate changes and prepare for the next recurrence of this stabilizing Jupiter-Saturn formation on **May 5**.

> **KEEP IN MIND THIS MONTH**
>
> *You can have the best of both worlds by giving yourself permission to cut loose, as long as you leave ample time for the serious work at hand.*

KEY DATES

APRIL 1–4 ★ *mixed messages*
These exciting few days can increase both mental and physical activity levels yet simultaneously restrain your emotional expression. The Libra Full Moon on **April 2** can be quite playful in your 5th House, yet Venus is uncomfortably square to stern Saturn and spiritual Neptune. Your romantic fantasies fall short of reality, isolating you from loved ones. You won't stay sad for long, however, for joyful Jupiter is also

wrestling with thoughtful Mercury. A wave of unrealistic optimism can cover your insecurities and get you into trouble if you speak too quickly.

APRIL 9 ★ *internal conflict*
Today, as Mercury squares intense Pluto, everyone postures for control, and you may find yourself in a battle of words with a formidable opponent. You might try to talk your way around conflicts, but could benefit much more by slowing down and dealing with the issues now. It is tempting to blame current problems on outside circumstances, but the real obstacle could be you. Don't waste energy attempting to coerce others to your point of view. Instead, look within yourself for a solution so that you can resolve the differences without having to struggle.

SUPER NOVA DAYS
APRIL 20–22 ★ *good to go*
Fast-thinking Mercury in innovative Aries is harmonizing with the long-term, stabilizing Jupiter-Saturn trine. You are able to present information in a way that others won't find offensive—even if it's something they don't want to hear. Although the Venus-Mars square on **April 22** can reduce your patience, fire up your creativity, and arouse your libido, this can be a rather productive phase, too. Put your life in good working order while your mind is functioning on such a practical level. This can be a financially savvy time, excellent for buying and selling property or just shopping with friends. All forms of communication, business, and travel are favored, as long as you don't avoid any tough details.

APRIL 26 ★ *imagine the unthinkable*
Get out your journal, think about your future, and then write whatever comes into your mind, for you are touching the tops of mountains and reaching into the heat of the lava today. Inquisitive Mercury harmonizes with volcanic Pluto, allowing you to think about the unthinkable. You can stretch your intellect into the underworld and bring back symbols laden with meaning. But beautiful Venus and thrill-seeking Uranus also conspire to draw you toward excitement and freedom, making you more eager to spontaneously flirt with the romantic edge. The danger of the day is only in how quickly and unconsciously you react to your own desires.

MAY

Hold on to your hats, Gemini, for May is like a spring breeze that can lift your spirits, hold you aloft, and capriciously shift when you least expect it. This wind can blow into your life in the guise of another person—a friend, coworker, spouse, or romantic interest—and is bound to open your mind to new perspectives and offer ample opportunities for growth if you are willing to get serious.

Grand old Jupiter is at home in Sagittarius in your 7th House of Partnerships for most of the year, but has long-lasting brushes with both unwavering Saturn and erratic Uranus. Jupiter trines Saturn on **May 5**, stabilizing relationships, and then squares Uranus on **May 10**, energizing an array of exciting possibilities in love and in your profession. Meanwhile, your key planet, Mercury, returns to its home sign of Gemini on **May 11**, remaining there until **May 28**; you can feel its presence amplifying your thoughts. Words are on the tip of your tongue, and you are eager to share them, whether you have something important to say or not. This communication feeding frenzy could peak when Mercury and Jupiter, the two idea planets, reach opposition on **May 20**, urging you to make mountains out of molehills.

A Scorpio Full Moon in your 6th House of Health on **May 2** opposes Mercury, deepening the connection between your body and your mind. Remember that you are what you think. Although diet and exercise are both important to your well-being, your positive attitude is essential. A practical Taurus New Moon square Neptune on **May 16** suggests the need for spiritual practice to center you. A rare second Full Moon occurring this month in Sagittarius on **May 31** conjoins Jupiter, blessing your life and your relationships.

> **KEEP IN MIND THIS MONTH**
>
> *It's certainly not time to retreat or withdraw. Although you usually engage life to the fullest, it's time to reach a dream, and then go beyond it.*

KEY DATES

MAY 2 ★ *talk your way through it*

You may try to think your way back to basics as mental Mercury conjoins the Sun in "keep it simple" Taurus, but there are complications from an intense Scorpio Full Moon. It is likely that a communication issue is the source of a conflict at work and that meaningful dialog may offer resolution, bringing the comfort you need to stay healthy and happy during the stressful Full Moon.

MAY 5-7 ★ *hold your ground*
You are quite distracted by your own internal process as rational Mercury dukes it out with foggy Neptune. Confusion arises from the strength of your fantasies as you see the hidden beauty in everything and desperately want to realize each possibility. Fortunately, the residual effects from the stabilizing Jupiter-Saturn trine on **May 5** will give you the tools to discern potential from fantasy in order to keep things real.

SUPER NOVA DAYS
MAY 14-16 ★ *the mind can do anything*
Your planet, Mercury, forms a magical quintile aspect with Saturn on **May 14**, allowing you to talk about unchangeable things in a way that changes them. Nothing is impossible now—although your style may be cramped by previous obligations. The restrictive thoughts also contain seeds for your progress. Don't accept defeat, even if you're overwhelmed. Today's discussions will set the stage for tomorrow's transformations when red-hot Mars shoots into Aries, igniting your booster rockets. You will happily find yourself more involved with friends over the days ahead. And the obstinate Taurus New Moon on **May 16** offers you a solitary moment to touch the ground in the midst of an exciting time.

MAY 20-21 ★ *connect the dots*
Your energy spreads out and shifts into high gear as Mercury in your sign is stimulated by high-frequency Uranus and buoyant Jupiter. Don't waste energy wishing for calmer days. Enjoy the crazy thoughts and unbridled optimism without holding anything back. Let your words fly like arrows; speak what's on your mind and write down your best ideas. Weave your story and hitch it to the nearest star.

MAY 27-31 ★ *unlock fear*
As you approach the Sagittarian Full Moon on **May 31**, it may feel like you are dancing as you skate over a thin sheet of ice. Beneath the veneer, however, is a pool of hot molten lava. With Mercury opposing intense Pluto on **May 27**, your concern is that if you stop moving, the ice will crack and down you'll go, right into the depth of your own fears. Nevertheless, slowing down allows you to overcome that which scares you. Your worries are more frightening when they are locked beneath the surface.

JUNE

LEAN BACK, BUT NOT TOO FAR

Your ruling planet, Mercury, resides in receptive Cancer in your 2nd House of Possessions all month. You may be concerned with financial issues, but the scrutiny will likely go beyond money and cut to the core of your self-esteem—after all, the most important thing you own is your self-respect. You may be extra sensitive to what others say, because you are feeling very vulnerable now. You receive much-needed support from friends, coworkers, and perhaps even a mentor, especially on the days prior to the empowering Gemini New Moon on **June 14**. There is, however, an undertow already strengthening, with soft-talking Mercury in watery Cancer turning retrograde on **June 15** and staying in reverse for the rest of the month. Mercury retrograde in sentimental Cancer has you remembering past feelings while also reorganizing your possessions and finances. And on the Summer Solstice, when the Sun enters moody Cancer on **June 21**, your normally buzzing mind calms down even another notch.

You will get more out of your life by slowing down throughout the month as a powerful tide swells, drawing you even deeper into your own personal reflecting pool. Somber Saturn opposes mystical Neptune on **June 25** for the third and final time, marking the end of a long-term phase of disappointment and self-doubt that began last summer and resurfaced around February 28. Make use of the additional fortitude you receive from willful Mars entering determined Taurus on **June 24**. Don't be too concerned if you are feeling a bit sad around the Capricorn Full Moon on **June 30** as sweet Venus runs into the Saturn-Neptune opposition. This is a chance to restructure your dreams as you get closure on your past.

> **KEEP IN MIND THIS MONTH**
>
> *Losses in money or love are temporary setbacks, reminding you of deeper underlying issues. Don't blame yourself or others; make adjustments and move on.*

KEY DATES

JUNE 2-5 ★ *overcoming anxiety*

Mercury's intellectual antennae are picking up eerie early warnings of the heavy Saturn-Neptune storm that gathers this month. You may feel it first in your pocketbook or perhaps as a subtle reminder of a particular failure that haunts you. Fortunately, an effervescent trine between eager Mars and joyful Jupiter on **June 4** makes it impossible for you to stay down too long. Friends come to your rescue, but something that's said may put you on edge. You may feel uncomfortable from a personal disclosure that threatens your established boundaries, but the possibility of love is too exciting for you to say no.

SUPER NOVA DAYS
JUNE 11-14 ★ *uplifting wind under your wings*

A series of harmonious aspects induces a sweet mixture of positive feelings, lovely fantasies, and very real events that can deeply inspire you. You are calm and collected, yet your ambitions are strong. Support arrives in many forms; everywhere you turn, someone shows up willing to help. Your concerns are not trivial; if something seems important, don't let it slip away without doing something about it. Your follow-through is dependable and swift, so you are capable of accomplishing much. Make sure to leave time for creative and metaphysical pursuits. Read or write poetry, lose yourself in music or dance, and escape into whatever beauty you admire. This phase culminates at the Gemini New Moon on **June 14**, launching you onward in your current quest for personal satisfaction in relationships and your career.

JUNE 18-21 ★ *endurance wins*

A powerful person could stand between you and your progress. Often, when thwarted, you become irritated. Your typical response is to strap on your roller skates and glide away, but now you are ready for a confrontation as you dig in your heels. In fact, you might even be enjoying the intense exchange. There is no hurry, for your endurance is strong, and what you learn from this encounter can stick with you for a long time.

JUNE 27-30 ★ *in the doldrums*

A sobering bout with dissatisfaction or even depression may be prompted by disturbing news you receive around **June 27**, when retrograde Mercury revisits the waning tension of the Saturn-Neptune opposition that was exact for the final time on **June 25**. But just because you know how you want to respond, this doesn't mean that you'll actually say it. There is a good chance you may be misunderstood, but you still must make the attempt. By the Capricorn Full Moon on **June 30**, your creative juices are flowing again, yet you could remain subdued for a few more days before bouncing back.

JULY

QUIET ON THE HOME FRONT

July begins on a melancholic note as it comes off an emotionally overwhelming Full Moon. The ongoing Mercury retrograde in hesitant Cancer continues until **July 9**, holding your thoughts in familiar yet retrospective patterns. And even after your key planet turns direct, it still remains in Cancer in your 2nd House of Self-Worth for the rest of the month. You are rather nostalgic now, perhaps a bit sad, especially with the Sun also in moody Cancer until **July 22**. The quiet Cancer New Moon on **July 14** invites you to look inward. As it falls in your 2nd House, you continue to be concerned about your finances. However, being overly protective of your money may only be a symptom of a deeper need to defend your core values against a seeming less than friendly world. It's a challenge now to feel safe, but you gain solace these days from the love and support of your friends and family.

Sweet pleasure may be hard to find as affectionate Venus contacts austere Saturn on **July 1**. You are more serious about love and can control your feelings for the sake of creating more mature relationships. Still, loneliness could be a part of the picture. Venus moves into critical Virgo at the New Moon on **July 14**, keeping your desires highly focused on what is most practical. But Venus doesn't make much progress this month, slowing down to turn retrograde on **July 27**. Moderate your expectations to avoid disappointment. An emotionally detached Aquarian Full Moon on **July 29** reflects your need for independence and can make you aware of the price you must pay to remain true to yourself. Again, you sense resistance to your plan; it's not easy now to reach your goals.

> **KEEP IN MIND THIS MONTH**
>
> *Listen to the deeper, richer planetary note behind the noise, reminding you to hold on to your present course. Know that you are making more progress than is outwardly apparent.*

KEY DATES

JULY 1 ★ *overcoming isolation*
Finances may be the source of worry as rich Venus squares immovable Saturn. Even if your bank account is in good shape, you still might need to cut a major expense. It may be that you just don't think you deserve anything extra now. This may also stimulate a communication problem in a relationship as one of you withdraws, thereby making the other person uneasy with the increased emotional

distance. You have the fortitude to meet most situations head-on with retrograde Mercury receiving support from determined Mars. Rely on your inner strategist while working hard to create a sensible path through this rather testy day.

SUPER NOVA DAYS
JULY 8-11 ★ *no retreat*

You still may be feeling vulnerable from sensual Venus's recent engagement with austere Saturn, but on **July 8** your desires deepen as passionate Pluto enters the scene. You'd like to get through these days without delving too deeply into your emotions, but this strategy may not work. A relationship hangs in the balance of what you say. The hesitation won't last, for highly energizing transits on **July 10** spur you on, tempting you to overreact. Don't take the easy way out by following your emergency escape route. If you do try to avoid a necessary confrontation with an intimate partner, a tense Mars-Pluto aspect on **July 11** will pull you right back. Work with the issues so that you can benefit from a healthy transformation.

JULY 20-24 ★ *answer the call*

An exhilarating Mars-Uranus sextile on **July 20** unleashes a flurry of events that affect your career or your role within the community, and when the Sun enters dramatic Leo on **July 22**, you proudly assume your new position. Still, you may not be happy about the additional responsibilities and might harbor feelings of insecurity. Self-directed Mars runs into a tense square with nebulous Neptune on **July 24**, strengthening your creative imagination. Putting it to practical use, however, can be tricky. Don't set your goals so high that you'll be disappointed when you cannot reach them.

JULY 28-31 ★ *reaching escape velocity*

Mercury harmonizes with revolutionary Uranus the day before an unorthodox Aquarian Full Moon on **July 29**. The lightning is striking and everything is shaking. You see better ways to realize your dreams, which could make for big changes to your work schedule or travel plans. Things that were holding you back are now letting go. But you are not home free, as assertive Mars must first overcome Saturn's resistance on **July 31**. Don't overdo during your first steps, or you will only be required to repeat them in a few days.

AUGUST

SLOW DOWN TO MAKE THE MOST OF LIFE

A slow-moving harmonious wave stabilizes the first part of the month, enabling you to concentrate your efforts on integrating both the accomplishments and the setbacks of the year. You don't get much breathing room, as this consolidation will require intense relationship work. You must walk your talk now, and this may involve changing how you think in order to become a more effective communicator. The powerful trine between persistent Saturn and regenerative Pluto on **August 6** strengthens your survival instincts and increases your stamina. You gain additional assistance from confident Jupiter, which turns direct the very same day. But don't waste energy, for Mars enters clever Gemini, making you fast to react. Your speed could cost you valuable time unless you plan your action carefully.

If you were unsure of yourself in July, this is a turnaround phase with self-directed Mars in your sign most of the month. Your ruling planet, Mercury, tells it like it is while in expressive Leo from **August 8 to 19**. The Leo New Moon in your 3rd House of Communication on **August 12** can increase the overall activity level in your life; you have so much to do that you feel like you're missing the fun. But even as stylish Venus retrogrades back into serious Saturn on **August 13**, you are a significant force now. Disappointment in love, a family squabble, or a lack of money should be taken in stride without letting these setbacks interfere with your overall plan. Your career is emphasized toward the end of the month as a Full Moon Eclipse in imaginative Pisces on **August 28** stirs unfulfilled dreams. Still, the tone is positive if you don't ignore the necessary details of your daily routine.

> **KEEP IN MIND THIS MONTH**
>
> *Keeping your options open can be a viable strategy, but narrowing your field of vision can give you much-needed clarity and peace of mind.*

KEY DATES

AUGUST 2 ★ *open the door*

An important person may enter your life as the Sun in big-hearted Leo trines bountiful Jupiter in your 7th House of Partnerships. This can improve your current relationships, but an irritable quincunx between sensitive Mercury and obsessive Pluto could make you wary of other people's motives. You may not wish to get involved because you are afraid of losing your own perspective, yet with Jupiter's beneficent presence, you'll be fine no matter how intense it gets.

AUGUST 9 ★ *say it with flowers*
This might be your lucky day if you want to invite someone special out on a date or ask for a raise from your boss. Within reason, whatever you want is yours as quick-witted Mercury receives encouragement from congenial Jupiter. You are more smooth-talking than ever, and with just the right flair, you could charm a snake with your clever one-liners. Beware of being so ingenious that no one understands what you say. If you overreach, you can lose your footing and your communication advantage.

AUGUST 13 ★ *a walk in the park*
Retrograde Venus conjuncts Saturn the Tester, increasing financial responsibility or creating complications in love. With Mercury and Neptune active, what you lack in mental clarity is made up in artistic potential. Your rationality is diffused, so forget about writing technical manuals; instead, enrich your soul by listening to music or relaxing in nature.

AUGUST 23–25 ★ *great expectations*
You think you can conquer the world with assertive Mars in your sign opposing overconfident Jupiter and squaring logical Mercury. It's challenging to maintain your balance today, because you are all fired up and primed for action. However, the biggest problem could be your own perspective; you may be deluding yourself. Assume that you are not seeing the real situation; instead, you're looking at your own excitement. If everything is as awesome as it appears, the opportunities will still be available in a few days.

SUPER NOVA DAY
AUGUST 28 ★ *it's all too much*
Events move too quickly today as the Pisces Full Moon Eclipse in your 10th House of Career fills your head with fantasies about your professional aspirations. You want to reach high for your dreams, but it's hard to make a practical decision, for you must stay on your toes to keep up with all of the surprises. You are normally pretty agile, but now with Mercury opposing Uranus, you may have to change your tune on a moment's notice. Forget about long-term plans for now. How well you respond to current challenges can set the stage for the weeks ahead.

SEPTEMBER

A RADICAL BREAK FROM THE PAST

A supercharged Solar Eclipse in Virgo on **September 11** can awaken forgotten memories and shake up the shape of your future. Unpredictable Uranus is opposite the Sun-Moon conjunction, which brings tremors of change from the depths of your 4th House of Home and Family. Assertive Mars in your sign and transformational Pluto in Sagittarius form tense squares to the eclipse and are a possible source of power struggles or outbursts of aggression. You can benefit from this wild ride, though, by letting go of long-held beliefs that keep you in a rut. Releasing old habits and expectations will prepare you for a sudden turnaround in your career and personal life. A flexible and patient attitude is necessary if confrontation arises now. Fortunately, there's more than one way to achieve your goals, so don't be afraid to experiment as you address any explosive issues.

Venus, the relationship planet, goes direct on **September 8** after turning retrograde on **July 27**. This forward shift, which occurs in your 3rd House of Communication, adds vibrancy to your already witty repartee, making for especially enjoyable conversations with your friends. This should also provide much-needed good humor to compensate for potential upsets triggered by the Solar Eclipse in Virgo. Peace becomes valuable from **September 17 to 21**, when the willful Sun, Mars, and Pluto form a series of hard aspects with one another. Tension can be very high this week as small disagreements turn into major conflicts. Impulsive Mars, in your sign until **September 28**, may provoke your pugnacious side. But while standing up for yourself is a good thing, Gemini, it's unlikely that anyone else is going to back down, so do your best to avoid any head-on collisions.

> **KEEP IN MIND THIS MONTH**
>
> *Victory comes from being gentle with yourself and working around resistance rather than struggling against it.*

KEY DATES

SUPER NOVA DAYS
SEPTEMBER 2-3 ★ *be spontaneous, not angry*
Serious Saturn enters Virgo, moving into your 4th House for the next two years. This long-term transit may indicate a change of address, but it is essentially about inner resolve. You're starting to build a foundation that may

define your future for years to come. More immediately, a square between chatty Mercury and no-nonsense Pluto on **September 2** can precipitate blunt exchanges. Tempers may be short with fiery Mars square intemperate Uranus on **September 3**, although innovation and spontaneity are possible benefits. On the same day, the proud Sun squares excessive Jupiter, with arrogance and overstatement as negatives and confidence a potential plus.

SEPTEMBER 8 ★ *unnecessary upset*
Your ruling planet, Mercury, clashes with supersensitive Neptune, a combination that engenders misunderstanding. What you're hearing might not be what was intended, so don't be quick to take offense. Venus turning direct adds vulnerability with self-worth issues, and you may feel less secure. Don't take things personally.

SEPTEMBER 13-14 ★ *masterful communication*
Your thoughts rise to a higher level of clarity with an intelligent sextile between fact-based Mercury and philosophical Jupiter on **September 13**. Their connection enhances your communication skills, enabling you to impress others with your eloquence. On **September 14**, Mercury forms a brilliant quintile with deep-seeing Pluto, adding potency to your thinking and your words. You can solve complex problems by cutting through unnecessary information and getting to the core of the matter. Your mental edge increases your powers of persuasion.

SEPTEMBER 17-18 ★ *sweet talk*
A mesmerizing way of expressing yourself gets your messages across in a lovely way. Talkative Mercury's helpful sextile with captivating Venus on **September 17** can be seductive, even if you're just reading a shopping list—romantic talk would, of course, work even better. Mercury's healthy trine with idealistic Neptune on **September 18** is great for communicating a delicate matter, since you are acutely sensitivity now.

SEPTEMBER 26-28 ★ *peer competition*
The Full Moon in energetic Aries on **September 26** sparks new ideas for group activities. Colleagues or friends may seem competitive, but a harmonious trine between Mercury and Aries's ruling planet, Mars, fills you with fast-thinking and sharp ideas to keep pace. On **September 27**, Mercury enters research-oriented Scorpio in your 6th House of Habits and Routines, giving you a more eagle-eyed perspective on work. On **September 28**, Mars enters Cancer in your 2nd House of Personal Resources, spurring you to upgrade skills that could raise your income.

OCTOBER

THE DEVIL IS IN THE DETAILS

A change of direction by little Mercury and two major aspects by gigantic Jupiter are the primary planetary events this month. On **October 11**, Mercury begins a three-week retrograde cycle that starts in deep, dark Scorpio and ends in light and airy Libra. These tri-annual reversals are times when data and details get lost or fuzzy and when gears of all types tend to malfunction. The message is always to double-check your facts, communicate more carefully, and maintain vital pieces of equipment. Reconnecting with people from the past, especially coworkers or classmates, is one of Mercury retrograde's gifts.

Generous Jupiter makes the last in a series of three dynamic squares with independent Uranus on **October 9**. This is earthquake energy that can shake the globe physically and politically. It's a period of upsets and radical change that took root with the first square back in January. The aspect's disruptive influence lasts as long as two weeks. Jupiter is in your 7th House of Relationships, and Uranus is in your 10th House of Career. Their collision, then, can mark conflict between these two areas of your life. An employment opportunity could separate you from a close friend, or a partner's needs might cause you to change your job. Still, there is an enormous potential for positive experiences, since helpful people can get you on the fast track to a higher level of success, perhaps in a new field. On **October 29**, Jupiter forms a sextile with idealistic Neptune. This constructive connection is also a long-lasting influence that should broaden your outlook on life. Spiritual awakening and increasing faith are two of its major properties. And you may be inspired to travel or study as ways to experience a wider vision of the world.

KEEP IN MIND THIS MONTH

Brilliant ideas have the best chance to produce concrete results when they are reinforced with careful attention to details.

KEY DATES

OCTOBER 1 ★ *well-organized thoughts*

Logical Mercury aligns comfortably with responsible Saturn, which brings you clear thinking and precise communication. This can be especially helpful when applied to work or organizing at home. Keep your mind on one task at a time. Take advantage of the efficiency available to you now, and demonstrate your productivity to a boss or coworker.

OCTOBER 10-11 ★ *put on a great show*

A New Moon in stylish Libra on **October 10** energizes your 5th House of Romance, Children, and Creativity. This is an excellent time to look your best and make an important presentation, whether for love or money. You know how to put on a show without seeming like a showoff, which is why others will respond to you so well. But charm without follow-through can cost you, with your ruling planet, Mercury, shifting into reverse gear on **October 11**. Promises made under the warm glow of the Libra New Moon can fall in the cracks without diligent effort and commitment.

OCTOBER 16 ★ *sensually speaking*

Mercury forms a supportive sextile with lovely Venus and a trine with passionate Mars that can turn an ordinary conversation into a sensual experience. The easy flow of communication, even with Mercury retrograde, makes it easy to connect with people. Enthusiasm is shared deeply but not loudly, allowing for an intimate feeling of complicity. Favorable reactions from others should be expected, as long as you're able to maintain a sense of fun, no matter how serious the subject. Flirt if you feel like it, and at least enjoy the playfulness now available.

OCTOBER 19 ★ *a return of respect*

A solid sextile between reliable Saturn and detail-oriented Mercury makes this a good day to go back and complete unfinished business. You express yourself well, appear sincere, and can regain trust where it has been lost. A serious private conversation can go a long way to repair a damaged relationship, especially at work. Getting face time can be difficult on a Friday, but make it a priority if you need to reestablish yourself with someone who counts.

SUPER NOVA DAYS
OCTOBER 23-26 ★ *truth works best in private*

Truth can pop out unexpectedly on **October 23** as mouthy Mercury joins the Sun and forms an edgy aspect with accident-prone Uranus. Under the right circumstances you could sound like a genius, but without careful planning you may look foolish. Tension builds toward the Taurus Full Moon on **October 26**; self-control is vital now. If you have to talk about unresolved grievances, do it in a quiet place to avoid embarrassing anyone, including yourself.

NOVEMBER

MORE OPPORTUNITIES THAN TIME

Ideas and information start flowing more freely this month, but taking action on them can be a slow process. That's because Mercury, the communication planet, turns direct on **November 1**, followed by the action planet, Mars, turning retrograde on **November 15**. The mind is speeding up, but then the muscles start to slow down. Mars is moving backward in self-protective Cancer in your 2nd House of Self-Worth through next January. This inward turn of the most forward-moving planet is a period in which careful assessment is recommended before committing your time, money, or energy to any significant project. Acting without consideration of the expenses involved can prove to be inefficient, costly, and exhausting. Don't overexert; instead, treat yourself tenderly and let your feelings have a greater role in determining where you put your efforts.

Vivacious Venus enters Libra in your sexy, fun 5th House on **November 8**, boosting your confidence and increasing chances for romance. This is an artistic and creative period when your talents and charms sparkle. This can open a new door to love or regenerate passion in a relationship that may have lost some glow.

The Sun enters outgoing Sagittarius in your 7th House of Partnerships on **November 22**. This is bound to brighten up your social life and earn you extra attention. You have the ability to make a strong impression, which is excellent for selling yourself to a potential employer or partner. Take notice of generous individuals appearing in your life with greater frequency, yet the quiet retrograde Mars is a reminder to be selective about the commitments you make, rather than spreading yourself so thin that you wind up resentful or worn out.

> **KEEP IN MIND THIS MONTH**
>
> *A flattering offer may tempt you, but unless it's important enough to replace another commitment, you may need to turn it down.*

KEY DATES

NOVEMBER 1 ★ *fun with friends*

Your ruling planet, Mercury, turns direct in your spontaneous 5th House of Play and Creativity, which gets the wheels of communication moving again. You're ready to catch up with friends or to plan a special evening with a romantic partner. Clever and imaginative ideas that have recently crossed your mind are finally ready to emerge in your personal life or on the job.

NOVEMBER 9-10 ★ *conserve your energy*
The Scorpio New Moon on **November 9** may complicate your work and mess with
your daily routine. Nebulous Neptune squares this Sun-Moon conjunction in your
6th House of Tasks and Health, which can drain energy with distractions or carelessness. Your desire to be of service is admirable, yet sacrifices that undermine
your own well-being are never in your best interest. Pay more attention to your
energy level during the next few weeks, being sure to replenish yourself with
nutritious food and plenty of rest. Mental Mercury enters penetrating Scorpio on
November 10 to narrow and deepen your focus.

NOVEMBER 16 ★ *effective information control*
A smart sextile between youthful Mercury and mature Saturn helps you to
communicate in a well-organized manner. Your patience for dealing with details
and complicated matters is excellent now, so attack those problems that require
the deepest thinking and the most delicate negotiations. A tense semisquare
between Mercury and overblown Jupiter attracts bogus data or inundates you with
too much information. Keep an open mind about what you're learning, but don't be
pressured to give a quick reply to a question best answered after further reflection.

NOVEMBER 19-21 ★ *the power of words and silence*
Three aspects involving communicative Mercury keep your mental wheels
spinning. An easy trine with Mars on **November 19** adds power to your words and
precision to your mind. However, a hard semisquare between Mercury and Pluto
on the same day can coerce you to reveal sensitive information. Share only what
serves your purpose now; when in doubt, keep your mouth shut until you know
exactly what you want to say. A trine between Mercury and inventive Uranus on
November 21 amplifies your intuition and feeds you with original ideas.

SUPER NOVA DAY
NOVEMBER 24 ★ *cover home base*
Today's Full Moon in your sign is normally a high-energy event, one that gets
the old feeling of restlessness cranked up again. You might even feel like
you're in the middle of a three-ring circus, with entertaining activities in every
direction. Yet stern Saturn forms a challenging square to this Gemini Full
Moon, which may present obligations at home that limit your playtime more
than you wish. Nevertheless, it's important to put practical concerns before
fun right now.

DECEMBER

RESHAPING YOUR VISION OF THE FUTURE

Major planetary action continues to energize your 7th House of Partnerships this month. The adventurous Sagittarius New Moon on **December 9** is almost sure to enliven relationships with new people and experiences. High-intensity individuals both shock and inspire you, with electric Uranus square the New Moon and spiritual Neptune in a supporting role. Still, lingering in the background is Saturn in exacting Virgo, burdening you with petty tasks like Cinderella when you're finally invited to the ball. Sagittarius's ruling planet, Jupiter, conjuncts mysterious Pluto on **December 11**, casting shadows of doubt over your high hopes. Encouragement from one quarter may be matched by discouragement from another, but this is no reason to give up your dreams. Dig deeply inside, decide what you want most, and then shape your beliefs to support this desire.

Philosophical Jupiter enters earthy Capricorn on **December 18**; then, the Sun enters this ambitious sign on **December 19** and joins up with Jupiter on **December 22**. All of these powerful events happen in your 8th House of Shared Resources, suggesting that you need to be more effective in enrolling the support of others to reach your goals. Jupiter is the planet of good luck, but in Capricorn, fortune is a reward for planning, patience, and hard work. This is not a time to wing it, especially when you're seeking material or emotional assistance from a tough-minded individual. If you state your intentions clearly, you can build the strong alliances that you need. On a lighter note, captivating Venus waltzes into your 7th House on **December 30**, just in time to add a festive touch to New Year's Eve. Celebrating is not an indulgence or a distraction, but a way to demonstrate that you are open to receiving love.

> **KEEP IN MIND THIS MONTH**
>
> *Let go of old assumptions that block your progress. What was true in the past might not be useful now.*

KEY DATES

DECEMBER 1 ★ *everybody's talking*

Mercury fires into Sagittarius, burning up the phone lines and stuffing your e-mail inbox. The communication planet is in your 7th House until **December 20**, filling your life with people, ideas, and information. A moment of truth with a partner or close friend may be required to set the record straight. Combine honesty with kindness to reestablish trust.

DECEMBER 6 ⋆ *be concise to be heard*

Intelligent Mercury is all over the place today. It forms an inspiring quintile with Neptune that sparks your intuition, but then makes tenser aspects with Saturn and Mars. It may take a sledgehammer to get your ideas across, no matter how creative or spiritual they are. Expect resistance from hard-liners who have their own agendas and don't want to hear what you have to say. If you can get a foothold by making one or two points, consider it a victory in this challenging environment.

DECEMBER 10 ⋆ *out-of-the-box ideas*

Mercury and Uranus hook up in a high-frequency square that can jangle nerves but may produce brilliant ideas. This hard aspect between two mentally charged planets does not engender calm. Sitting still and keeping quiet don't come easily, either. Originality is strength now, although sharply divergent perspectives tend to produce stressful conversations. Compromise is difficult to achieve, so you might want to tone down the rhetoric before a verbal spark ignites a fire.

SUPER NOVA DAYS
DECEMBER 17-22 ⋆ *deliver the truth gently*

A Sun-Mercury conjunction on **December 17** usually aligns will (the Sun) with words (Mercury). But with shape-shifting Pluto lurking nearby, these are not times of breezy conversation. Every thought and feeling intensifies as the powerful planet of transformation is joined by Mercury on **December 19** and the Sun on the following day. Mercury conjuncts exaggerating Jupiter on **December 20** with the Sun following suit on **December 22**, fanning the flames even higher. Extreme opinions and unrelenting attitudes can be great for moving mountains, but delicate egos can be easily bruised by the force of the words. Look within to deepen understanding, rather than compensating for doubts by trying to prove your beliefs to others.

DECEMBER 25-27 ⋆ *reason and rivalry*

A cooperative trine between Mercury and Saturn makes for logical thinking and clear communication on **December 25**. Yet no matter how sharp your calculations, a hyperactive Mars-Jupiter opposition on **December 26** can force facts out of the way. This competitive pair can turn almost anything into a contest. A semisquare between garrulous Mercury and gentle Venus on **December 27** triggers misunderstandings and a sense of being underappreciated, even when that isn't what the speaker intended.

CANCER

JUNE 21–JULY 22

CANCER OVERVIEW

Ready or not, here you grow! This is a dynamic year for you Crabs as you grow in sudden spurts, whether you are ready for the ride or not. And although there may be events that leapfrog you forward, your challenge is to keep a steady pace throughout the year. Opportunistic Jupiter blesses you with the most potential, along with a few headaches. While visiting the far reaches of Sagittarius, the planet of optimism opens your eyes to the distances that beckon with possibilities of great adventure. You may be eager to board the jet plane with ticket in hand and head out into the vast unknown, but this also raises your greatest fears. You long for the safety of what you know and the security of what you have. Anything that threatens these known comforts is not easily welcomed, even if it offers potentially great rewards. Your current life may be far from ideal, but at least it's familiar, offering you safe refuge from a sometimes hostile world. You will need courage to take risks, but this isn't a license for foolishness. Take advantage of Jupiter's harmonious trine to stabilizing Saturn in mid-March and early May by blending a healthy dose of common sense with ambition to create adventure, even at work.

The difficulties you encountered when Saturn was in your sign from 2003 until mid-2005 initiated changes that have taken root. Stern Saturn, moving through your 2nd House of Money and Self-Worth until September, continues to be a taskmaster, forcing you to firm up your foundations and consolidate your finances. You could face obstacles along the way, especially if the opposition from diffusive Neptune—around February 28 and again around June 25—sends you running back into the safety of your cave. **Don't waste energy feeling sorry for yourself if an investment—financial or emotional—doesn't pan out as expected.** Instead, analyze the situation, learn what you can, and move on with your newfound wisdom. But by autumn, as this planet of maturity enters your 3rd House of Immediate Environment, expect increased responsibilities to place limitations on your activities as you reevaluate your goals. There's no need to hurry; you'll have plenty of time for serious self-examination then.

A series of four eclipses zaps your travel houses, so be ready to hit the road. You can also explore within your mind, so diversionary reading or academic studies can also be emphasized. The Lunar Eclipse on March 3 is with erratic Uranus, indicating a surprise coming your way. The Solar Eclipse on March 18 involves powerful Pluto, suggesting a power struggle on the job. The second Lunar Eclipse, on August 28, involves restrictive Saturn, testifying to the hard work that must be done. The Solar Eclipse on September 11 again points to electric Uranus, proclaiming the instability of the times. The harder you try to grip the status quo, the more the routines of your life will change.

MAKE IT REAL

You self-protective Crabs have a hard shell and a soft, sensitive inside. You tend to take your relationships quite seriously, and although you have high ideals, you'll choose a partner who is authentic, though imperfect, over an unrealizable dream lover. You do, however, have your fantasies, especially this year as imaginative Neptune opposes the "make it real" planet, Saturn. Your heart is easily wounded, not because of increased sensitivity but because you are likely to reach farther than usual, thereby setting yourself up for romantic disappointment. Don't get discouraged during the summer when Venus, the love planet, does her retrograde dance. If someone special doesn't live up to your unrealistic expectations, reevaluate the situation and move forward once you know the truth. But don't use this as an excuse to withdraw emotionally, or you may isolate yourself from the very love you so strongly desire.

AWAKENING AMBITION

Accepting increased responsibility early in the year can better your chances for a promotion later on, giving you additional freedom without sacrificing the security you need. You are drawn to big ideas and could get involved with a rather grandiose project—not the regular work style for you sometimes timid Cancerians. Your 6th House of Work sees quite a lot of planetary activity this year, with expansive Jupiter providing the vision and powerful Pluto supplying the drive. Their conjunction on December 11 can be the payoff for your hard work. But all is not smooth, for the eclipses in late winter and late summer can arouse a whirlwind of activity, testing your ability to perform your job with the expected skill and regularity. Your most reliable path to success comes from the relentless concentration on details along the way.

NO GET-RICH-QUICK SCHEMES

You get what you pay for with karmic Saturn in your 2nd House of Money for most of the year. It may feel as if you are working harder without receiving adequate financial compensation. Somber Saturn won't prevent you from having what you want; it just makes the material world a bit less satisfying. Your inability to trust your imagination, especially during the first half of the year, can get in the way of fiscal success. Change the way you think, for seeing failure in your mind's eye can be problematic. By early August, money could be flowing more easily, but you might have to make a hard decision that limits your future possibilities for advancement. Don't be afraid to say no to an opportunity that doesn't feel right. There are no quick fixes to your finances, so it's wise to keep doing your best at your current job.

 THINK PREVENTION, NOT CURE

Energetic Mars in your 6th House of Health jump-starts your year with plans for more physical activity, but good intentions aren't enough to guarantee your well-being. You'll need to fine-tune your diet and make improvements to your exercise program throughout the year. Start making healthy choices in March and April; don't wait for any problems to manifest as symptoms. Deal with issues on an emotional or spiritual level when they first surface, thereby avoiding unnecessary sickness or fatigue.

 THERE'S NO PLACE LIKE HOME

You are nurtured and sustained within the safety of your walls, whether it's a beautiful estate or simply your own room. From March through June, work or school responsibilities may pull you away from your home and family. Still, making time to be with your loved ones helps you maintain essential mental and emotional balance. The tide shifts by early September, giving you more flexibility in your personal life. When assertive Mars enters cautious Cancer on September 28—where it stays for the rest of the year—you begin a cocoon phase, spending many productive hours doing household projects, taking care of the kids, and scurrying around like a crab inside its cave. No matter how busy you may be this year—possibly even telecommuting or studying online—your home is always more than just a place to hang your hat.

GO FAR; GO OFTEN

An unusual travel year is in store for you normally stay-at-home Cancerians. Freedom-loving Uranus hangs out in your 9th House of Journeys and is activated by a slow-moving square to big-thinking Jupiter. Opportunities for an exciting trip, possibly job-related, arrive at your doorstep without prior warning. You may not have much time to make up your mind, so say yes and sort out the details later. If you've been thinking about going back to school to complete a degree or take an advanced study course, this is your year. Whether you are flashing your passport to a customs official or a transcript for admission, think of them as your tickets to expanding your life experience.

METAPHYSICAL SOLUTIONS TO PHYSICAL PROBLEMS

The first part of this year may be spent completing the spiritual lessons that the Saturn-Neptune opposition already started last summer as the ground beneath your feet shifted. Your personal growth was stimulated as you ran into mundane and material setbacks. Throughout March, April, and May, you can begin to realize that the solution to your malaise is within your mind. By summer, you will have to absorb what you've learned and apply it to your life as you take the next steps on your path. Be open to new ways of looking at each situation, for your potential is limited only by your thoughts.

RICK & JEFF'S TIP FOR THE YEAR:
Believe in Yourself

As you dream about the possibilities for your future, remember that if you reach too far, you could fall short of your goals, only to face disillusionment and disappointment. However, if you don't reach far enough, you'll never know what you could have accomplished. The opportunities are yours for the asking, but to sustain the advancements you can make this year, you will need to conquer self-imposed limitations. Your meticulous preparations and cautious deliberation can give you the self-confidence that you need. Armed with optimism and a willingness to establish healthy routines, you can overcome obstacles that may appear in your path.

JANUARY

BREAKING FREE FROM OLD PATTERNS

A dynamic, slow-moving square between amplifying Jupiter and unpredictable Uranus is exact on **January 22** yet charges the entire month with an underlying restlessness, making you less likely to tolerate an uncomfortable situation at work. In fact, anything that restrains your freedom of expression now may stir you to action. But this goes beyond your personal preferences, for you may be quite ready to also take on a larger cause to create a better life for others. Be careful about your choices, though, because anything started now could turn into more work than you want. Ultimately, this can be a positive influence that brings opportunities to break out of tired old patterns as long as you don't overcommit your time and resources. Take calculated risks and you just might find the additional meaning you are seeking in your daily life.

Your dedication to issues of renewal, both global and personal, increases throughout the month as the planets stack up in your 8th House of Regeneration. Sultry Venus enters this powerful house on **January 3**, followed by logical Mercury on **January 15** and the Sun on **January 20**. Whether you become more involved in community politics or pursue an intimate relationship, emotional commitments are involved. The sensitive Cancer Full Moon on **January 3** requires you to reflect on your unfulfilled needs, not just those of a partner. Acknowledge your own feelings before taking care of everyone else. The subdued Capricorn New Moon in your 7th House of Partnerships on **January 18** can limit your responses until you've fulfilled your obligations. This may be your last chance to straighten out your current relationship issues before moving on to what comes next.

> **KEEP IN MIND THIS MONTH**
>
> *Liberate yourself from the expectations and judgments of others. What you think and feel are more important than how they react.*

KEY DATES

JANUARY 2–3 ★ *clear the air*

The moody Cancer Full Moon in your 1st House of Personality demonstrates its power without using words, but talkative Mercury and erratic Uranus are also in the picture, so your fear of rejection may not be enough to keep you quiet. Nevertheless, you cannot easily share your feelings with others now, for they are more interested in the nuts and bolts of what you must do than in learning more about your inner emotional landscape. Say what you must without self-censorship to clear the air of underlying tensions.

JANUARY 8–13 ★ *fine-tune plans*
What begins as a sound idea on **January 8**, when constructive Saturn receives an energetic boost from Mars, can become too much of a good thing by **January 12**. Your organizational skills are adept, but you still may need to make adjustments to your plan along the way. The intensity builds throughout these days, reaching a crescendo on **January 13** as Mars runs into powerful Pluto. Hold your temper if someone opposes you; treat them with the same respect you want for yourself. You cannot win by fighting fire with fire. Instead, self-control coupled with unflagging determination will serve you best in the long run.

JANUARY 16–18 ★ *you don't have to be alone*
Mars enters ambitious Capricorn in your 7th House of Relationships, granting you the fortitude to keep moving forward even when you face adversity. You are not about to give up, even if it feels that something is about to change. The Capricorn New Moon on **January 18** also falls in your 7th House, reminding you that you are not alone. Although partners can make your situation more complex, they must be taken into consideration as you develop your plan. Keep cool now; take whatever time you need before jumping into action.

SUPER NOVA DAY
JANUARY 22 ★ *listen, then dance*
Sweet Venus opposes restrictive Saturn today, making it difficult for you to fully appreciate your life. Boredom motivates you into action as opportunistic Jupiter dynamically squares freedom-loving Uranus. Although you may be eager to make big changes in your life, it will probably take some time for the long-term effects of this transit to work their way through your system. This Jupiter-Uranus square colors much of your year, repeating this theme on **May 10** and **October 9**. Sure, you are listening to a different drummer these days, but it may be best to shrewdly wait before wildly dancing to your own rhythms. Be patient; once these cosmic changes are put into motion, they will take on a life of their own.

FEBRUARY

MATERIAL CONCERNS ARE REAL

Taking material concerns seriously this month won't necessarily alleviate feelings of pessimism and doubt, but it can soothe what seems like an irresolvable problem. You probably have been working hard to stabilize your finances, yet even as you conserve resources, you still might face fiscal uncertainty. The long-lasting opposition that began last summer between Saturn the Tester and Neptune the Dissolver comes back into focus this month, slowly rolling in a fog of confusion. You can react with fear, scrambling to hold on to your core beliefs, or you can focus on pursuing the greatest potential, trusting that clarity will return once the weeds of resistance have been pulled from your garden. The choice is yours; play the role of an escape artist, succumb to the malaise, or trust the unfolding changes while maintaining your values. Avoid temptations to retreat behind rigid defenses. Your hope and courage will chase the dark clouds from the sky.

You could feel financially overwhelmed right from the start of the month. Beginning on **February 1**, with the Leo Full Moon in your 2nd House of Resources, you may spend too much time worrying about money. Although you should deal with any bookkeeping issues that surface at this time, the real juice come from reevaluating your own self-worth. And with Mercury just entering mystical Pisces, you might have a hard time wrapping your mind around the practical ramifications of your current actions. Still, it's critical that you concentrate on tying up loose ends, for Mercury turns retrograde on **February 13**, forcing you to retrace your steps and revisit unfinished business. The inventive Aquarius New Moon on **February 17** in your 8th House of Joint Holdings gives you one more chance to reorganize your finances.

> **KEEP IN MIND THIS MONTH**
>
> *Handle mundane and financial matters early so that you can luxuriate in the sharing of your dreams later.*

KEY DATES

FEBRUARY 1–3 ★ *reflect and break free*

Although the Full Moon on **February 1** activates your money houses, wealth extends way beyond the material. Your most important possession may be the personal values you use to guide your interactions with others. Since the Sun in Aquarius is now in your 8th House of Joint Holdings—including shared feelings—this Leo Full Moon reflects a recurring dilemma about the relationship between your emotional needs and your obligations to others. By **February 3**, supportive aspects to optimistic Jupiter and independent Uranus give you the confidence to break away from complex entanglements that don't support your basic philosophy.

SUPER NOVA DAYS
FEBRUARY 7-10 ★ *dream the original dream*
The Sun in quirky Aquarius shines upon imaginative Neptune, electrifying your dreams. Additionally, sweet Venus conjoins eccentric Uranus, sending currents of desire throughout your body. Together, they dynamically square jovial Jupiter, removing normal concerns for self-restraint. Be careful, for not much holds you back now, and you may not even care what others think as you indulge your weirdest fantasies. On **February 10**, however, the Sun runs into opposition from Saturn the Taskmaster. If you've gone overboard in your search for sensual satisfaction, there may be consequences for your excessive behavior.

FEBRUARY 13-14 ★ *sidestep unnecessary conflict*
These tricky days require your utmost attention to avoid miscommunication or misunderstanding. You may not say exactly what you mean as talkative Mercury turns retrograde on **February 13**. But it's the rare configuration between Venus and Mars—the cosmic lovers—both in irritating quincunx aspects with restrictive Saturn that makes what is usually a love fest between Venus and Mars at best an awkward social situation. Nothing you do is quite right and you can't easily discuss it, for that makes matters worse. Delay important conversations and decisions, and move through these days with as much grace and dignity as you can.

FEBRUARY 24-28 ★ *no time for tears*
You must act on the dynamic aspects from Venus and Mars on **February 24 and 25** to stand up for your core beliefs, for integrity is more important than comfort at this time. Both Mars and Mercury enter emotionally detached Aquarius on **February 25 and 27**, respectively, allowing you to see your personal drama more objectively. Make necessary changes so that you don't find yourself back in a similar position a few months down the road. It could feel as if the whole month unravels to a less than satisfying outcome during these last few days. If you have not been working on your inner resolve, the discouraging opposition between realistic Saturn and dreamy Neptune on **February 28** gives you no time for self-pity or isolation.

MARCH

STEADINESS IN THE FACE OF UNEXPECTED CHANGES

You may feel your physical strength returning pretty quickly at the beginning of the month as the dreamy influence of Neptune grows weaker. And as this planet moves away from its recent opposition with ambitious Saturn, confident Jupiter steps into the picture, offering much-needed reassurance. The Jupiter-Saturn trine on **March 16** blesses the entire month, supporting your hard work with well-earned opportunities and rewards. With both planets in fire signs, you might feel unusually industrious, as if you had a reservoir of stored energy available to you. Jupiter in your 6th House of Health increases your vitality, as long as you exercise regularly and stick to a healthy diet.

Intelligent Mercury goes direct on **March 7** in your 8th House of Shared Resources, turning your best recent ideas about investing time or money into reality. Then on **March 17**—just a day after the harmonizing Jupiter-Saturn trine— your imagination sweeps you off your feet when pensive Mercury enters spiritual Pisces. Lovely Venus enters her comfortable home sign of Taurus on the same day, so your desires begin to simplify, clearing a path to satisfaction.

As Crabs, you are particularly attuned to a pair of eventful eclipses in March that can either propel you toward success or just churn your life with increased distractions. The Full Moon Eclipse on **March 3** rattles your brain and awakens you from a dream. Suddenly, you can see the shimmering possibilities ahead of you that were previously blocked. The New Moon Eclipse on **March 18** is a different story; it's part of a whirlwind of activity that requires you to overcome your resistance to success. Put in extra effort every day until you have the confidence necessary to achieve excellence.

> **KEEP IN MIND THIS MONTH**
>
> *Make healthy changes; creating consistent daily routines in work and play will have lasting positive ramifications throughout the entire year and beyond.*

KEY DATES

MARCH 3-7 ★ *rapid release*

The Virgo Full Moon Eclipse on **March 3** in your 3rd House of Communication illuminates the forgotten details that have the power to unravel what you recently accomplished. However, getting lost in endless analysis won't lead you to the heart of the real issues. You need to talk about your feelings with a close friend, but with unpredictable Uranus aligned with the eclipse, there's no telling what may happen. Although Mercury's retrograde phase ends on **March 7**, you cannot wait. Don't hold yourself back; if something's been bugging you, let it out of the closet now.

MARCH 8-9 ★ *self-assuredness is your ally*

Sensual Venus trines both optimistic Jupiter and realistic Saturn, bestowing your life with harmony and grace. Relying on common sense works effectively now as you establish the authority needed to further your cause. Others respond to you in a friendly manner, encouraging you to share more of yourself than usual. This is an opportune time to ask for a promotion, a new job, or a raise—assuming you deserve it. Keep in mind that these days cast a bright light forward to **March 16**, so concentrate on bringing your current goals to fruition over the next several days.

SUPER NOVA DAYS

MARCH 16-19 ★ *holding the keys to your future*

The Pisces New Moon Eclipse on **March 18** in your 9th House of Big Ideas may activate your desire to learn, and enrolling in a course is only one way to satisfy this urge. Your openness to ancient philosophies or metaphysics can set the stage for a variety of mind-expanding experiences. The slow-moving trine between ambitious Saturn and rewarding Jupiter creates a magical blend of enthusiasm and perseverance. Showing up with the right attitude all but ensures success. Additionally, harmonious aspects among pleasing Venus, passionate Pluto, and innovative Mercury tilt reality in your favor. As long as you don't abuse your current power with selfish demands, you are in a position to make your dreams come true.

MARCH 22-25 ★ *don't surrender*

You were encouraged to charge ahead, but you run into a wall of resistance on **March 22** as assertive Mars opposes authoritative Saturn. Don't make the mistake of watering your doubts with the very real obstacles you must face. A lack of resources isn't reason enough to stop pursuing your goals. Someone working against you can slow you down but shouldn't prevent you from reaching your destination. Your enthusiasm waxes and wanes as diffusive Neptune dissipates your excitement as quickly as it comes. Hold steady and let the discouragement pass without taking it as a personal defeat.

APRIL

INTROSPECTION LEADS TO A NEW DIRECTION

Although April begins and ends with a bang, the middle of the month provides you with less turmoil. In particular, you can solidify the mundane aspects of your life, thereby increasing the security you derive from your career or daily work routines. However, shocking Uranus has something to tell you right away as it aligns with wordy Mercury on **April 1**—just one day prior to the Full Moon in your 4th House of Home and Family. Restless discontent has nowhere to go and can threaten a delicate balance at home. If you don't say something, someone might upset the applecart by giving voice to what you know yet attempt to avoid mentioning. By **April 6**—when assertive Mars floats into watery Pisces—you may already be feeling somewhat more relaxed. Your confidence continues to grow, even if you don't yet make any apparent changes, for this is more about introspection and your intentions than it is about taking action externally.

The pace of forward progress picks up on **April 10**, when logical Mercury shouts its way into impulsive Aries, placing your previously hidden thoughts on the table for all to see. Additionally, lovely Venus enters socially adept Gemini on **April 11**, alleviating your concerns about whether to act on your feelings. The New Moon on **April 17** in your 10th House of Career confirms your high standards and establishes your new direction. Be firm and proceed with determination, for this is a time to muster up enough courage to stand in a place of power. Don't allow yourself to be knocked off course by an unsettling but thrilling conjunction between fiery Mars and electrifying Uranus on **April 28**.

> **KEEP IN MIND THIS MONTH**
>
> *Decide what you want early, but wait a couple of weeks before taking any action. Maintain inner strength while you work out the details.*

KEY DATES

APRIL 1-4 ★ *think before you speak*

Your mind races ahead of your common sense, and if you don't rein it in, there could be trouble. There may be too much mental noise at home, but this doesn't give you the right to spew your unresolved emotions onto anyone else. The Libra Full Moon on **April 2** encourages you to be fair and just, yet satisfactory solutions are elusive. You are like Goldilocks, finding either too much or too little. Don't give up in your struggle to find a position that is just right.

APRIL 7-9 ★ *inner strength*
The practical houses of your chart are fueled with the light of the Sun in fiery Aries as it harmoniously trines the regulators, expansive Jupiter and restrictive Saturn. You exude a graceful balance, combining dogged independence with a healthy respect for cooperation. Temper your flights of enthusiasm with moderation and smart thinking. But beware; beneath a socially smooth veneer lays a tense square between thoughtful Mercury and dark Pluto. Even if you'd rather focus on the good news, don't be afraid of exploring the shadows for the treasures they have to offer.

SUPER NOVA DAYS
APRIL 17-18 ★ *harnessing the power*
The Aries New Moon on **April 17** is about beginnings and endings, both of which may be simultaneously happening. You may be eager to reveal more of yourself than usual, for you realize that no gains will be made without taking appropriate risks. But this New Moon is agreeably linked with powerful Pluto, attracting you into the dark recesses of your unconscious mind. Your feelings are intense, and others will quickly recognize your inner power. However, don't try to control anyone else's emotions, or your own journey could end before it even starts.

APRIL 20-21 ★ *cautious optimism*
The power of positive thought can serve you extremely well now, for intelligent Mercury in self-directed Aries forms cooperative trines with planetary heavyweights Jupiter and Saturn. On one hand, you think that anything is possible. On the other hand, you are logical and cautious. This combination of eagerness and prudence provides an excellent foundation for your future success.

APRIL 27-30 ★ *flights of fancy*
You are all over the emotional map these days with an explosive Mars-Uranus conjunction on **April 28** that blows the covers off anything hidden as it receives the go-ahead from enthusiastic Jupiter. You might want to keep your intentions secret, but you cannot control the emotional leakage once the dam breaks. Additionally, overindulgent aspects with pleasurable Venus and imaginative Neptune may blur the fine line between enough and too much.

MAY

WAITING IS THE HARDEST PART

May is an unusual month for you lunar-sensitive Crabs, with two Full Moons that can overwhelm you with the power of your own dreams—the first in emotional Scorpio on **May 2** and the second in philosophical Sagittarius on **May 31**. A New Moon in solid Taurus on **May 16** is an anchor in an otherwise transitional period that motivates you to grab hold of the social opportunities coming your way.

The ongoing opposition between hardworking Saturn in your 2nd House of Possessions and fantasy-driven Neptune in your 8th House of Transformation won't reach its last peak until the end of June, but financial issues may already be critical this month as Mercury and the Sun tensely square both Saturn and Neptune between **May 5 and 12**. It may feel like you've stretched your budget as far as possible, and you see no easy way out of your current dilemma. Benevolent Jupiter comes to the rescue, creating a lovely trine with Saturn on **May 5**. This gives you a concrete place to stand as you attempt to expand your vision of the future by taking on an additional project while still fulfilling current obligations. Life gets crazy as these alternating currents of expansion and contraction wash back and forth, especially with unstable Uranus entering the equation around **May 10**. A sudden opportunity is presented, and you might be ready to seize the chance, whether it makes sense or not. Do yourself a favor and hold out until after energetic Mars enters "just do it" Aries on **May 15** and the New Moon on **May 16**, giving you a shove toward your goals between **May 21 and 24**.

> **KEEP IN MIND THIS MONTH**
>
> *Use the second half of the month to make necessary revisions to your plan and to build on what you have already established.*

KEY DATES

MAY 2 ★ *stifled passion*

The Scorpio Full Moon in your 5th House of Fun and Games might not bring much playful activity today, for you must keep your life in order. Your dreams are filled with passion now, but they don't manifest easily; all four fixed houses of your chart are activated, indicating a resistance to movement. You desire change, but it won't come without struggle. Neptune is in the picture, encouraging your fantasies; Saturn is here, too, testing you along the way. Maintain an open mind while extinguishing brush fires, but don't force changes at this time.

MAY 5-7 ★ *change your attitude*

Thoughtful Mercury in determined Taurus crosses words today with authoritative Saturn, making communication difficult as you argue to get your point heard. But you have the power now to change the course of your life by changing your attitude. Persistent optimism combined with serious work is generously rewarded by Jupiter as it harmonizes with the hopeful Sagittarian Moon. Ultimately, Saturn the Taskmaster is working on your behalf as long as you don't forget the details. Don't let unconscious motives undermine your honorable intentions, for Venus slips into self-protective Cancer on **May 7** and your insecurities can lead to less than ideal choices.

SUPER NOVA DAYS
MAY 12-16 ★ *time of reckoning*

The days preceding the New Moon can rattle your foundation, yet eventually make you stronger. Instability emanates from the Sun squaring imaginative Neptune on **May 12**; you question or even doubt what you previously thought was true. Then on **May 13**, an aggressive Mars struggles with influential Pluto, creating a volcanic surge of energy. Your intensity can rouse strong reactions from others, which in turn stimulates your survival instincts. You become uncharacteristically forceful when Mars plows into impulsive Aries in your 10th House of Career on **May 15**. Dynamics shift abruptly on **May 16** with the solid Taurus New Moon in your 11th House of Goals. Cut through the noise and turmoil; focus on your destination of choice and head out with determination in your chosen direction.

MAY 27-31 ★ *successful launch*

It may feel as if others are working against you as wordy Mercury opposes compulsive Pluto on **May 27**. It's also possible that you appear too controlling as you relentlessly make your case. You can quickly come to your senses on **May 28**, when Mercury enters sensitive Cancer, assuming a less aggressive position. You become much more hopeful as the optimistic Sagittarian Full Moon conjoins buoyant Jupiter on **May 31** in your 6th House of Daily Routines. With cooperation from "me first" Mars in Aries, you are launched toward success and recognition for your work.

JUNE

TAP INTO YOUR DREAMS

The biggest event of the month is the final occurrence of a slow-moving opposition between serious Saturn and illusory Neptune on **June 25** that brings issues of personal values and finances to the front burner. Look back to last summer and around **February 28** of this year for the origins of any current disillusionment. Additionally, fair-minded Venus joins Saturn at the end of the month and may apply pressure until you take ownership of your feelings, your loved ones, and the possessions you treasure.

Supportive Saturn supplies stability, although the source might not always be obvious with the Sun in your 12th House of Secrets until **June 21**. Broad-minded Jupiter in your 6th House of Work encourages you to demonstrate your good intentions in every little thing you do. Although you may not show all your cards, it's easier to express yourself in the community with front-runner Mars in Aries in your 10th House of Public Status until **June 24**. You can deal with career matters most effectively on **June 4, 11, and 21**, but it's better to push ahead prior to the Gemini New Moon on **June 14** with Mercury turning retrograde the following day. Due to its retrograde cycle, mental Mercury spends the entire month in your sign, placing increased importance on the security of your home and feelings.

Your attachment to family and your past is deeper now. Invite those you love over for a backyard barbecue after the Summer Solstice on **June 21**, for the Sun enters emotionally nurturing Cancer. And you may not feel so rushed when Mars settles down and enters practical Taurus on **June 24**. The Capricorn Full Moon on **June 30** recalls a familiar struggle of yours as you weigh your own needs against the responsibilities of relationships.

> **KEEP IN MIND THIS MONTH**
>
> *Don't be afraid to receive what you justly deserve. If you struggle too hard, you can frighten your dreams away instead of seeing them turn into reality.*

KEY DATES

JUNE 4–5 ★ *your time has come*

A vital and harmonious trine between energetic Mars and adventurous Jupiter can fill your sails with the winds of progress, setting a positive tone for the days ahead. Don't be afraid to reach out, for your actions are quite well received now. If you have been quietly withholding your desires as you wait for the right moment, rest assured that your time has arrived. Remember, however, that you can get so carried away by the possibilities that you could overstep your limits. Go for the gold, but exercise a touch of restraint as needed.

JUNE 11-14 ★ *step up to the plate*

A series of supportive sextiles and terrific trines can turn life into Easy Street, but this is no time to get lazy. With assertive Mars harmonized to authoritative Saturn on **June 11**, you have a keen sense of what needs to be done, and you can take the right baby steps to execute a grand and masterful plan. Don't be afraid to take on a leadership role at work and manage a significant project to a successful conclusion or to orchestrate a memorable social event. Whatever you attempt now will meet less resistance than if you wait to start until after the Gemini New Moon on **June 14**.

JUNE 19-21 ★ *you've got the power*

Sensual Venus combines with joyful Jupiter on **June 19**, creating one of the most enjoyable days of the year. Whether you experience the loveliness through beautiful music or art, sweet romance, gourmet food, or fine wine, you will likely be happily indulged. But the Sun tensely opposes compulsive Pluto while forceful Mars joins in the hookup, adding depth and intensity to an otherwise lightweight event. The Summer Solstice on **June 21** is an annual marker for you as the energizing Sun's rays return to your sign. Claim your own power and be confident in showing others a more commanding side of your personality.

SUPER NOVA DAY

JUNE 30 ★ *recognizing limits and moving beyond*

The goal-oriented Capricorn Full Moon in your 7th House of Partnerships—opposite the Sun in your sign—reflects your desire for stability. It also makes you painfully aware of the feelings you suppress to maintain the harmony of personal and business relationships. Additionally, with loving Venus conjunct restrictive Saturn—and both opposed to nebulous Neptune—you may feel as if you have reached an impasse. Something needs to give, for you can no longer sustain the illusions that brought you to this point. You have seen the truth; now respond to the situation by taking decisive action.

JULY

SLOW AND STEADY

Perhaps you won't win a race this month, but that's just because you may not feel very competitive. This is fine, for July is a month of emotional integration that leads to long-awaited transitions. However, temporary isolation or financial hardship will only make you work harder to manifest the change you desire. Mercury, the planet of perception, is more receptive than usual while in sensitive Cancer, and with the Sun also in your sign until **July 22**, it's time for you to take a "wait and see" approach. Watch the consequences of past actions as they shape your summer. Although Mercury turns direct on **July 9**, freeing you to think about what's ahead, you aren't too quick to jump into anything new. The emphasis on Cancer encourages you to bide your time. Mars in slow-moving but determined Taurus doesn't light a fire under you, either. Instead, it supports caution, rewards steadiness, and can even make you lazy. Even attractive Venus lacks luster now as she slows down to begin her retrograde phase on **July 27**.

The quiet Cancer New Moon on **July 14** rolls out the lazy, hazy days of summer, reminding you once again that you don't need to go outside your comfort zone. Happiness may just be right where you live—or at the beach. But a niggling quincunx to nebulous Neptune can have you doubting your choices, making you wonder if there isn't something else that you should be doing. Keep in mind that you will get your chance to swing into action next month. There's no need to worry about hurry. By the time the Moon grows full on **July 29**, you should be ready to start seeing the fruits of your previous labors.

> **KEEP IN MIND THIS MONTH**
>
> *Don't judge yourself too harshly if it feels like you aren't getting much done, for rest and relaxation are more important now than external accomplishments.*

KEY DATES

JULY 1 ★ *love is hard to find*

A strained meeting between warm Venus and cold Saturn withholds pleasure and makes love seem distant. If this sounds like a bleak picture, remember that possible negativity may actually be a much-needed dose of realism. Self-restraint clarifies your needs, and isolation can actually bring you peace of mind. Don't complain about what you do not have romantically. Instead of seeking immediate gratification, make a plan for a more satisfying connection.

JULY 8-10 ★ *don't hold back*

Powerful emotions motivate you to express what's in your heart as sensual Venus receives support from passionate Pluto on **July 8**. Your needs run deeper now and you are ready to play for keeps. Then, as Mercury turns direct on **July 9**, you begin to see a way to your heart's desire. You may be so excited that you misjudge the amount of effort or commitment required to reach your goal, but as the Sun harmoniously trines brilliant Uranus on **July 10**, you are blessed with the ability to unambiguously hit the nail directly on the head.

SUPER NOVA DAY

JULY 14 ★ *state your wishes aloud*

The Cancer New Moon receives electric intensity from a trine to Uranus, emphasizing your unsatisfied needs for emotional security. But energetic Mars dynamically squares wounded Chiron, reminding you of unsuccessful attempts to get what you want. And with loving Venus moving into picky Virgo, you have to be specific about your romantic desires. Still, it's uncomfortable to say them aloud. Whether you are embarrassed about your unconventional needs or just afraid of rejection, overcoming your own resistance now is the first step toward experiencing more pleasure.

JULY 24-27 ★ *temporary setback in love*

This is a bit of a confusing period as self-directed Mars squares imaginative Neptune on **July 24**, increasing your creativity but reducing your certainty about how to interact with others. Additionally, nostalgic Venus in your 3rd House of Communication begins her retrograde cycle on **July 27**, making you less able to talk about your feelings. Give it a couple of days; it's not necessary to force any relationship issues now.

JULY 29-31 ★ *surprising revelations*

The Aquarius Full Moon in your 8th House of Intimacy on **July 29** may encourage you to reveal your heart as you strive to manifest your individuality. A trine from erratic Uranus to chatty Mercury—now in emotional Cancer—has you setting your fears aside so that you can talk about your needs. And although this is the beginning of a more outgoing cycle for you Crabs, a trying square between assertive Mars and resistant Saturn on **July 31** may heighten your frustrations for a few more days.

AUGUST

SWING INTO ACTION

It's time for you Crabs to climb out of your shells and show the world what you have to offer. The relentless Leo Sun is illuminating your 2nd House of Self-Worth until **August 23**. Talkative Mercury is proudly showing off your thoughts while also in dramatic Leo from **August 4 to 19**. Even diva Venus—traveling retrograde all month—is strutting its stuff in expressive Leo from **August 8** through the end of the month. And pushy Mars enters versatile Gemini on **August 6**, making you more eager to engage in whatever comes along. It is, however, in the 12th House of Secrets, so you might be inclined to initiate projects alone, showing others your work only after you have made some progress.

Perhaps the most important aspect—the effects of which impact the entire month—is a long-lasting trine between heavy hitters Saturn and Pluto, exact on **August 6**. Unfinished business can be completed as you experience higher levels of practical ambition combined with an intense concentration. This harmonious aspect revitalizes your houses of money and work. You are prepared to overcome anything standing in the way of success, even if it means facing your own demons.

KEEP IN MIND THIS MONTH

Accepting the faith that others have in you is crucial, but having the courage to trust your own convictions is even more critical for your creative success.

The grand Leo New Moon on **August 12** pits your belief in yourself against a fear that others may not share your confidence; however, you've reached a point of no return. With five planets clustered in fiery Leo, state your position and hold steadfast. Take your best ideas to the next level at the Full Moon Eclipse in Pisces on **August 28**, which features a surprising connection between erratic Uranus and mental Mercury in your communication houses.

KEY DATES

AUGUST 2-4 ★ *expand your horizons*

This is an uplifting period, even if you must process leftover negativity from a recent power struggle. The Sun's illuminating trine to jolly Jupiter on **August 2** helps you focus on the positive side. Don't second-guess your intuition, for quicksilver Mercury is keenly attuned to your needs. Invest in yourself—perhaps by enrolling in a training course—to improve finances. But remember that you must communicate your ideas for them to have value.

AUGUST 7-9 ★ *looking for love*

Forceful Mars—just having entered restless Gemini—can wastefully scatter your energy. However, harnessing Mars as it dynamically squares loving Venus on **August 7** can prove to be fun, especially if you are artistically inclined or are willing to playfully transform conflict into romantic endeavors. An optimistic trine between Jupiter and Mercury in heart-centered Leo on **August 9** encourages you to declare your love, so be willing to risk exposure to receive the affection you desire.

SUPER NOVA DAY
AUGUST 12 ★ *stand by your choice*

A New Moon in dramatic Leo in your 2nd House of Possessions suggests making a personal statement by treating yourself to something special. But money is ruled by Venus, aligning with austere Saturn and making resources scarce or, perhaps, sweet love difficult to find. Either way, this can be a turning point. You'll need to batten down the hatches to fend off resistance or overcome your lack of clarity. Additionally, an unstable quincunx between Mercury and Uranus puts your nervous system on high alert, for now there are no easy answers. Nevertheless, you still must make a decision—however unsatisfactory it feels—and then walk resolutely down your chosen path.

AUGUST 23 ★ *cool your jets*

Sometimes you Crabs are hesitant to commit to a cause or a project, but now you are ready to go before you even have all the facts. Although the Sun has just entered critical Virgo, a super-confident opposition between "get up and go" Mars and grandiose Jupiter tricks you into forgetting about the details and just saying yes. Be careful; all is not as rosy as it appears.

AUGUST 28 ★ *dangerous currents ahead*

If you have overextended yourself financially or overindulged recklessly, today's Pisces Full Moon Eclipse may require you to make immediate adjustments to your lifestyle. Because this dynamic eclipse activates your mind, you could experience something significant enough now to change your perspective and your direction. Take contrary data in stride and sort it out later when you aren't as overwhelmed.

SEPTEMBER

STEPPING OUT CAREFULLY

A powerful planetary passage sends deep ripples through your life as slow-moving Saturn enters detail-oriented Virgo on **September 2**, shifting its focus into your 3rd House of Communication, where it remains until October 2009. If you've paid attention to stern Saturn's lessons for the past couple of years, take your hard-earned self-worth—both financial and psychological—and build stability in your immediate environment. Precious Venus turning direct on **September 8** affirms that you must demonstrate your core values by expressing yourself creatively. The Virgo New Moon Eclipse on **September 11** is a catalyst that energizes critical thinking and careful communication, establishing your foothold as you move ahead with cautious determination. With a square to active Mars in flexible Gemini, your greatest challenge comes from wasting physical energy as you chase down all of the possibilities in order to weed out the extraneous noise. Don't be afraid to say no to a good idea, for it is more productive now to concentrate your actions instead of scattering them.

You may doubt the choices you make around **September 20** as you run into a domineering person who appears to frustrate your intentions. An intense opposition between red-hot Mars and compulsive Pluto is stressed by the Sun, pushing you right to the edge of your limits. You might not want to be confrontational at work or within your family, but you come to the realization that you must anyhow. Expressing your truth is healthy; just do not overreact or you'll be cleaning up the mess you make over the days ahead. The impulsive Aries Full Moon on **September 26** can bring these issues to a head. Process them quickly and move on.

> **KEEP IN MIND THIS MONTH**
>
> *Feeling the strength of your convictions doesn't mean you should share your perspective with everyone. Talking to the right person at the right time can increase your power.*

KEY DATES

SEPTEMBER 3-4 ★ *no place to hide*

An exciting yet tense square between fiery Mars in jumpy Gemini and unorthodox Uranus awakens your nervous system with an unexpected thunderbolt. If you were trying to squeak by without facing the full truth, you suddenly realize that you cannot hide behind a protective wall of denial. As the Moon joins volatile Mars on

September 4, tempers may explode, whether or not you are ready. Whatever temporary inconveniences are created by an emotional outburst, the discomfort will pass and you can respond without fear of being rejected by someone you love.

SUPER NOVA DAYS
SEPTEMBER 8-11 ★ *lightning strikes twice*
Even if you've taken steps to ease tensions, you still could feel discouraged, as if your efforts have been in vain. Your indecision, however, creates a disarming neutrality that settles even the prickliest emotions. Mars is working its magic with diffusive Neptune, so beware of getting lost in your fantasies. By **September 9**—just two days prior to a destabilizing Solar Eclipse—the lightning strikes again as the Sun opposes uncontrollable Uranus. You may have thought that you found safe harbor, only to realize you are in the midst of another communication storm—this one, perhaps, right in your own backyard. Trust your instincts; life will return to normal once the air has cleared.

SEPTEMBER 18-21 ★ *difficult issues require moderation*
Intense feelings are underscored on **September 18** by a conjunction of the Moon in idealistic Sagittarius with the underworld boss, Pluto. This highly charged emotional meeting is fired up by their mutual opposition to angry Mars. Fortunately, charming Venus and intuitive Neptune come to the rescue, serving a vision of ideal love. You can use your dreams as a model for a gentle approach while confronting the more difficult issues, or you could use them as an escape hatch. Unfortunately, your fantasies and indulgences are quite tempting, and it will take concentrated willpower on your part to keep your head clear of the beautiful illusion that could be mistaken for reality.

SEPTEMBER 26-28 ★ *turning point*
The Impetuous Aries Full Moon in your 10th House of Career on **September 26** marks a turning point in your drive to achieve recognition at work or in the community. On one hand, your stamina is maxed out and you're ready to begin a retreat, with assertive Mars entering passive Cancer on **September 28**. On the other hand, retreating may not be an act of defeat or weakness; your apparent withdrawal can be part of a long-term strategy to regain control of your feelings and to reestablish a path to achieve your ambitions.

OCTOBER

TIME TO REFLECT

Although there are specific times this month for you to open your eyes wide and take in as much as you can, this is predominately a period for you to review your recent experiences, integrate your accomplishments, and restore your sense of balance. Self-directed Mars just entered mild-tempered Cancer, where it stays for the remainder of the year. Mars in your sign can fire you up, but you may have difficulty expressing the heat of its anger, choosing instead to hide behind passive-aggressive behavior. It's important to direct your energy into physical activities, lest your feelings stagnate and turn into depression or even manifest as undesirable ailments. Mercury's retrograde phase from **October 11 to November 1** intensifies this inward movement. In addition to sharing what's on your mind, this is a time for healthy reflection and rethinking your relationships, perhaps writing your thoughts in a journal or blog. The social Libra New Moon, also on **October 11**, is in your 4th House of Family, suggesting that you don't have to leave home to be with the people you love the most.

However, you aren't ready to shut out the outer world. In fact, on **October 9**, a dynamic square between jovial Jupiter in adventurous Sagittarius and radical Uranus in your 9th House of Higher Education sends you on an exciting journey of the mind. You can see opportunities even on distant horizons and are willing to risk your highly coveted safety to escape boredom and explore the plausibility of doing something extraordinary. On **October 26**, a deliberate Taurus Full Moon in your 11th House of Groups and Friends can further pull you out of your shell as you seek fellowship within your community.

> **KEEP IN MIND THIS MONTH**
>
> *Use your energy to maintain the status quo instead of driving for more change. Relax and give yourself permission to indulge in a bit of "you" time.*

KEY DATES

OCTOBER 1–3 ★ *draw upon inner certainty*

On **October 1**, a supportive sextile between close-mouthed Mercury in emotional Scorpio and disciplined Saturn in focused Virgo can place a wise smile on your face. You know more than you are willing to say, and others won't take offense now, because you exude personal integrity as you keep a secret. When seductive Venus harmonizes with compelling Pluto on **October 3**, you express your intense feelings, although you won't need words to show someone what you want. Dispense with the lengthy explanations; just go for it with quiet confidence.

OCTOBER 11–13 ★ *quiet your mind*
There's little need for flagrant demonstrations of your feelings or fancy verbal footwork, for the well-mannered New Moon in Libra on **October 11** picks up on the spiritual visions of Neptune while retrograde Mercury turns you introspective. You can travel to the far reaches of the cosmos while sitting quietly in meditation. Still, possible loneliness comes from a conjunction between warmhearted Venus and harsh Saturn. By **October 13**, you have no patience left for casual social niceties. Instead, create peace of mind by calming your inner world.

OCTOBER 16–20 ★ *fortunate action*
Your soul is revitalized by an interrelated series of harmonious aspects between several planets, including energetic Mars in nurturing Cancer, verbally magnetic Mercury in passionate Scorpio, and sweet Venus in picky Virgo. You may feel as if you have nothing to prove—and you don't—yet any positive action taken now has a fortunate outcome. Acknowledge your inner purpose and strength of character by letting others know your honorable intentions.

SUPER NOVA DAY
OCTOBER 26 ★ *anything goes in the name of love*
You don't seem to be able to escape the recurring astonishing actions of Uranus the Awakener—and today's Full Moon is no exception. Although you have been lulled into a quieter and gentler state of mind this month, now you are adamant about getting what you want. Romantic Venus has been careful about revealing your needs since entering timid Virgo on **October 8**, but as the planet opposes rebellious Uranus today, your need to be with friends or your desire for love overcomes your fears of rejection or impropriety.

OCTOBER 29 ★ *imagination rules*
An overindulgent square between sensual Venus and inflated Jupiter blurs your regular boundaries. If it feels good, you want more. But Venus forms a nagging quincunx with diffusive Neptune, further confusing the limits of acceptability. Ultimately, your good intentions will overcome any befuddlement. Your imagination is powerful, and if you can dream it, there's a chance that you can make it real.

NOVEMBER

PUSH ME; PULL ME

The tides wash back and forth this month as intellectual Mercury turns direct on **November 1** and energetic Mars turns retrograde on **November 15**. You may be done making your holiday plans and are ready for the fun. If you have family, you're eager to gather them near. If not, your friends can fill the void. Either way, the nurturing of loved ones is extra important at this time of year. Unfortunately, Mars may not be assertive enough to kick you into gear, so you might not follow through with timely execution. If you stall mid-month, remember that it's important to take a moment to regain your confidence. The intense Scorpio New Moon in your 5th House of Fun on **November 9** can plant a seed for more merriment later in the month, especially since this lunation is emotionally excited by physical Mars and erratic Uranus.

Be patient; you may have to wait until the positive trine between Mercury and Mars on **November 19** feeds you another boost of much-needed self-assurance. This energizing transit receives voltage from outrageous Uranus by **November 21**, encouraging you to further risk exposure by spontaneously expressing what's in your heart. The timing of this sudden predilection for play is perfect, preparing you for an energetic jump as the Sun enters adventurous Sagittarius on **November 22**. Ride the surge of energy toward the Gemini Full Moon on **November 24** and right through Thanksgiving weekend. You may feel a bit of post-holiday blues around **November 30** as the Sun moves toward a difficult square with pessimistic Saturn. For example, your boss may require you to put in a few days of extra hard work, especially if you dodged any responsibilities the previous week.

> **KEEP IN MIND THIS MONTH**
>
> *Nurturing others can make you feel better about yourself, but watch your motives. Remember that love must be given freely for it to be well received.*

KEY DATES

NOVEMBER 4–7 ★ *transparent intentions*

This is the first of two periods this month—**November 19 to 21** is the next—when you feel stable enough to easily express your feelings. It's more difficult to hide your intentions, for your emotions bubble over into action. Meanwhile, an exact square between foxy Venus and obsessive Pluto can force a control issue with a romantic partner. Defend your right to feel your deepest emotions, even if they are inconvenient for your mate, but don't lash out with hurtful accusations that could be difficult to retract.

NOVEMBER 9-10 ★ *fight the inclination to withdraw*
The secretive New Moon in Scorpio on **November 9** indicates that more is going on than is apparent on the surface. When issues are too complex, you tend to withdraw until you have a plan. Mercury the Messenger enters sphinx-like Scorpio on **November 10**, pulling your thoughts into deeper places as you obsessively search for meaning. You could sink to the bottom of your own well and hope that no one notices, but this isn't in your best interest. Pick out the most important feelings and share them before it's too overwhelming. Don't seek resolution now; it may take weeks for a conversation to reach fruition.

SUPER NOVA DAYS
NOVEMBER 19-21 ★ *risk vulnerability*
You can pluck the energy right out of thin air as mental planets Mercury and Uranus harmoniously trine defensive Mars in Cancer. Feelings that would normally remain hidden can be easily expressed. If you've been running in circles and worrying about the same old things, this is an opportunity to jump off the hamster wheel. However, there is risk, for lovely Venus tensely squares feisty Mars, and you could impulsively make a romantic advance that you later regret. While your words represent only one dimension of how you feel, others could treat them as the ultimate truth. Still, it's always worth taking a chance and sharing what's in your heart.

NOVEMBER 24-26 ★ *confused enlightenment*
A rather disorganized Gemini Full Moon on **November 24** heralds a confusing weekend as illusive Neptune takes center stage. Mercury forms a tense square to this evasive planet, putting your common sense at odds with your intuition. The more you try to use language to rationalize your fuzzy feelings, the more unwieldy and incoherent it becomes. But Neptune also receives a magical trine from desirable Venus, giving you an opportunity to feel your emotions without saying anything about them. Spiritual enlightenment can be yours if you are willing to separate yourself from needing approval. Detachment is essential, but don't slip down the slope into denial.

DECEMBER

WORK FOR WHAT YOU WANT

As the holidays roll around, you Crabs face a familiar dilemma: retreat or engage. You are drawn toward the security of your tribe as you celebrate family traditions, but with the Sun in far-reaching Sagittarius until **December 21**, you may wish to travel somewhere exotic. On **December 1**, chatty Mercury also enters Sagittarius, giving you a more philosophical outlook on life. With the Sun, Mercury, Jupiter, and Pluto all in your 6th House of Employment, you surely will be busier than usual and also could receive extra attention for the inspiration you now are to others. The rowdy Sagittarius New Moon on **December 9** rouses excitement on the job and elsewhere. Still, there is an irresolvable difference between your desire for quiet solitude at home and your need for recognition at work. A rare conjunction between powerful Jupiter and Pluto on **December 11** can tilt the balance, spurring you on toward greater ambitions than ever.

On **December 18**, big old Jupiter—having spent the year being as large as possible in its home sign of Sagittarius—faces the need to contract to fit within the strict rules of Capricorn, thereby limiting your options. This entrance by Jupiter into your 7th House of Partnerships signals a distinct shift in your energy as you become open to opportunities that come through those closest to you. Jupiter's arrival in ambitious Capricorn in your relationship house is followed by Mercury on **December 20** and the Sun on **December 21**—the Winter Solstice in the Northern Hemisphere. You are eagerly leaving the safety of your shell as you happily engage in a variety of relationship dances, especially around the Mars-charged Cancer Full Moon on **December 23**.

> **KEEP IN MIND THIS MONTH**
>
> *There's little time for self-doubt. Apply yourself whole-heartedly to the tasks at hand, and you'll soon be harvesting the fruits of your labor.*

KEY DATES

DECEMBER 1–3 ★ *a positive spin*

Mercury's movement into philosophical Sagittarius on **December 1** lifts your thoughts from the deep emotional waters of Scorpio. In addition, charming Venus receives support from optimistic Jupiter and powerful Pluto, giving you good reason to smile. Remember that you'll feel less isolated if your close friends know what you are feeling.

SUPER NOVA DAYS
DECEMBER 7-11 ★ *on a mission*
Everything is magnified around the intensely resourceful conjunction of Jupiter and Pluto on **December 11**. But the noisier squares to erratic Uranus illuminated by the Sun on **December 7** and tricky Mercury on **December 10** create an attraction/repulsion dilemma that can tear you in half or show you a brilliant solution. If you express your affections for someone, you might lose your precious freedom. Hiding your feelings can block the possibility of shared intimacy and of gaining the emotional security you crave. Similarly, you may be vacillating between issues at home and with your career, but you cannot cover both simultaneously. The extroverted New Moon in Sagittarius on **December 9** is a positive force for change that will likely blast you outside your safety walls, so do what you must prior to heading out on your mission.

DECEMBER 19-20 ★ *stick to the facts*
Mercury in casual Sagittarius confronts dark Pluto on **December 19** before changing into more serious clothing to enter the ambitious land of Capricorn on **December 20**, where it runs into Jupiter. Your acute perceptions, combined with an inclination to dig beneath the surface, grant you sufficient information to make excellent decisions, especially relating to business or personal dealings. You begin by thinking of all of the reasons why you cannot do something. By the time you've overcome initial obstacles, you could become so confident that you commit to more than you should. Keep coming back to the facts, and your breadth of vision will support the organization of the various factors into an all-encompassing plan.

DECEMBER 22-26 ★ *take it to the edge*
An especially intense Full Moon in self-protective Cancer on **December 23** is activated by a conjunction with red-hot Mars, agitating your emotions and driving you out of your own comfort zone. Additionally, Mars is opposite a boundless Sun-Jupiter conjunction, supplying you with unlimited enthusiasm. It may seem backward, but as your optimism pushes you outside your protective shell, you'll actually feel safer rather than at risk. You are being supported now by a stabilizing trine between thoughtful Mercury and authoritative Saturn. Take time to write an important e-mail or make a long-overdue phone call. Take advantage of your powers of concentration by cleaning off your desk to get ready for the New Year.

LEO

JULY 23–AUGUST 22

LEO OVERVIEW

It's all about hard work, Leo, and it might not feel like you've made a lot of progress for all of your effort. Fortunately, 2007 is likely to tell a happier tale. There's still a great deal demanded of you this year, but it's much more likely to propel you forward than to simply keep you going in circles. In fact, with the two final oppositions between reality-based Saturn and fantasy-loving Neptune in late February and late June, **the dreams that were percolating in your mind last summer may finally come to fruition**. When you shoot for the stars, it's easier to sustain your commitment and creativity. A big goal that you establish for yourself gives you the motivation that you need to live up to your highest expectations.

Jupiter, the planet of growth and good fortune, in its enthusiastic home sign of Sagittarius occupies your 5th House of Self-Expression this year. **This is a time to take risks and push the envelope in terms of what you're willing to give the world.** A creative drive can take you far, as long as you don't allow doubt to slam on the brakes and take you out of the race. Yes, planning is appropriate, and there will be some tough turns where caution is necessary to keep you from skidding off the road. Still, **being bigger, bolder, and more dramatic in what you say and do is right on target now**. It isn't about showing off or trying to prove yourself to others. This is about filling your heart with hope, loading your head with dreams, and living up to your full potential.

Saturn, the planet of making it real, is in your sign again this year, which can be a test of your commitment and your resolve to work for what you want. **You are in control of your fate now, Leo, which can be both exciting and scary.** Start by giving yourself all the respect that you can. It's easier to grow when you begin with a foundation built on positive self-esteem. Even if you haven't lived up to your expectations in the past, this is your time to construct a life that's more reflective of your true gifts. It can take a while to develop the healthy habits you need to fully exploit your talents, so measure your progress from where you've come, not from how far you have to go. Keep inching along steadily and you will travel many miles on the road to success.

Jupiter and Saturn form constructive trines in mid-March and early May. These are key periods for aligning your vision of the future with the work required to make it real. Both of these planets are ideal for reshaping your life on a grand scale since they combine the principles of possibility and necessity in a productive way. **Good judgment and a canny sense of strategy are allies** as your fiery zest for a fuller life blends seamlessly with a practical view of what's really possible.

EXPAND YOUR HEART'S DESIRE

The giant planet Jupiter is moving through your 5th House of Romance this year. This is a great sign for opening your heart and being honest about what it desires. What you express can seem unrealistic at first and might even feel unreachable. By allowing your deepest feelings to emerge, however, you may discover important clues that point you in a more favorable direction to find a fulfilling partnership. Generosity is a key theme as well, one that applies both to yourself and others, including children. Treat yourself royally, and do the same for those you care about as a way to widen the path of love. A little bit of extravagance is healthy when it is motivated by joy; there's no such thing as too much when it comes to happiness. Regardless of how busy you are, clear space on your calendar for physical and social delights.

BE YOUR OWN BOSS

You're not the type who dances well to someone else's tune, and this year is no exception. Trying to perform to please the boss is likely to stir resentment rather than strengthen your commitment to work. But when you are self-motivated, you can advance your career considerably now. Activities that use the power of your personality, such as selling, teaching, and working in the arts, are most likely to prove rewarding. Pride and discipline will be invaluable to getting ahead, but you may need to double-back and pick up some extra training or patch up a professional relationship from July 27 to September 8. Venus, the ruling planet of your 10th House of Career, will be retrograde and could require remedial work to upgrade your skills.

TRUST YOUR INSTINCTS

You have to spend money to make money now, Leo. Certainly, there are short-sighted expenses that deplete your bank account without giving you much in return. But investing in leisure activities that bring out your creative and playful sides can pay priceless dividends. It's certainly wiser this year to follow your own financial instincts than to hitch a ride on someone else's dream. Fanciful Neptune in your 8th House of Shared Resources is opposed by Saturn in late February and late June, times when you may be forced to pay for the foolishness of others. Your cash flow is likely to increase if you trust your instincts and make all of your own decisions.

SELF-DISCIPLINE WORKS

Practicing self-control is a must with Saturn in your sign this year. The planet of discipline in the 1st House of Physicality will reward you for healthy habits but punish you just as readily for your unhealthy ones. This is a time when the patterns you set are likely to have long-term effects. You can work hard to overcome any weaknesses by approaching them in a methodical way. You can even reshape your body. The extra time and attention you pay to exercising and eating well are worth the effort. Ultimately, though, the essential ingredient for wellness is a positive attitude. Anything you do to increase your vitality and improve your appearance is a gift to yourself, not punishment. Treat your body like the temple that it is and you'll be proud of how you look and feel.

A PLACE TO PLAY

Think of your home as a playground, an artist's studio, or a lover's lair. Your environment is most enriching when walking in the door puts a smile on your face and fills you with the joys of life. Perfect order is less important than a festive atmosphere, one in which all of your toys are easily accessible. Brighten up the old abode with colorful objects and images that inspire you. If the place is more like a cave than a movie set, plan a party to motivate you to redecorate. Family matters, too, can benefit from a lighter approach this year. Stretch the rules; heck, it's probably time to eliminate some of them completely. Allowing yourself and those you love more freedom to be who you are can make even the smallest house seem spacious now.

LEARN BY DOING; TRAVEL WITH PURPOSE

The best education comes from direct action, so avoid courses and classes that rely more on theory than practice. One exception is any program that arms you with information you can use to battle for a political, religious, or social cause. Active Mars will be in your 9th House of Higher Thought and Faraway Places from May 14 to June 24, a particularly active time for moving mind and body. Physical or mental challenges suit you best then. Lounging on a beach chair can be an appealing idea, but it's bound to bore you by the second day. Work-related travel from February 13 to March 7 and October 11 to November 1 can be especially tricky, so be vigilant regarding transportation, reservations, and appointments during these periods.

CLOSE RELATIONSHIPS RAISE CONSCIOUSNESS

Personal and spiritual growth derives primarily through relationships this year. Dealing with disappointment in others is a test of faith as well as a challenge to be forgiving while remaining true to your feelings. A compassionate and flexible attitude will help you bridge this apparent divide. Active Mars will be retrograde in your 12th House of Divinity from November 15 until the end of the year. This is a favorable time frame for going on a vision quest, joining a prayer group, connecting to nature, and tuning into the unity of all things.

RICK & JEFF'S TIP FOR THE YEAR:
Concentrate on You

Aiming high is appropriate, but it takes a narrow focus to reach your goals this year. There will be plenty of distractions from a partner, friends, or colleagues who have needs and dreams, but you have to put your own plans first. Don't lose sight of what you are trying to accomplish, regardless of the seductive stories of others. This apparent self-absorption can be your greatest contribution to the rest of humanity, because the strength and satisfaction you attain will be an enduring inspiration to all.

JANUARY

UNUSUAL IDEAS ACCELERATE YOUR PROGRESS

Relationships are likely to get your year off to an exciting start as three planets enter your 7th House of Partnerships this month. Sweet Venus lights up your life with unconventional individuals beginning **January 3**. Mercury supplies plenty of mental stimulation from others on **January 15**, and the Sun attracts courageous people as of **January 20**. All of these planets are in intelligent Aquarius, though, a sign that favors collective concerns rather than self-interest. Finding ways to be cooperative while sharing the load—without giving up control of your own life—can be a challenge. Assertive Mars's entry into your 6th House of Work on **January 16** may require adjustments to your routine on the job. Feeling constrained by a rigid system is the downside, although adding efficiency and upgrading your productivity are potential pluses.

One of the year's major planetary events, a tense square between expansive Jupiter and eccentric Uranus, occurs on **January 22** (to reoccur in May and October). Optimistic Jupiter is cruising through your ever-so-happy 5th House when it slips on the banana peel of Uranus. Surprises in love, brilliant but weird ideas, and unexpected turns in creative projects are all constructive expressions of this transit. The last week of January should be a little wild with a crackle of electricity in the air. You may be tempted to hunker down to hold off interruptions of your reality, but that will simply increase tension. Instead, take a breath, open your mind, and let your intuition do the work. A flash of insight could derail a plan, but if you can jump the track without wrecking your project, it's likely you will discover a time-saving shortcut.

> **KEEP IN MIND THIS MONTH**
>
> *A person or thought that seems odd at first can trigger a stroke of genius that takes your game to a higher level.*

KEY DATES

JANUARY 2–3 ★ *new answers to old questions*
Practical concerns are best resolved with unconventional solutions. A smart Sun-Uranus sextile on **January 2** boosts intelligence and sparks inventiveness. The Full Moon in reflective Cancer on **January 3** stirs issues of security, perhaps work-related. But Venus's entrance into Aquarius on the same day can attract an individual with a taste for experimentation who values original thinking and eclectic tastes.

JANUARY 6–8 ★ *responsible communication builds trust*
A mature conversation can keep a relationship on track as a Sun-Mercury conjunction in your 8th House of Intimacy allows a touchy subject to be handled responsibly. A trine between go-go Mars and stable Saturn on **January 8** aligns methods and goals to create a highly productive environment. Clear directions allow you to operate in a systematic way so that you can knock down a mountain of work and turn it into a manageable task.

JANUARY 13 ★ *desire works best with sensitivity*
An incredible depth of desire makes you unstoppable with a super-potent Mars-Pluto conjunct in your house of creativity. If you want something (or someone), you're able to concentrate all of your force to get it. But if you fail to consider someone else's feelings, what you think of as mere passion can come across as bullying. Temper your intensity based upon the circumstances in order to avoid stirring resentment.

SUPER NOVA DAYS
JANUARY 18–20 ★ *romantic dreams morph into reality*
This is a highly transitional period. The New Moon in orderly Capricorn on **January 18** is big on commitment. But on the same day, pleasure-loving Venus conjuncts Neptune, which is more suitable for romance than reality. It's easy to project your fantasies onto a potential partner. What you're seeing, though, is not a promise of what you'll get, but an ideal image of what you want. On **January 20**, the Sun's entry into Aquarius can help clear your head, allowing you to back away from the dream of endless bliss so that you can recalibrate your expectations.

JANUARY 26–28 ★ *faith filled with facts*
Intellectual Mercury shifts from an imaginative conjunction with spiritual Neptune on **January 26** to a deadly serious opposition with Saturn on **January 28**. Illusions can come crashing to earth as clouds disappear and the light of reason returns. Yet if you blend logic with desire, this will be a time when you can advance your hopes with the help of a supportive partner. On **January 27**, Venus enters Pisces, which is more about faith than facts and carries a strong romantic impulse. Make the most of this message of compassion that softens judgment, raises trust, and increases your chances for intimacy.

FEBRUARY

RECONSIDER YOUR COMMITMENTS

Thinking clearly and planning carefully can be major challenges now. Mercury, the information planet, enters impressionistic Pisces on **February 2** and turns retrograde on **February 13**. The boundless emotional field of Pisces makes it hard to communicate precisely, and Mercury's backward turn mid-month adds another layer of complexity to mental processes now. This planetary reversal occurs in your 8th House of Intimacy and Shared Resources, stirring deep waters in these delicate areas of life. While the three-week retrograde period gives you a chance to reflect on your emotional and financial commitments, it's also possible that a partner may want to back out or change the terms of your relationship. However, it's probably best to avoid finalizing any agreements until after Mercury turns direct on **March 7**.

On **February 28**, slow-moving Saturn and Neptune form the second of three long-lasting oppositions that began late last August and will finish on **June 25**. This is the single most important astrological event of the year, especially with karmic Saturn in your sign. The planet of order and control struggles against the dissolving waves of Neptune. Frustration can arise with others who are either unclear or unreliable, leading you to lose faith in them. The harder you push for clarity, the fuzzier reality gets. Nevertheless, there is potential to refine a dream or an ideal that has been taking form since last summer. Although you could feel farther from that goal than ever now, the point is not to give up but to readjust your sights and alter your tactics. If you're unhappy about a lack of support from others, don't let despair lead to finger-pointing. It's best to allow your thoughts to simmer for a long time before sharing them with others.

> **KEEP IN MIND THIS MONTH**
>
> *Use body language, music, poetry, and other creative art forms to communicate ideas that words alone cannot fully describe.*

KEY DATES

SUPER NOVA DAYS
FEBRUARY 2–3 ★ *a convincing speaker*
A Full Moon in your sign on **February 2** is bound to bring drama into your life. Small matters can feel like major issues, little desires like desperate needs.

You want attention and should get it, but make sure it's for being creative, playful, and generous rather than demanding and loud. A supportive sextile between the Sun and confident Jupiter on **February 3** inspires a new vision that you can enthusiastically share with others. The power of your belief is so strong that people will be extremely receptive to what you have to say.

FEBRUARY 8-10 ★ *the price may be too high*
The Sun conjuncts Neptune on **February 8**, bringing out the sensitive side of your personality and drawing you closer to a gentle person. Be cautious, though, about buying into an idea that sounds too good to be true. A tense Venus-Jupiter square on **February 9** can lead to overestimating the value of someone or something. An opposition between the Sun and Saturn on **February 10** is a day to come back down to earth and make practical matters a priority in your dealings with people.

FEBRUARY 17-18 ★ *reconnecting with your past*
The New Moon in progressive Aquarius on **February 17** falls in your 7th House of Partnerships. A close connection with Pluto, the resurrection planet, could bring someone from your past back into your life. Experience shows you how to handle the situation differently to get the most out of it this time around. On **February 18**, the Sun swims into oceanic Pisces, pulling you into a wider world of feelings and intuition and allowing you to lower your guard, increase your vulnerability, and share your emotions honestly.

FEBRUARY 21-22 ★ *fresh ideas*
Sociable Venus enters impulsive Aries on **February 21**, activating your desire to learn something totally new and travel someplace you've never been. Explore fresh ideas and unknown environments to satisfy your interest in others and how they live. These fascinating experiences, in turn, can stimulate new connections. A Sun-Mercury conjunction on **February 22** can find you deep in thought as you revisit recent events in your mind and see them in a different light.

FEBRUARY 25 ★ *pushing playfully*
Passionate Mars enters your 7th House of Partnerships, which can bring out your competitive side or attract aggressive individuals. Fighting and flirting may be closely linked, as long as you're both playing fairly. The planet of initiation crossing the horizon in your chart may also trigger your desire to launch a project or make a romantic move. Step cautiously until you're sure that you're on solid ground.

MARCH

REASSESS RESOURCES AND SELF-WORTH

Two eclipses rock the money sectors of your chart this month, compelling you to reevaluate your long-term financial plans. A total Lunar Eclipse in discerning Virgo on **March 3** occurs in your 2nd House of Income, which can suddenly alter the frequency of your cash flow. But if interruptions do occur, there are prospects that can more than compensate for any losses you might incur. A partial Solar Eclipse in mutable Pisces on **March 18** in your 8th House of Investments and Shared Resources can lead to changes related to community property, inheritance, or business partnerships. The influences of these eclipses can last for months, but decisions made now can be critical in maximizing returns and reducing risks for the entire year.

Informative Mercury turns direct on **March 7**, bringing you communications that have been lost in the channels for the past three weeks. Constructive trines from wealth-attracting Venus to big-thinking Jupiter and responsible Saturn on **March 8 and 9** supply a new perspective on opportunities that may come from foreigners, faraway places, or risk-oriented entrepreneurs. Venus's transit into her earthy home sign of Taurus in your 10th House of Career on **March 17** could raise your professional status by garnering well-earned appreciation for your accomplishments. Mars makes a series of significant aspects from **March 22 to 25**. First, it opposes Saturn in Leo, possibly in the form of an independent-minded person who doesn't want to play by your rules. Setting limits without stifling his or her creativity requires patience on your part. On **March 23**, Mars sextiles Jupiter, an aspect that puts wind in your sails with the support and encouragement of enthusiastic allies. And on **March 25**, Mars conjuncts Neptune—great for a Sunday escape of imagination and adventure.

> **KEEP IN MIND THIS MONTH**
>
> *Explore new ways to make money; even if the first one doesn't work, you should hit a winner eventually.*

KEY DATES

MARCH 3–5 ★ *a little change produces big results*
Wild and crazy Uranus is conjunct the Sun during the total Lunar Eclipse in picky Virgo on **March 3**. Panicky people worrying about petty details can put your life into a spin. Stay flexible and light on your feet—you might land in a better place. There could be an innovative approach to solving problems, even when dealing with an

eccentric boss, an insecure lover, or a nervous financial partner. A small shift on your part can produce surprisingly powerful results, so be subtle but brilliant now.

MARCH 9–10 ★ *going too far*
The Sun forms a hyperactive square with "more is better" Jupiter on **March 9**. You may give more than you can afford or promise more than you can deliver. Trying to impress or cheer someone up is fine, Leo, but "get real" Saturn is just around the corner and will force you to back off very quickly if you've overdone it.

MARCH 16 ★ *visualize the future*
The first of three creative trines between the career-related planets Jupiter and Saturn motivates you to visualize your future. Don't worry about filling in all the details just yet; this stabilizing aspect will return in early May and again in January 2008. This gives you plenty of time to align your sights and transform your concept into concrete reality.

SUPER NOVA DAYS
MARCH 18–20 ★ *out with the old, in with the new*
A Solar Eclipse in your 8th House of Intimacy and Transformation on **March 18** will probably push some powerful emotional buttons. Deep, dark Pluto's tense square to the Sun and Moon brings hidden fears and desires to consciousness and may threaten to shake your world. But the Sun's entry into fiery and fresh Aries on **March 20** turns your attention away from the past and toward the future. A whole new tomorrow seems possible as excitement about what's next overcomes worries about what may be left behind.

MARCH 24–26 ★ *play your way to the top*
Your ruling planet, the Sun, is triggering the confusing opposition between Saturn and Neptune that dominates your life this year. You can shift from doubt to hope and back again as you encounter the gap between where you are and where you wish to go. A Mars-Neptune conjunction on **March 25**, though, is a reminder that the magic is within you. An inspired friend, an imaginative partner, or a free-spirited stranger shows that you don't have to struggle to reach your goal. Play is a powerful vehicle to free you from fears. Expressing your imagination can reveal creative ways to bypass any obstacles.

APRIL

SPEAK LOUDLY AND CARRY A SOFT STICK

An intuitive style of action and an assertive way of talking make for an interesting combination of experiences this month. The warrior planet, Mars, slips into watery Pisces on **April 6** in your intimate 8th House of Regeneration. Small nudges can feel like vicious shoves. It's wise to encourage others gently, if at all, and try not to overreact if you feel that someone is pressing you too hard. Chatty Mercury enters blunt Aries on **April 10**, which often leads to a less than diplomatic communication style. Your excitement about a new idea or discovery can blurt out of your mouth before you consider the hurtful consequences of your words. This direct approach is great for charging people up and motivating the troops as long as they don't feel bullied. Fortunately, socially conscious Venus bounces into easygoing Gemini on **April 11**, bringing you a lighter touch and playfulness that can be useful for cooling off heated situations.

Expect pyrotechnics near the end of the month when Mars conjuncts volatile Uranus on **April 28** and squares excessive Jupiter on **April 30**. Impulsive, impatient, impetuous, and irritable attitudes are likely, especially when it comes to the delicate matters of sex, self-worth, and money. A restless partner or close friend will probably surprise you with a sudden change of plans or an odd shift of behavior. You could feel abandoned by this unexpected turn of events, but there's also a chance that you will be thrilled, or at least intrigued, by a new sense of freedom as well. Connecting with a person in a totally different way can feel risky, yet might rekindle the flame of a waning relationship. A dreamy Venus-Neptune trine adds gentleness and compassion to this potentially explosive period, providing opportunities for forgiveness if things should go awry.

> **KEEP IN MIND THIS MONTH**
>
> *A fast mind with a slow trigger finger gives you the tact to express your innovative ideas without provoking opposition.*

KEY DATES

APRIL 1–2 ★ *lead by listening*

You may have the responsibility to make everyone happy on **April 1**, but don't be a martyr about it. If you are in a position of leadership, spread the work around so that it's not all on your shoulders. The Full Moon in fair-minded Libra on **April 2** falls in your 3rd House of Communication, making this a good time to initiate a conversation about delicate matters, since you know when to press your point and when to step back and let the other person talk.

> **SUPER NOVA DAYS**
> **APRIL 8-9** ★ *grace under fire*
> If you believe in it, you can sell it now. People easily trust you because your ruling body, the Sun, forms reliable trines with realistic Saturn and optimistic Jupiter. This Grand Fire Trine lights up your chart with clarity and vision that inspire you to take charge without taking yourself too seriously. Confidence that you can achieve any goal, given the time and resources, gives you a calm demeanor even in the midst of stressful situations.

APRIL 11 ★ *inspiration comes easily*

The Moon is moving through your partnership zone as the Sun and psychic Neptune are linked by an intelligent sextile. This can bring a spiritually oriented person into your life, one who knows the meaning of compassion and who accepts you unconditionally. You're gifted as well, with the capacity to inspire others, even lifting their hopes when they feel that all is lost. You have abundant opportunities to share your knowledge with kindness and generosity. Use your intuition to gently open your mind to new concepts.

APRIL 17-20 ★ *passion with practicality*

The New Moon in speedy Aries on **April 17** puts high-octane fuel in your tank, adding extra power to any endeavor you undertake. Support from intense Pluto makes it possible to direct that force with purpose, cut out distractions, and demonstrate your strength. Aries is an outgoing fire sign like yours, so blaze a trail where you've never gone before. Solid ground rises up to meet you as reliable Saturn turns direct on **April 19** and the Sun moves into earthy Taurus in your 10th House of Career on **April 20**.

APRIL 22-24 ★ *intelligence without compromise*

The Sun illuminates the hard Jupiter-Uranus square, throwing off sparks of genius that can light your world with brilliant ideas. But the drive to make your own choices can lead to conflict with authority figures. You may be so convinced that your way is the only right way to go that considering any kind of compromise might feel like defeat.

LEO

MAY

QUIET TIME BALANCES AN INFORMATION OVERLOAD

May starts and ends with Full Moons on **May 2 and 31**. These are high-energy events that can pull you out of a rut at home or at work and send you traveling to the other side of the world. But even if you don't get out of your own hometown, you're likely to start looking at your life in a bigger way. Far-reaching Jupiter in Sagittarius forms its second creative trine with practical Saturn in Leo on **May 5** (the first was in mid-March). The planets of hope and reality work well together to support your good judgment, making this a positive time to recalibrate your view of the future. On **May 7**, sociable Venus slinks off into your 12th House of Privacy, suggesting a need for more peace and quiet in your life before the planet struts into Leo and pulls you back into the spotlight in early June.

Sparks fly with a dynamic Jupiter-Uranus square on **May 10** and Mercury the Messenger's entry into its chatty home sign of Gemini on **May 11**. Strong opinions can bring stress to a friendship, a working group, or an organization. Avoid forcing a showdown based on a so-called principle that's more of a work in progress than a well-founded philosophy. Since assertive Mars is entering its fiery sign of Aries on **May 15**, it won't take much to ignite a conflagration that can damage team spirit. Make room in your mind for conflicting ideas so that lively debate works to energize rather than destroy cohesion. The overdose of information should be reduced when Mercury enters caring Cancer on **May 28**. An emotional filter between mind and mouth can tone down the rhetoric as sensitivity leads to a more cautious approach to communication.

> **KEEP IN MIND THIS MONTH**
>
> *Recognize that there is more than one right answer to most questions, thereby reducing the risk of conflict among friends and colleagues.*

KEY DATES

MAY 2 ★ *it's safer to be open than closed*

Today's Full Moon in comfort-seeking Taurus may raise security concerns that put you in a defensive mode. Serious Saturn's stressful square to the Sun-Moon opposition could provoke self-doubt that freezes you in your tracks. If you feel yourself shutting down, take a deep breath, get up, move around, and shake up your energy until you put yourself in a more flexible state of mind.

MAY 8-9 ★ *reality reshapes a brilliant proposal*

An inventive idea requires some adjustments before it can be applied in a practical way. Take an original thought and test it out with others before going overboard with it. The Sun's easy connection with exciting Uranus on **May 8** can set your mind aflame, but hard solar aspects with both Jupiter and Saturn follow, imposing real-world conditions on an untried concept.

MAY 12-13 ★ *sweet until pushed*

The Sun's 90-degree angle to dreamy Neptune can make for a fuzzy Saturday. This is a good time for fantasy, faith, and breaks from reality. But there is a vulnerable side to this aspect as well, one that can be provoked by the hard-edged Mars-Pluto square on **May 13**. Concentrate your efforts to be effective in one area, rather than scattering energy everywhere. If attacked by someone, defend yourself with clear, concise statements instead of a vague verbal rant.

MAY 21 ★ *cracking the code*

The Sun enters mentally agile Gemini while forming a clever quintile with Uranus. This 72-degree aspect enriches your mind with cutting-edge ideas that can help you overcome obstacles in working with others. Your ability to adapt to changing conditions without surrendering your core principles can be very impressive now. You're a problem solver who is able to complete the most complicated puzzles, even when you're dealing with highly eccentric or uncooperative individuals.

SUPER NOVA DAYS
MAY 30-31 ★ *feelings fly in all directions*

Relationships are characterized by a greater degree of uncertainty now. Venus, the planet of personal value, is in a tense angle to the Sun on **May 30**, opening cracks of doubt about your importance or abilities. The Full Moon in adventuresome Sagittarius on **May 31** is in the 5th House, the playpen of the chart. This indicates a joyous attitude with romantic overtones. Impulsive Mars in Aries supporting the Full Moon ignites your interest in new games and people. However, there's instability in the air that can quickly turn hilarity to hysteria as confidence flies right out the window. Temper your passions a bit to reduce the likelihood of an emotional crash and burn.

LEO

JUNE

PLEASURE AND PRIVACY

A blend of sweet and strange describes this month, Leo. Sweetness comes on **June 5** in the form of Venus, the planet of love and pleasure, entering your sign, where it will reside for about five weeks. This is a time to feel your inner beauty and have it reflected back to you by a more appreciative world. Indulging yourself in sensory delights and splurging on a new wardrobe are worthwhile endeavors. There can also be more self-consciousness and the feeling that people are looking at you even when they're not. Please yourself instead of being too concerned with making everyone else happy. The New Moon in networking Gemini on **June 14** falls in your 11th House of Groups and Friends. This often initiates a fresh cycle of social activity, yet some unresolved issues with colleagues or pals may also surface now. Underworld kingpin Pluto opposes and "shake it up" Uranus squares this Sun-Moon conjunction, which can alter the makeup of your team.

Mercury turns retrograde in the deep recesses of your super-secret 12th House of Fantasies on **June 15** and will continuing moving backward until **July 9**. You might not have the time to go on a three-week silent meditation retreat, but taking a few moments a day to quiet your mind and listen to your heart is a good way to reduce stress caused by missed flights, computer glitches, and lost messages. On **June 25**, Saturn opposes Neptune for the final time in a series that began last August. This may be a period when old dreams or illusions hit the end of the road. But it also presents a groundbreaking opportunity to put your ideas into action and build a more inspiring life for yourself and a partner.

> **KEEP IN MIND THIS MONTH**
>
> *Seek pleasure but do it intelligently, and you will find it at a price that suits you financially, physically, and emotionally.*

KEY DATES

JUNE 5 ★ *a little bit more is just about right*
Venus enters proud Leo as the Sun opposes Jupiter, the planet of overdoing. Your appetite for life is large, but your need for approval can be excessive. There is nothing wrong with putting on a show to get what you want, but consider the long-term cost of making promises that you may not want to keep. Asking for more from others is appropriate and can work well if you balance your heart with your mind now.

JUNE 9–12 ★ *a fresh vision made real*

A tough square between the Sun and jumpy Uranus on **June 9** speeds up your nervous system. Seeing yourself in a new light is much more creative than rebelling against someone else. The Sun forms favorable sextiles with initiating Mars and constructive Saturn on **June 11**, both of which give you a blueprint for turning inspiration into reality. A spiritually rich Sun-Neptune trine on **June 12** empowers you with faith even if you encounter resistance to your plans.

JUNE 17–18 ★ *digging deeper in relationships*

Your ruling planet, the Sun, makes hard aspects to Venus and Pluto, a potentially jealous pair. Relationships can be rocky if you don't feel like you're getting your fair share. Someone close to you might not be thrilled with your behavior, either. Discontentment may not be pretty, but when it reveals deeper desires, it paves the way to greater fulfillment.

JUNE 21 ★ *seek emotional comfort*

The Sun enters self-protective Cancer while making a difficult aspect with wounded Chiron. Wanting to hide under the covers is a more likely response to a misunderstanding than working hard to make yourself heard. Self-pity, though, does not ennoble the soul. Blame is equally futile. Judgment of yourself or others may be toxic. An environment where raw emotions can be expressed safely is ideal. Share your feelings with a supportive individual, and you'll quickly be on the fast track to healing whatever ails you.

SUPER NOVA DAYS

JUNE 28–30 ★ *a thousand-mile journey starts with a single step*

Retrograde Mercury passes between the Earth and the Sun on **June 28**, making you conscious of what's been motivating your recent behavior. The Sun and Mercury both aspect the slow-moving Saturn-Neptune opposition. This can lead to feelings that vacillate between doubt (Saturn) and hope (Neptune). The Full Moon in responsible Capricorn on **June 30** falls in your 6th House of Health, Work, and Daily Routines. It's time to come down to earth and take concrete steps to upgrade your life. You don't have to conquer the world; just add some constructive order and discipline on a small scale, and the larger pieces will fall into place.

JULY

VULNERABILITY REDUCES ISOLATION

Two planets changing directions are key events this month. Mercury the Communicator turns direct on **July 9** after three weeks in backward mode. It begins its forward movement in your 12th House of Secrets, which helps to get information flowing more freely. Conversations and negotiations that were put on hold can start up again. Facts that you've been seeking may finally appear, and feelings that you've been keeping to yourself should be more easily released. There's no need to shout from the rooftops, but give yourself permission to talk privately with someone you trust. This is an ideal time to open up and overcome some of your shyness about revealing your innermost thoughts.

Vivacious Venus, the planet of love, tells a complex story now. It leaves your sign for prudent Virgo on **July 14**, commencing a more cautious approach when it comes to relationships. On **July 27**, Venus turns retrograde until **September 8**. This adds another layer of complication to partnership, self-worth, and income-related issues. Revisiting your romantic past is one possibility; making adjustments with a current companion is another. Since this transit begins in your 2nd House of Money and Resources, reworking unfinished financial matters can be expected. Rediscovering enthusiasm in a forgotten talent or interest has positive income potential now.

Late this month, active Mars empowers the long-lasting Saturn-Neptune opposition. It squares spacey Neptune on **July 24** and unforgiving Saturn on **July 31**. Investing your energy carelessly under the first aspect can lead to frustration during the second one. Mars is moving through your 10th House of Career and Public Responsibility, so problems on the job or in any leadership position may be expected. Consider your workload carefully before adding anything else to the pile, no matter how appealing the task or its reward.

> **KEEP IN MIND THIS MONTH**
>
> *An honest conversation will lighten your load when it's done in a safe setting with a caring individual whom you really trust.*

KEY DATES

JULY 1 ★ *respect yourself*

This is a serious Sunday with a Venus-Saturn conjunction in your sign. Your confidence may not be as high as usual, so you may work extra hard to prove yourself to someone. Simplify your plans to satisfy yourself, rather than trying so much to please others. If you're not feeling sociable, there's nothing wrong with being alone for now. Attending to your own needs builds self-respect, which will ultimately have a positive long-term effect on all of your relationships.

JULY 10 ★ *shake up the team*
Inventive Uranus is hooked up in a healthy trine with the Sun, a combo that sharpens your intuition. Unorthodox ideas pop up when you least expect them and might not sound very practical at first. But don't throw them out, because there is a method to this madness. Original concepts for working with a group are especially hot now, making it possible to get value out of a team member who has been more of a problem than an asset to you lately.

JULY 13-14 ★ *tender loving care*
A slippery Sun-Neptune quincunx on **July 13** is quickly followed by the New Moon in moody Cancer on **July 14**. Emotions can leak out unexpectedly, bringing tears or profound feelings of vulnerability. You need to be babied now, Leo, and if there is no one else to rub your feet or make you dinner, be sure to pamper yourself somehow. A long bath, a day reading in bed, or eating some comfort food can be ideal for soothing your weary soul.

SUPER NOVA DAY
JULY 22 ★ *it's your job to have fun*
It's your season as the Sun enters warmhearted Leo and lights up your sign for the next month. It's time to celebrate and to make a toast to life. There's no need to limit the birthday party to just one day. Take the loving feeling you have and share it proudly and loudly. But if you're feeling blue, wake up the urge to splurge in whatever way brings joy back into your heart. Be playful; cross out everything serious on your to-do list, and have fun any way you can.

JULY 29 ★ *distance can bring clarity*
The Aquarian Full Moon in your 7th House of Partnerships can bring some unexpected behavior from a lover or close friend. If you're chilled by a sudden cooling of interest, don't try to overcome it by being too aggressive. Maybe you two need to step back and look at things from a fresh perspective to add more excitement into the relationship.

AUGUST

GIANT STEPS INTO YOUR FUTURE

The planets are moving in big ways, which can make this a time of monumental shifts in your life. On **August 6**, Saturn in Leo trines Pluto in Sagittarius, signaling an enduring commitment to your deepest desires. Saturn has patience; Pluto has depth and power. Their creative connection can build a blueprint for defining your future. Don't overwork yourself, but effort spent on study, discipline, and planning now can pay dividends for the rest of your life. Joyful Jupiter in Sagittarius turns direct on **August 6** as well, adding a wave of optimism to carry you forward. Even little Mercury joins the party by entering its idea-rich home sign of Gemini on the same day. Friends and colleagues stimulate your thinking, but avoid chatterboxes who provide more clutter than clarity. Memories of the glory days are stirred when Venus backs into Leo on **August 8**. Draw inspiration from these recollections to create your future instead of getting lost in the "what-ifs" of times past.

A total eclipse of the Moon in mystical Pisces winds up the month with a dramatic flourish on **August 28**. It lasts only a few hours, but this uncommon occurrence will resonate for months, perhaps even years, to come. This powerful event lands in your 8th House of Deep Sharing, which can touch your sex life, trust issues with a partner, or financial matters. Stirring these delicate issues may provoke strong reactions; the impulse to take action immediately is natural. Yet it is difficult to assess the possible effects of your choices if you're under duress. Somewhere between being frozen in your tracks and leaping to conclusions, there's a more moderate level of response that will ultimately produce the most effective results.

> **KEEP IN MIND THIS MONTH**
>
> *Strategic, precisely planned steps will land you closer to your goal than impetuous leaps based on faith alone.*

KEY DATES

AUGUST 2-4 ★ *lower expectations*

A buoyant trine between the Sun and Jupiter on **August 2** builds confidence and encourages risk taking. But even your best intentions can lead to unexpected consequences when the Sun forms a cranky sesquisquare with Pluto on **August 4**. Instead of holding your ground based on earlier hopes or promises, make adjustments and pare down your plans if a lack of resources or a balky partner proves to be a problem. Half a loaf is better than none, and if the bread is really tasty, one slice can be quite satisfying.

SUPER NOVA DAYS
AUGUST 12–13 ★ *new dreams are quickly tested*

The proud Leo New Moon on **August 12** opposite Neptune, the fantasy planet, directly impacts your self-image. Unreliable individuals can give you faulty feedback that proves misleading. Whether they are singing your praises or putting you down, take what you hear with a grain of salt. Positively, this event touches your soul, inspiring greater love and forgiveness. Retrograde Venus joins Saturn in Leo on **August 13**, bringing a quick return to reality in your relationships. Disappointment can lead to cynicism, but commitment to your core values can ensure that the dream will last.

AUGUST 17–19 ★ *mirror, mirror, on the wall*

Narcissistic Venus passes in front of the Sun on **August 17**, an event that can increase self-consciousness, especially about your appearance. Don't let vanity get the best of you. Observant Mercury joins stern Saturn on **August 18** and then moves into critical Virgo the following day. Flaws become magnified, little details blown out of proportion. A healthy Sun-Pluto trine on **August 19**, though, puts practicality before pride, enabling constructive action instead of futile fretting.

AUGUST 21–23 ★ *calculate your risks*

There's a practical turn of events now as the Sun joins Saturn on **August 21** before leaving Leo and entering Virgo on **August 23**. Feelings of responsibility are useful unless they paralyze you with guilt. Assess yourself honestly and recognize your accomplishments. Saturn is great for setting goals; Virgo is helpful for developing resources to reach them. All is far from glum, though, since Mars opposing Jupiter on **August 23** can fill you with passion. Competitive Mars can stir your juices, but don't let overextravagant Jupiter pressure you into taking foolish chances.

AUGUST 28 ★ *an emotional wash*

Jupiter square the total Lunar Eclipse may exaggerate emotions, accentuate fears, and make you feel farther than ever from getting what you want. Don't believe it! This is just a time when feelings flow beyond the bounds of reason. Let 'em go, since a good cleansing can clear out worries and ready you for a bright new start.

SEPTEMBER

CHANGES IN THE FLOW

Venus, the planet of attraction, turns direct in your sign on **September 8**, which can put the sizzle back into your social life. This is an excellent time to update your look as well as your outlook on relationships. Unresolved issues are ready for the light of day, so you can repair a wounded partnership or move on to seek love elsewhere. Venus is also associated with money, so its newfound sense of direction can help your finances as well. This could be a critical issue with a Solar Eclipse in your 2nd House of Income on **September 11**, an event that can suddenly impact your pocketbook.

A wave of intensity arises just after the middle of the month with a series of very potent aspects. Demanding friends or a challenging group activity can take you to extremes with an opposition of combative Mars and powerful Pluto on **September 21**. You could feel like you're being coerced to do more than you should, perhaps even compromising your principles. But if you're passionate about what's happening, you can find the strength to overcome any obstacle. Whether this is about work or play, if your heart's into it, you'll dig deep within to find what you need to reach your goal. An opposition between Venus and Neptune on the same day matches power with vulnerability, making for a volatile mix. This combination of hard-driving force and hypersensitivity easily leads to situations where one party seems like a bully and the other feels like a victim. Yet when tenderness toward others is blended with desire, you can experience the magic of depth and delight that turns an ordinary Friday into a day you will never forget.

> **KEEP IN MIND THIS MONTH**
>
> *Focus on the intention and execution of your creations, rather than worrying about what others might take from you.*

KEY DATES

SEPTEMBER 3 ★ *electricity in the air*

A tense square between active Mars in Gemini and electric Uranus in Pisces puts a buzz into your day. Tempers may be hair-trigger quick, especially with supposed allies. Another stressful square, between the Sun and expanding Jupiter, adds more noise. Everyone wants to be heard, but no one wants to listen. Competing points of view take on an exaggerated degree of importance, potentially turning small differences into major battles. Taking yourself lightly, though, won't cut your power but brings you the flexibility to avoid head-on collisions. This will free you to experiment with new methods without having to prove anything to anyone.

SUPER NOVA DAYS
SEPTEMBER 9–11 ★ *show me the money*
The Sun's opposition to shocking Uranus on **September 9** can incite explosive reactions to others' comments. Whether the statements are critical or comical, you might not be in the mood to laugh about what others think of you. The upside, though, is a breakthrough in awareness about a personal or financial partnership. On **September 11**, the New Moon in Virgo is a Solar Eclipse, with Uranus still very much in the picture. Since the eclipse falls in your 2nd House of Finances, you may encounter unexpected expenses or a reevaluation of your worth. The possible benefit is a new plan for earning income or upgrading your skills. Shaking the money tree, any way you can, could bring a rewarding harvest.

SEPTEMBER 17–19 ★ *the battle within*
The Sun squares aggressive Mars on **September 17** and transformational Pluto on **September 19**. Power struggles in which no one gives an inch are an undesirable possibility now. But if you focus the considerable force you're feeling in an original way, you can perform miracles. A situation that looks like a total loser can be turned into a winner. The battle is not against an external enemy; it is the struggle to dig deep in yourself to find the creative key that unlocks your full potential.

SEPTEMBER 26–27 ★ *discovering inner knowledge*
The Full Moon in hot-to-trot Aries on **September 26** occurs in your 9th House of Travel and Higher Education. The most educational journey, though, can be into your own psyche. Mercury, the information planet, enters emotionally profound Scorpio on **September 27** in the private 4th House of Inner Landscapes. Looking deep within yourself by revisiting family patterns can reveal where knots of doubt or denial can be untied. This is knowledge worth more than a Ph.D. Enlightenment of the soul leads to greater awareness of your purpose and increases your ability to fulfill it.

OCTOBER

THE DEVIL IS IN THE DETAILS

Enthusiastic Jupiter makes two major aspects this month that broaden your spirit and stimulate your sense of adventure. The last of three Jupiter-Uranus squares occurs on **October 9**. This completes a mind-blowing series of discoveries that can shake your vision of the future. Electric, eccentric Uranus shatters an old picture of possibilities for yourself and the world, freeing you to create a new and improved vision. Gain comes from loss in unexpected ways—perhaps in love, with children, or through different forms of self-expression. You may not be clear on the rules of this emerging reality quite yet, Leo, so allow yourself to move tentatively as you explore unknown territory. On **October 29**, Jupiter forms a sextile with boundless Neptune. This positive blend gives a feeling of faith in where you're going, even if you lack the facts to fully map the trail.

Mercury, the communication planet, turns retrograde on **October 11** in your 4th House of Home and Family. This backward turn could help you dig up long-forgotten stories of your past that clear up mysteries in your personal history. Every Mercury retrograde cycle marks a three-week period in which important e-mail can be deleted, data is mangled, printers are jammed, and other snafus with technology and details occur. Double-check your facts to avoid the frustration caused by incomplete information and mental blind spots. Take time to reorganize your living space by clearing up clutter and ridding yourself of objects that have outlived their usefulness. Lovely Venus in fastidious Virgo on **October 7** will appreciate you for being extra clean and tidy. If you give your place a simpler, more Zen-like feeling, you make room for your mind to quiet itself and discover secrets that can be heard only in silence.

> **KEEP IN MIND THIS MONTH**
>
> *Big changes may occur suddenly, but managing the small stuff well enables you to keep your balance when surprises happen.*

KEY DATES

OCTOBER 7–8 ★ *trust your intuition*

Intuition guides you through choppy waters now. The Sun forms a creative quintile with penetrating Pluto and a harmonious sextile with wise Jupiter, giving you good sense and judgment. But a quixotic quincunx between the Sun and Uranus can produce some irregular bounces, so stay calm if your plans veer off course. You don't have to take the easy way out to reach your goal, as long as you're open enough to improvise, adapt, and make adjustments on the fly.

OCTOBER 10–13 ★ *listen with your heart*

The New Moon in friendly Libra on **October 10** falls in your 3rd House of Communication. Normally, this would open channels of information, but with Mercury turning retrograde on **October 11**, what you hear may not be what you get. Key information is not in the words, but in their tone. The Sun forms hard 45-degree angles to a Venus-Saturn conjunction peaking **October 13**. This adds seriousness to relationships that can constrict the flow of love. Fragile feelings increase uncertainty, but a Sun-Neptune trine brings compassion and hope.

OCTOBER 20 ★ *soft but strong words*

A savvy Sun-Pluto sextile occurs while the Moon is moving through your 7th House of Relationships. You get the best out of others by overlooking their imperfections and acknowledging their strengths. This allows you to draw closer to people, whether in an intimate one-to-one or in a public forum. You needn't shout to be heard since the clarity of your intention empowers your words, even if you whisper.

SUPER NOVA DAYS
OCTOBER 23–26 ★ *setting a lasting pattern*

This is a meaningful time with the Sun entering emotionally powerful Scorpio and crossing retrograde Mercury on **October 23**, followed by the Full Moon in stubborn Taurus on **October 26** in your 10th House of Career and Public Life. If you're feeling threatened at home or on the job, you're likely to dig in your heels. Holding your ground can be the best way to go, as long as your stance is based on conscious values rather than habitual patterns. The choices you make now are likely to have a long-lasting effect, so consider them carefully.

OCTOBER 29 ★ *desire within reason*

An impulse to spend more than you should will probably be checked by common sense now. The long-term Jupiter-Neptune sextile is encouraged today by an inflationary Venus-Jupiter square that widens your field of desire. Simultaneously, a stable Sun-Saturn sextile restrains excess. This combination can stimulate your taste for people or experiences that you've never encountered, but gives you the patience to pursue at a pace that matches your financial and emotional capacities.

NOVEMBER

FASTER THINKING, SLOWER ACTING

Planets are shifting gears again this month with Mercury the Messenger turning direct on **November 1** and energizing Mars going retrograde on **November 15**. The communication planet begins moving forward in your 3rd House of Information, making this a rich period for learning, gathering data, and picking up unfinished business. On **November 10**, Mercury will return to Scorpio in your 4th House of Roots and Family, a good time for physical changes at home as well as deep conversations to address difficult personal issues. Mars is the igniter, the planet that sets things in motion, but it has been languishing in your 12th House of Secrets since late September. Its backward turn in the middle of this month will last until late January. The most important work you do may not be visible to the world. It can be private, inward, spiritual, or in a support position where your services go unrecognized. Yet this is also a period in which your heightened intuition and vivid imagination can serve to widen your view of life's possibilities.

The Sun enters happy-go-lucky Sagittarius on **November 22**, shining brightly in your 5th House of Love, Children, and Creativity. The upsurge of energy that this represents runs counter to retrograde Mars, suggesting that you can feel pulled in two opposite directions. While the Sun encourages risk taking, romanticism, and bold behavior, Mars wants to keep you under wraps. Ideally, you can combine the two by drawing on careful private preparation that gives you the training and confidence to show yourself more openly. The stage can be your workplace, a disco dance floor, a romantic bedroom, or an artist's studio. Whatever venue you choose, your performance is sure to be sensitive, subtle, and sublime.

> **KEEP IN MIND THIS MONTH**
>
> *Give new ideas enough time to germinate before putting them into practice. A longer than usual period of gestation will ensure better results.*

KEY DATES

NOVEMBER 4 ★ *stronger than you think*

You pack a wallop today with the Sun in a high-capacity trine with still-direct Mars and a tense semisquare with potent Pluto. You might not even know your own strength; just a little nudge can throw someone off balance. You might not look like you're trying hard, but you can blow through tasks that make others sweat. Tackle the tough stuff; you can get more done with less apparent effort now.

NOVEMBER 9-11 ★ *dive deeply*

The Scorpio New Moon on **November 9** is an emotionally powerful event that can drive you to the depths to pierce the dark corners of your soul. Desires may be stirred, shame awakened, and doubt doubled. But spiritual Neptune squares the New Moon, spilling the light of compassion into the shadows. Faith and forgiveness bring you up from the bottom, release guilt, and help you put a painful family story behind you. Purged of fear, your potential is enriched by this complex journey within.

NOVEMBER 19-20 ★ *handle sensitive relationships with care*

The Sun forms challenging angles with the lovers, Venus and Mars. Relationships can be complicated by misread intentions and unclear signals. Pressure only muddles the picture, but a more sensitive and patient approach to others can build trust and intimacy. Mutual vulnerability must be shared with tenderness that takes time to fully express. This is only the beginning of a negotiating process that may involve taking many steps backward before forward progress is ensured.

NOVEMBER 24 ★ *reduce noise*

The Full Moon in flighty Gemini in your 11th House of Groups and Friends can overload your social calendar. Trying to be in more than one place at a time is impossible, so avoid overbooking yourself. You might feel like everyone is talking at once and that messages are bombarding you from every direction. Stern Saturn's square to the Full Moon says that there's a limit to how much you can take. But avoid slamming the brakes on someone, as that would seem rude. Instead, leave space in your schedule for some quiet activity so you can hear yourself think again.

NOVEMBER 29-30 ★ *creativity meets reality*

A clever quintile between the Sun and Neptune on **November 29** opens your imagination like a giant umbrella. Colorful ideas and images fill your mind—some practical, others not. On **November 30**, the Sun bangs into a hard square with tough guy Saturn, putting the halt to fantasy and letting pass only those concepts that can be made real. Be sure you have the resources required to pay for any of your creative plans.

DECEMBER

BELIEF SYSTEMS WILL BE TESTED

Buckle your seat belt and get ready for a rocket-ship ride. On **December 11,** Jupiter conjuncts Pluto—a once-every-thirteen-years meeting of the planets of big and extreme. This major event fills the month with powerful opinions that can tear apart friendships or lead to breakthroughs in terms of long-term plans. Jupiter relates to beliefs and visions for the future. Its union with transformative Pluto increases the pressure to know what you want and where you want to go. If you're on track, you can tap into a deep well of material and psychological resources to carry you a long, long way. But if you're stuck with a model that no longer fits, you may have to tear it down and start all over. On **December 18,** Jupiter leaves playful Sagittarius and enters businesslike Capricorn. This could lead to professional growth and achievement if you're willing to develop your skills with additional training. Saturn turns retrograde in your 2nd House of Possessions on **December 19,** which means that discipline has to come from within, beginning with a hard look at your finances and resources.

Mercury enters Capricorn and conjuncts Jupiter on **December 20.** Serious thinking is in store, but overloading on data can lead to confusion rather than clarity. The Sun conjuncts Pluto on the same day, enters Capricorn on **December 21,** and conjuncts Jupiter on **December 22.** This planetary pileup in Capricorn can mean more than the usual holiday hustle and bustle. Rather than planning an elaborate celebration, stick to the essence for simplicity's sake. The planets are in your 6th House of Work and Service, so you may feel performance pressure to show everyone a good time.

> **KEEP IN MIND THIS MONTH**
>
> *Allowing emotions to get out of hand will not lead to a positive solution, so do your best to stay cool in the midst of any disagreement.*

KEY DATES

DECEMBER 7–9 ★ *respect yourself*

A Sun-Uranus square on **December 7** is followed by the New Moon in Sagittarius on **December 9.** Normally, this Sun-Moon conjunction is a jolly event that puts you in a playful mood. However, the hard right angle from nervous Uranus can produce a high-strung atmosphere that makes compromise and cooperation difficult. You might need space to act independently so that you're not boxed in by someone else's rules. Romantic impulses can run hot and cold now as your unconventional behavior shakes up a relationship.

DECEMBER 17 ★ *curb that tongue*

The Sun and Mercury join up to get your mind buzzing and your mouth moving. Being honest is a good thing, as long as you're sensitive to what others are able to absorb. Being spontaneous is fun when you are playful, but an unconscious comment could go astray and hit someone where it hurts. A little caution will keep the conversation from turning caustic.

SUPER NOVA DAYS

DECEMBER 20–24 ★ *'tis the season for intensity*

On **December 20**, the Sun joins penetrating Pluto, which can cause some deep soul-searching and, perhaps, some self-doubt. Yet with patience and a sense of purpose, you can turn around situations that seem hopeless. Mercury enters responsible Capricorn on the same day and joins big old Jupiter. You'd better have your act together if you're trying to impress someone. If you don't have all of the facts or can't present them in a well-organized way, you might want to delay an important meeting until you are more prepared. The Sun then enters ambitious Capricorn on **December 21** and conjuncts Jupiter on **December 22**. Showing authority without arrogance will earn you respect, especially at work. The Full Moon in Cancer on **December 23** is joined with aggressive Mars, followed by the Sun's conjunction to the warrior planet on **December 24**. This is quite an intense prelude to the holidays, a time when insecurities often push buttons and lead to conflict. If you're feeling the slightest bit edgy, it's best to process emotions privately, rather than dumping them indiscriminately on others.

DECEMBER 30 ★ *play within bounds*

A healthy trine between the willful Sun and responsible Saturn brings more common sense into your life. You demonstrate maturity by overlooking petty matters to keep your attention on your priorities. Venus enters joyful Sagittarius in your sexy 5th House of Fun and Creativity and forms a wicked quincunx with Mars. Go ahead and have a delightful time, but watch your boundaries. Fortunately, this dangerously playful energy is balanced with Saturn's wisdom and restraint.

VIRGO

AUGUST 23–SEPTEMBER 22

VIRGO OVERVIEW

T his is a critical year for you as one phase of your life draws to a close, allowing a new you to emerge. You have seen your share of instability since 2003, when Uranus, the champion of the unexpected, entered watery Pisces in your 7th House of Partnerships. It may seem as if the important developments in your life have been in response to circumstantial surprises that were outside your control. These unpredictable events—affecting both business and personal relationships—are likely to continue, keeping you on your toes until Uranus leaves Pisces in 2010.

Your need for freedom intensifies this year—at times creating anticipation and eagerness—but you may be confused by the wide range of choices. With Jupiter, the planet of expansion and reward, in your 4th House of Home and Family this year, you might not want to leave the house. Still, **your desire for grand adventure is stimulated** by a long-lasting dynamic square between optimistic Jupiter and erratic Uranus. Don't try to restrain your need for independence much, or you might find yourself vicariously living out your life through the actions of unconventional people. Your attraction to unorthodox and even irresponsible friends or lovers can, in turn, vitalize your spirit at the expense of reducing your serenity.

Four eclipses this year fall along the Virgo-Pisces axis, mobilizing the cosmos and acting as electrifying catalysts for change in your life. **You won't be able to hold on to the status quo, so embrace the transformations as they arrive.** The first, a Lunar Eclipse involving Uranus on March 3, stimulates the sudden release of pent-up tensions. On March 18, a Solar Eclipse in your relationship house squares passionate Pluto, agitating deeply rooted fears and jealousy issues. On August 28, a Lunar Eclipse with Saturn indicates the need to meet your obligations at any cost. The last, on September 11, is a Solar Eclipse opposite Uranus that again awakens an urgent sense that life may pass you by if you don't take action right away. Each eclipse has a different flavor, but together they make a convincing story for personal metamorphosis.

Much of your attention now is about a serious reevaluation of where you are in your life, what parts of it are working, and what parts are not. There is no need for panicky decisions if you begin this process early in the year. However, by September, when the stern taskmaster, Saturn, enters Virgo, you will feel the pressure to take responsibility and redirect your focus, if necessary. **You may already see your freedom of choice being limited by circumstances, so you must eliminate everything that isn't critical to your future.** Wherever you have fallen short of your expectations, it may be time to cut your losses. Unfortunately, if you wait until autumn, it will be too late to methodically plan for this powerful time that will continue for the next couple of years.

ROCK AND ROLL

Excitement rocks your relationship world with hit-or-miss Uranus in your 7th House of Partnerships all year. You can have the best and the worst wrapped up in one special person now. Also, four eclipses portend alternating elation and distress. One thing is certain: you are in for a few surprises. Your eyes open to untapped potential in a current love affair or the possibilities of a new one starting in mid-January. Mars, in your 5th House of Love until February 25, offers an opportune time to make your move, creating a temporary island of romantic stability in a sea of change. Be ready for sensational action around February 8, March 5, and April 29. But a feeling of being misunderstood may create unwanted isolation toward the end of June. And although Jupiter's entrance into your house of romance doesn't arrive until December 18, it bodes well for the holidays and on into 2008.

NEARING THE SUMMIT

A chapter in your professional life is coming to a close and a new one begins in September, when ambitious Saturn enters your sign. Your career may generate deep satisfaction, but you sense an impending shift. Make long-term decisions in mid-March, early May, and early August, when persistent Saturn receives support to help you execute plans with self-discipline. Your ruling planet, Mercury, is connected to your work, and its retrogrades can suggest communication problems. Others may fall short of your expectations from February 13 through March 7, so try not to demand too much at this time. The retrograde period from June 15 through July 9 might raise challenges about working as part of a team, when you prefer to be alone. Between October 11 and November 1, keep intense thoughts to yourself. You are reaching toward a culmination, and whether or not you've achieved your professional goals, you must adapt and integrate them to the other changes unfolding in your life.

 ## NO SURPRISES

You may not rake in the bucks, but it's a reliable year when you get what you expect. One source of worry stems from how you are fiscally tied to a partner while not having control over his or her activities. However, the harder you work, the greater the payoff—so focus on what you do instead of worrying about what's beyond your reach. You could make extra money from a family business or working on the Internet from home with entrepreneurial Jupiter in your 4th House. Stash money aside under favorable Venus aspects during the first part of March and the end of April. You may need to draw on those funds, possibly during the Venus retrograde July 27 through September 8.

 ## IMAGINE THERE'S NO ILLNESS

A year filled with eclipses in your sign will require you to stay on your toes when it comes to issues of health and vitality, for instant karma can get you if you slack or it can cure you if your lifestyle is clean. There's no need to go overboard. Daily yoga, organic food, and dietary supplements are fantastic, but the magic potion is your imagination with Neptune in your 6th House of Health. You might dream your way to well-being through a variety of mental disciplines such as meditation or hypnosis. Of course, proper diet and regular exercise are still highly advised.

 ## BIG PLANS

Jupiter magnifies everything it touches, and this year it visits your 4th House of Home and Family, opening doors to rooms you've never visited. This can indicate a major remodeling, which can increase your home's value. Take decisive action from March through May, during a stabilizing trine between optimistic Jupiter and realistic Saturn. Deeper changes are unfolding that are tied to an ongoing process of renewal as Jupiter conjuncts powerful Pluto in December. The makeover isn't only about your living space; it's also about you.

HOME SWEET HOME

You have a practical outlook on travel now and shouldn't waste energy running off to faraway places. By March, as Venus enters your 9th House of Higher Education, you may start to think about the benefits of additional schooling—especially how it could positively impact your income. It could, however, be May before your plans get off the ground. Schedule a relaxing vacation in July, while Mars in sensual Taurus is in your 9th House. Travel in August, however, may be more business-related. Jupiter is quite content this year in having its grand adventures while staying safely at home in the 4th House of Roots.

 ## SURRENDER TO THE MYSTERIES

Normally, you like to know the details of what you are doing and why you are doing it. This year, as Saturn contacts your 12th House of Spirituality and Fantasy, you could become frustrated as you attempt to solidify that which cannot be known. Also, Saturn's long-term opposition with indeterminate Neptune makes this even more challenging. Your greatest source of growth emerges from the fear of not being able to rely on your keen sense of analysis and applied logic. Don't even try to think your way to enlightenment now; it won't work. Instead, surrender to the netherworld of your imagination, for this is where your life can be enriched beyond your wildest dreams.

RICK & JEFF'S TIP FOR THE YEAR:
Work Toward Completion

Your life is approaching a major crossroads, a time when the choices you make will have very long-term consequences. Until September—when constructive Saturn enters your sign—you won't be able to stand in the middle of this intersection to see where these various roads lead. Accordingly, you'll need to wait until autumn to make the most important decisions, but this doesn't mean you can be lazy until then. Get ready for the hard work ahead by cutting back extraneous activities and finishing old business. Make sure not to start any significant new projects until you truly know which road you are going to take.

JANUARY

GO OUTSIDE YOUR COMFORT ZONE

A nurturing Cancer Full Moon in your 11th House of Groups and Friends on **January 3** activates your need to be with like-minded people during the first part of the month. You seek support from others, yet you may have concerns about how to safely express yourself within your group. Excitement during these first days of the year fills your head with far-out ideas as your key planet, Mercury, aligns with the Full Moon, the Sun, and erratic Uranus. This may stimulate an avalanche of brilliant thoughts that are too much and too fast, presenting you with the challenge of sorting through it all. This mental exercise sets the tone for the weeks ahead as the planets pile up in quirky Aquarius in your 6th House of Details, culminating just a couple of days after the self-contained Capricorn New Moon on **January 18**. At this time, you'll need to take notice of what brings you pleasure so that you can incorporate it into the busy days ahead.

The Aquarian parade begins when sensual Venus leaves reserved Capricorn and tempts you with uncommon delights on **January 3**. You may be somewhat hesitant to act on these desires, for they could be atypically unconventional. The cascade continues as mental Mercury zaps into futuristic Aquarius on **January 15** and the Sun joins the pack on **January 20**. Although this is an intellectually active phase, the emphasis on conceptual rather than practical thought can put you on edge. A long-lasting dynamic square between adventurous Jupiter and unpredictable Uranus on **January 22** affects you all month by enticing you to take risks you might otherwise let pass. Reach beyond your limits, but don't overextend or you could lose your balance.

> **KEEP IN MIND THIS MONTH**
>
> *Transform theory into practice any way you can. Having a great idea is not enough; you need to turn it into a useful action.*

KEY DATES

JANUARY 6-8 ★ *mental magic*

There are disagreements brewing, even if they aren't quite ready to surface yet. In the face of turbulence, you sincerely want to act on your highest principles as rational Mercury and the Sun form an intelligent biquintile with rulemaking Saturn. You can brilliantly think your way through a complex array of obstacles, but conceptual logic won't solve everything; you must also rely on your common sense.

Self-directed Mars harmoniously trines Saturn on **January 8**, giving you a firm foundation on which to build. Rely on your own practical and efficient manner to make progress.

SUPER NOVA DAYS
JANUARY 11-13 ★ *feel the power*
Your ruling planet, Mercury, is rather agitated now, intensifying an already awkward situation with a family member or romantic partner. Face your fear of being out of control, for you are riding an intense emotional wave as fiery Mars conjuncts passionate Pluto on **January 13**. You may not like the extreme emotions you are experiencing, feeling powerful and passionate one moment and then rationally detached the next. Although you might be desperate to find a middle ground where you can intellectually respond to the pressures, your resistance to your own feelings could be the greatest impediment to the breakthrough you need. Accept your own power and ride it like a surfer. It will be easier than trying to control the wave itself.

JANUARY 22 ★ *make it real*
You can turn sour grapes into sweet wine if you are willing to think about the potential gain instead of a failure in the present moment. Logically, you know that what's happening now is probably best for you, even though it may not feel great. If, for example, a beautiful romance has morphed into a more practical arrangement, the passion isn't necessarily gone. It's merely transforming into a more stable form of energy. Avoid the temptation to use this as an excuse to withdraw. Instead of building a relationship on fantasy, commit to making love real.

JANUARY 26-28 ★ *learning your lesson—again*
An all-too-familiar scene is replaying in your life as you build a beautiful fantasy when Mercury conjuncts dreamy Neptune on **January 26**, only to have your illusions crash to the ground when Mercury opposes stern Saturn on **January 28**. Last week, this sequence starred Venus and affected your pocketbook or your heart. This time around—with Mercury involved—it's more mental and could even affect your health. Take care of yourself by staying aware of what is happening. If you go into denial or even become too detached from your thoughts now, you're likely to get yourself into trouble.

FEBRUARY

DELAYED SATISFACTION

On **February 2**, the melodramatic Leo Full Moon in your 12th House of Endings brings opportunity for emotional and spiritual growth, but not without giving up something at work. You may have reached a temporary peak at your job, and now it's time to shift your attention to other matters. This month does have a few surprises in store for you, especially around **February 7**, as romantic Venus contacts wild Uranus in your 7th House of Partnerships. Someone could suddenly explode onto the scene, turning your heart inside out. Or perhaps a business associate makes you a bit crazy by refusing to be tied to a mutually agreed-upon schedule. Communication mogul Mercury is also in the neighborhood but turns retrograde on **February 13**, indicating that a deal you want to wrap up may not be completed as expected. Satisfaction may be delayed while you spend the remainder of the month working out the details and trying to negotiate a sensible arrangement. Part of your current dilemma is knowing when to trust your intuition versus your common sense.

The futuristic Aquarius New Moon on **February 17** marks a shift from dealing with practical issues to working with more conceptual ideas in your imagination. As the Sun enters emotionally sensitive Pisces on **February 18**, it draws closer to retrograde Mercury, activating all forms of communication. There can be problems stemming from misunderstandings with your spouse, coworkers, or friends, so pay attention to the meaning you ascribe to someone else's words. Meanwhile, beneath the surface of spoken or written words, a powerful opposition between serious Saturn and soulful Neptune weighs heavily as you face disappointment yet also can inspire you to reach beyond the limitations of your daily life.

> **KEEP IN MIND THIS MONTH**
>
> *Careful analysis of the facts can point you one way, but don't ignore your feelings, even if they indicate a different path.*

KEY DATES

FEBRUARY 2 ★ *to the edge of the imagination*
The demonstrative Leo Full Moon illuminates your need for recognition while Mercury stimulates your imagination as it enters the dreamy world of Pisces. This is a time of increased emotional sensitivity. You are more open to the thoughts and feelings of everyone around you now, but you might have a challenging time as you

attempt to integrate their fuzzy ideas into your practical perspective. Don't try to analyze everything ad infinitum. Instead, kick back and enjoy the trip into your fantasies without having a specific goal in mind.

SUPER NOVA DAYS
FEBRUARY 7-10 ★ *balance freedom with responsibility*
You are in a carnival funhouse, complete with moving floors and mirrors that distort reality. It starts when a close friend or lover surprises you with a sudden disclosure, yet you may enjoy the excitement once you get over your initial reaction. Your imagination overrides your common sense as the Sun joins illusory Neptune on **February 8**. You are likely to throw caution to the wind, overindulging your senses or spending beyond your budget. However, the messages are mixed, and it's difficult to know what to do. You're ready for fun one minute; the next, you are obsessively responsible. An uneasy feeling that you are missing the boat may wash over you, but in reality there is still time to get it right. Honor your spiritual and creative leanings, but don't skip out on your previous commitments or you will have serious trouble on your hands as the Sun opposes karmic Saturn on **February 10**.

FEBRUARY 19-21 ★ *embrace the darkness*
Four planets gather in mysterious Pisces, flooding your mind with fanciful images from deep in your subconscious. But sensual Venus dynamically squares intense Pluto on **February 19**, bringing hidden feelings into the open. Relationships become complex as erotic desires and neurotic fears mix within your imagination. Your lack of rationality scares you, but you cannot control your fantasies. Building intellectual dams does more damage than letting your emotions flow naturally. Embrace the shadow as part of yourself and watch the intensity settle back down.

FEBRUARY 27-28 ★ *loss of faith*
Retrograding Mercury backs into quirky Aquarius, increasing your concern about completing a project. But it's deeper than just meeting a deadline, for the ongoing opposition between stable Saturn and diffusive Neptune is exact on **February 28**. Even if you thought you could lean upon certain dependable institutions—such as a government agency or a medical service provider—they may not prove trustworthy. You could even doubt your own ability to choose wisely now. Avoid making any long-term decisions. Your confidence will return in the days ahead.

MARCH

RECLAIMING YOUR PURPOSE

Although you might be somewhat more relaxed this month than last, there may not be a lot of leisure time to enjoy your newfound composure. On **March 3**, a Full Moon Eclipse in level-headed Virgo opposite invigorating Uranus lights up your nervous system and releases you from any recent discouragement. You begin to realize that your planning days are over when analytical Mercury turns direct on **March 7**. It's time now to turn your thoughts into actions. Don't be afraid to start small, as Mercury is in your 6th House of Details until **March 17**.

This month is securely anchored by a very slow-moving and long-lasting trine between expansive Jupiter and contractive Saturn. Although this stabilizing aspect is exact on **March 16**, it sets the tone for all of March and lasts through the beginning of May. These two giant, gassy planets counterbalance each other and support you as they smoothly regulate the growth in your life. Gone now are any frantic feelings of urgency and the doom and gloom of depression. Presently, while you are self-assured, calmly assess where you are, where you want to go, and how you can best get there.

A second eclipse this month on **March 18**—this one a Solar Eclipse in your 7th House of Partnerships—is another opportunity to break free from the restrictions of the past. You won't necessarily have to end a relationship to stand up to someone else's control, but it is a last option. With all the forward movement, it may not be surprising that you have obstacles to overcome, especially around **March 22**, when feisty Mars runs into the walls of authoritative Saturn's rules. Slow down, but don't give up.

> **KEEP IN MIND THIS MONTH**
>
> *Don't let the satisfaction of small accomplishments lull you into a state of placidity. Instead, use your current gains as a foundation for future growth.*

KEY DATES

MARCH 3–5 ★ *sudden intervention*

The Full Moon Eclipse on **March 3** in Virgo brings a whirlwind of activity that temporarily overtakes your life. Your greatest assets are your sharply focused mind and analytical capabilities. But if you don't take care of business, you still may get zapped by unexpected lightning bolts of awareness as the Sun conjuncts maverick Uranus on **March 5**. If you are afraid of expressing your need to be free, someone may act out your unspoken desires, leaving you no choice but to react as best you can.

MARCH 8–9 ★ *pleasant company included*

Mercury just turned direct, and you may feel as if you are on your way to success. A couple of days of sweet indulgences, however, might distract you from your real work, for what you do now can have lasting value. Venus is harmonizing with the rock-solid Jupiter-Saturn trine, so it's important that you find a balance between enjoying yourself and doing meaningful work on the job or at home. Even if you are worried about inappropriate feelings, go ahead and express them anyhow. Sensual Venus holds the key to your current happiness; trust it and move sensibly toward that which attracts you. You are safely swimming in protected emotional waters now, so it's likely that a lovely encounter manifests as financially profitable or romantically delicious.

SUPER NOVA DAYS
MARCH 16–17 ★ *go for it*

Imaginary fears dissipate now as your confidence rises. The Jupiter-Saturn trine, exact on **March 16**, creates a graceful symmetry in your life, and it's up to you to put it to work. There's no need to hold back from taking a calculated risk. Within reason, your current actions will prove to be fortunate as long as you balance the potential benefits with the amount of work that will be required of you. This supportive aspect is exact again on **May 5**, so you will have time enough to proceed cautiously before making your final commitment. You are receiving additional strength from regenerative Pluto, so don't be afraid to rework old ideas into new ones or even start from scratch. Do your research thoroughly, and you will be well equipped to make the best choices now.

MARCH 20–22 ★ *pause to regroup*

You may face frustration as obstacles appear to thwart your advancement, but consciously reining in your own energies first can put you one step ahead of the game. If you blindly push forward, you might have to learn a lesson the hard way. Even if it feels like you're not accomplishing much at work, more progress is being made than you realize. Stay focused and you'll see the positive results next month.

APRIL

CONTINUING THE PROGRESS

April is another month of substantial progress for you, but it may not be apparent to everyone else. It's not necessarily about receiving a promotion or a raise—yet both are possible. The growth you experience now is a reflection of your inner dynamics as the powerful Jupiter-Saturn trine that began on **March 16** is brought back into play on its way toward culmination early next month. This is a great time to center yourself through spiritual disciplines such as yoga, meditation, and prayer while Saturn the Teacher is in your 12th House of Destiny. Additionally, you receive fantastic support from bountiful Jupiter in your 4th House of Security. It would benefit you to make positive changes in your private life by getting more involved with family activities or initiating projects to improve your residence. You might also consider a distance-learning course that you can take on the Internet. Around **April 8**, the Sun activates this trine, favoring you with the ability to clearly see the outcome of your current choices. Then, around **April 21**, when fast-thinking Mercury activates the same pattern, you will be able to confirm your recent decisions.

The ambivalent Libra Full Moon in your 2nd House of Possessions on **April 2** can point to financial problems, especially if you jointly hold property with a partner. Keep a cool and balanced approach to any issues that surface at this time, for it probably isn't advantageous to take significant action yet. The Aries New Moon in your 8th House of Intimacy on **April 17** can jump-start a new romance or rekindle an existing one. Its trine to emotionally transformative Pluto can stimulate a very intense sharing of feelings that deepens and strengthens any relationship.

KEEP IN MIND THIS MONTH

This is a truly powerful time in your life. Whatever you undertake now can have long-lasting consequences, so make your decisions carefully and act on them with great intent.

KEY DATES

APRIL 1-3 ★ *fast thinking*

It's not an April Fool's joke when warm Venus crosses paths with cold Saturn, making you feel rejected or excluded. But even with limited money or withheld affections, you can still turn bad fortune around quickly, as your key planet, Mercury, downloads brilliant Uranus into your 7th House of Partnerships. You are keenly aware of what's happening, and you can think your way through any challenging relationship situation. The Libra Full Moon on **April 2** may bring too much information about your emotions, but your mind is fast enough now to keep your head above water. Try a different approach by trusting your intuition, and you could discover new solutions to old problems.

SUPER NOVA DAYS
APRIL 9-10 ★ *keep it simple*
You may have to face familiar demons as Mercury squares shadowy Pluto on **April 9** before it charges into pioneering Aries, giving you a totally new mental framework on **April 10**. But even with this heady activity, it could be useful to set logic aside and act more spontaneously. The Sun now harmonizes with both beneficent Jupiter and austere Saturn. Jupiter tells you to let the cascade of images flow into awareness without applying your normal filtering activity. Simultaneously, Saturn requires you to be serious and to the point. Together, they inform you that you're on to something really big and that you must go public. Don't inflate your ideas now, for you will have greater impact by understating the benefits of your plan.

APRIL 20-21 ★ *get to the point*
This is the second time this month that the Jupiter-Saturn trine is supported by another planet; this time, it's your friend Mercury in the mix. It starts with Saturn demanding that you concentrate your attention on communicating your plan coherently. But it's possible for you to say too much when Mercury trines Jupiter on **April 21**. Unfortunately, you cannot pull the words out of the air and stuff them back into your mouth. If you do speak your mind too freely, you will probably be able to do sufficient damage control. Still, it's more efficient to think twice before you utter your next word.

APRIL 26-28 ★ *truth wins*
There may be power struggles going on close to home. If you pay attention, you can end up on top without a major battle. Remember that your strength is to pay attention to the little things, but not at the expense of the principles at stake. Voice your needs in a rational way that demonstrates your commitment to cooperation, as sparks could fly too easily. Maintain your integrity and the discussion will likely come around, surprising you with the results.

MAY

RIDE THE MENTAL ROLLER COASTER

Positive changes that began to materialize around **March 16** during a wave of stabilization may go through another level of evolution this month. Expressive Jupiter harmoniously trines suppressive Saturn on **May 5**, mixing just the right amount of common sense with your optimism. Projects you began during the past six weeks and the plans you made—especially during April—must now evolve or fall to the wayside. A separate long-term Jupiter aspect culminates on **May 10** as it squares unconventional Uranus. Although this might surprise you with unexpected events affecting your relationships and family interactions, it also opens previously closed doors. This is a thrilling time, but be careful about overestimating the potentials and underestimating the amount of work that will be required.

Your ruling planet, Mercury, is flying through the cosmos now at maximum speed and taking your thoughts along. The messenger planet enters its other home sign, Gemini, in your 10th House of Career on **May 11**, creating a flurry of mental activity throughout the rest of the month. You can make the most of this phase by actively sharing your ideas on the job, even if they are not as concrete as you normally prefer them to be.

The powerful Scorpio Full Moon in your 3rd House of Communication on **May 2** helps you talk about your feelings, even the most uncomfortable ones. The practical Taurus New Moon in your 9th House of Higher Learning on **May 16** could motivate you to enroll in a basic course that can bolster your career. A rare second Full Moon in enthusiastic Sagittarius in your 4th House of Roots on **May 31** bodes well for joyous gatherings at home with intimate friends or family.

KEEP IN MIND THIS MONTH

As you analyze opportunities that arrive at your door, pursue only the most significant ones. You could lose focus by spreading yourself too thin.

KEY DATES

MAY 5–7 ★ *a softer focus*

Overall, your life should be running smoothly as Jupiter and Saturn push and pull in sweet harmony, warming up your heart and gracing your life with good fortune. But Mercury is stirring up trouble as it first squares constrictive Saturn on **May 5** and then squares spaced-out Neptune on **May 7**. Saturn helps you pinpoint what's wrong, even if you cannot fix it. Your mind is like an out-of-focus camera, and the more adjustments you make, the fuzzier it gets as Neptune's influence spreads. As much as you want concrete solutions, you will be happier and more productive if you free yourself from rules and tap into the wellspring of your imagination.

MAY 13 ★ *inner transformation*
Forceful Mars in your 7th House of Partnerships is resisting the unpleasant intensity of a square from coercive Pluto. Someone may be pushing against you now, and it could feel like he or she is trying to undermine your best efforts. Look carefully at what's motivating you and what you've done to arouse such animosity. It's possible that unexpressed anger or resentment is driving you too hard. And although you may have to confront this person about what he or she is doing, it will be to your advantage to alter your own course, too. If you don't change your attitude, you won't be able to easily overcome the external resistance.

SUPER NOVA DAYS
MAY 20-21 ★ *moderate extreme thinking*
Quicksilver Mercury, now buzzing all around in fickle Gemini, activates the destabilizing Jupiter-Uranus square that was exact on **May 10**. This is a particularly tricky time as you juggle a variety of things that affect your home, relationships, and career. Information is streaming into your consciousness faster than you can categorize the data. Suddenly, in a stroke of brilliance, you see how to organize all of the little facts that you have been collecting. You may get totally hyped up on your own ideas, but this wave of confidence can cause you to gloss over important details and make errors in judgment. Taking a more conservative approach, however, can prevent you from falling off the edge of the map.

MAY 27 ★ *probing mind*
Your ruling planet, Mercury, is in a cosmic standoff today with Pluto, the lord of darkness. And although this may not sound good, Mercury is like a ferryman who goes back and forth into the shadows of the subconscious, retrieving hidden thoughts and expressing them in the real world. Let Mercury do its job now, even if this precipitates intense and uncomfortable communication. You will be better off when more of how you truly feel is in the open.

JUNE

EMOTIONAL CONNECTIONS STEADY YOUR COURSE

You jump into June with a great attitude and a burst of energy as forceful Mars harmonizes with optimistic Jupiter on **June 4** and attractive Venus dances into playful Leo on **June 5**. Although you may be stretched out to the max between commitments both at work and at home, you are ready to take on even more when necessary, especially if the possibility of fun is attached. Your career is emphasized through the middle of the month as both Mars and Saturn aim their attention on the Sun in your 10th House of Career. Even if you aren't employed, your status may climb, and others will look up to you as an inspiration. But all is not rosy this month, and the Gemini New Moon on **June 14** may be a turning point as it stands opposite powerful Pluto. Someone or something may be working against you, but you still have strong allies in Mars, Jupiter, and Neptune as long as you don't overestimate your ability to deliver on what you promise.

Your ruling planet, Mercury, turns retrograde in your 11th House of Groups and Friends on **June 15** and continues its backward movement until **July 9**. This is a great time to reevaluate your relationships with others and to clear up any misunderstandings that have developed in the past few weeks. How you handle communication snafus now can have great impact on your overall state of mind in the coming weeks. Serious Saturn reaches opposition to diffusive Neptune on **June 25**, but this slow-moving aspect can create problems all month. You may feel less certain about practical matters that you normally wouldn't question at all. Your possible discouragement may arise from circumstances that began to brew last summer and were revisited around **February 28**.

> ### KEEP IN MIND THIS MONTH
>
> *Listening carefully to others and remaining openhearted can help you create new visions to replace the ones that must be left behind.*

KEY DATES

JUNE 4–5 ★ *too much of a good thing*

It can be a challenge to know how much is too much now, for you are probably feeling more optimistic than usual as Jupiter trines Mars on **June 4** and opposes the Sun on **June 5**. Meanwhile, exacting Mercury tangles with indefinite Neptune, making it difficult to define your limits. Family members might have problems with your lack of boundaries as your overconfidence gets in the way of a clear perspective. Turn the volume down on all aspects of your life. It won't be any less fun, and it will help you in the long run.

SUPER NOVA DAYS
JUNE 11-15 ★ *no time for fantasy*
Your life may be operating smoothly now as the assertive energy of Mars harmonizes with the stabilizing principle of Saturn on **June 11**. Others watch you put your best foot forward as you walk steadily toward your goals. You are acting on higher principles, and everyone appreciates your intelligence and radiant grace. But don't plan on accomplishing all that you set your sights on, for distracting Neptune is floating around now, too, fueling your fantasies and softening your resolve on **June 13**. These are pleasant days, and you may be tempted to leave some commitments unfulfilled. Remember, however, that the New Moon on **June 14**, followed by Mercury turning retrograde on **June 15**, will not let you escape from your responsibilities. Whatever you don't do now is likely to resurface quickly.

JUNE 19-21 ★ *reveal complexity*
A lovely trine between Venus and Jupiter on **June 19** arouses your desires and is likely to bring you the sweet rewards of love or other sensual delights. But the beautiful feelings deepen now as physical Mars hooks up with passionate Pluto on **June 21**. Your emotions may become so intense that it's difficult to hold back the tide. It's important to find the right level of expression, for if you try to hide your needs, someone will notice anyhow. Revealing your innermost fears and desires can create a strong foundation for a new relationship or repair damage to an existing one.

JUNE 27-30 ★ *overflowing confusion*
The days leading up to the ambitious Capricorn Full Moon in your 5th House of Romance on **June 30** bring a variety of communication challenges. You may be trying to stabilize your love life, or you could be dealing with parenting issues. Either way, Mercury retrograde creates tension that arises from lack of clarity. You might be trying so hard to get it right that others become tangled in your words. Be concise and try not to say more than you must.

JULY

LESSONS IN SELF-DISCIPLINE

The month starts on a low note as sensual Venus joins restrictive Saturn on **July 1**. You may face relationship uncertainty, possibly even wondering if you'll ever receive the satisfaction you seek. But this month's lesson is about remaining true to your needs while having enough confidence to persevere for the long haul. Your determination may be tested when Mercury in cautious Cancer turns direct on **July 9**, aiming your thoughts, however tentatively, into the future. Your impatience is further aroused by the Sun's harmonious trine to freedom-loving Uranus on **July 10**. The sensitive Cancer New Moon in your 11th House of Dreams on **July 14** picks up confusing signals from Neptune, activating your fantasies and making you less sure of yourself. But this is no time to doubt the sensibility of your intentions. Accept the mental fog as a temporary weather condition, and rest assured that it will clear.

Venus enters discerning Virgo on **July 14**, raising specific issues of love and money. Investing in a makeover by coloring your hair or purchasing new clothing not only makes you feel great, but can also stimulate someone's interest in you. Don't expect too much to change quickly, as Venus is slowing down and preparing to turn retrograde on **July 27**. Persistence will be rewarded eventually, but you may deal with recurring bouts of loneliness or low self-esteem now and over the coming months.

> **KEEP IN MIND THIS MONTH**
>
> *Prepare and wait, for thinking of all of the possibilities ahead can be both exciting and frustrating. It's not yet time to put your best ideas into action.*

The Aquarius Full Moon in your 6th House of Health on **July 29** can overwhelm you with choices about your diet and daily routines. As tempted as you may be to do something crazy for quick results, self-restraint and self-respect are the greatest gifts you can give yourself at this time.

KEY DATES

JULY 1 ★ *delayed pleasure*

Mental Mercury receives creative juice from Mars today, giving you the power to put your ideas into motion. Meanwhile, stylish Venus meets up with authoritative Saturn, reminding you of your social obligations. You'll need to follow through with your commitments, even if you'd rather do something more exhilarating. Don't expect to have much fun now, for this aspect can delay gratification. Accept the seriousness of the current circumstances so that you can get on with the better times just around the corner.

SUPER NOVA DAYS
JULY 8-10 ★ *high emotional IQ*
Provocative Venus harmoniously trines powerful Pluto on **July 8**, setting the stage for deep emotional transformation. You are not afraid to step into the shadowy realms of your suppressed desires. Additionally, the Sun trines shocking Uranus on **July 10**, sharpening your intellect and allowing you to express yourself with originality. In the midst of this, Mercury turns direct, encouraging you to move forward. With these conflicting signals, it's tough to decide exactly what actions are the most sensible. Rely on your instincts, but remember that it's not necessary to act on every hunch.

JULY 22-24 ★ *no direction home*
The Sun enters Leo on **July 22**, lighting up your 12th House of Spirituality. This can activate your fantasies, making you somewhat uneasy, for you prefer concise thinking to the diffusive wanderings of your imagination. It's hard to get a clear fix on the truth now; whatever you think is real can change from moment to moment. Mars dynamically squares spacey Neptune on **July 24**, distracting you with an easy escape route—something you rarely take. Your nervous energy can get the best of you as your thoughts run all over the map, without direction or purpose. Even if you have work to do, make time to meditate, listen to music, or get out to enjoy nature. Your sharp analytical skills will return soon enough.

JULY 31 ★ *don't give up*
Mars, the planet of hot, crosses swords today with Saturn, the planet of cold. You are eager to swing into action, yet reality says not yet. The frustration may be unbearable as you reach the end of your rope. It feels as if there's nowhere left to go and nothing left to try. But all is not lost. In fact, although you may be irked by the resistance you are facing, at least you know what's going on. This is a vast improvement over last week, when you were still in the dark. Remember that even the most brilliant concepts must prove themselves worthy. Don't get discouraged; just improve your ideas and then try again.

AUGUST

CLEAN UP AND CLEAN OUT

Profound changes at home and on the job this month are grounded by a long-lasting harmonious trine between reliable Saturn and transformative Pluto on **August 6**. Still, this doesn't diminish the gravity of the upcoming shift. Saturn has been in Leo in your 12th House of Endings since July 2005, forcing you to cut your losses and eliminate nonessential activities. Now, as Saturn receives a power boost from Pluto, you must act with swift determination—for time really is running out. This may not be simple, because your ability to concentrate will be tested by a variety of distractions at work that seem only to get louder, building to a crescendo as energetic Mars in your 10th House of Career opposes bigger-than-life Jupiter on **August 23**. However, when Saturn enters Virgo on **September 2**, you will lose the luxury of being able to plan your future. Instead, you'll be required to live it.

Venus is retrograde in practical Virgo, backing into dramatic Leo on **August 8** and joining restrictive Saturn on **August 13**, delaying personal gratification and perhaps limiting the availability of money. The seriousness of these times is emphasized when ponderous Mercury conjuncts Saturn on **August 18** and the Sun joins Saturn on **August 21**. All of this activity, along with the Leo New Moon on **August 12**, occurs in your not-so-public 12th House, keeping you out of the spotlight. Thoughtful Mercury returns to your sign on **August 19**, as does the Sun on **August 23**, so now you can depend on your innate razor-sharp analysis to figure out what to do. A Pisces Full Moon Eclipse on **August 28** marks the end of one phase and the initiation of a whole new direction to your life.

> ### KEEP IN MIND THIS MONTH
>
> *Stay on top of what's important while finishing old projects. Tie up loose ends while you can.*

KEY DATES

AUGUST 4 ★ *better left unsaid*

Your ruling planet, Mercury, enters dramatic Leo while moving into your 12th House of Secrets, where it remains through **August 19**. You are more likely now to take pride in what you say, for you want to impress others with your creativity and with the substance of your thoughts. Yet there are private spiritual or religious issues that prevent you from sharing too much. Don't let this become a burden. Instead, use your discretion when deciding what you can share.

AUGUST 9 ★ *talk fast; think later*
Mercury harmonizes with far-reaching Jupiter, carrying your thoughts beyond their usual orbits and making you less practical and more philosophical. Normally, you are pretty careful about what you say, but you are tempted to throw caution to the wind and express feelings that you might otherwise keep to yourself. Tomorrow may be a bit more embarrassing when you must acknowledge what you said in anticipation of immediate gratification.

SUPER NOVA DAYS
AUGUST 14–18 ★ *through the looking glass*
Your imagination is highly active as Mercury contacts five planets from your spiritual 12th House. On **August 14**, Mercury opposes spacey Neptune, placing reality slightly out of reach. You may be less discriminating than usual as images float across the movie screen of your inner mind. Mercury and Venus conjunct the Sun and trine dark Pluto over the next few days, touching deep memories and activating intense desires. Trust the process, even if you have to leave data untouched. Life may get overly serious by **August 18** as Mercury conjuncts authoritative Saturn. It might seem easier to shut down, but denial will cause much greater problems later on.

AUGUST 23–25 ★ *overreaction creates conflict*
A highly charged opposition between energetic Mars and overoptimistic Jupiter is stressed by analytical Mercury, encouraging you to think and talk big. Social activities may pull you out of your comfort zone, but suppressed anger could make you overly ready to defend yourself against someone's challenging words. Your too-swift reaction may be overstated. As confusing Neptune contacts sweet Venus on **August 25**, keep reminding yourself that making love is really more fun than making war. Avoid getting involved in a needless confrontation.

AUGUST 28 ★ *shock and awe*
Today's Pisces Full Moon Eclipse can turn your world upside down, as your planet, Mercury, is electrified by Uranus. The lightning creates brilliant flashes in your brain, and it may take a lot of energy just to keep up with your own thoughts. Catch the best ones in your net of consciousness, but let the crazy ones slip away. Forget about mundane mental tasks for now; just go wherever your mind takes you. You'll land safely back on Earth tomorrow.

SEPTEMBER

MAKE IT REAL AND MAKE IT LAST

On **September 2**, Saturn enters logical Virgo, seriously impacting your world for the next couple of years. You may not feel the weight immediately, but something is different now and you know it. Your preparation phase is complete; it's time to make major decisions that can affect the course of your life. You get what you deserve; if you have been diligent at work, you can begin harvesting the fruits of your labors. But Saturn will also show you where you've been slacking, whether on the job or at home. Accept additional responsibilities relating to current projects, but avoid new obligations that distract you from your primary purpose. If you haven't been taking care of yourself physically or emotionally, Saturn may require that you make significant and healthy changes in your lifestyle.

September isn't only about hard work; it also delivers on the social front. Your ruling planet, Mercury, enters companionable Libra on **September 5**, and amicable Venus in playful Leo turns direct on **September 8**—both planets adding zest to your love life. Additionally, a Solar Eclipse on **September 11** in your sign can force you to pay close attention to personal issues that you have been avoiding. This New Moon in analytical Virgo is in a tense opposition to Uranus the Awakener in your 7th House of Partnerships. An eccentric friend or lover may have a surprise in store that opens your mind to a new way of relating. On **September 21**, Venus and Mars are each involved in an opposition, again emphasizing your need to interact with others to learn more about yourself. The Aries Full Moon on **September 26** fuels your confidence, so explore your romantic options while you have both the energy and the interest.

> **KEEP IN MIND THIS MONTH**
>
> *Focus your efforts like a laser beam, concentrating your energy instead of scattering it. State your intentions, and then apply your best efforts toward reaching your goals.*

KEY DATES

SEPTEMBER 2–3 ★ *temporary dark clouds*

Your thoughts can fall deep into the underworld as mental Mercury squares off with dark Pluto. Be ready to discover new meaning in your life from your own personal mythic quest into the subconscious realms. Simultaneously, assertive Mars squares erratic Uranus, crossing enough high-frequency wires that you could experience a short circuit if you don't monitor your hair-trigger reactions.

Remember that your passions are obsessively strong now, yet you will be better off for having taken the journey into the darkness.

SUPER NOVA DAYS
SEPTEMBER 8-11 ★ *beyond logic*
These intense days culminate in a Virgo Solar Eclipse that rattles your world. The lights of awareness are suddenly shining on critical relationship issues, and with freedom-loving Uranus in the picture, you must be willing to break through anything that keeps you from your highest purpose. Whatever makes you feel tense needs to be brought to the surface, where you can deal with it in the open. Additionally, forceful Mars trines spiritual Neptune, so rational analysis may not be useful. Don't get trapped by the binds of logic. Dance, sing, or meditate—anything to activate your imagination. This may make you a bit nervous, but you'll have to trust the truth that exists beyond words.

SEPTEMBER 18-21 ★ *dream or reality?*
A challenging opposition between pushy Mars and obstinate Pluto can set up a no-win situation unless you are willing to back away from the heat of conflict. Retreat may not be simple, but you can play the mystery card now by keeping a secret, even if it seems as though you are telling all. The problem is accentuated by a second opposition—this one between sweet Venus and diffusive Neptune—making it impossible for you to see things as they truly are. With clever Mercury releasing the pressure, your idealism can get in the way of a sensible solution. Dreaming about a lovely outcome is one thing, but keep your feet firmly on the ground. The answer is not somewhere over the rainbow; it's right in front of you.

SEPTEMBER 26-28 ★ *make a difference*
The Aries Full Moon in your 8th House of Transformation on **September 26** is a signal for dramatic changes that are ready to take place. Your life is about to shift into more emotional realms, but as Mercury harmonizes with assertive Mars, everything you say now can have more impact than you realize. It doesn't even matter whom you talk to; you can make a difference. You may act more outgoing now, but will mellow as Mercury enters emotional Scorpio on **September 27** and Mars enters sensitive Cancer on **September 28**.

OCTOBER

TWO STEPS FORWARD, ONE STEP BACK

This month begins with a positive acknowledgment of your past hard work. The emotional landscape warms up even more as sweet Venus enters your sign on **October 8**, attracting friends or lovers—as long as they meet your stringent requirements. Although you might not normally take risks, a powerful repeat performance of the exciting Jupiter-Uranus square—previously on **January 22** and **May 10**—encourages you to take a chance now. This energizing aspect, exact on **October 9**, can have you buzzing for days.

The exciting edge, however, is tempered by two planetary events around the socially active Libra New Moon on **October 11**. First, on the same day, Mercury the Winged Messenger, still in passionate Scorpio, stops in its tracks to begin a bothersome retrograde that lasts through the rest of the month. During this time, you could find yourself reconsidering a commitment, rescheduling a trip, or redoing work you thought was completed. Then, loving Venus meets authoritative Saturn on **October 13**, possibly throwing cold water onto a developing romance or business deal. Either way, you must reevaluate the situation before going forward.

By mid-month, a series of supportive Mercury aspects finds you capable of communicating what you learned from the recent Venus-Saturn conjunction.

Don't worry if you aren't accomplishing as much as you wish. Remember that Mercury is still retrograde, and you may be forced to bide your time while preparing for the real gains next month. The practical Taurus Full Moon that falls in your 9th House of Higher Education on **October 26** suggests that you could improve your work prospects by taking a class or attending a job-related seminar.

> **KEEP IN MIND THIS MONTH**
>
> *Follow your emotional compass if you are on unfamiliar ground. Take a chance with a personal or business relationship; even if it doesn't last, you'll still gain from the encounter.*

KEY DATES

OCTOBER 1 ★ *plan for the future*
Your logic is sound enough to build a foundation for the rest of the year as steady Saturn supports clever Mercury. Take advantage of your coherent thoughts by writing them down or sharing them with others. Although these days may be

relatively free of conflict, it's no time to get lazy. Apply yourself wholeheartedly, and you'll have an easier time bypassing any obstacles later in the month.

OCTOBER 8 ★ *make a list and check it twice*

Charming Venus enters picky Virgo, remaining there until **November 8**, marking a time to make a list of your goals with respect to love and intimate relationships. Ask yourself the tough questions now about what you desire, and make a plan to get it. Energetic Mars is sextile to rock-solid Saturn, so trust your mental powers of reasoning and discrimination. Push for what you want now. But an annoying quincunx between quirky Uranus and the Sun can trash your best-laid plans. Don't throw in the towel too quickly, or you will lose before you even begin.

OCTOBER 13 ★ *no escape*

Practical issues rule your world with a Libra New Moon falling in your materialistic 2nd House of Possessions. You may be pressured to make a commitment as Venus conjuncts rulemaking Saturn. It feels as if you are being coerced and there's no way out. With escape artist Neptune also in the picture, you may be tempted by your own fantasies. Use your creative vision to imagine a more fulfilling future, but don't try to sidestep the present dilemma.

SUPER NOVA DAYS
OCTOBER 16-19 ★ *supported in all that you do*

These are effortless days, confirming that you are on the right path. Solutions are within reach as Mercury harmoniously trines Mars. What you couldn't say just days ago can float right to the surface and be expressed without the layers of guilt that have plagued you. You are playing on an emotional field, but with Mercury sextile to no-nonsense Saturn, you can still think clearly and engage in open discussion about whatever is needed, including your feelings.

OCTOBER 27-29 ★ *set logic aside*

You normally know your limits and color within the lines, but a wildly positive Venus-Jupiter square washes over you, transforming your normally cool and collected demeanor into blind optimism. Don't count your chickens yet; there are many factors to consider before you reach your goals. Still, this may not be the best time to use analysis and logic. Sometimes, when the music moves you, you just have to dance.

NOVEMBER

BUILDING MOMENTUM

There's an odd push/pull influence this month that has you making exciting plans during the first part of the month and then canceling them later as you get cold feet. Mercury's considerable influence in your life places your thoughts on the future and quickens the pace throughout the month. The action begins right away as quicksilver Mercury turns direct on **November 1** in creative Libra and then enters magnetic Scorpio on **November 10,** leaving you with deep thinking to do as you plan for the coming winter. Meanwhile, the undertow is building in intensity as normally assertive Mars—now slowly crawling along in passive Cancer—reverses direction on **November 15.** You know what you want, but you may have trouble reaching your goals. Intellectually, you race ahead, but your ideas are not easily translated into successful action.

Active Mars and surprising Uranus—both in emotional water signs—are locked in a harmonious trine all month that never quite culminates. You crave stability but may not be able to tame your erratic feelings. You are constantly tempted to agitate the status quo and step beyond your normal boundaries. Turn up your passion and take a risk when this expressive trine is stimulated by both the Sun on **November 4 to 9** and by Mercury on **November 19 to 21.** The intense Scorpio New Moon in your 3rd House of Communication on **November 9** can portend an over-the-top weekend schedule where you take on too many activities yet somehow manage to do it all. A disorganized Gemini Full Moon in your 10th House of Public Status on **November 24** can suggest uncertainty as to your career goals, especially since nebulous Neptune is squaring Mercury. Work hard at what you are doing, even if your heart isn't always in it.

KEEP IN MIND THIS MONTH

Leading with your heart can be frightening, for you value facts over emotions. Now, however, it's time to turn the tables and develop faith in the wisdom of your feelings.

KEY DATES

NOVEMBER 4-7 ★ *negative feelings stir positive changes*
The Sun harmonizes with Mars in your 11th House of Groups and Friends on **November 4** and then with wild Uranus on **November 7** in your 7th House of Partnerships. It may seem as if the emphasis isn't on you alone but mainly on your relationships, which is refreshing these days. But in the midst of these two fun

aspects, sexy Venus squares passionate Pluto on **November 5**, stirring up feelings of jealousy or control. It may suddenly feel as if you are fighting for survival, but the stress can motivate you to make much-needed changes. Don't waste time defending your territory or trying to hold on to the past.

NOVEMBER 15-16 ★ *conserve energy*
These may be a couple of frustrating days as assertive Mars turns retrograde in emotional Cancer. There is a certain security to be gained over the next couple of months with this backtracking, yet it may be somewhat discouraging. Additionally, your ideas don't flow as quickly now, as Mercury is restrained by the authority planet, Saturn. It's tough to make much progress now, so you might as well accept the flow of events as they happen instead of trying to go against the grain. Save your energy for next week, when you'll really need it.

SUPER NOVA DAYS
NOVEMBER 19-21 ★ *impatient brilliance*
Your life lights up like a sky filled with celebratory fireworks as probing Mercury in Scorpio completes a grand trine with energetic Mars and explosive Uranus. Although you may have trouble sleeping because your mind is wired, you'll be able to figure out how to get what you want. But your impatience can create problems, too, because others won't be able to keep up with your fast pace and you may be willing to quickly tell them of their failures. Watch your temper; a lovers' quarrel could turn ugly if you aren't willing to give a little. However, sweet love can be an unexpected reward for resolving a sticky issue.

NOVEMBER 24-26 ★ *fantasy time*
The chatty Gemini Full Moon on **November 24** can make it difficult for you to get much accomplished during this long holiday weekend as fuzzy Neptune's square to mental Mercury throws your perceptions out of focus, while its trine to sensual Venus allows you to view the world through rose-colored glasses. You can easily gloss over important details or be deceived by your misinterpretation of the facts. Your dreams can, however, tell you something significant about your future. Remember that you may not know exactly what's happening, but you can at least enjoy the illusions.

DECEMBER

TAKE YOUR CELEBRATIONS SERIOUSLY

An active holiday month is kick-started by your planet, Mercury, entering fun-loving Sagittarius on **December 1**, where it joins the Sun, Jupiter, and Pluto. This comic gathering occurs in your 4th House of Home and Family, which suggests an emphasis on domestic activities. The inspiring Sagittarius New Moon on **December 9** reaffirms the emotionally nurturing 4th House emphasis in time for holiday preparations. It also indicates a bit of unexpected turbulence from a square to Uranus, so fasten your seat belt and enjoy the homespun adventure as it unfolds. Fortunately, from **December 8 to 12**, a series of stabilizing aspects to Saturn allows you to maintain control and still join in the fun.

A once-every-thirteen-years conjunction between philosophical Jupiter and mysterious Pluto on **December 11** is the planetary highlight of the month. This can magnify your greatest dreams for success but can also arouse fears of the unknown. Let yourself be guided by a desire for abundance without getting lost in the details of planning. On **December 18**, joyous Jupiter begins an exodus from easygoing Sagittarius and moves into calculating Capricorn. Mercury and the Sun follow Jupiter into your 5th House of Play on **December 20 and 21**, respectively, favoring you with a keen sense of organization—especially when celebrations are involved. On **December 23**, the emotionally charged Cancer Full Moon has energetic Mars pressing you to take charge of a group—perhaps a team of coworkers or your friends and family. And with Mars' powerful opposition to Jupiter on **December 26**, you might just overextend your energy and take on more than you can handle. This is a perfect time to reconnect with your Virgoan need for simple perfection in order to balance your current desire to reach beyond your limits.

> **KEEP IN MIND THIS MONTH**
>
> *Prevent unnecessary stress by moderating your enthusiasm. You can still have a fantastic holiday season with your feet planted firmly on the ground.*

KEY DATES

DECEMBER 6 ★ *back to the drawing board*

Your planet, Mercury, is forming a tense square with Saturn the Tester and an irritating quincunx with Mars the Energizer. You are likely to feel resistance to what you say, which can make you rethink your current position on an important family issue. But the disapproval doesn't need to come from the outside, for you may well be your own harshest critic now. Although your ideas may be carefully thought out, you still could be hesitant to share them because you are afraid of rejection. If you do run into problems, don't get discouraged; take it as a sign that you still have more work to do.

SUPER NOVA DAYS
DECEMBER 10-13 ★ *courage to change*
The long-lasting Jupiter-Pluto conjunction on **December 11** sets the tone for these days, creating powerful waves of evolutionary transformation. You are quite resourceful; don't be afraid to commit to lofty goals. A hyper Mercury-Uranus square on **December 10** issues a storm warning as hurricane-force mental winds blow through your mind. You feel the rush of adrenaline as you begin your high-wire act without the safety net of all of your facts and figures. But support arrives through a series of fortunate sextiles and a wonderful trine between Venus and Mars. Even if you don't think you need one, a knight in shining armor may offer assistance. You can be your own saving grace, but either way, this transit favors relationships. The planetary pressures drive you into deeper emotional realms where fear can get in your way, yet your courage assures your successful journey into new and uncharted regions of the mysteries of life, love, and loss.

DECEMBER 18-20 ★ *cautious confidence*
Your enthusiasm will be modified over the months ahead by a wave of cautious realism, beginning on **December 18** as idealistic Jupiter enters conservative Capricorn. Your feelings become the source of a difficult situation as Mercury joins passionate Pluto on **December 19**. It's as if your heart won't cooperate with the finely tuned logic that you prefer to use to run your life, but your emotions don't follow orders from your rational mind. Then suddenly everything seems better on **December 20**, when Mercury enters ambitious Capricorn and conjuncts fortunate Jupiter. Within limits, careful planning can produce whatever results you desire.

DECEMBER 25-26 ★ *a balancing act*
You could act like Scrooge one moment and feel like a philanthropist the next as Mercury harmonizes with somber Saturn while Mars activates joyful Jupiter. Seek that elusive middle ground where you can be serious even as you enjoy the party. Give yourself permission to have fun, but don't forget about your obligations.

LIBRA

SEPTEMBER 23–OCTOBER 22

LIBRA OVERVIEW

You're the peacemaker, the diplomat who tries to keep everyone happy, but that might be a tough role to play this year. **You might want to get out of the line of fire and let opposing parties settle their own issues.** Unless you're in a position of responsibility where harmony is required to get a job done—or to keep your sanity—some breaks from the battlefield of human relations can do you a lot of good. There are four eclipses this year; two of them fall in your behind-the-scenes 12th House of Privacy and two in your nose-to-the-grindstone 6th House of Work and Service. These suggest that you could use more time to yourself, as the demands of work may be heavier than normal. Usually, you're so responsive to others that solitude can be the remedy for an overdose of discussions, negotiations, and endless bargaining with people. **This isn't about running away from reality; it's about finding enough peace and quiet to hear your own thoughts without interruption.**

Your ruling planet, Venus, is retrograde from July 27 until September 8, a period of revisiting old relationships. The reverse cycle of the partnership planet can pull you back into a group you thought you had left behind or return someone from your past to your present-day life. Whether this feels like a second chance to get it right or a rerun of a show you didn't like the first time, **standing up strongly for your own values is the surest way to achieve a better outcome**.

Serious Saturn is spending the first eight months of the year in your 11th House of Groups and Friends. Saturn's presence here demands that you be clear about expectations of others if you want to avoid disappointment with pals or as a member of a team. **It's time to be a leader and play a more active role in directing events socially or on the job.** You gain a higher level of respect when you state your goals, make a plan, and stick to it. There's a shift on September 2 when Saturn enters modest Virgo and your 12th House of Privacy. Your proudest achievements may not be widely seen or recognized, but you can gain great satisfaction by assisting those in need and by furthering your spiritual development. You won't become invisible during this period, but an inner sense of purpose and dedication can be so rewarding that the approval of others will become less important to you.

Lucky Jupiter in Sagittarius is shining brightly in your 3rd House of Communication, making this an excellent year to get your messages across with more power and pizzazz. You should be able to express more passion when you speak, as yours is a voice that will be heard. When you believe in something, your ability to sell it rises considerably. This house is also associated with learning, so expect to be quicker to pick up information and ideas now. Broaden your mind with new fields of interest, and you will grow into a more multifaceted and intriguing individual.

 ### THE END OF ILLUSION

Idealistic Neptune, in the midst of a long, slow transit of your 5th House of Love, is opposed by no-nonsense Saturn in late February and late June. If you're living in a romantic fantasy world, the ringed planet will most likely bring you back down to earth. Hopes and dreams are fine; they're necessary nourishment for your heart. Yet chasing rainbows can keep you turning in circles with no place to land. The end of illusion might come in the form of a reluctant lover, a less than committed partner, or the realization that the object of your affection is not the person you thought. On the plus side, this is a time when you can be more direct about what you want from others. You might not be able to have the "perfect" mate, but Saturn helps you realize that you have the power to take a more active role in shaping your future.

 ### SHOWCASE YOUR SKILLS

Tooting your own horn may not be your favorite thing to do, but it should boost your professional life significantly this year. Outspoken Jupiter in the communication zone of your chart says that this is no time to be shy. It's all about selling, yet that doesn't mean selling out. Just be a little prouder and louder than usual, but only if you've got the goods to back up the gab. If you don't feel secure enough to promote yourself more actively, get the help of a friend or colleague who can give you some coaching. You don't need to come across as pompous or a know-it-all; confidence and enthusiasm will carry the day. Take some risks to speak out—not to make noise or just to be noticed, but when you have something important to say. Eclipses in your 6th House of Work in March and August could show that you need to learn new skills to advance yourself or to find a totally different field of employment.

 ## SLOWER IS SMARTER

Think long-term when it comes to money this year. Investing in property and projects that can take months or years to pay off is wiser than spending your cash on the vacation of a lifetime. Definitely avoid get-rich-quick schemes that are more likely to diminish your savings than put you in a higher tax bracket. Aggressive Mars in your 8th House of Shared Resources from June 24 to August 8 may attract individuals who pressure you to join them in a business venture, but don't rush your decision. The right partner will be patient and prudent. When Venus, the planet of values, is retrograde from July 27 to September 8, you may need to straighten out unfinished financial business.

 ## LET GO TO GET MORE

Major changes in diet and daily habit are highly recommended this year. Two eclipses in your 6th House of Health—one in March and one in August—are not causes for alarm, but signals that you can significantly upgrade your energy level by making adjustments to your lifestyle. The Solar Eclipse on March 18 is in a formidable square with transformational Pluto. This is the planet of "addition by subtraction" that rewards letting go. Cutting out one unhealthy substance or a pattern of negative thinking can pay off in big ways. A key to making this work is to remember that this is a gift to yourself and those who love you. Any short-term sense of deprivation is a small price to pay in comparison to the vitality you will gain in return. And if you fall off the wagon, don't be too harsh with yourself; guilt is a lousy long-term motivator. Just gently remind yourself that your well-being is worth the effort, and start all over again.

 ## MAKING MAGIC

Use your highly developed sense of style to transform your home into an inspirational place this year. Creative decorating can make a studio apartment in Winnipeg feel like a beach in Tahiti. Creating a space for spiritual activities such as prayer and meditation is another way to transform your environment. Harmony within the household is especially important now, which also means being gentle with the dreams of those who share your home. There's a delicate balance between the ideal and the real that will require all of your diplomatic skills to navigate. Expressing practical concerns about others' projects or plans without discouraging them may be essential for the peace you seek.

JOURNEY OF THE MIND

Professor Jupiter's transit in your 3rd House of Learning makes it easy for you to grasp new languages this year. Your vocabulary and comprehension should expand quickly, whether you are studying a foreign tongue or technical jargon. Save money on travel plans now, since exotic adventures may be found close to home. There are undiscovered treasures not far from where you live that should be every bit as fascinating as a trip around the world.

NEW TOOLS FOR ENLIGHTENMENT

A pair of eclipses in your 12th House of Spirituality is likely to alter the way you experience your faith and view your dreams this year. If you encounter a loss of connection with your source of inspiration, don't surrender. There are new methods that can take you to an even higher level of awareness. Specific practices and techniques to align your consciousness may seem complicated and strange at first, but a disciplined approach will produce divine results.

RICK & JEFF'S TIP FOR THE YEAR:
Be the Boss

When you are in a position of responsibility this year, make sure that you have the authority to carry out the task at hand. The burden of leadership can be uncomfortably heavy if you don't have a clear sense of the power you hold. In order to be a successful leader, you need to follow your heart first. Listening to others is fine, of course, but you needn't be democratic in the group process. You're not in a popularity contest when you have obligations that involve other people. Be kind, but be firm for the good of the team and the sake of the goal.

JANUARY

HOME VERSUS CAREER

The balance between your personal and professional lives is likely to be a major issue at the start of the year. The Full Moon in domestic Cancer on **January 3** is in a tense opposition between the Sun in your 10th House of Career and the Moon in your 4th House of Family. Finding a way to meet your public responsibilities and your personal needs can be a challenge. Fortunately, inventive Uranus forms a creative trine to the Full Moon, which reveals unexpected ways to bridge this gap. Perhaps you can meet your spouse or child for lunch, or work at home to spend more time with those you love. Another favorable trine between active Mars and organized Saturn on **January 8** could spur ideas about teamwork or job sharing that make you more efficient.

Mars entering your 10th House on **January 16** is another signal that you may need to put in more effort to keep pace with the demands of your job. But then the New Moon in dedicated Capricorn on **January 18** can reveal a unique approach for taking care of business that could even lead to an eventual change of profession. New duties and ambitions require careful management of your time and energy.

Expansive Jupiter forms the first of three tense squares with wild and crazy Uranus on **January 22**. Restless feelings can make it hard to concentrate on current tasks during the latter part of the month. Your mind can leap to faraway places and far-out ideas. Most are distractions, but at least one could ignite a plan for radical change that may grow into a blazing fire when this same aspect returns in May and October.

> **KEEP IN MIND THIS MONTH**
>
> *Take time for yourself. It's important to step back from the hectic pace to avoid exhaustion.*

KEY DATES

JANUARY 1–3 ★ *start the year with a buzz*
You could be feeling a little restless on New Year's Day as your ruling planet, Venus, forms a tough 45-degree angle with electric Uranus. On the plus side, it's a chance to wake up a relationship that's grown stale and discover a new form of fun. On **January 3**, Charming Venus encourages a stylish new look and attitude, adding joy to this work-heavy month as the planet enters your 5th House of Romance and Self-Expression.

SUPER NOVA DAYS
JANUARY 12-14 ★ *take it to the limit*
This is a very passionate weekend as sensual Venus dances deliciously with "more is better" Jupiter on **January 12**. This romantically expansive pair is matched with a feverish conjunction of assertive Mars and powerful Pluto on **January 13**. Venus makes aspects to both of these bad boys on **January 14** to bring the level of intensity even higher. There's no gray zone about feelings now; it's a high-contrast world of emotional extremes that leaves little doubt about where you stand.

JANUARY 18-20 ★ *caught in a dream*
A conjunction between sweet Venus and spiritual Neptune on **January 18** heightens your innate sensitivity in relationships. Your boundaries are wide open, allowing attraction to take you more easily but also letting criticism hit you harder than usual. You may be inspired by your dreams of love, but a reality check is recommended to keep you from spending your heart or money foolishly. The Sun enters your 5th House of Love and Creativity on **January 20**, lifting your confidence and enabling you to make a lasting impression on others.

JANUARY 22-23 ★ *know what you want*
An opposition between Venus and no-nonsense Saturn on **January 22** feeds you a strong dose of reality. But this can stabilize your position in a personal or professional connection if you can approach it in a down-to-earth way. When you're clear about your goals, the chances of success are much higher now. If you encounter resistance, a clever quintile between generous Jupiter and Venus on **January 23** stirs your intuition and creates a way around any obstacle.

JANUARY 26-27 ★ *desire empowers you*
Your key planet, Venus, slides into a highly efficient sextile with masterful Pluto on **January 26** and then enters intuitive Pisces on **January 27**. You'll know exactly where to apply pressure to get what you want from others. This subtly powerful aspect may also save you from a loss by repairing a partnership or escaping from a potentially costly situation. Desire opens your awareness and shows you how to make your next move. Trust the feeling in your gut, even when logic tells you that the odds are against you.

FEBRUARY

BALANCING COLLECTIVE NEEDS AND PERSONAL DESIRES

Friends and lovers could be your theme as the second of three oppositions—the first occurred on **August 31, 2006**—between earnest Saturn and dreamy Neptune falls in your 5th House of Romance and your 11th House of Pals on **February 28**. But the Sun's aspects to these planets on **February 8 and 10** can trigger their influence in advance. Idealistic plans can be stifled by uncooperative colleagues or churlish chums who put practical matters first. It's up to you to either show them a way to overcome their doubts or simply ignore their objections. Group demands can get in the way of your blissful visions of love or creative fantasy. Conscientious management is required to make time in your busy schedule to address both of these collective needs as well as your personal desires. The Full Moon in dramatic Leo on **February 2** and the New Moon in detached Aquarius on **February 17** involve both Saturn and Neptune, so a balancing act between the ideal and the real is likely to remain a consistent issue throughout the month.

On **February 13**, Mercury, the information planet, turns retrograde in your 6th House of Health and Work, a three-week period when carelessness with small details can produce big complications. Be extra alert on the job to avoid errors associated with miscommunication by double-checking important messages and data. Watch out for the quality of what you eat and drink, as your system might be more susceptible to upset now.

KEEP IN MIND THIS MONTH

Don't let others' seriousness get in the way of your need to play. Creating joy for yourself is essential.

On **February 25**, impulsive Mars goes into Aquarius and stimulates your fun-filled 5th House. This passionate planet encourages saucy behavior and a playful, flirtatious attitude through the first week of April. Participating in extreme sports, enjoying an unconventional nightlife, and exhibiting originality in appearance are all possibilities.

KEY DATES

SUPER NOVA DAYS
FEBRUARY 7–9 ★ *over the top*
Your energy is electric with a conjunction between alluring Venus and eccentric Uranus on **February 7**, followed by an overindulgent Venus-Jupiter

square on **February 9.** Impulsiveness with love or money can be immensely exciting, but could turn out to be very costly. While taking risks is appropriate, leave yourself some margin for error. Venus-Uranus explodes with surprises that can rock your world, and expansive Jupiter inflates whatever you're feeling. Drama in appearance, resources, or relationships is to be expected. Be the director of the show by initiating something new rather than simply overreacting to someone else's changes.

FEBRUARY 13-14 ★ *less than perfect*

A sexy sextile between the lovers, Venus and Mars, on **February 13** can put more bounce in your step, but be cautious about the moves you make now. Retrograde Mercury can trip you up whether you're asking for a date or a raise. Don't play your hand too strongly; a clunky quincunx from strict Saturn to sensitive Venus on **February 14** can throw up a detour that feels like rejection, even if it's just a temporary delay in getting what you want. This can make for a somewhat awkward Valentine's Day, as it is not an easy task matching tastes and desires with others for mutual satisfaction.

FEBRUARY 19-21 ★ *getting to the bottom of desire*

A tense square between mysterious Pluto and loving Venus can complicate relationships on **February 19.** No matter what's given or received, it may not be fully appreciated. Pluto is about insatiable hunger, so awareness of what's missing can be acute, sometimes resulting in jealousy and dissatisfaction. Yet this can also deepen awareness of what you really want and don't want from others. Be totally truthful with yourself about this whether it's "nice" or not, because when you recognize what's most important, you can act more effectively. On **February 21,** Venus enters Aries and your 7th House of Partnerships, beginning a fresh cycle in relationships. Cleaning out your emotional closet in advance is especially valuable because it's so much easier to move ahead when you've unburdened yourself first.

FEBRUARY 25 ★ *don't think; just act*

Your planet, Venus, forms hard aspects to the Saturn-Neptune opposition and places you on an emotional seesaw—first hope, then doubt, then hope, then doubt again about your self-worth or an important connection. You can feel like you're in a bind, but there is a way out. Mars entering quirky Aquarius in your 5th House of Play is a signal to amuse yourself without worrying about what others think. Innocent self-indulgence can set you free from calculating every move.

MARCH

SAY GOODBYE TO OLD HABITS

Deep rumblings from your subconscious bring an important shift to your life this month. A total Lunar Eclipse in your 12th House of Secrets on **March 3** can suddenly awaken you, as if from a dream. The outdated workday habits that keep you plugging along without question are brought into the spotlight, illuminating the need for alternative ways to live. Radical Uranus opposing the Moon may bring a shock of awareness or an unexpected change of circumstances. Additionally, a Solar Eclipse in your 6th House of Work on **March 18** suggests that a job shift might be in order. A spiritual discovery is also possible, one that can free you from old doubts and insecurities, emboldening you to strike out on a more adventurous professional path. On **March 7**, mental Mercury turns direct, paving the way to forward thinking in the weeks ahead. Then, when the communication planet returns to sensitive Pisces on **March 17**, your intuition kicks in, and your feelings can tell you just as much as your thoughts.

On **March 16**, a slow-moving trine between visionary Jupiter and practical Saturn comes to a peak. This is an extremely positive aspect for long-range planning. The wide base of new knowledge that Jupiter's been downloading into your 3rd House of Data Collection blends well with the support of reliable friends or colleagues through steady Saturn in your 11th House of Teamwork. Big projects that start to percolate will take on another degree of reality when this aspect returns in early May. Before then, energizing Mars triggers these giant planets with an opposition to Saturn on **March 22** and a supportive sextile to Jupiter on **March 23**. Be patient; your excitement level is high, and there's a lot to assimilate now.

> ## KEEP IN MIND THIS MONTH
>
> *An unexpected loss can be a real blessing in disguise. Stay calm if your world starts to shift, because it's most likely taking you to a bigger and better place.*

KEY DATES

MARCH 2–3 ★ *light and steady*

An edgy Mercury-Venus semisquare on **March 2** and the Uranus-shocked Lunar Eclipse on **March 3** can make you a tad nervous. The stressful Mercury-Venus aspect can make even the most innocent comment feel like an insult, so avoid overreacting to what others say. The sense that your world is changing in ways you can't control may lead you to try to hold on tighter. A more relaxed attitude will successfully guide you through the bumpy surprises.

SUPER NOVA DAYS
MARCH 8-9 ★ *good sense builds relationships*
Your ruling planet, Venus, forms creative trines with Jupiter on **March 8** and Saturn on **March 9**, providing you with good judgment about people and the resources needed to achieve your goals. These three planets form a grand trine, a dynamic yet stable pattern that attracts support from innovative individuals. You have the perfect balance between openness and caution, optimism and practicality. People trust you because you're able to quickly assess any situation accurately and handle relationships with maturity.

MARCH 16-18 ★ *take power in partnerships*
A helpful trine between lovely Venus and transformational Pluto on **March 16** allows you to express power in relationships with the right amount of force. This is a good time to eliminate patterns or people who don't serve your needs. And a slick sextile between Mercury and Venus on **March 17** helps you find gentle yet persuasive ways to express yourself. Venus enters sensual Taurus on the same day in your 8th House of Intimacy. Its semisquare to surprising Uranus signals your readiness to break old bonds and explore a more exciting path to vulnerability. The Solar Eclipse on **March 18** square Pluto repeats that it's time to grow by letting go.

MARCH 20-22 ★ *speeding to a crashing halt*
The Sun's entry into Aries on **March 20** marks the first day of spring and lights up your 7th House of Partnerships. A Venus-Jupiter semisquare on **March 21** increases your appetite for pleasure, but a tense opposition between impatient Mars and Saturn, the planetary stop sign, on **March 22** is liable to force you to slam on the brakes if you've gone too far or too fast.

MARCH 29-31 ★ *connect with the truth*
Another Venus-Pluto aspect on **March 29** can bring blunt truths to a relationship. And while you, a partner, or a close friend can feel shaken, rapid recovery is on the way. A bright sextile between sweet Venus and innovative Uranus on **March 31** reveals an unorthodox approach that puts old issues behind you and ignites a fresh spark to an important connection in your life.

APRIL

TAKE THE LEAD

This is a dramatic time of year, especially when it comes to your connections with others. The Full Moon in accommodating Libra on **April 2** is a reminder to take care of yourself in relationships, rather than giving too much of yourself just to make someone else happy. Chatty Mercury enters your 7th House of Partnerships on **April 10**, a shift that encourages your spunky side and a more direct way of communicating with those closest to you. Then, on **April 17**, the New Moon in Aries in your 7th House aligns favorably with powerful Pluto, making it easy for you to uncover the core of an issue concerning matters of the heart. You can be strong because you're clear about what you want. You are still willing to compromise, but not at the cost of your principles. Letting go of a person or pattern that's no longer satisfying isn't necessarily easy, yet doing it now is better than waiting.

Jupiter, the planet of wisdom, turns retrograde on **April 5** in your 3rd House of Communication. While you will continue to learn in the months ahead, it may be more efficient to deepen your understanding of material already covered than to overload yourself with lots of new information. Concepts that may still feel a little strange should start to sink in and take root, making you more confident about your knowledge base. By contrast, practical Saturn turns direct in your 11th House of Groups and Friends on **April 19** by demonstrating your considerable leadership talent. Projects that involve teams, friends, and organizations can be a positive outlet for your networking skills.

> **KEEP IN MIND THIS MONTH**
>
> *Trust your own opinions first. Even if others have a valid point, it doesn't negate the value of your perspective.*

KEY DATES

APRIL 1–4 ★ *emotional drama*
Stern Saturn stresses Venus on **April 1**, which tends to take some of the fun out of life. Rewards and recognition come grudgingly, if at all, so be patient if you're feeling underappreciated. The Full Moon in your sign on **April 2** may lead to emotional drama, especially with tough aspects from Venus to extravagant Jupiter on **April 3** and supersensitive Neptune on **April 4**. Going to extremes isn't recommended, but if you do, at least everyone will know how you truly feel.

APRIL 10-11 ★ *talk freely and meaning will follow*

Mouthy Mercury makes it hard to keep silent on **April 10**, but why shouldn't you speak your mind? Your concerns about a significant relationship aren't necessarily easy to explain, but it's healthier to start talking than to clam up due to fear or embarrassment. Your ruling planet, Venus, comes to the rescue on **April 11** when it enters lucid Gemini in your 9th House of Higher Learning. Passions will cool as reason returns and real dialogue becomes possible.

APRIL 17 ★ *turn up the volume*

The New Moon in fiery Aries draws assertive people into your life. This might inspire you, as long as they offer fresh ideas rather than belligerent attitudes. Whether dealing with a friend, boss, partner, or total stranger, standing up for yourself is easier and easier. You can be cool and calculating when you choose, but you also know how to turn up the volume to make yourself heard. Initiate a connection with someone new, or prod your current relationship in a more adventurous direction.

APRIL 22 ★ *a very hot sunday*

Passions run high with a superheated square between Venus and Mars. The planets of receiving and giving hook up in a tense way, sparking disagreements about style, manner, and social activities. But if you can take conflict in a playful way, you can have a very stimulating time. The banter of teasing and joking may bring you to the edge of anger, yet can just as easily result in laughter or passion.

SUPER NOVA DAYS
APRIL 26-30 ★ *every emotion under the sun*

The month ends with a diverse flurry of astrological events that can have you bouncing all over the place. Venus square erratic Uranus on **April 26** feels restless, yet a sextile with solid Saturn on **April 27** can put you back on solid ground. But on **April 28**, Venus opposes excessive Jupiter; desire tends to go too far, skewing your judgment. An explosive Mars-Uranus conjunction on the same day increases the likelihood of risky behavior, and then a sensitive Venus-Neptune trine arrives with a calming effect on **April 30**.

LIBRA

MAY

A WILD IDEA THAT WORKS

Gigantic Jupiter makes two major aspects this month that can shake your world and reorient your professional life in a more constructive direction. On **May 10**, this planet of opportunity makes the second of three tense squares with erratic Uranus. The air is electrified with a buzz of instability that can crack open a vision of your future involving new and different work. Whether you're excited or threatened, there's no need to jump into action right away. The third and last of these aspects, occurring in October, is when you may have to make a choice between a safe but stale position and a stimulating and more up-to-date job. Fortunately, Jupiter aligns creatively with reliable Saturn on **May 6**, essentially giving you two flavors of expansion at once: wild and crazy or clear-headed and calculating. Reliable friends offer practical advice, and trusted colleagues chime in with solid support, all to help you find ways to turn an inspired idea into a workable reality.

The Full Moon in Scorpio on **May 2** falls in your financial houses, so resource issues are likely. You could feel squeezed for cash or time as restraining Saturn squares this Sun-Moon opposition. If you need help, ask for it. There are people willing to pitch in as long as you state the problem succinctly and demonstrate your ability to pay back the favor. On **May 15**, Mars, a planetary hottie, enters your 7th House of Partnerships, initiating more passionate interaction with others. You have the ability to attract aggressive people, but the real fun is for you to be more assertive yourself. Strive for what you want in your private or public life, and you might be surprised at the positive results.

KEEP IN MIND THIS MONTH

It's better to be a leader than a follower. Don't wait for others to take the initiative, even if it ruffles a feather or two in the process.

KEY DATES

MAY 6-7 ★ *relationship secrets revealed*
Sweet and friendly Venus clashes with deep, dark Pluto on **May 6**, which often makes for complications in relationships. Jealousy and distrust are possible as buried feelings rise to the surface. It's common to get caught between blame and guilt, but condemnation is not the purpose. The point is to be brutally honest about your desires. Rejecting behavior that you don't like and calling for the affection

that you need may be uncomfortable but can bring you closer to fulfillment. A square between logical Mercury and ethereal Neptune on the same day can make for some fuzzy communication. Before going off on someone, be sure that what you think you heard or said is clearly understood. On **May 7**, Venus enters cautious Cancer. It's time to start healing any pain caused by recent revelations.

SUPER NOVA DAYS
MAY 11-14 ★ *contradictory signals*

Mercury enters curious Gemini on **May 11** and opens your mind to thoughts about faraway places and new ideas. This would normally make for a chatty and casual Friday, but Venus's 45-degree angle with testing Saturn can put an edge on relationships. Words expressed carelessly can land with a thud and put a chill in the atmosphere. A supersensitive Sun-Neptune square on **May 12** adds uncertainty and a greater degree of vulnerability. On **May 13**, a powerful Mars-Pluto square may come in the form of bullying from an inconsiderate individual. But this is also a signal to put a stop to behavior that wears you down without giving enough in return. On **May 14**, a semisquare between Venus and Neptune is a time when dreams can blur reality and lead to poor judgment.

MAY 22-24 ★ *delight in discovery*

Your beautiful planet, Venus, brings much-needed inspiration now. On **May 22**, Venus creates a magical aspect with imaginative Neptune, promising romance and pleasure in relationships. You'll be able to find delight in ways you haven't experienced. On **May 23**, a slippery quincunx between Venus and Jupiter leads to excess spending or overestimating someone, especially if you're feeling needy. But on **May 24**, a brilliant trine between Venus and Uranus may shake you out of a rut at work and put some fun back into the job.

MAY 28 ★ *whistle while you work*

Mercury the Messenger enters Cancer and your 10th House of Career. Worrying about everyone and everything is possible, so it's important to counter negative thinking with positive actions. Allow yourself to be playful, even silly, while you work. Pleasant distractions won't reduce your efficiency if they make you happy. Taking a break to enjoy conversation or engage in some light shopping will give you renewed energy.

JUNE

ADVENTURE BECKONS

You could be feeling restless and ready for major movement this month, Libra. The Sun in your 9th House of Faraway Places opposes Jupiter in the traveling sign of Sagittarius on **June 5**, and the New Moon falls in this mobile section of your chart on **June 14**. Feet get itchy and minds wander under such conditions, but travel of body or spirit can also be tricky now due to Mercury retrograde. This speedy planet hits the brakes on **June 15** and goes backward through **July 9**, marking a period when schedule snafus, message mix-ups, and communication errors are common. If you do hit the road, take a class, or teach a course, paying extra attention to details can keep you from wasting precious time and energy.

An opposition from penetrating Pluto to the inquisitive Gemini New Moon on **June 14** is a source of confrontation about beliefs and principles. Differences of opinion may cause you to reexamine your basic philosophy and make some alterations in your view of the world. If you put the emphasis on learning rather than having to prove that you're right, it can be a positive, mind-expanding experience. This wider perspective comes in handy because of the third and last opposition between solid Saturn and wispy Neptune, which occurs on **June 25**. This major aspect that began late last summer defines the approach you need to make dreams real over the next few years. Saturn in your 11th House of Groups and Friends suggests that you can't do it alone or just for your own self-gratification. Connecting your creative, romantic, and idealistic visions with helping others makes an unbeatable combination. You will, in turn, be supported when your personal fulfillment serves the community.

> **KEEP IN MIND THIS MONTH**
>
> *Take care of practical matters to ensure that you have a strong enough foundation to reach your long-term goals.*

KEY DATES

JUNE 5 ★ *voracious appetite*

An edgy semisquare between Venus in Cancer and larger-than-life Jupiter expands your appetites. One bite is rarely enough, nor is one kiss, one modest purchase, or one small bit of praise. Excessive Jupiter amplifies the desire for pleasure and approval, yet at the same time can distort your judgment. Later, Venus enters self-indulgent Leo, just as this fire sign's ruling body, the Sun, opposes Jupiter, furthering the cause of excess. Enjoy the drama, but don't lose sight of the cost of the show.

SUPER NOVA DAYS
JUNE 9-13 ★ *surprise, discipline, and faith*
Rebellious Uranus stresses Venus and the Sun on **June 9**, inciting impulsiveness and unexpected shifts of social activities and attitudes. Spontaneity is delightful, as long as your nervous system can handle surprises. On **June 11**, the Sun's harmonious aspects to active Mars and disciplined Saturn—while the two planets are favorably hooked up to each other—is excellent for productivity. A trine between the Sun and spiritual Neptune on **June 12**, followed by Mars' sextile to this gentle planet on **June 13**, gives you a light hand to motivate others gracefully or to express your own feelings creatively.

JUNE 17-19 ★ *oasis in the desert*
The Sun (identity), Venus (self-worth), and Pluto (power) connect with challenging aspects during these three days. Mistrust is possible as personal comments can be taken in the worst way. You could sense a lack of love or a limit of resources that stresses relationships. The truth about your deepest desires can emerge out of this struggle, but facing painful revelations will reward you richly and quickly. On **June 19**, Venus and Jupiter, astrology's traditional benefics, form a generous trine that turns a desert of emotional dryness into a fertile meadow of comfort and fulfillment.

JUNE 26 ★ *unexpected turn of events*
A quirky quincunx between accommodating Venus and independent Uranus can throw a monkey wrench into your plans. A store might not have an item you ordered, or a colleague can let you down. Prepare to operate on your own if others fail to live up to their commitments in your professional or personal life.

JUNE 29-30 ★ *business before pleasure*
High tension is in the air with a wild and crazy Mars-Uranus connection on **June 29** and the Full Moon in somber, ethical Capricorn on **June 30**. Unexpected responsibilities at home can test your patience. If you feel like a victim, an escapist Venus-Neptune opposition on **June 30** can put you in a state of denial. Recreational shopping and romantic fantasies may temporarily soothe the pain, but reserve the bulk of your time and energy to address the real issues at hand.

LIBRA

JULY

REFLECTIONS ON LOVE AND MONEY

Your ruling planet, Venus, is slowing down as it approaches its retrograde station in Virgo on **July 27**. Venus will continue to move backward until returning to forward motion in Leo on **September 8**. Subjects associated with Venus, such as love, relationships, and material resources, tend to advance less quickly during this period. This cycle marks an inward turn—a reflective time in which to review many of these critical issues. There are, however, opportunities to reconnect with old sources of pleasure, including individuals from your past. And reevaluating your life in spiritual terms is another possibility, since Venus's turn occurs in your 12th House of Soul Consciousness. The usual needs for affection, appreciation, and pleasure can be seen from a wider, less personal perspective.

Mercury the Messenger turns direct in your 10th House of Career on **July 9**. Work-related projects that have been delayed should start to pick up speed. If you've been waiting for important information related to a job, your chances for getting an answer start to increase now. "Do it now" Mars forms tough squares to opposing Neptune and Saturn on **July 24 and 31** respectively. The impatient warrior planet is a bit less rushed in sure-footed Taurus, but can also engender stubbornness. The square to squishy Neptune may spur conflict caused by confusion. If you go into battle mode, make sure that you know exactly what you're fighting about. The square to rigid Saturn may result in a standoff in which the harder one side pushes, the more the other side resists. Cooperation, though, is possible—when the rules are crystal clear to both parties. Time spent planning in advance will help you to avoid the frustration that comes from working with an obstinate partner.

> **KEEP IN MIND THIS MONTH**
>
> *Some tasks are more easily done solo. When working with difficult people, find a way to complete the job by yourself.*

KEY DATES

JULY 1 ★ *heeding good advice*

The month could start on a somber note as desirable Venus joins restrictive Saturn. Love may flow less freely, and pleasure can be limited by duties, doubts, or responsibilities. Yet a trusted friend can offer you support that helps you better understand a relationship. And while praise is unlikely to be given easily, you can earn respect by standing up for your convictions even when it's not popular.

JULY 8-9 ★ *the power of persuasion*

Venus lines up in a constructive trine with powerful Pluto on **July 8**, showing you how to influence others without force. Your sense of what buttons to push is very strong, enabling you to go beyond old limits and deepen a relationship. You're attractive in a subtle way that's noticeable only to those whose attention you want. Mercury's direct turn on **July 9** is a good time to put your cards on the table when it comes to a work project, money, or sex. Taking on a delicate subject in a calm and steady manner makes you very persuasive now.

JULY 14 ★ *sweet solitude*

Slow-moving Venus crawls into Virgo two weeks before turning retrograde and illuminates your heart with a more universal vision of love. Satisfaction doesn't require a partner as you enter the 12th House of Inner Peace. Quiet time for reflection, meditation, or prayer proves fulfilling and releases your need for approval from others. A New Moon in Cancer, though, lands in your 10th House of Career and Public Responsibility, adding obligations outside the home. Spacey Neptune quincunx this Sun-Moon conjunction represents ill-defined duties that can drain your energy. However, innovative Uranus kicks in with a clever trine that can spark a sudden solution.

JULY 22 ★ *bright but shy*

The Sun enters generous Leo to brighten up your 11th House of Groups and Friends. Outgoing pals and confident colleagues are a joy at play and at work. Your capacity to shine in the midst of a crowd is also likely to thrive, although your need for alone time is still fairly strong now.

SUPER NOVA DAYS
JULY 27-29 ★ *both bold and bashful*

Venus turns retrograde on **July 27**, followed by a hypersensitive Mercury-Venus semisquare on **July 28**. Neutral words can sound like criticism when that was not the speaker's intention. The unconventional Aquarius Full Moon on **July 29** brings out a quirky and playful side of your personality. Your need for fun and attention may increase, possibly creating tension with your desire for privacy. But you have the right to be on center stage and then retreat. As long as you have an escape route, it's fine to take the spotlight sometimes.

AUGUST

SOCIAL CONNECTIONS

Your key planet, Venus, is still retrograde this month, kicking up old memories about love and loss, but its shift into friendly Leo on **August 8** should lighten your emotional load. That's because even when moving backward, Venus is more joyful in the sign of the Lion. Your key planet is out of your secretive and spiritual 12th House and among friends and groups in the sociable 11th. Pals who've been out of touch for a long time may reappear, and a renewed interest in an organization can be rekindled. It's still wise to be cautious about any commitments you make with Venus retrograde, since your feelings may change when it goes direct next month. Optimism, though, is to be expected when happy-go-lucky Jupiter shifts out of reverse on **August 6**. Its expansive nature overflows your life with positive ideas and lots of local travel as it moves through your mentally active 3rd House of Information. On the same day, Saturn and Pluto's supportive trine adds depth to your perceptions and strength to your friendships. This long-lasting aspect is a subtle powerhouse that earns you trust and increases your influence over others.

The New Moon in Leo on **August 12** may stir some drama in your personal life. It's exactly opposite supersensitive Neptune in your 5th House of Self-Expression, so others' reactions to you are magnified in your mind. You can feel like you're onstage with a row of critics taking notes on your every move. But if you have your act together and are ready for the attention, this can work to your advantage. With the Sun entering detailed Virgo on **August 17**, knowing your material well before making a presentation is essential. Practice makes perfect.

KEEP IN MIND THIS MONTH

A generous act can lead to complications, so weigh carefully what you put in motion before giving someone a hand.

KEY DATES

AUGUST 7-8 ★ *quality control*

A sharp square between Venus in fussy Virgo and Mars in flighty Gemini on **August 7** can be quite stressful. Taking on several tasks that require careful attention could lead to cross words with someone who isn't as committed to quality as you wish. Either accept the weaknesses of this individual, or take care of your responsibilities alone. Venus moves back into Leo on **August 8**, which could bring you the support and encouragement of friends and colleagues.

AUGUST 13 ★ *surreal life*

Venus joins authoritative Saturn to make this a rather formal day, but Neptune's alliance with the Sun adds an air of fantasy everywhere you turn. Still, you might feel a little stiff, not as trusting, and less open than normal around people. There's an air of emotional sterility that makes festive events seem unreal, as if you are in a kind of Disneyland where every act has been preplanned. But if you have important business to discuss, the sober circumstances could be just right for a mature and respectful exchange of ideas.

SUPER NOVA DAYS
AUGUST 15–18 ★ *refined personal power*

You're super-alert on **August 15** as penetrating Pluto lines up favorably with resourceful Venus. You can untangle knotty situations from the past, fix relationship problems, and motivate others to dig deep within themselves. You make this happen so gracefully that no one feels pushed or exploited. On **August 16**, Mercury joins your lovely ruling planet, Venus, and on **August 17**, Venus sweetly connects with the Sun. You hold others in the spell of your charms, knowing how to use a gesture, touch, or look to make your point discretely but powerfully.

AUGUST 22–25 ★ *trial and error*

A clever quintile between the planetary lovers, Venus and Mars, on **August 22** grants you the ability to turn conflict into play and to solve problems with your creativity. Let your intuition guide you, even if it leads you astray at times. Active Mars opposes far-reaching Jupiter on **August 23**, followed by squares from Mercury to both planets. Making mistakes is unavoidable, even as the Sun's entry into perfectionist Virgo on the same day resists the idea. But the point is to take chances, try a number of approaches, and accept failure as part of the journey to success. Sweet Venus opposes Neptune on **August 25**, a day when dreams and pleasure set reason and practicality aside.

AUGUST 28 ★ *less is more*

The Full Moon in compassionate Pisces is a total eclipse in your 6th House of Health and Work. Jupiter's square to the Sun and Moon indicates a likelihood of overextension. Control your desire to be helpful when your plate is already full. Protect yourself by pulling back from situations that are going to demand more time and energy than you can give.

SEPTEMBER

Big changes start this month with sober Saturn entering analytical Virgo on **September 2**. For the next two years, the planet of necessity will be in your 12th House of Spirituality. Your most important work during this period can take place behind the scenes while you tune into meditation, prayer, yoga, and other practices that connect you to your higher self. Regardless of the demands of work, friends, and family, take time to tap into the divine spirit that is the source of all life. On **September 5**, perceptive Mercury enters your sign, bringing clarity to your purpose and a greater ability to explain it. Venus, your ruling planet, turns direct on **September 8**, which marks an energetic shift that will pick up steam as you head toward your birthday. The love planet is back on track, and your love life should be, too. Pick up the pace socially and financially to capitalize on the change of direction.

The Virgo New Moon on **September 11** is a high-powered Solar Eclipse in your 12th House. Eccentric Uranus, aggressive Mars, and gigantic Jupiter all form tense aspects with the eclipse and are bound to hype up your energy. There's a nervous feeling that can lead to impulsive actions. You might want to turn your life upside down, but don't be in a hurry to make radical changes. Sit down, take a deep breath, and think this through carefully. You need to bring a method to this madness and come up with a constructive plan to avoid creating chaos. When the Sun enters your sign on **September 23**, you're more likely to find your equilibrium and be able to skillfully cut loose of the past without damaging your future.

> **KEEP IN MIND THIS MONTH**
>
> *A lasting sense of freedom comes from going toward what you want rather than running away from what you don't.*

KEY DATES

SEPTEMBER 3 ★ *wit wins over warfare*

Your sense of humor can defuse a potentially explosive situation. Intemperate Mars forms an incendiary square with unpredictable Uranus while the prideful Sun squares exaggerating Jupiter. Differing opinions can blow up into a heated clash that you can calm with a light touch. Diplomatic Venus's savvy sextile with Mars graces you with the ability to apply charm and wit to cool down all parties involved.

SUPER NOVA DAYS
SEPTEMBER 8-9 ★ *rock the status quo*
Venus turns direct on **September 8**, and you're not likely to waste any time waking up your social life. An edgy quincunx with unconventional Uranus shows that you're ready for a change of style and pleasure. A fashion experiment may lack your usual panache, and a relationship move could be less than elegant. Yet with the Sun opposing Uranus on **September 9**, this is no time to stick with the status quo. In fact, if you're forced to play nice in a boring situation or listen to a pompous person you don't respect, you might just get up and leave.

SEPTEMBER 17 ★ *say it kindly*
A tight square between the Sun and pushy Mars compels you to say something that you'd prefer to keep to yourself. You don't want to hurt or embarrass anyone, but it's better to speak up than clam up. Fortunately, communicative Mercury forms a favorable sextile with sweet Venus, allowing you to take even bad news and wrap it up in a pretty package. You're not covering up the truth; you're presenting it in a creative form in which it's most likely to be understood.

SEPTEMBER 21 ★ *complex emotional cocktail*
This is a day of high contrast that can complicate relationships yet also take you to the heights of delight. A Venus-Neptune opposition is soft and romantic, while a Mars-Pluto opposition is intense and persistent. This is like a sweet-and-sour sauce of love, one that makes a rich and complex meal or causes conflict—or both. A partner who knows how to be up front and gentle is a highly desirable playmate.

SEPTEMBER 26 ★ *know what you want*
The Full Moon in impulsive and independent Aries opposes the Sun in deliberate, cooperative Libra. This can intensify your interactions with others as the struggle to balance self-interest with sharing burns stronger. You can flip-flop from one side to the other or attract individuals who play both sides. But if you start with a clear sense of what you really need, rather than just trying to make someone else happy, your negotiations are bound to be more successful.

OCTOBER

LONG-RANGE VISION

It's time to gaze far into the future to find meaning and inspiration and to pay less attention to the day-to-day issues that usually fill your thoughts. Jupiter, the planet of the higher mind, makes major aspects to Uranus and Neptune that lift your thinking from the mundane to the magical. On **October 9**, Jupiter makes the last of three form-breaking squares with inventive Uranus and throws lightning bolts of brilliance into your head. Your ideas about work may change radically as you seek more excitement from your job. Further education is a key that will open the door to more fulfilling employment. On **October 29**, Jupiter sidles up to a gentle sextile with Neptune that supplies vision and faith just as this spiritual planet of the seas is about to turn direct and fill your heart with hope.

The New Moon in peace-loving Libra on **October 10** will realign your intentions for the next twelve months. This fresh wave can take you for a very long ride with big Jupiter and boundless Neptune making supportive aspects to the Sun-Moon conjunction. A newfound belief in yourself doesn't have to be based on logic, since imagination and faith in your creative powers can carry you as far as you want. Mercury, the planet of the lower or concrete mind, turns retrograde on

October 11 in your 2nd House of Money and Resources. Throughout the three weeks of Mercury's backward cycle, you may need to reexamine your financial commitments. This is a time to look at the relationship between your income and expenses to make alterations to your budget. Avoid making any major purchases until Mercury turns direct on **November 1**. If you must spend any serious money, be a very careful shopper.

> **KEEP IN MIND THIS MONTH**
>
> *Dreaming about a brighter tomorrow is not escapism, but an appropriate investment of time as well as your inspiration for a more fulfilling future.*

KEY DATES

OCTOBER 3 ★ *potent partnerships*

A sly trine between pleasing Venus and potent Pluto grants you more power than usual in relationships. You're able to motivate friends and colleagues, and you know how to appeal to the deepest interests of your partner. You can get right to the point and express your desires without stirring resistance because of your acute sense of the situation. Repairing a damaged connection with someone, hooking up with an old lover, and rediscovering pleasures from your past are possible as well.

OCTOBER 10 ★ *don't take it personally*

Venus returned to retiring Virgo on **October 7** and forms an anxious semisquare with the Sun today. Pride is easily bruised under these conditions as you bristle at comments that are less than laudable. Try not to let insecurity cause distrust of someone who's on your side or to allow vanity to dampen a pleasant social occasion. Show more self-confidence by actively participating.

SUPER NOVA DAYS
OCTOBER 13-16 ★ *from productive to playful*

A heavy Venus-Saturn conjunction on **October 13** is better for one-on-one time than for a busy social situation. Quiet conversations to address serious issues may not be pleasant but can be quite productive. The mood is quite different on **October 16**, when sextiles from Venus to chatty Mercury and spicy Mars tickle your playful side. An easy flow of conversation is perfect for teasing and flirting without the danger of taking things too seriously. There's a relaxed atmosphere and an accepting spirit that makes it easy to talk about anything without bruising anyone's ego.

OCTOBER 24-26 ★ *full moon fever*

These can be stressful days when a Mercury-Venus semisquare on **October 24** can be a cause for possible miscommunication, followed by an emotional Full Moon in your 8th House of Intimacy and a high-tension Venus-Uranus opposition on **October 26**. It's natural for feelings to change quickly and take you from the highs of excitement to doubt-driven lows. If you don't like the mood you're in, relax, because another one is coming soon. The upside can be breakthroughs in relationships that free you from the limiting patterns of the past.

OCTOBER 29 ★ *foolish and forgiving*

A lusty Venus-Jupiter square increases your need for pleasure and can even push you across the line of good taste. But it can be healthy now to go too far as long as you don't break the law, exceed your credit limit, or make a promise you can't keep. Fantasy-loving Neptune is quincunx Venus, which can also provoke some slippery social behavior or bad purchases. Yet the deeper message is that you are human and that all mistakes are forgivable.

NOVEMBER

IDEAS FLOW, BUT ACTIONS SLOW

Information starts to flow more freely on **November 1**, when Mercury, the communication planet, turns direct in your sign. This can be an opportune time to make a pitch if you have an idea or a plan that you want to sell. Additional support arrives when your ruling planet, the lovely and charming Venus, returns to her home sign of Libra on **November 8**, where she will be holding court until early December. The planet of attraction in your sign puts you in a glowing light that highlights your strong points and masks your weak ones. Some pampering is recommended, because treating yourself well is a wise investment. When you demonstrate your worth by taking care of yourself and nurturing your talents, you become much more appealing to others.

On **November 9**, the New Moon in possessive Scorpio falls in your 2nd House of Income. Supportive trines to the Moon from Mars and Uranus initiate new ideas for making money, but a challenging square from wobbly Neptune suggests that when it comes to material matters, what you see isn't necessarily what you get. On **November 15**, assertive Mars turns retrograde in your 10th House of Career. The backward cycle of this most forward-moving of planets makes it difficult to get new projects off the ground. If your professional burdens are too heavy, consider rearranging your schedule to lighten your load until Mars turns direct on **January 30, 2008**. You can advance during this period, of course, but each step should be carefully measured to avoid mistakes. The travel bug may be biting when the Full Moon in restless Gemini lights up your 9th House of Voyages on **November 24**. Widen your horizons by exploring new places, learning a foreign language, or reading about distant lands and cultures.

> **KEEP IN MIND THIS MONTH**
>
> *Invest your resources carefully. Better to miss an opportunity than to leap too quickly and lose what you've earned.*

KEY DATES

NOVEMBER 5 ★ *necessary repairs*

You might not be at your gracious best and prefer to be left alone with sweet Venus square grumpy Pluto today. The tendency is to be more aware of what's wrong than what's right in your life. If you are dissatisfied, don't waste time grumbling about it. Take a good, hard look at the issues, and start thinking about making improvements. If you don't have a clue, find someone who does and ask for advice.

NOVEMBER 11-12 ★ *romantic escape*
Nebulous Neptune makes hard aspects to the Sun on **November 11** and to
Venus on **November 12** that can lead to confusion, illusion, and fantasy. A lack of
confidence about yourself may drive you to look for a savior, if you imagine that
someone else has the answer for you. If you're feeling vulnerable in relationships
now, you might make sacrifices that aren't in your best interests. Enjoy a romantic
escape if you can, but don't make any serious commitments unless you're positive
that you're standing on solid ground.

SUPER NOVA DAYS
NOVEMBER 19-22 ★ *unsettled feelings*
A square between Venus and Mars on **November 19** is a very provocative
aspect. You can be frisky and flirty, but may be easily offended if someone is
aggressive with you. A Venus-Sun semisquare on **November 20** tilts you in a
sensitive direction that can lead to unexpected reactions on **November 21**. It's
hard to relax with the agitating quincunx between Venus and unpredictable
Uranus. But a magical quintile from Venus to powerful Pluto on **November 22**
turns it all around by showing you how to get what you want and eliminate
what you no longer need.

NOVEMBER 26 ★ *unconditional love*
Peace, love, and understanding are possible with a beautiful trine between
Venus and spiritual Neptune. This favorable meeting connects earthly values with
heavenly ones, a delightful pairing for pleasure without guilt. Feelings flow easily,
and trust grows with your faith in the generosity of the universe. You can give and
receive without keeping score, because you know that the joy you're experiencing
is beyond measure and without limit.

NOVEMBER 29 ★ *demand respect*
Responsible Saturn semisquares Venus to bring relationships back to hard, cold
reality. You could be feeling the chill of rejection or a lack of appreciation. Perhaps
your cash flow is low. Whatever the circumstance, the remedy is to take a serious
look at those around you and ask if they're treating you fairly. If not, don't be coy,
but speak directly about your expectations. Act firmly and be prepared to make a
tough decision for the sake of self-respect.

DECEMBER

RELATIONSHIP REGENERATION

Big wheels are turning as Jupiter, the largest planet of them all, is making major noise this month. The planet of expansion joins transformational Pluto in your 7th House of Partnerships on **December 11.** This slow-acting transit awakens deep questions about your beliefs and long-term goals. If you're in a primary relationship, you may discover that the two of you are not on the same page with respect to your visions for the future. It's time to recommit, make adjustments, or move on. If you're single, your ideas about what it means to be part of a couple could change. Either way, you are likely to be much more passionate, even extreme, in expressing your opinions. On **December 18,** jolly Jupiter leaves sunny Sagittarius and moves into responsible Capricorn for the next year. This puts the opportunity planet in your 8th House of Intimacy, a sign of emotional maturity and a greater ability to address complex personal issues.

The heat is on for the holidays as the Sun joins Jupiter on **December 22** and opposes moody Mars on **December 24,** which then opposes Jupiter on **December 26.** This action takes place in the relatively temperate signs of Capricorn (the Sun and Jupiter) and Cancer (Mars), but the nature of all three planets is fiery. Celebrations can be loud and hearty, but the odds favor conflict as well. When confrontation breaks out on the home front, you're the one who usually steps in to keep heads cool. Yet the tension can be so high that you're drawn into battle yourself. If you can handle a little combat, it might help to let off some steam. While that's risky, repressing your feelings could be even worse.

> **KEEP IN MIND THIS MONTH**
>
> *Allow yourself to disagree without becoming disagreeable. Different views can spice up a relationship as long as emotions and egos don't get out of hand.*

KEY DATES

DECEMBER 1–3 ★ *make a convincing case*
Smart sextiles from Venus to confident Jupiter on **December 1** and compelling Pluto on **December 3** increase your powers of persuasion. You can apply some pressure to get your way without coming across as too aggressive. This is also a fortunate time to address a delicate issue that you've been reluctant to discuss. Be honest about your desires, and you may be surprised at the positive responses.

DECEMBER 9-12 ★ *relationship roller coaster*
The New Moon in Sagittarius on **December 9** sparks brushfires in your 7th House
of Partnerships. Circumstances can change in the blink of an eye, but stay cool if
you're the one whose world is being rocked. There's more room for compromise
than you think. Consider your words carefully, since unformed thoughts can pop
out of your mouth. Socially sophisticated Venus forms a happy trine with Mars on
December 11 and a supportive sextile with Saturn on **December 12**, helping you to
find your equilibrium in a volatile environment. Your people skills are solid under
pressure and can quickly turn a dangerous situation around.

DECEMBER 17 ★ *originality counts more*
A Venus-Jupiter semisquare may cause excessive spending with overindulgence
a real possibility. Seek alternatives before you buy a budget-busting gift. A Venus
trine with inventive Uranus reveals unconventional ways to please someone and
yourself without breaking the bank. Unlike your credit card or bank account,
creativity has no limit.

SUPER NOVA DAYS
DECEMBER 22-24 ★ *holiday heat*
A Venus-Neptune square on **December 22** can be a cause of uncertainty.
There's plenty of pressure to perform, and you might feel like you're faking it.
But an inventive quintile from Venus to Saturn shows you solutions to even
the trickiest problems, while a Sun-Jupiter conjunction blesses you with luck
when you act like a leader. The Full Moon in protective Cancer on **December
23** is conjunct Mars in your 4th House of Home and Family; the Sun opposes
Mars on **December 24**. Tempers could be short, but the real problem is about
old issues bubbling under the surface that can erupt unexpectedly. Mix your
reactions with humor to move through these hot spots without a blowup.

DECEMBER 30-31 ★ *handle with discretion*
Venus enters outspoken Sagittarius and quincunxes Mars on **December 30**, which
can produce some awkward moments. Accidentally spilling the beans may prove
embarrassing, so watch what you say now to keep a playful conversation from
turning serious. Mars backs into Gemini on **December 31** to make New Year's Eve
especially lively. Some innocent flirting, though, could provoke a jealous response,
so stay conscious of whom you play with and who might be watching.

SCORPIO

OCTOBER 23–NOVEMBER 21

SCORPIO OVERVIEW

An ongoing struggle between career aspirations and your personal dreams can color this year with disappointment and accomplishment. Although this dilemma began stirring last summer at the standoff between serious Saturn and dreamy Neptune, the issues are emphasized again in the first half of 2007. **It will be your job to conquer discouragement by facing your limitations rather than ignoring them.** You began a reevaluation of your life's goals in July 2005 and must now be ready to put your new plan into action. These considerations may be tied to decisions you made in 1999 and 2000, when Saturn was last stressing your chart. Fortunately, this year you have the confident support of expansive Jupiter, which forms harmonious trines to constructive Saturn on March 16 and May 5. Accept this powerful cosmic gift of equilibrium by striking boldly, and your courage will lead you to future success.

Last year, when Jupiter was in your sign, you may have pursued a career opportunity that aimed you in a particular direction. Now it's time to build long-term stability as lucky Jupiter spends the year in your 2nd House of Self-Worth. **Financial rewards may be forthcoming**, especially if you continue to dedicate yourself enthusiastically to your work. And although your vocation is currently more lucrative, there are distractions on the romantic or creative front. Surprising Uranus in your 5th House of Love and Play dynamically squares Jupiter throughout the year, making it tough for you to commit to your personal relationships. You desire more freedom than you may be able to find.

Mars and Pluto are your key planets, but since Mars moves quickly, it tends to have short-lived effects, while Pluto moves so slowly that it impacts long-term cycles. Pluto has been in your 2nd House since 1996, transforming your values and your relationship to money. By early August, career-oriented Saturn trines Pluto, granting you the power to change the course of your professional life and blessing you with a deep understanding of how to apply your personal power without overstepping boundaries. **You can accomplish great things now if you are willing to work passionately for your deep convictions.** This is the last year of intense Pluto's stay in fearless Sagittarius, and it culminates with an awesome, once-every-thirteen-years conjunction to Jupiter in December. Be specific about what you want, as the potential for fulfillment looms closer.

The pace of your life shifts in September as Saturn enters your 11th House of Groups and Friends, linking your long-term goals to social or political issues. You are more likely now to get involved with an organization, whether for community action, professional advancement, or just plain fun. Four eclipses this year—on March 3, March 18, August 28, and September 11— activate your houses of friends, children, and lovers. **Changes in relationships, some quite unexpected, can rock your year with excitement and hand you the ticket to personal satisfaction that you have been seeking.**

EXCITING DEVELOPMENTS

Uranus in your 5th House of Romance may destabilize your love life, but the release of pent-up tensions can be exhilarating if you are willing to accept overdue changes. The action begins in late January as a square from Jupiter tempts you to take a risk. By early February, sensual Venus and thoughtful Mercury are in the picture, but Mercury's retrograde can delay fulfillment until early April. On March 3, the Virgo Full Moon Eclipse lights up your social life, and you must remain open to unconventional experiences if you want to strengthen your current relationship. Your unwillingness to wait for what you want can create trouble. This theme of impatience is roused again by the New Moon Eclipse on September 11, yet an ongoing connection between the love planet, Venus, and responsible Saturn through late summer and early autumn can place work obligations in the way of sweet romance. Venus returns to your sign in December, paving the way for holiday happiness.

SHIFTING GOALS

The foundations on which you built your professional life can shift like sand beneath your feet, leaving you uncertain about your accomplishments. With diffusive Neptune tensely opposing stable Saturn in your 10th House of Career, even the most reliable jobs can change. You get what you deserve this year, yet your efforts at key times can have a very positive impact on your success. Saturn receives substantial assistance from opportunistic Jupiter and piercing Pluto. Redefine your goals and advance steadily by making well-considered decisions around March 16 and May 5. Put your plans into action by early August, and you could be on your way to getting the job of your dreams.

 CAUTIOUS OPTIMISM

Expand on your previous efforts and you can find yourself smiling all the way to the bank. Fortunate Jupiter is in your 2nd House of Money this year, which indicates increased material wealth. You must be careful, though, for this planet of bigger and better can also be the planet of too much, suggesting that you could overestimate the potential of an investment, which is great if you are selling but not okay if you are buying. Watch your pocketbook around March 8 and April 30. If you overspend, you may be particularly stretched when Venus runs into restrictive Saturn at the end of June. Days when your financial judgment will be especially keen include April 11, June 19, and August 2.

 HEALTHY HEART, HEALTHY BODY

With active Mars as the ruler of your 6th House of Health, your well-being is tied to how you move energy throughout your body. Exercise is one essential way to maintain good health, but your physical expression of love can also be significant. If you fearfully withhold emotional communication, the negativity is likely to express somatically when Mars is stressed, as it is around March 22, April 22, and September 21. The best time to shake up your workout routine for maximum impact is around March 16 and May 5. Improvements to your diet at the beginning of August can help to eliminate toxins and increase your overall stamina, but the regenerative power of Pluto is strongest during the first half of December, when it aligns with bountiful Jupiter.

 SEEK TRUTH OVER FANTASY

There is a lot of activity on the home front early in the year, especially when Mars keeps you hopping from February 25 until April 6. You continue to be under a long-term Neptune influence in your 4th House of Home and Family, making it tough to maintain clarity about your dreams. But an opposition to stern Saturn culminating on June 25 can burden you with responsibilities that force you to see the truth, even if it is discouraging. Once you accept reality, however, it is easier to improve upon it—and this becomes your primary task during the rest of the year. Remember that Neptune can turn up the volume on your spiritual practice, too, so creating and utilizing a space at home for yoga, meditation, or relaxation can provide a calming influence this year.

FREQUENT FLYER

You are motivated to travel this year for a variety of reasons. First, Jupiter, the planet of long journeys, is strong in its home sign of adventurous Sagittarius, so you may have free-floating wanderlust all year long. Jupiter harmoniously trines Saturn in your 10th House of Public Status, suggesting that you may get on an airplane for work-related responsibilities or perhaps to fulfill family obligations. Jupiter also dynamically squares eccentric Uranus in your 5th House of Play throughout the year, so you may be inclined to take a vacation for sheer pleasure. If so, this trip could happen on an impulse, especially around late January, mid-May, or early October. Since the 5th House is also related to children and romance, either could trigger your desire to escape.

SOMETHING VENTURED, SOMETHING GAINED

You are curious about the mysteries of the universe, and this year your need for metaphysical exploration is stronger than usual. With Jupiter squaring unorthodox Uranus, you are inclined to study a variety of teachings. However, with Saturn opposite spiritual Neptune, you are pulled back to earth if you are not practical in applying what you learn. Be willing to risk your intellectual security in anticipation of learning something new and enlightening.

RICK & JEFF'S TIP FOR THE YEAR:
Be True to Yourself

If you get distracted by someone else's vision, you might falter and lose your center of power. On the other hand, remain true to your core beliefs, and you will have an opportunity this year to create a wonderful equilibrium between your desire for new experiences and your need for long-term stability. Be conscious, however, that whatever you do now will impact your life in very practical ways for a long time to come. Even if you must make choices that limit your freedom of expression, rest assured that the rewards will justify the temporary sacrifice.

JANUARY

CONTROL YOUR PASSIONS

Your year begins with an emotional Cancer Full Moon in your 9th House of Big Ideas on **January 3**, arousing dreams of grand adventures and stimulating your desire to share these visions with loved ones. But your escape plans may not get far when energetic Mars receives a reality check from authoritative Saturn on **January 8**. Mars may be saying "go," but Saturn the Boss says "slow down and make it real." The real problems, however, continue to grow through **January 13**, when Mars runs into powerful Pluto. Mars and Pluto are your two key planets, and their alignment can fill you with such intense passion that you can scare off meeker souls. You can also unconsciously express anger that mobilizes others to resist your efforts. This is a tricky time, and you must overcome negativity to get the most positive results from your unending source of physical energy now.

On **January 16**, self-directed Mars enters ambitious Capricorn in your 3rd House of Communication, where it stays until **February 25**. Mars is quite effective here, granting you extra stamina and the willingness to work hard. Use this time to solidify your plans and to move methodically toward your goals. The Capricorn New Moon on **January 18** reconfirms your commitment to your profession and community. But it also signals a shift of emphasis to your 4th House of Home and Family that's bound to create conflict with work responsibilities. On **January 22**, a dynamic square between far-reaching Jupiter and erratic Uranus sets up a long-term cycle that lasts throughout the year, imparting a combination of restlessness and adventure into your life. Be open to changes that can increase your freedom, but you may have to take a calculated risk with money or in love to make the most of this time.

> **KEEP IN MIND THIS MONTH**
>
> *You can become so compulsive that you forget that others may not feel as intensely. If necessary, go off by yourself until your emotions settle.*

KEY DATES

JANUARY 8 ★ *frugal actions*
Practical issues about money might alter your long-term planning as Mars in your 2nd House of Possessions harmonizes with conservative Saturn, giving you a keen organizational sense. Bold action positively impacts your career. Don't waste time on frivolous endeavors, for you won't always have as much energy at your disposal.

JANUARY 13 ★ *transform fear*

Mars and Pluto—your two key planets—come together today in your 2nd House of Values, showing you what passion is really all about as it intensifies your love energy. You might attempt to hold back a tidal wave of feeling for fear of what may happen if you tell the truth. But controlled anger can easily turn into resentment, which is even more destructive in the long run. Replace blame with practical solutions, and above all, use your willpower to keep from succumbing to negativity.

SUPER NOVA DAYS
JANUARY 16–18 ★ *spiritual retreat*

You can finally settle down to work on **January 16,** when fiery Mars enters disciplined Capricorn, encouraging you to take a more serious approach to accomplishing your goals. Your ambitions are reemphasized by the steady Capricorn New Moon on **January 18.** However, you temporarily may not have your feet firmly on the ground while romantic Venus is contacting illusory Neptune in your quiet 4th House of Home and Family. You might be rather confused about a personal issue, and it may not be productive to try to clarify the situation. Although you could find time for spiritual retreat by withdrawing into fantasy, you may feel uneasy because you are missing the depth and detail that normally makes you comfortable. Be careful about falling into escapist behaviors, especially the overuse of sex, drugs, and alcohol.

JANUARY 22 ★ *don't give up*

Today, as the liberating Jupiter-Uranus square culminates, you can also feel the isolation of an emotionally restrictive opposition between the love planet, Venus, and the karmic planet, Saturn. It's tough to experience sensory pleasure now without fully considering all consequences of your desires. There's no playful romance today without engaging serious issues. No matter what, hold on to your long-term dreams, for the current limitations will not outlast your passion.

JANUARY 26–28 ★ *strengthen your plan*

Mercury contacts nebulous Neptune on **January 26** and constrictive Saturn on **January 28,** first diffusing your thoughts into the realms of imagination and then precipitating your dreams into reality or dispelling the fantasies with the hard, cold truth. It can be frustrating, but the key is to use the obstacles that Saturn places in your path to tighten your thinking and strengthen your communication skills.

FEBRUARY

SET NEW GOALS

Discouragement may resurface now as the second of three oppositions between confusing Neptune and rock-solid Saturn distorts your perceptions of reality. You might discover that the foundations of your home life or career are not as stable as you thought. These issues began to surface last summer during the first Saturn-Neptune contact and will intensify all month as the aspect culminates on **February 28**. But there is a higher spiritual purpose to the changes you are now contemplating. If you feel as if you have lost your purpose, it is time—between now and the final opposition on **June 25**—to move through your disappointment and create new dreams to inspire the next phase of your life.

The dramatic Leo Full Moon in your 10th House of Career on **February 2** can galvanize your professional prospects. Although responsibilities weigh heavily on you, replenish your soul by setting time aside to have fun or to just be alone in quiet meditation. A particularly powerful few days between **February 7 and 10** can captivate your imagination with an exciting dream, but it may just turn into a distracting detour. Retrospective contemplation is assisted by mental Mercury's retrograde from **February 13 to March 7**, but you must be extra careful to avoid misunderstandings during this period. While Mercury is in imaginative Pisces until **February 27**, you are more inclined to rely on spiritual wisdom and your own dreams than on facts. The emotionally detached Aquarius New Moon on **February 17** poses a dilemma, placing your passions at odds with logic. This New Moon can clear your mind of excessive emotional drama. Plus, in the weeks ahead, your intuition is strong and your compassion deep as the Sun joins a pileup of planets in watery Pisces.

> **KEEP IN MIND THIS MONTH**
>
> *Don't judge yourself harshly if you can't measure up to your rigid idea of perfection. Reality can be clouded by fears, even when you struggle to get your facts straight.*

KEY DATES

FEBRUARY 3 ★ *soften your approach*

This is an uplifting day as you express your feelings with your closest friends and family. The Sun's sextile to joyous Jupiter revives your optimism and confidence as you share your goals. But direct Mars's sextile to shocking Uranus has you forcing your ideas on others before they are ready to hear more. You are on a roll but need to take things slower, or you may alienate your greatest supporters. Remember that gentle persuasion is more effective than coercion.

SUPER NOVA DAYS
FEBRUARY 7-10 ★ *opposites at work*
Opposing forces spark emotional wildfires, fan the flames, and douse them with cold water. Venus conjuncts wild Uranus on **February 7** and then squares joyful Jupiter on **February 9**, reactivating the exciting potential of the long-lasting Uranus-Jupiter square that was exact on **January 22**. Unconventional desires ripple through your system now, and you are tempted to take almost anything further than needed. You eagerly move yourself right to the edge of rationality. Simultaneously, however, the Sun conjuncts fanciful Neptune and then opposes austere Saturn on **February 10**. You are awakened from your dream by an obstacle blocking your progress at work. This is a test; whatever withstands this phase will prove to be valid and have long-term significance. Forget about the big picture; for now, just take one small step at a time.

FEBRUARY 18-19 ★ *spontaneity creates vulnerability*
Waves of creativity and joy wash through your life as the Sun swims into inspirational Pisces on **February 18**. With five planets now in your 5th House of Romance, you may be drawn toward anyone and anything that allows you to be more spontaneous while playfully revealing what's in your heart. Activities with children can turn into fun for all. But beautiful Venus in Pisces harshly squares your key planet Pluto, drawing you into a complex web of feelings. Behind any power struggle, there may be compulsive relationship issues, along with the opportunity to expose your deepest desires if you are willing to face your fears.

FEBRUARY 24-25 ★ *truth sets you free*
Once again, conflicting planetary pressures challenge you to find comfort amid mixed messages. A tense aspect between impulsive Mars and electric Uranus tempts you to take unnecessary romantic risks, while a similar aspect from sexy Venus to stern Saturn cautions you to keep your desires to yourself. You feel as if you are damned if you do and damned if you don't. Relief, however, arrives as Mars enters progressive Aquarius, encouraging you to share the truth with less concern for the consequences. You feel cleansed from your past experiences, enabling you to tackle what's next.

MARCH

LEAN INTO THE WINDS OF CHANGE

You now must reconsider your personal needs with respect to those around you. A Full Moon Eclipse on **March 3** in astute Virgo is opposite a highly expressive Sun-Uranus conjunction in your 5th House of Fun. You know exactly what to do to enjoy yourself. You are in touch with your inner child and possibly with real kids. How spontaneous can you be without upsetting the status quo? The answer comes from the increasing steadiness of optimistic Jupiter's harmonious trine with level-headed Saturn. You can probably get away with more outrageous behavior, for rocking the boat these days won't necessarily tip it over. You can rely on the ballast of good judgment as this aspect occurs on **March 16** for the first time, setting up career opportunities that can be back on your plate when it is repeated on **May 5**.

Mercury turns direct on **March 7**, indicating that you are finished with your necessary review and can now begin to turn your revised plans into action. The propitious Jupiter-Saturn trine on **March 16** is reinforced by several aspects to powerful Pluto. You are standing at the very edge of change. Push firmly and resolutely against the resistance you face; your persistence now is critical if you are to reach your goals over the following months. An intense Solar Eclipse in boundless Pisces tensely squares compulsive Pluto on **March 18**, raising control issues around money, love, or children. It may feel as if you are fighting for survival, but the intensity will fade and the struggle will settle down soon after "just do it" Mars opposes restrictive Saturn on **March 22**. Relax if you can, and float along for a few days without having direction.

> **KEEP IN MIND THIS MONTH**
>
> *Don't overreact early in the month; your sense of urgency will fade. Make your big move mid-month to utilize the great potential for growth.*

KEY DATES

MARCH 3–5 ★ *spontaneous fun*
The discerning Virgo Full Moon Eclipse in your 11th House of Groups and Friends on **March 3** makes for a hectic weekend. Although practical, you are also attracted to something new and different. The Sun conjuncts unconventional Uranus on **March 5**, pulling you off course and preparing you for radical change. Spontaneous emotional expressions can catalyze a romantic situation. Make the changes you have been considering, especially if the tension has become unacceptable.

MARCH 8-9 ★ *steady as it goes*

Sweet Venus harmonizes with both Jupiter and Saturn as they move closer to their alignment on **March 16**. Fortunate Jupiter feels the love planet first on **March 8**, blessing a romantic or financial situation. Then on **March 9**, Saturn seals the deal with an agreement that can sustain you through thick and thin so that both love and money are stabilized. Don't, however, be more forceful than necessary. You may overestimate your ability to make it all happen right now. You needn't hurry as much as you think. Just keep everything moving along steadily in anticipation of what is ahead.

SUPER NOVA DAY

MARCH 16 ★ *make magic now*

An easygoing trine between the cosmic regulators—expansive Jupiter and contractive Saturn—sets the stage for positive developments in your career. It's a struggle, however, to find balance when you are being tempted by opportunities that look too promising. Luckily, Mercury the Communicator assists psychologically intense Pluto, allowing you to dig deeply into your subconscious mind for guidance about complex issues. Mysteries that were unknowable are now fully accessible. Magic is ready to happen if you act on what you believe.

MARCH 22-23 ★ *work through frustration*

You might find yourself in a situation where you have bitten off more than you can chew, and it's exasperating that you can't do everything. But if you're willing to put in the effort as impassioned Mars opposes authoritative Saturn on **March 22**, you can overcome the resistance by the weekend. It's up to you to turn an apparently unsolvable dilemma into a more manageable situation. Optimistic Jupiter supports Mars on **March 23**, allowing you to feel great about a job well done.

MARCH 25 ★ *clouds of illusion*

Your ego drive dissipates as willful Mars meets diffusive Neptune. You thought you knew where you were going, but now unsettling uncertainty shrouds your destination in the mists of your imagination. The separation between reality and fantasy is thin, so use this day to retreat into spiritual interests instead of applying your energy to worldly pursuits.

APRIL

HOLD STEADY TO THE COURSE

You are adjusting to a subtle change of tides as the stabilizing trine between Jupiter and Saturn that began last month continues to positively impact your professional and social standing. Unrestrained Jupiter turns retrograde on **April 5** and contractive Saturn turns direct on **April 19**, creating alternating waves of optimism and realism. Although several aspects can widen your horizons, your caution prevents you from overstepping boundaries or expecting too much too soon. Accepting the good news without getting carried away will allow you to maintain a healthy perspective on the work that is still ahead of you. The Full Moon in even-keeled Libra on **April 2** can help you temper the extremes by reminding you to keep your eyes on the distant goal instead of being frustrated by what is presently just out of reach. A supportive sextile between your two ruling planets, Mars and Pluto, on **April 4** can give you a shot of powerful determination and drive, giving you the ability to conquer temporary obstacles. Act quickly, for forceful Mars enters watery Pisces on **April 6**, and you might lose your sense of direction for a few days.

You will make steady progress toward your goals throughout the second part of the month with the go-getter Aries New Moon in your 6th House of Work on April 17, marking an energetic shift to your ongoing efforts. You receive a powerful boost from Pluto as it trines the New Moon. This is the best time to set your plans into motion, especially as harmonious aspects between mental Mercury and the ongoing Jupiter-Saturn trine grant you clarity of thought and depth of perception between **April 20 and 27**.

> **KEEP IN MIND THIS MONTH**
>
> *Don't lose sight of long-term goals, for you're laying the key groundwork that can take months to reach fruition.*

KEY DATES

APRIL 4 ★ *strong but silent*

Sensual Venus forms a tense square with confusing Neptune, confronting you with the differences between your attractions and reality. This could be a fuzzy kind of day where your feelings may leave you in an emotional mess. Fortunately, Mars forms a supportive sextile with intense Pluto, positively impacting actions that can speak louder than words. It's easy to become enamored with a fantasy; however, weighing all of the factors can ensure that your decision will be a wise one.

SUPER NOVA DAYS
APRIL 8-9 ★ *follow your intuition*
A mixture of positive and negative forces morphs into a productive energy as dark thoughts are alchemically transformed. The Sun harmonizes with both Saturn and Jupiter now, giving you a clear and optimistic view of reality. Your current feelings are based upon very practical issues, so don't let anyone talk you out of your perceptions. Meanwhile, thoughtful Mercury in dreamy Pisces harshly squares dark Pluto, bestowing power and intensity onto your words. You can compulsively seek answers to questions about love or blindly project your fears onto others as you deny the secret feelings within yourself. If you are involved in a power struggle, remember that communicator Mercury wants your thoughts spoken out loud or written down on paper to avoid any misunderstandings. The bottom line is that this is no time to hesitate; trusting your intuition is essential.

APRIL 20-21 ★ *hard work ensures success*
Good news about your career can improve your life now, indicating the possibility for increased financial stability. Your mind is sharply focused on bettering your position as intelligent Mercury activates the Jupiter-Saturn trine from your 6th House of Work. With Saturn in the picture, you are quite serious about elevating your professional status. Don't talk yourself out of success before it arrives. You have specific tasks that must be accomplished, and you just need to do them without making a big fuss. Others will notice your competence, and you will get your just rewards.

APRIL 28-30 ★ *calculated risk*
The wild and crazy planet Uranus is set ablaze on **April 28** by the heat of Mars in your 5th House of Play. This can be disruptive and uncomfortable if you are fearful of change, yet it can be spontaneous and pleasantly surprising if you are willing to take an emotional risk. Be careful, though, about taking action on every whim or desire, for the tense Mars-Jupiter square on **April 30** encourages you to believe you can get away with just about anything. Heightened anxiety may propel you toward action, but don't overdo it just to impress others.

SCORPIO

MAY

WAKE UP AND SMELL THE FLOWERS

This is an intense month filled with significant changes—some are expected, but some may certainly surprise you. The ongoing trine between buoyant Jupiter and weighty Saturn, which peaks on **May 5**, enables you to persevere while taking your work to the next level. Even if you have little to show for your efforts, it's still not too late to seek positive growth in your career and to add stability to your finances. No matter how well you have applied yourself during this time, another long-term aspect—this one between Jupiter and erratic Uranus—can issue a wake-up call on **May 10**, when it is exact. This dynamic square began opening your eyes to ways of creative expression back on **January 22**. Whether you pursue them or not, joyful opportunities awaken your inner child. Activities with kids and the playfulness of romance are highlighted. Don't assume, however, that your exhilaration will last unless you make a commitment.

This month is unusual because there are two Full Moons. The first, an emotionally expressive Scorpio Full Moon on **May 2**, can be a bit upsetting, as your intensity might rub someone the wrong way. It's not that you are being difficult; you are simply trying to bring suppressed issues into the open. Even if you turn things a bit topsy-turvy for a while, life will sort itself out by **May 16** at the grounding Taurus New Moon in your 7th House of Partnerships, allowing you to rely on others when you need them. The second Full Moon, on **May 31**, is in philosophical Sagittarius in your 2nd House of Values. You are full of inspirational ideas that can be effectively put into moneymaking action over the weeks ahead.

> **KEEP IN MIND THIS MONTH**
>
> *Whatever happens is not separate from a much larger series of events. Remember that the structures you are building can support your growth throughout the year.*

KEY DATES

MAY 5–6 ★ *more than meets the eye*

Your strong organizational skills may elicit praise and widen your career path. Although hardworking Saturn receives encouragement from joyful Jupiter, someone may block your next move. You can do solid work under the pressure of clever Mercury's square to restrictive Saturn on **May 5**. This may not be so tough if you are actively pursuing opportunities for advancement; it's harder if you resist the changes. Attractive Venus opposes compelling Pluto on **May 6**, possibly dragging you into a complex emotional drama. Don't be afraid to jump into the deep water to uncover a vital truth.

SUPER NOVA DAY
MAY 13 ★ *emotional moderation needed*
Your energy level is exceptionally high as assertive Mars and obstinate Pluto are squaring off today in a tense showdown. You may be supercharged with feelings that are even more than you want to manage, but deal with them you must. Even if you feel at odds with an individual, don't push the conflict to the max. If you do, there may not be a winner. You are overreactive as you fight for survival, so be on the lookout for ways to salve open wounds. All will be much less intense if you can channel your passion into physical expression.

MAY 20 ★ *shocking words*
The wide-angle lens of the Jupiter-Uranus square that was exact on **May 10** is reactivated today by inquisitive Mercury as it opposes bigger-than-life Jupiter and squares unorthodox Uranus. Problems may seem magnified, but so will the potential opportunities. Your logic is keen, but you can easily make more out of what's happening than is necessary. Your opinions might be extreme, inciting others to action, and this is probably what you want. There's something about the shock value of what you say that carries power. It's like you're pushing the buttons of others for your own amusement and excitement. Be aware that your actions could backfire on you with a surprise.

MAY 27-31 ★ *significant conversations*
The days leading up to the powerful Sagittarian Full Moon on **May 31** can be quite challenging as the conversations in your life sink into the mysterious unknown. Chatty Mercury in glib Gemini is prepared to discuss anything, including sex and death, as it opposes dark Pluto on **May 27**. This is a time of great transformation when your basic perceptions about yourself continue to evolve. Your passions are volcanic and you may feel a confrontation building, but Mercury becomes less communicative as it slips into watery Cancer on **May 28**. Avoid holding your feelings in. Make use of the expressive trine between Mars and the Full Moon by passionately sharing what's in your heart.

JUNE

SHIFTING SANDS

The deepest planetary current of the year—one that began on **August 31, 2006,** and repeated on **February 28**—culminates on **June 25** as Saturn the Taskmaster opposes metaphysical Neptune. Saturn in proud Leo in your 10th House of Career requires that you have absolute integrity in the workplace and the community. Neptune in Aquarius in your 4th House of Roots softens your inner world and fuels your desire to escape into fantasies of an ideal home life. Their opposition turns the most solid bedrock into shifting sand. You may not feel very secure now if you have previously focused only on material acquisitions and achieving status. On the other hand, a strong spiritual orientation can grace you with much-needed inner strength at this time. Remember that even if you haven't reached your destination yet, you have gained much wisdom along the way.

Both Mars and the Sun harmonize with the intensifying Saturn-Neptune opposition between **June 11 and 13**, temporarily relieving the pressure if you are willing to take the initiative to approach your daily work routines in new ways. The mentally active Gemini New Moon in your 8th House of Intimacy on **June 14** falls right in line with this planetary support network. Shadowy Pluto's involvement with the New Moon reminds you to delve into the unknown, for that's where your most significant growth originates. But then, on **June 15**, Mercury turns retrograde in your 9th House of Travel and remains in reverse until **July 9**, marking a time to reconsider vacation plans for the rest of the year. The cautious Capricorn Full Moon on **June 30** finds you reflecting upon your recent progress and regrouping as you set new goals.

> **KEEP IN MIND THIS MONTH**
>
> *Allow your unfulfilled wishes to slowly fade away so that they can be replaced by new and more meaningful dreams.*

KEY DATES

JUNE 4 ★ *blend enthusiasm with realism*

Your attitude is on an upswing and contributes to your productivity today as willful Mars harmoniously trines bountiful Jupiter. You probably realize that your current wave of enthusiasm won't last, but hopefully you are wise enough to make the most of it while you can. Accept recognition for your hard work—maybe even an overdue bonus—graciously. But keep in mind that even this positive influence has a shadowy side, for impulsive actions can have unexpected consequences.

JUNE 11–13 ★ *on target*

Fiery Mars trines cold Saturn on **June 11**, and although these two hard energies are contradictory, now they work exceedingly well together, allowing the practical execution of your well-considered ideas. Even though Mars then sextiles dreamy Neptune on **June 13**, your ambitions clearly direct your actions. Neptune's positive role now is to add vision, rather than confusion, to your plan. The right mixture between hard, cold reality and illuminated imagination strengthens your intuition. Your willpower is strong, and your hunches are right on target. Don't waste the awesome potential by escaping reality.

SUPER NOVA DAY
JUNE 18 ★ *there's more than one way*

The Sun makes its annual opposition to relentless Pluto, and the tension may become temporarily unbearable, but you cannot fully express what you're feeling without offending someone. Burying the intensity doesn't work, either. Even if you know you are right, remember that you must allow for multiple points of view. Instead of trying to come out on top, finding common ground allows everyone to win.

JUNE 21 ★ *go for the gold*

Aggressive Mars and passionate Pluto combine their significant forces in a harmonious trine today, and you could quickly overwhelm others without even realizing it. Mars can be selfish as it moves through Aries, so it's critical to use your energy for the good of all. Restrain your drive for personal power now, and you could be rewarded with what your heart desires. Others are ready to jump in to help as long as you include them in your upcoming success.

JUNE 30 ★ *dream a little dream*

The calculating drive of the Full Moon in ambitious Capricorn today is somewhat dissipated by an opposition between sensual Venus and spiritual Neptune. These two planets of love can make an unusually sweet combination, yet tensions may surface at work arising from unrealistic expectations on the home front. It's a real challenge to acknowledge your personal needs in the outer world. Still, it's a dreamy day, but be careful about self-deception, as pleasure-loving Venus must answer to the harsh judgment of Saturn within the next couple of days.

SCORPIO

JULY

FOUNDATIONS AND TRANSFORMATIONS

Another deep wave from the cosmos laps upon the shores of your consciousness this month as karmic Saturn steadily moves toward a harmonious trine with your powerful ruling planet Pluto. Although this transformational aspect won't reach completion until **August 6**, it continues to stabilize your life, potentially increasing financial security or self-esteem. At the least, your confidence should allow you to advance professionally while gradually shifting your long-term goals to include more meaningful activities. However, the month may begin on a difficult note with lovely Venus feeling the cold judgment of Saturn. This can be a healthy attitude adjustment, and by **July 8**, when Venus trines Pluto, you know that you are on the right path. Your new direction is confirmed over the days ahead as messenger Mercury turns direct on **July 9** to bring you thoughts of the future rather than of the past. Things are looking up for you, even with a minor meltdown on **July 11**, when combative Mars and Pluto could drag you into a skirmish.

The sensitive Cancer New Moon on **July 14** may be somewhat confusing as it amplifies your emotional strength, yet an irritating quincunx with fuzzy Neptune makes it a real challenge to describe your feelings. Additionally, feisty Mars crosses swords with Chiron the Wounded Healer, possibly raising old fears of inadequacy tied to prior relationship difficulties. Emotional satisfaction may be elusive as Venus slows her forward motion to turn retrograde on **July 27**, initiating a period of challenges in love. The quirky Aquarius Full Moon on **July 29** may surround you with alternatives. You know it will work out fine, but the frustration might take a few more days to play out as Mars squares cold Saturn on **July 31**.

> **KEEP IN MIND THIS MONTH**
>
> *Relationship issues can open old emotional wounds. Don't place your fears between you and the happiness that may be just around the corner.*

KEY DATES

JULY 1 ★ *create functional boundaries*

Today, as beguiling Venus meets up with resistant Saturn in your 10th House of Career, consciously restrain your own intensity so that you don't have to deal with difficult consequences. Being a tough negotiator is one thing, but your insecurities may push you to make too many demands. Consciously softening your position can put others at ease so that everyone feels like a winner.

SUPER NOVA DAYS
JULY 9-11 ★ *make peace within the storm*
Mercury is more sensitive than usual as it turns direct in moody Cancer on
July 9. Although your summer plans may begin to take concrete shape, you
still might want to steer clear from too much social activity while restoring
equilibrium to your emotional and spiritual life. On **July 10**, hotheaded Mars
and overbearing Jupiter push you overboard when reacting to someone else's
aggression. Mars and Pluto form a tense sesquisquare on **July 11**, so counter
any unpleasant encounters with gentleness rather than anger.

JULY 14 ★ *the power of choice*
Today's quiet Cancer New Moon bodes well by providing an opportunity to harness
your own emotional power and increase your ability to manage change. Even if it's
challenging to verbalize your desires, don't give up. Venus, the love planet, enters
analytical Virgo, so being selective about what you want may be what you need.

JULY 20 ★ *unsettling changes*
Life may feel very uncertain with many undecided issues up in the air. Energetic
Mars is forming a sextile with exciting Uranus, releasing creative blockages and
arousing romantic needs. Circumstances can change quickly, but it's not all going
to happen overnight. Nevertheless, now that the catalyst has been added to the
solution, you must let the reaction play on through.

JULY 24 ★ *blocked fantasies*
With action-packed Mars dynamically squaring unrealistic Neptune, the conflict
between your outer world and your spiritual world may come to a climax. Although
you have access to a deep well of wisdom, it may not be tied to the demands of
your everyday life. Don't force your will upon others. Instead, engage with external
circumstances as honestly and directly as possible. You'll have time later to attend
to your magic and dreams.

JULY 31 ★ *temporary angst*
Others may think you are being stubborn, yet you see them as the source of the
problem. Expressive Mars and restrictive Saturn square off today, making you less
flexible than you prefer and more likely to project blame onto a friend or partner.
Whatever your frustrations are at this time, rest assured that they will diminish
over the next few days, even if it seems as if you can do nothing about them now.

SCORPIO

AUGUST

AT THE CROSSROADS

This month opens with mixed signals from your two ruling planets, Mars and Pluto, as they form an unstable quincunx on **August 1**. It can be hard to tell how much pressure to apply while attempting to impose your will on others. But a temporary lack of sound judgment gives way to deep certainty as authoritative Saturn harmoniously trines evolutionary Pluto on **August 6**. You are standing at the edge of a great transformation, and your lack of fear is your greatest strength. Although you may not be able to tell where your current path is taking you, there is no reason for concern. As long as you possess complete integrity, whatever happens now is preparing you for a stabilizing career shift as you look farther into the future.

Retrograde Venus backtracks into rough territory as it squares scattered Mars in Gemini on **August 7**. Even if you know what you want, satisfaction may be out of reach. Then, just one day after the dramatic Leo New Moon on **August 12**, Venus runs into judgmental Saturn, possibly reactivating a frustrating scenario from the beginning of last month, when Venus and Saturn had their first clash. If issues weren't resolved around **July 1**, you may have to wait for their final conjunction on **October 13**. Now can be rather somber with serious Saturn blocking thoughtful Mercury on **August 18** and the Sun on **August 21**. But by **August 23**, a new wave of optimism washes through your life, leading up to a fantasy-driven Full Moon Eclipse in Pisces on **August 28**. This eclipse in your 5th House of Love can be a profound reality check if you are too detached from your passions and dreams.

> **KEEP IN MIND THIS MONTH**
>
> *The more you try to keep things the same, the more stress you will face. Embrace the changes ahead by being flexible instead of fearfully resisting what could prove to be most beneficial.*

KEY DATES

AUGUST 1–3 ★ *holding pattern*
Aggressive Mars irritates intense Pluto, compelling you to take bold action, but you may annoy others instead of being an effective leader. And although logical Mercury and Mars work together to make your words quite convincing, Mercury also quincunxes Pluto, perhaps adding a lack of clarity to your communication. It's best to ease up for a few days until the emotional environment is more receptive.

AUGUST 9 ★ *know your value*
Mercury trines effervescent Jupiter, boosting your spirit and cheering you on to think big. This harmonious aspect links your career and resources houses, reinforcing the balanced optimism you currently bring to your job. Don't be afraid to ask for that overdue raise. You just might get what you are worth. But even if there's no financial involvement now, you can still feel satisfied about what you do.

AUGUST 12–14 ★ *quiet celebration*
The outgoing Leo New Moon joins a party of four planets in your 10th House of Career and Community. You could receive recognition now, but karmic Saturn in the mix may subdue the celebration. Nebulous Neptune opposes the proud Leo parade, indicating that dreams may need to be denied while you are directing your energies to the outside world. No matter what, listen to your small inner voice throughout this time.

AUGUST 17–18 ★ *thinking like a detective*
Mental Mercury trines mysterious Pluto on **August 17** and conjuncts authoritative Saturn on **August 18**. You can probe right to the core and uncover the essential truth. But Saturn can be a stickler now for detail, requiring you to follow the rules exactly. Also, with sweet Venus conjunct the Sun, admiring the beauty around you will help the tensions quickly pass.

AUGUST 23 ★ *exaggerated expectations*
Fiery Mars opposes buoyant Jupiter, expanding your optimism enough for you to steamroller most any negativity. But your tendency to overreact makes it tough to know what your limitations are until you have gone too far. You could spend more energy or money than you should. Don't get carried away by your own enthusiasm.

SUPER NOVA DAY
AUGUST 28 ★ *creative juice*
The intuitive Pisces Full Moon Eclipse can flip a switch in your creative process and open a brand-new channel to your imagination as analytical Mercury opposes lightning-like Uranus. It's as if you are racing your mind on an open road, eager for the excitement of the upcoming twists and turns. Your mental responses are highly tuned today, and you feel like you can navigate through anything that comes your way. Consciously slowing down your thoughts, however, can make your intellectual touring less dangerous and more thrilling.

SEPTEMBER

BE CAREFUL WHAT YOU WISH

On **September 2**, hardworking Saturn enters practical Virgo in your 11th House of Friends and Wishes, shifting your attention from the 10th House of Career and Community, where your primary focus has been for the last two years. You have established a place in the world based on your past work performance. If you have lived up to the responsibilities placed upon you, it's now time to consolidate previous gains while dreaming about what comes next. This is not about idle fantasies; Saturn in Virgo is about precision. It marks the beginning of a two-year phase when social engagements can modify the direction of your life. Your best friends, work associates, and acquaintances gain importance as they reflect your dreams back to you. Instead of working harder to get the next promotion, you take other things such as meaning and purpose into deeper consideration.

Your energy is somewhat scrambled with assertive Mars in undisciplined Gemini, especially when it squares freedom-loving Uranus on **September 3** and trines imaginative Neptune on **September 8**. An exciting new romance may be activated on **September 11** by the Virgo New Moon Eclipse opposite Uranus in your 5th House of Love and Creativity, but this can also play out through matters with children. Dealing with unexpected events can gobble up your valuable time and money, so keep an eye on your purse strings. Your two driving forces, Mars and Pluto, stand opposed on **September 21**, with the Sun tensely squaring both. Although these are dangerous emotional waters, a little self-restraint combined with kindness can grant you the power to accomplish more than you realize. The Aries Full Moon in your 6th House of Work on **September 26** reminds that you shouldn't sacrifice creative expression to get a job done.

> **KEEP IN MIND THIS MONTH**
>
> *Harder work may bring greater success, but your efforts might be best applied toward personal, rather than material, rewards.*

KEY DATES

SEPTEMBER 2–3 ★ *preemptive expression*

Your words can sting like a scorpion as Mercury squares off with obsessive Pluto on **September 2**. Energetic Mars activates unconventional Uranus on **September 3**, creating an electrified environment of excitement and impulsiveness. You may feel like you're ready to explode, but the worst thing you can do is hold it in, because suppression just doesn't work now. The emotional energy must express itself, so try to let it out consciously and gradually, rather than waiting for something or someone to precipitate a meltdown.

SEPTEMBER 8-11 ★ *tensions require compassion*
There is more happening than meets the eye during these days preceding the intensely focused Virgo New Moon Eclipse on **September 11**. Although you may be dealing with a minor annoyance at work over creative styles, inflexibility will make matters worse. The opposition to explosive Uranus increases stress in personal relationships now as you obsess about freedom or what you've sacrificed for love. You're ready to forgive, yet Mars's trine to mysterious Neptune on **September 8** can also make you unrealistic or confused, so put off major decisions until next week.

SEPTEMBER 17 ★ *move your body*
The Sun squares impetuous Mars, driving you to the edge of your patience and escalating the potential for ego skirmishes. You may not get your way and are quite ready to fight for your cause. Unfortunately, aggression is counterproductive, bringing only unhappiness and stress. Create healthy outlets for your physical energy through exercise, dance, or even sex so that it doesn't get bottled up inside.

SUPER NOVA DAYS
SEPTEMBER 19-21 ★ *emotional intensity*
Your two key planets—fiery Mars and passionate Pluto—now stand at opposite ends of the sky. There may be intense drama in your life, perhaps a clash over values or a disputed piece of property. You may get caught in your own web of intrigue as you try to prevail in a relationship struggle originating possibly from jealousy or possessiveness issues. You can consciously apply this power positively toward deep transformations as you convert negativity into love.

SEPTEMBER 26 ★ *less is more*
A reckless Aries Full Moon today is somewhat restrained by an annoying quincunx to serious Saturn, making you feel as if you cannot get away with anything that isn't exactly according to the system. But you really want to speak your mind now instead of blindly following rules with mental Mercury being dared by opinionated Jupiter. And with today's Mars-Mercury trine, your words can be exceptionally forceful. Downsizing your message and lightening your touch can effectively convince others to adapt to your point of view.

OCTOBER

STRONG EMOTIONAL CURRENTS

Your world becomes even more emotionally charged this month with planets in each of the water signs—Cancer, Scorpio, and Pisces. Assertive Mars is hesitant now as it slows down in sensitive Cancer, where it stays for the rest of the year due to its retrograde beginning **November 15**. You are more patient these days and are willing to wait for optimal conditions before starting something new. In fact, you may be so tentative that you delay until someone else initiates action, forcing you to respond accordingly.

Messenger Mercury, now in impassioned Scorpio, adds intensity to your words as they explore hidden feelings. Mercury turns retrograde on **October 11**, submerging your thoughts even deeper and dredging up memories to help you gain perspective while you wrestle with a current spiritual dilemma or problems at home. And although Mercury backs up temporarily into a gentler Libra on **October 23**, the Sun reinforces the water element as it enters your sign on the very same day. Additionally, eye-opening Uranus in compassionate Pisces completes the emotional circuit. Your passions are stronger these days, and you're revitalized and inspired rather than agitated by your deepening awareness.

On **October 9**, the third and last square between grandiose Jupiter and shocking Uranus increases your spontaneity and expands your nonconformity as you dream of taking daring risks. Romantic or financial issues dating back to January 22 and May 10 are again on your plate and spur you on to make a move. Then the pleasant Libra New Moon in your 12th House of Secrets on **October 11** activates your fantasies and further stimulates your unorthodox desires. By **October 16**, a series of harmonious aspects brings several smooth-sailing days, but the stubborn Taurus Full Moon on **October 26** can stir up relationship dynamics and create yet another whirlwind of excitement.

> **KEEP IN MIND THIS MONTH**
>
> *You are swimming in strong emotional currents, so remember that when you get caught in a riptide, don't exhaust yourself by struggling against the flow.*

KEY DATES

OCTOBER 3 ★ *fulfilled desires*

Pluto symbolizes the hidden treasures buried within your subconscious mind, and although these mysteries are often unreachable, now the doors are unlocked. Your feelings are the key, and as sensual Venus harmonizes with Pluto, you have the power to create deep satisfaction for yourself and an intimate partner. You know what you want and are ready to go for it. Don't fall into the trap of setting your expectations too high, or you may end up being disappointed.

OCTOBER 8 ★ *eyes on the prize*

As energetic Mars forms a supportive sextile with stabilizing Saturn, your ability to organize complex projects into manageable tasks is razor-sharp. You might even assume a supervisory role to set things right on the job or at home. Focus on the long-term goals rather than specific events while you continue inching forward.

OCTOBER 13 ★ *one last look back*

Sweet Venus conjuncts harsh Saturn, closing an emotionally restrictive phase that began on **July 1**. Even if you have tucked your feelings away for safekeeping, they may again rise back up to the surface. Don't take yourself too seriously now, for your past efforts will begin to pay off soon enough. If you must make a significant purchase or sign a contract, make sure you feel certain about it. If you don't, then let it slide for a few days, for your attitude and your finances are about to improve.

SUPER NOVA DAYS
OCTOBER 16–20 ★ *wide-open road*

You can be productive while having fun this week as the tides turn in your favor. It feels as if the tough days are behind you and that your creativity has returned. Don't hold back; let your active mind run like wild horses. You can see your future yet are flexible enough to incorporate the views of others, too. But if you must take a stand on a point that is personally important, make certain that you are fighting for the right cause before you burn your bridges.

OCTOBER 26 ★ *be patient*

The Taurus Full Moon is in your 7th House of Partnerships, arousing your needs and presenting you with a romantic dilemma. On one hand, the Taurus Moon attracts you to the simple pleasures of love and the delights of the senses. On the other hand, a Venus-Uranus opposition stimulates your desire for freedom. This creates an approach/avoidance issue that certainly influences your behavior in relationships. Even if you think you know what you want, your emotions are in flux, so what you wanted last month may differ from what you will want next month.

SCORPIO

NOVEMBER

ANYTHING CAN HAPPEN

This month tempts you with the euphoria of love, the thrill of playful interactions with children, and the rush of your own creative process. Still, something is missing, as total gratification may not be achieved easily. Artistically expressive Mercury in Libra turns direct on **November 1** and reenters intense Scorpio on **November 10**. You are relentless as your sharp mind now probes for the secrets beneath the surface. Physical Mars in self-protective Cancer turns retrograde on **November 15**, building power behind the scenes by delaying immediate action and slowing the forward progress in many areas of your life. It is this backward motion of your traditional key planet that can also leave you feeling slightly unsatisfied until it turns direct early next year.

Regardless, your month is filled with several surprising and enchanting experiences. A volatile Scorpio New Moon on **November 9** creates emotionally active trines with both sexy Mars and "anything goes" Uranus. Your world could be turned topsy-turvy from a new romantic interest, or you might revitalize an existing relationship. Spontaneity can be your best friend; enjoying the moment is its own reward. From **November 19 to 21**, rational Mercury reactivates these lovely trines, bringing another round of pleasant surprises as you make plans and anticipate the possibilities of the long holiday weekend. Elation may turn to concern by **November 24** as the hectic Gemini Full Moon in your 8th House of Shared Resources stirs up uncomfortable relationship issues. Significant choices must be made, but they are not yours to make alone. Active communication now is more urgent than solving any one problem. Forcing a decision prematurely can create a frustrating end to a stimulating month, but relinquishing control prepares you for the big changes ahead.

> **KEEP IN MIND THIS MONTH**
>
> *Life's pace is quickening, and you may feel intoxicated by the possibilities. Your happiness, however, may depend on not expecting too much too soon.*

KEY DATES

NOVEMBER 5 ★ *make room for love*

Your sexual urges are stronger than usual and may provoke relationship issues as romantic Venus squares passionate Pluto. But it's not just about physical gratification; power struggles over love or money demand your attention, too. You feel as if you must fight for survival now with deeply rooted feelings interfering with your sensual pleasures. Don't let this opportunity pass, even if you are uncomfortable. Dig into the root causes of your fears so that you can loosen their emotional ties to allow the transformation to occur.

NOVEMBER 7 ★ *outside the box*
The magnetic Scorpio Sun illuminates brilliant Uranus, wiring your already strong feelings. Events will not unfold according to your plan, but if you make adjustments to your attitude, amazing things can happen. Paths will appear before your eyes where previously there was no possibility of passage. Go ahead and express your emotions without regard for social convention. It's time to clear the air of resistance as you step over the edge—a wondrous experience awaits your arrival.

NOVEMBER 11 ★ *dream power*
The Sun's square to diffusive Neptune can be somewhat confusing, but there is also something about the craziness of it all that amuses you today. Common sense just cannot withstand the pressure from your creative imagination. Give yourself permission to set logic aside while you entertain your fantasies. Rest assured that the real world will intrude and force your return just in time so that others may not even realize that you have been on an inner journey.

NOVEMBER 19–21 ★ *let go of your fear*
This might begin as a stressful period, but the outcome will probably be pleasant. On **November 19**, sweet Venus in social Libra is square to not-so-assertive Mars, which is retrograde in defensive Cancer. Your actions may not support your desire, and you could even push satisfaction away. But as insightful Mercury harmoniously trines Mars later in the day and then Uranus on **November 21**, your thoughts are connected and your actions are clear. Your physical energy is positively wired by what you think; the skies clear and you can soar with the eagles.

SUPER NOVA DAY
NOVEMBER 24 ★ *carve out time for solitude*
Your logical mind fights with your intuitive faculties as mental Mercury's square to dreamy Neptune is overstimulated by the scattered emotional energy of today's Gemini Full Moon. Perhaps an overabundance of holiday conversation has made it difficult to integrate all of the new information. It may get louder before it settles down, so stay focused on the here and now. Enjoy the chatter of friends and family without worrying about what's coming next.

DECEMBER

TRANSFORMATION ABOUNDS

Seeking adventure this month elevates your spirits and improves your self-esteem as planets congregate in fiery Sagittarius in your 2nd House of Self-Worth. This can also focus your attention on financial plans that go beyond holiday shopping, such as purchasing furniture, a new car, or even a home. Whether the changes are psychological or material, you are nearing the end of a growth-filled year. Buoyant Jupiter, moving through big-thinking Sagittarius this year, has encouraged you to widen your perspective. It makes a once-every-thirteen-years conjunction with your ruling planet Pluto on **December 11** and then steps into practical and ambitious Capricorn on **December 18**. You have the power needed to transform your environment into a more supportive and healthier place that will serve you well for the future. You should take advantage of this tidal wave of change by working extra diligently throughout the first half of the month.

The highly inspirational Sagittarius New Moon on **December 9** provides a clear vision of your future, along with the impetus to break free from your own judgments that can limit your growth. Although you may feel a bit crazy from the square to erratic Uranus, you are receiving organizational support from a stabilizing Mars-Saturn aspect. Try not to get discouraged between **December 18 and 21** as Jupiter, Mercury, and the Sun each leave the party world of Sagittarius and enter Capricorn's world of hard work and social obligation. You could, however, also feel relief, for you may be eager to get started with the many ambitious projects on your plate. The emotionally fulfilling Cancer Full Moon on **December 23** colors your holidays with an abundance of activity as energetic Mars and opulent Jupiter turn even a small gathering into a significant social event.

KEEP IN MIND THIS MONTH

Your positive attitude is crucial as you eliminate outdated aspects of your life in preparation for next year. Concentrate on the potential of the future instead of mourning the loss of the past.

KEY DATES

DECEMBER 1–3 ★ *new vistas*
Your life's horizon widens and your vision extends as Mercury enters philosophical Sagittarius on **December 1**. Venus adds a bit of sweet optimism to the day as it sextiles Jupiter. You have a good chance to get what you desire, but a difficult Mars

aspect on **December 2** can make you unsure of your plans. Reconsider your priorities before committing to a project. A Venus-Pluto sextile on **December 3** brings an opportunity to create magic by exploring the shadowy world of your unexpressed feelings. Darkness is not evil; it's just more complicated than daylight, where things are easily visible. Shining the light of awareness into rarely touched emotional places transforms fear into love.

SUPER NOVA DAYS
DECEMBER 9-12 ★ *this is it*
A spiritually uplifting Sagittarius New Moon on **December 9** heralds the powerful Jupiter-Pluto conjunction on **December 11** that drives you to achieve financial success and to demonstrate your worth to others. Making a critical decision can be challenging, because there is potential everywhere. With Pluto's involvement, you must choose by a complex process of elimination, but you receive support in the form of a series of trines and sextiles. You are in a most fortunate position, so make the most of these days. Although a high-tension square from mental Mercury to electric Uranus can have you running too quickly, rest assured that you are being guided by spirit. Follow your intuition, and convert your great ideas into momentous action.

DECEMBER 17-19 ★ *creative breakthrough*
Romantic Venus harmoniously trines unconventional Uranus on **December 17,** arousing sensual desires and new avenues for creative expression. You love the unusual and might purchase avant-garde art or unique clothing. But Jupiter's entrance into conservative Capricorn on **December 18** may have you wondering if you've gone too far. Wait until **December 19,** when Mercury conjuncts probing Pluto, before finalizing decisions about recent purchases or relationship potential.

DECEMBER 23-26 ★ *practice moderation*
The family-oriented Cancer Full Moon on **December 23** aligns with feisty Mars and stands in opposition to joyful Jupiter. This can be a creative and fun-loving time if you are willing to temporarily set aside your long-term responsibilities. Don't miss the opportunity to have a good time and enjoy yourself, even if you feel like you have too much work to do. Your self-discipline may be temporarily lost, making it hard to place limits on your indulgences. Your job is to be present, but try not to make any promises in the heat of the moment that you cannot keep.

SAGITTARIUS

NOVEMBER 22–DECEMBER 21

SAGITTARIUS OVERVIEW

This is the year that you have been waiting for as your key planet, Jupiter, makes its once-every-twelve-years return to your sun sign, bestowing grace and opportunity onto your life. As the Archer, you aim your arrows of intent high; your targets are often far in the distance. Now you can see even farther, and your power is even stronger. Jupiter's influence works like a magnifying lens by making your life even bigger. But you like grandiosity, so this will feel quite comfortable, even familiar. There are other planetary influences this year, but jovial Jupiter in your sign—from November 23, 2006, until December 18, 2007—will likely be the most obvious and should provide a fortunate underpinning for a very successful year. Jupiter was last in your sign in 1995, which may have been the beginning of the opportunity cycle that is currently coming to a close. **You see good news now everywhere you turn, yet this will also require you to make a number of long-term decisions.**

Although this may be a truly wonderful time, there are potential pitfalls that demand your attention. First, because Jupiter can make anything appear better, be careful about accepting an opportunity before you really check it out. Whether it's a fantastic job offer or an exciting new romance, the joy of Jupiter will eventually pass, perhaps leaving you with less than what you imagined. Second, because Jupiter encourages you to overextend yourself, be cautious about making a commitment that you cannot keep. Third, because Jupiter widens your perspective, you can gloss over important details. Remember that sloppy work and hasty thinking will not be rewarded, so use extra diligence.

The slow wave of the Jupiter tide recedes from April 5 until August 6. Shore up your plans and conserve your energy during this retrograde period. Jupiter dynamically squares erratic Uranus three times—on January 22, May 10, and October 9—creating an exhilarating yet destabilizing sequence of interrelated events. With Uranus in your 4th House of Home and Family, **unexpected changes, a physical move, or even the purchase of a new home is not out of the question.** Meanwhile, serious Saturn harmoniously trines Jupiter on March 16 and May 5, balancing the melodramatic Uranus scenario with clear thinking and patience. Still, you may feel dissonance between the commitments you willingly make and the freedom you wish you didn't have to sacrifice.

An ongoing opposition that began last summer between Saturn the Task-master in your 9th House of Higher Education and Neptune the Dreamer in your 3rd House of Communication can temporarily take the wind out of your sails around February 28 and June 25. This may be a crisis of confidence, making you wonder if you really have what it takes to reach your profession-al goals. Avoid critical decisions around these times, unless they involve going back to school or taking courses that can positively impact your career. A life-changing conjunction between "more is better" Jupiter and evolutionary Pluto on December 11 places you on the threshold of a new chapter of your life. Get ready for an incredible ride as you aim your next vol-ley of arrows twelve years into the future.

REALISTIC LOVE

Your enthusiasm fuels the vagaries of your heart, but generally speaking, this is a rather straightforward year for you in the department of love. Saturn is in demonstrative Leo, demanding that you methodically express your feelings. Its ongoing trine to Jupiter balances your romantic expectations with the hard, cold reality of the truth. There is less room for ungrounded fantasy now than for creating a stable relationship that functions efficiently. Your charm is intoxicating when Venus is in assertive Aries from February 21 until March 17. Your physical energy is superhot when Mars is in fervent Aries from May 15 until June 24. Seek stability instead of excitement when Venus is in relentless Leo from June 5 until July 14 and again from August 8 until October 7.

BUILD LASTING SUCCESS

Success may come easily now, but it won't last unless you consciously create a foundation. Unfortunately, attracting a great job or a profitable deal isn't enough. Your glory can fade as quickly as it arrives. Jupiter tricks you into believing that all will work out for the best; however, Saturn's positive presence reminds you that your persistence will pay off even more than your positive attitude. The efficient Virgo Full Moon Eclipse in your 10th House of Career on March 3 can turn your job responsibilities upside down. Don't struggle against the changes; they may open a path in a new direction. The Virgo New Moon and Solar Eclipse on September 11, also in your 10th House, again indicate unexpected changes that release pent-up tensions and free you to be more productive.

 ## REAP YOUR JUST REWARDS

Though your earning potential is likely to increase with Jupiter in your sign, do not overestimate your income or underestimate your expenses. As the ruler of your 2nd House of Money, Saturn holds your purse strings, and its move into your 10th House of Career on September 2 can portend success. Jupiter-Saturn trines on March 16 and May 5 present investment opportunities. Much depends on how you've handled karmic Saturn's rise toward your 10th House over the past decade. Take responsibilities seriously and work hard without cutting corners, and you'll be ready to receive the financial rewards you seek.

 ## REINVENT YOURSELF

This year, nurturing your overall health and positive attitude may be your best ally in your desire for increased vitality. Jupiter in your sign encourages you to set goals early in the year and then create the daily routines to support your healthy new lifestyle. Physical exercise is significant, but don't overlook the value of an optimum diet and moderation in your choices. Overcome temporary negativity or malaise at the end of both February and June with nature hikes, sporting activities, and even yoga. The conjunction on December 11 between powerful Jupiter and regenerative Pluto can be the final touch to your transformation, so don't wait until then to begin your process of renewal.

 ## SURPRISES ARE BREWING

Unpredictable Uranus in your 4th House of Home and Family is a long-term transit that began in 2003. However, big-thinking Jupiter dynamically squares Uranus throughout this year, making you restless and rebellious. Your high spirits long for additional excitement within your home. Shaking up the status quo seems like a good idea as you consider a major remodel, a change of residence, or even a new roommate. Whether you choose them or not, there will be disruptions to the flow of your life, yet this whirlwind provides the exhilaration you seek. The hectic pace may become extra distracting when Uranus is further stimulated by Venus on February 7, by Mercury on April 1, and by Mars on April 28, but will settle back down by mid-May.

TAKE YOUR TRAVEL SERIOUSLY

Adventure may not happen as easily this year as others, but you may still do serious traveling as long as you are willing to work hard to make it happen. Even the simplest trips will require serious planning now. Austere Saturn is moving through your 9th House of Journeys, so chances are that you will be flying economy rather than first class. And travel for business or study may take precedence over a vacation. However, once you get going, Saturn's trines to Jupiter in mid-March and early May can indicate prosperity resulting from your travels. The Saturn-Pluto trine in early August may be the right time for a summer getaway, especially if you want a memorable experience.

WORK AT TRANSFORMATION

Mystical Neptune learns from disciplined Saturn this year. You can further your spiritual studies by sticking to tangible goals. This is the final year of a long-lasting metamorphosis that gives you a deeper understanding of the mysteries of the universe as authoritative Saturn trines Pluto on August 6. You may need to narrow your focus to advance your practice, but it is easier now to eliminate distractions. Your metaphysical journey culminates with a once-every-thirteen-years Jupiter-Pluto conjunction on December 11. Don't wait until then to try to reach your goal. The sooner you start, the more wisdom you gain.

RICK & JEFF'S TIP FOR THE YEAR: Create Balance

The changes that you make this year are opening the way to a road that you'll travel for the next twelve years. Even though you're used to thinking big, it's time to move beyond previous limitations. Dream of lofty but attainable goals, for you must have something inspirational to work toward. Don't let this year slip by along with the incredible potential that it offers. Yet aiming too high can be problematic, generating failure and disappointment that dampen your enthusiasm. Don't be afraid to create parallel plans and to adjust them based upon your experiences throughout the year.

JANUARY

FREE YOURSELF

The Full Moon in caring Cancer on **January 3** lands in your 8th House of Intimacy and Shared Resources. This can touch a nerve as accountability for financial and emotional matters develops into a sensitive issue. If you are disappointed in a partner's performance, it's best to bring it up gently than to stay silent. On the other hand, if someone says you are not meeting his or her expectations, don't let defensiveness block an honest exchange that can get the relationship back on a more positive track. The New Moon in conscientious Capricorn on **January 18** in your 2nd House of Money should trigger an ambitious yet practical idea about increasing your income. The message is that prudence, not impatience, will be the most effective path to profitability.

Jupiter, your ruling planet, gets the year off to a rollicking start with its major aspect to rebellious Uranus on **January 22**. This first of three squares sets the stage for a series of inner shifts and changes that can alter the shape of your future for years to come. The tense right-angle relationship between the principles of expansion and revolution affects your appearance, attitude, and home life. While restlessness is to be expected, it's better to apply it by creating a new relationship, image, or living situation than to express it through resistance to and resentment of your circumstances. Invent and go forward instead of complaining and hanging back. The power to free yourself is in your hands, and the starting point is to let your imagination awaken a more fulfilling vision of your future. Think of this as a first draft; a revision will come with the second Jupiter-Uranus square in May and the final adjustment in October.

> **KEEP IN MIND THIS MONTH**
>
> *Original ideas for change flood your mind, but don't take serious action until you have finished careful deliberation.*

KEY DATES

JANUARY 3 ★ *ask for what you need*

The tender Cancer Full Moon brings out your cuddly side and an uncharacteristic need to feel protected. At the same time, however, loving Venus enters cool and detached Aquarius, making it harder to show your vulnerability. Helping you can make someone else's day, so go ahead and ask for what you need. A lover, friend, or family member will not be put off by your request, but will be happy to get closer to you by being able to offer whatever support you desire.

SUPER NOVA DAYS
JANUARY 12-13 ★ *strictly confidential*
Your planet, Jupiter, receives a sweet sextile from sociable Venus on **January 12** that enriches your social life and enhances your sense of self-worth. On the same day, a stressful semisquare from chatty Mercury to Jupiter suggests indiscretion due to spilled secrets. Respect the privacy of others, and demand the same. Mercury's conjunction to serious Pluto on **January 13** indicates that the consequences for breaking trust can be severe. With the right person, this can be an appropriate time to discuss highly personal issues, but do it in a safe setting with the strictest rules of confidentiality in effect.

JANUARY 16 ★ *reality check*
A semisquare between the Sun and optimistic Jupiter increases self-confidence and promotes salesmanship. Yet offers made or heard might not stand up to close scrutiny. Promoting yourself is smart as long as you can deliver on your promises or commitments. Active Mars enters result-oriented Capricorn, so concepts will be measured against reality very quickly. A thoughtful plan to manage any new projects should be in place before asking others to cooperate.

JANUARY 22-23 ★ *persistence wins*
The Jupiter-Uranus square is exact on **January 22**, sending ripples of excitement through your day. A wise Mercury-Jupiter sextile gives you the capacity to put your ideas together effectively and communicate them with enthusiasm. Resistance may come with a Venus-Saturn opposition that attracts skeptics who are reluctant to say yes, no matter how compelling your plan. But a magical quintile between delightful Venus and magnanimous Jupiter on **January 23** gives you the social skills to overcome any resistance.

JANUARY 27-30 ★ *tender feelings*
Venus enters intuitive Pisces and your familial 4th House of Security on **January 27**, providing you with a safe and dreamy environment at home. Adding ethereal beauty to your surroundings is sure to inspire you. An opposition between Mercury and responsible Saturn on **January 28** is a time for a significant conversation with a family member. If you run into a serious bump in the road, a clever quintile between Mercury and Jupiter on **January 30** opens your mind and shows you an explainable solution that should resolve any concerns.

SAGITTARIUS

FEBRUARY

A BIT OF HEAVEN ON EARTH

On **February 2**, the Full Moon in generous Leo brightens your 9th House of Truth, Travel, and Higher Education. A supportive trine from expansive Jupiter in your sign widens your eyes with visions of exotic places, inspiring you to manifest a more fulfilling future. Invest in a better tomorrow by reading and taking courses designed to improve your professional skills and motivate your creative impulses.

Mercury hits the brakes and turns retrograde on **February 13**, staying in reverse mode until **March 7**. The cycle begins with the communication planet in your 4th House of Home and Family, where it is likely to dig up unresolved issues from the past. But finding the words to express these muddled feelings may not be easy, and listening to someone close to you who tries to explain things can be even harder. Be patient with slow talkers, fuzzy speakers, and those who lack the facts, because clarity can be hard to come by now. Pay attention to tone and tempo, and meaning will reveal itself on another level. This poignant poetry will tell you more about the soul than about the world to reconnect you with a vital part of yourself.

The inventive Aquarius New Moon on **February 17** crackles with bright ideas and unexpected connections. Seek more intellectually stimulating company to fan the flames of curiosity for a wide variety of unconventional subjects. On **February 28**, practical Saturn and mystical Neptune form the second of three oppositions, a process that began late last August and finishes in late June. Saturn could ground wasteful flights of fancy so that you can attend to the business of making dreams real. A tangible piece of paradise, no matter how small, is worth more than a vision of heaven you cannot reach.

KEEP IN MIND THIS MONTH

Breaking habitual patterns of thinking may produce short-term disorientation but will help you find the answers you seek in the long run.

KEY DATES

FEBRUARY 3 ★ *doors are wide open*

The Sun and Jupiter align in a cooperative sextile, an empowering aspect that allows you to make a big impact without looking like you're showing off. The Sun represents your ability to shine, and unabashed Jupiter's support increases self-confidence, enhancing your ability to sell yourself and your ideas. Your words carry extra weight now, so choose them carefully, rather than allowing unbridled enthusiasm to pull you off message. Opportunities to impress others can open doors, but backing up your pitch with a clear plan ensures that your follow-up won't let them down.

SUPER NOVA DAYS
FEBRUARY 7-9 ★ *a wild and crazy mood*

Sweet, sociable, and sometimes sexy Venus puts you in a spunky mood with a conjunction to wild Uranus on **February 7** and a lively square to "bigger, better, more" Jupiter on **February 9**. The love planet's transit of this hot zone of the zodiac may spark some unconventional and erratic behavior on your part. You can find yourself attracted to the strange and unusual as well as terribly bored by predictable people and events. Avoid impulse purchases. Think twice before you paint your living room bright red. It makes sense to shake up your wardrobe or a relationship with stylistic experimentation, but starting small is more logical, since the urge for change can pass as quickly as it came.

FEBRUARY 17-19 ★ *big-picture remake*

The Aquarius New Moon on **February 17** always sparks new ideas, but instead of passing fancies, the ones you get now have an excellent chance to endure. That's because Jupiter forms an integrating quintile with the New Moon that helps you weave any fresh insights into a comprehensive picture of reality. A sextile between resourceful Pluto and the New Moon is another positive influence for pulling together diverse bits of data into a meaningful whole. You know which information is usable and which you can ignore. On **February 19**, Venus squares Pluto, an aspect that may require tough choices about relationships or resources by eliminating who or what rewards you least. Think of it as addition by subtraction.

FEBRUARY 27 ★ *brilliant deduction*

Mental Mercury retrogrades into intelligent Aquarius and forms a quintile with Jupiter. This inventive aspect between the planets of facts and philosophy is excellent for clever thinking and skillful communication. You're able to connect the dots from different parts of your life to recognize a larger pattern of meaning. What appeared as random experiences in the past starts to make sense, enabling you to solve a puzzle that's been bothering you.

SAGITTARIUS

MARCH

INVEST IN YOUR FUTURE

The planetary highlight this month is a trine between your key planet, Jupiter, and karmic Saturn on **March 16**, providing you with a solid foundation for an otherwise dynamic month that includes two eclipses. On **March 3**, the Full Moon in hard-working Virgo is a total Lunar Eclipse that could shake up your professional life. It falls in your 10th House of Career and is directly opposite explosive Uranus. A falling-out with your boss, a sudden change of position, and the realization that it's time to radically alter your work life are strong possibilities. Rapid adjustments to new responsibilities can be exciting but require flexibility and fast thinking to keep pace. On **March 7**, Mercury, the planet of communication, begins moving forward in the zodiac after its three-week retrograde cycle. Information that's been lost may reappear, important messages hung up in transit could finally reach you, and ideas you've been trying to share will eventually get the recognition they deserve.

The New Moon in compassionate Pisces on **March 18** is a Solar Eclipse that stirs emotional waters in your 4th House of Home and Family. Transformational Pluto's hard right-angle square to this Sun-Moon conjunction may force you to remember events you wish to forget. Attend to a gnawing feeling caused by unfinished business with relatives; don't let it linger in silence and undermine trust within your household. Facing the skeletons in the closet can bring enormous relief as shame or doubt is lifted, freeing up your mental and emotional resources to create a better future. If you're tempted to renovate your living space, keep it simple to avoid unpredicted costs and complications.

> **KEEP IN MIND THIS MONTH**
>
> *Maintain a lighter load, as unexpected events are likely to demand extra attention that will fill up your schedule.*

KEY DATES

MARCH 1 ★ *have fun instead*

Your adventurous spirit may take you on a wild goose chase today. Impetuous Mars meets extravagant Jupiter in a miscalculating semisquare that can lead to overestimating your resources. Activities take more time than planned or offer more promise than they can deliver. If you have extra energy, spending it on a recreational event is bound to produce more fun and less complications than investing it in an overly ambitious work project.

MARCH 8-9 ★ *luck is on your side*
Venus in risk-taking Aries trines fortunate Jupiter to give your personal life a boost on **March 8**. Be the initiator in organizing a gathering of friends or an intimate tête-à-tête with the object of your affection. Take a chance on love, as a gambling heart is bound to win. Venus trines stabilizing Saturn on **March 9** while the Sun squares Jupiter. These contrasting aspects also suggest that pushing your luck appears to be a safe bet. Trust your instincts even if you feel like you're teetering on the brink of disaster, because if you don't feel like you're going too far, you're not going far enough.

MARCH 16 ★ *strategic superiority*
Optimistic Jupiter trines pessimistic Saturn in the first of a series of aspects that will continue on and off through late 2008. This perfect alignment of the planets of growth and prudence is excellent for long-range planning, especially associated with career and education. You have a strong strategic sense that allows you to seize an opportunity and see it to its successful conclusion. Trust your realistic vision and your ability to commit to your goals.

SUPER NOVA DAYS
MARCH 20-23 ★ *beware of overindulgence*
The Sun fires into spontaneous Aries on **March 20**, the first day of spring and the springboard to romance and creativity in your chart. Make room in your day to play like a child and imagine a more exciting world for yourself. A Venus-Jupiter sesquisquare on **March 21** could lead to excess, but just don't spend the rent money and you can enjoy a little extravagance. Mars opposes disciplinarian Saturn on **March 22**, an arresting aspect that disapproves of excessive behavior. But a supportive trine between the action planet, Mars, and generous Jupiter on **March 23** reveals that limits are being imposed not to punish you, but to turn your grandiose vision into reality.

MARCH 28 ★ *easy magic*
A clever biquintile between charming Venus and Jupiter gives you magical powers of persuasion and a gift for turning a dull day into a festive one. You can make sad people smile with a silly joke or make a drab outfit look classy with a surprisingly simple but creative tweak.

SAGITTARIUS

APRIL

ALL SYSTEMS GO

Your growth is tempered this month as your key planet, Jupiter, reverses direction while ambitious Saturn turns forward. Beneficent Jupiter turns retrograde on **April 5** and will continue moving backward until **August 6**. Optimism won't disappear, but this marks a time to reevaluate your schemes and dreams, checking in with your gut instincts to see if your plans still make sense. Digest your experiences more slowly before signing on for any big adventures. Serious Saturn turns direct on **April 19**, meaning that it's time to face the music about educational issues and your strong convictions. When it comes to religion or politics, actions count more than words. If you aren't willing to put yourself on the line, it could be that your faith is flagging and that reconsidering your position is necessary now.

The Full Moon in diplomatic Libra on **April 2** occurs in your 10th House of Career, which helps you handle relationship issues on the job. Repairing your connections with coworkers and establishing new alliances to advance in your profession are likely possibilities. In any case, refining your people skills could be a key component to stabilizing and raising your status in the workplace. The New Moon in trend-setting Aries on **April 17** arrives in your playful 5th House of Self-Expression. This monthly conjunction of the Sun and Moon in a dynamic fire sign can push you to make dramatic alterations in your appearance. If you're feeling restless or bored, try a different look, and don't be afraid to be even sassier than usual. Regenerative Pluto's creative trine to the New Moon shows that pushing emotional limits isn't destructive, but can purge negative feelings and clear the way to a fresh start. Reinventing yourself, even through conflict, will turn out to be empowering now.

> **KEEP IN MIND THIS MONTH**
>
> *Fighting can be healthy if you play fair. Take responsibility for your feelings, be honest, and no hitting below the belt.*

KEY DATES

APRIL 3–4 ★ *objects are smaller than they appear*
Evaluative Venus and analytical Mercury form hard aspects with enthusiastic Jupiter on **April 3**, skewing your good judgment. A tendency to overrate someone, pay more than you should for something, or believe an exaggerated tale is to be expected. You, too, can overstate your case, overextend, and overindulge. An even fuzzier Venus-Neptune square on **April 4** continues to favor fantasy over reality,

but a hyper-efficient Mars-Pluto sextile on the same day can cut through the fog of illusion and reduce unwarranted magnification where necessary.

APRIL 8-9 ★ *make your move*
Don't let little uncertainties hold you back, because you're on very solid ground now. The Sun forms trines with Jupiter on **April 8** and Saturn on **April 9**, making a powerful grand trine in your fiery element, an awesome mix of creative energy and competence. Think big, look far, and count on leaps of faith to land you in the right places. A Mercury-Pluto square on **April 9** can plant a seed of doubt that requires tackling a knotty issue, but don't let imaginary problems derail your master plan.

APRIL 17 ★ *spontaneity rules*
The Aries New Moon could spark a fire of desire that opens your heart to love. Whether you're rekindling the flame for your present partner or starting up with someone new, it's appropriate to feel like a teenager again. The same passion can be applied creatively through the arts or simply in the art of making others happy. Being cool and self-contained is so yesterday. Let the impetuousness of the moment be your banner now.

APRIL 20-21 ★ *the sharpest mind in the drawer*
Mentally mobile Mercury in Aries tosses thunderbolts of fresh ideas onto fertile ground with constructive trines to practical Saturn on **April 20** and strategic Jupiter on **April 21**. You've got a gift of gab that's like a laser beam of light—a wave of unmistakable intelligence that's perfect for making a point, setting a plan, and keeping a promise, no matter how bold and far-reaching.

SUPER NOVA DAYS
APRIL 28-30 ★ *exceeding the speed limit*
Loading up on luxuries could be more costly than you think on **April 28**. Venus seeks extravagance with an opposition to overdoing Jupiter, while Mercury's perceptions are distorted by a sesquisquare to Venus. A high-frequency conjunction between impulsive Mars and lightning-strike Uranus tosses caution to the wind. But a rapid course correction is likely on **April 29**, when racing Mars bounces off a quincunx with speed bump Saturn, and accelerates again on **April 30** as it squares Jupiter. With Venus also trining imaginative Neptune, you're in store for a magical mystery tour, but you need to try to apply the brakes to keep from falling over the edge.

MAY

ORDER AND CHAOS

The planets are popping for you this month with two Full Moons and a pair of major aspects from your key planet, Jupiter. On **May 2**, the relentless Full Moon in Scorpio shines light on your 12th House of Secrets and Spirituality. You may have to face the music to a song you prefer not to hear again, but doing so can dissolve an old fear and allow you to breathe more freely. The practical Taurus New Moon in your 6th House of Work on **May 16** helps you focus on your day-to-day activities. The **May 31** Full Moon in Gemini is exciting and explosive, especially when you are interacting with others; it falls in your 7th House of Partnerships with aspects from extroverted Jupiter and experimental Uranus, bringing rapid changes on the relationship front. Your own restlessness can lead to breaking rules about whom you connect with and how. But solid support to the Full Moon from Mars and Saturn, the kings of competence, indicates that you'll be able to skillfully handle whatever or whomever you attract.

Jupiter's two major aspects contrast order and chaos. A reliable trine with Saturn on **May 5** repeats a productive pattern that began in mid-March. This highly strategic alignment between the planets of expansion and contraction is perfect for combining risk and reason to manifest your vision. Their well-choreographed dance continues through 2008 in practical earth signs that are likely to bring you more professional recognition. On **May 10**, though, the second of three Jupiter-Uranus squares crackles the air with mind-blowing thoughts and an impulse to radically change your life. But before you pack the car and head for parts unknown, you might want to stop and make a plan to take you where you want to go instead of just escaping from where you are.

> **KEEP IN MIND THIS MONTH**
>
> *Patience is your ally, because it allows you time to digest the explosion of information coming your way.*

KEY DATES

MAY 5 ★ *unproductive detours*
The slow-moving Jupiter-Saturn trine operates in the background while a less stable Mercury-Jupiter quincunx takes the lead. Conversations slide around the point, requiring more time to get your message across. What a person presents as a critical issue might be only a distraction, turning a small matter into a major waste of time. Choose how you spend yours carefully now.

SUPER NOVA DAYS
MAY 8-11 ★ *flashes of clarity*
The Sun makes tough aspects to Jupiter on **May 8** and Saturn on **May 9** prior to the big Jupiter-Uranus square on **May 10**. A Sun-Jupiter quincunx can overload you with work, so don't add to the pile voluntarily. A Sun-Saturn square puts a sudden stop to unrealistic plans and overinflated expectations. The struggle to prove yourself can bring an inner sense of purpose and clarity that will help you capture the Jupiter-Uranus lightning in a bottle. Be at your best, with Zen-like concentration and focus. Stay calm, even if people around you are panicking, and you can receive a brilliant gift of awareness.

MAY 15-16 ★ *let the games begin*
Fun is heading your way as willful Mars fires its way into go-getter Aries in your 5th House of Romance on **May 15**. The urge for action brings out an even bolder side of your personality. Artistic, social, and sporting endeavors are terrific outlets for spontaneous play. Take risks by expressing your inner child and showing your feelings. This blunt display of your desires could ruffle the feathers of overly sensitive individuals, but don't let their fears hold you back. The New Moon in down-to-earth Taurus on **May 16** may bring a relaxed attitude on your job and, hopefully, inspire you to seek more fulfillment through your work.

MAY 20-21 ★ *talk, talk, talk*
Fact-based Mercury opposes philosophical Jupiter and squares eccentric Uranus on **May 20**, bringing an overflow of information that can stress your nervous system or bring an unexpected revelation. The Sun's entry into communicative Gemini on **May 21** attracts chatty people in your 7th House of Partnerships. This is a very busy time when your social life crowds private time out of your calendar, which could suit you just fine.

MAY 28 ★ *repair relationships*
Loving Venus and wise old Jupiter meet in a magical biquintile that can help you heal a wounded relationship. You find value in others and in yourself that may have been previously difficult to recognize. Don't be put off if you feel misunderstood or unappreciated. You can overcome someone's lack of respect for you with a surprising show of talent and social skills.

JUNE

FIXING RELATIONSHIPS

The sheer intensity of your passion inflates your optimism to an impractical size as impetuous Mars harmoniously trines Jupiter on **June 4**. This extravagance is legitimate, and a series of integrative aspects from **June 11 to 13** helps you regain control of your overindulgences. On **June 15**, Mercury in emotional Cancer turns retrograde, churning up unsettled relationship issues through the rest of the month. Exposing vulnerabilities about your needs and fears can build a strong bridge of trust. Whether the connection is sexual, professional, or a close friendship, repairs may be required to maintain what you have and, perhaps, take it to the next level. As always with Mercury retrograde, double-check details and messages to avoid misunderstandings and mistakes.

On **June 14**, the New Moon in friendly Gemini brings activity to your 7th House of Partnerships. New people can pop into your life, and you may be ready to go public in ways that you haven't done before. Powerful Pluto's opposition to this Sun-Moon conjunction may force you to make a difficult choice. Jealousy over your availability could pressure you to cut back with one person to free up more time with another. Erratic Uranus square the New Moon might put you on edge, making it difficult to feel settled. But solid Saturn and mighty Mars forming favorable aspects supplies you with plenty of good judgment and physical resources. Just don't be led by others' priorities; set your own agenda. The deeper truth of your own desires will be your most reliable compass for finding happiness. Crystallizing Saturn makes its third and final opposition to idealistic Neptune on **June 25**, completing a long process of committing yourself wholeheartedly to a dream that began late last August. The steady Capricorn Full Moon on **June 30** reflects your need to clarify your values and put your financial house in order.

> **KEEP IN MIND THIS MONTH**
>
> *Being real about your feelings is more important than being right when it comes to strengthening your bonds with others.*

KEY DATES

SUPER NOVA DAYS
JUNE 4–5 ★ *larger than life*
A trine between dynamic Mars in Aries and boundless Jupiter in Sagittarius fills your tank to the top on **June 4**. High enthusiasm and an abundance of

energy make you an unstoppable force. You can work and play hard enough to fill two days in one. Your charisma sizzles, and you're successful at promoting yourself and your ideas. The fire continues to burn on **June 5** with a Sun-Jupiter opposition and an indulgent Venus-Jupiter sesquisquare, followed by the love planet's red carpet strut into showy Leo. You could overpower mere mortals who can't match your strength and endurance, so remember to turn it down a notch in a delicate situation.

JUNE 11–13 ★ *an irresistible force*

Your self-control is admirable on **June 11** with a remarkable pair of sextiles from the Sun to Mars and Saturn, which are trine each other as well. This coherent connection of purpose, passion, and planning is extremely productive. Yet the force of your will is tempered with tenderness as the Sun trines compassionate Neptune on **June 12** and Mars sextiles Neptune on **June 13**. Incredible strength matched with finesse makes you almost irresistible when you set your sights on a specific target now.

JUNE 18–21 ★ *calculated risks*

A Sun-Pluto opposition on **June 18** can put you in a power struggle, a game you don't especially like to play. But a Venus-Pluto sesquisquare on **June 19** can show you the high cost of avoiding confrontation when your needs are at stake. Sweet Venus is also trine generous Jupiter, so don't be afraid to ask for what you want or to give openly if it suits your purpose. A Mars-Jupiter sesquisquare on **June 21** is usually associated with going overboard, but active Mars also forms a creative trine with Pluto on the same day. This combination of excess and control favors risk taking. You're pushing the limits yet have the sharpness to avoid real danger. Just be aware that others may need to be more cautious and won't be able to match your desire for adventure now.

JUNE 30 ★ *due diligence*

The Full Moon in reliable Capricorn opposite the Sun and Mercury awakens you to financial realities today, especially those involving shared resources or property. If you've been careless with money or lack training for a job you want, that's likely to become obvious to you. However, fanciful Venus also opposes Neptune, a pair that prefers romance and fantasy to dealing with practical matters. Take care of necessities first so that you can play later with a clear conscience.

SAGITTARIUS

JULY

This is a relatively quiet month astrologically, making this a favorable time for getting away from it all, especially when the Sun struts into its home sign, outgoing Leo, in your 9th House of Travel on **July 22**. Life does have its challenges, of course, but they appear to be less stressful than usual now. In fact, good judgment and self-control can go a long way toward making your life run more smoothly. Two fast-moving planets are changing directions: Mercury goes forward on **July 9**, and Venus turns retrograde on **July 27**. Messenger Mercury begins chugging forward in your 8th House of Shared Resources, opening channels of communication that concern financial matters and intimacy issues. On the other hand, attractive Venus's reversal later in the month could have you returning to untangle old relationship concerns connected to your career. Venus will reengage forward gear on **September 8**, which could trigger a deeper interest in both higher education and faraway places.

The New Moon in sensitive Cancer on **July 14** can open tear ducts in your 8th House of Intimacy. Your relatively unsentimental sign might not be happy with histrionics about who's done what for whom lately, but don't disrespect your emotions. They may not be logical in an ordinary sense but might reveal their own meaning, which is essential for understanding partnerships of all kinds. Brilliant Uranus making a creative trine to this New Moon can incite a fresh perspective on the complexity of human relationships that allows you to feel deeply without feeling trapped. The Full Moon in Aquarius on **July 29** crosses your 3rd and 9th Houses, areas associated with questions and answers. It's great to be right, but avoid getting caught up in philosophical disputes in which one side has to be wrong.

> **KEEP IN MIND THIS MONTH**
>
> *Opinions are just ideas with attitude. Share your thoughts without taking yourself too seriously for the best results.*

KEY DATES

SUPER NOVA DAYS
JULY 2–3 ★ *cool down the rhetoric*
Assertive Mars can be stubborn in Taurus, but its cagey biquintile with big-minded Jupiter on **July 2** can help you work around obstinate individuals

who think they know it all. Such flexibility will be needed on **July 3**, when the willful Sun tangles with Jupiter in a clunky quincunx. Egos puff up, pride exceeds prudence, and differences of opinion get blown out of proportion. Back off before overheating occurs and rash statements are said.

JULY 9–10 ★ *brain power*

The Sun's biquintile with Jupiter on **July 9**, the day Mercury goes direct, can broaden your perspective on working with others. Trust your instincts, especially when they tend toward openness and generosity. There's no need to drive a hard bargain when you can engineer a smart deal. On **July 10**, though, macho Mars rubs against Jupiter in an irritating quincunx that can produce friction on the job. This is no time to dig in your heels and match force with force. An ingenious Sun-Uranus trine is present to raise the level of your game, so you can take care of business with more brain and less bravado.

JULY 18 ★ *more than you think*

A dicey sesquisquare between the Sun and Jupiter can make for shaky judgment. Double-check any estimates regarding how much time it will take to complete a task or how great a return you'll get on an investment of energy or money. Keep your workload light if you can, because one small task could unexpectedly grow into a more burdensome responsibility than expected. Less is better than more; it will rapidly turn into more than enough.

JULY 22–24 ★ *blind faith*

Handle sensitive information carefully on **July 22** as Mercury's eye for detail is pushed out of focus by a quincunx from Jupiter. Data may be wrong, or your understanding of what someone said can be off target. The Sun's entry into head-strong Leo, though, heightens pride at the same time. Yet with Mars in a stressful square with slippery Neptune on **July 24**, acting on faith could lead you down the wrong path. Check your progress regularly to be sure that reality is in sight.

JULY 27 ★ *fair market value*

Your financial smarts are cooking with the Moon in your 2nd House of Resources and a masterful Mercury-Jupiter biquintile lighting up your mental circuits. You can handle tough negotiations with a light but controlling hand; be confident that you can work your way out of any difficult situation. If you're not happy with the pay you receive for your hard efforts, it's time to broach a discussion on your compensation package.

SAGITTARIUS

AUGUST

BUILDING A BRIGHTER FUTURE

An enormously powerful aspect enables you to focus your intent and conquer any obstacle that gets in your way this month. The two heaviest planets, Saturn and Pluto, align on **August 6** in a perfect trine for choosing a goal and discovering exactly what you must do to reach it. This slow-moving aspect will be in effect for at least two weeks, during which time you can actualize your potential to operate at a very high level. In fact, with sufficient motivation, you can tap into talents you didn't even know you had. There's time for play now, too, but don't let too much fun distract you from the tremendous opportunity to reshape your body and redefine your future. Your ruling planet, Jupiter, turns direct on the same day, another green light for aiming for the stars.

The New Moon in demonstrative Leo on **August 12** occurs in your 9th House of Future Vision, filling you with hopes and dreams for a better tomorrow. Mental Mercury conjunct the New Moon spews more creative ideas than you can use. And idealistic Neptune opposite the Sun-Moon conjunction tempts you with fantasies just beyond your reach. Take inspiration from these images, but then allow the discipline of Saturn and the concentrated power of Pluto to forge the best image into a realistic plan. The Pisces Full Moon on **August 28** is a total Lunar Eclipse that falls in your 4th House of Home and Family. This can awaken old patterns of escapism rooted in a lack of self-confidence. If you pass through a cloud of self-doubt based on past failures, just let it go by. The eclipse burns off these memories if you don't hold on to them too tightly.

> **KEEP IN MIND THIS MONTH**
>
> *Honor your lofty aspirations with commitment and hard work, because fulfilling your dream is a gift to yourself that can also inspire others.*

KEY DATES

AUGUST 1-2 ★ *believe it and others will, too*

A sesquisquare between Mercury in cautious Cancer and Jupiter in adventurous Sagittarius on **August 1** can magnify problems. You don't need to tackle it all to move toward resolution. On **August 2**, a Sun-Jupiter trine raises your confidence, perhaps as a result of well-earned recognition. You're a motivating leader who can lift the energy level of an entire team with your fiery exuberance, good judgment, and sense of strategy. Your passion excites others, which could brighten up your personal life.

SUPER NOVA DAYS
AUGUST 6-9 ★ *big fun in the summer sun*

This can be an extremely exciting period with Jupiter turning direct on **August 6** while spirited Mars enters your 7th House of Partnerships. A rush of new energy rises as relationships grow livelier with more flirting and teasing. Your life cannot be boring now as romantic games and creative contests come into play with a highly charged Venus-Mars square on **August 7**. You may cross swords with someone whose values or tastes differ from yours, but you can keep it light and sexy and enjoy the contrasts. On **August 8**, lovely Venus warms up in Leo, potentially heating things up to another level of pleasure. On **August 9**, a smooth-flowing trine between Mercury and Jupiter suggests the possibility of travel while increasing your ability to grasp new ideas quickly to eagerly teach others.

AUGUST 15-17 ★ *intimate conversation*

Your ability to assess people is excellent with a Venus-Pluto trine on **August 15** as the Sun and Mercury join each other in your 9th House of Big Ideas. You're able to look past the surface and see great potential in both yourself and others. You may not bother with superficial chatter now, since you value your time too much to spend it carelessly; you have more substantial ideas. Mercury conjuncts Venus on **August 16** and you delight in conversation with passionate people. Mercury trines Pluto while the Sun conjuncts Venus on **August 17**, continuing the talk about serious subjects, including love.

AUGUST 23-24 ★ *easy does it*

An opposition between combative Mars and excessive Jupiter on **August 23** brings out the feisty side of your personality. But instead of spending this force in conflict, take up the challenge of bettering yourself. Push forward to make connections with potential partners or customers. Mercury's square to Jupiter on **August 24** could lead to overexplaining yourself or being overloaded by more details than you can handle. Simplify long stories and prioritize tasks to make the day a bit more manageable.

SEPTEMBER

DIFFICULT CHOICES

Your job may demand more time and energy from you all month long, but this is really just the beginning of a two-year phase with a strong emphasis on your vocation and public status. Saturn the Taskmaster enters perfectionist Virgo in your 10th House of Career and Community on **September 2**, requiring you to be more serious about your place in the world. Whether you have earned recognition in your community or church, a chosen profession, or a position within your family structure, additional duties are assigned to you—and you must be responsible and fulfill your obligations. But Saturn's journey through discerning Virgo can also be problematic as it squares your sun sign. Tough decisions must be made as you confront the parts of your life that are not working out the way you wish.

The practical Virgo New Moon Eclipse in your 10th House on **September 11** opposes explosive Uranus in your 4th House of Home and Family. You are suddenly released from an emotional predicament as hidden information comes to light; however, your newfound awareness may not make life any easier. Nevertheless, you must integrate what you learn into your plans. The gains you make at work can compensate for the temporary loss of stability on the home front.

The intensity of an ongoing power struggle may reach a climax on **September 21**, when aggressive Mars opposes obstinate Pluto. Know when to walk away from a situation that is not winnable. The expressive Aries Full Moon in your 5th House of Play on **September 26** may push you right to the edge. Although you are ready to dive into something new, even a small amount of self-restraint is a good idea now, for there are greater shifts coming your way.

> **KEEP IN MIND THIS MONTH**
>
> *Although you may be forced to manage more detail work than you prefer, it is best to finish it now than to have to deal with it later.*

KEY DATES

SEPTEMBER 3 ★ *contain yourself*

You are highly motivated and ready for action now as the Sun squares enthusiastic Jupiter. And with Mars also squaring impulsive Uranus, you can have a somewhat short fuse. Everything appears as a wonderful opportunity with huge potential. If you use your energy wisely, you'll be able to accomplish a great deal. This is both a strength and a weakness, for you may be tempted to put your efforts toward a project that is better left undone. Since you love to court the big adventures, try paring back your plans and you will be even more effective.

SUPER NOVA DAYS

SEPTEMBER 8-11 ★ *catalytic awakening*

Venus turns direct while forming an irritating quincunx with erratic Uranus on **September 8**, making it difficult to control your desires. Simultaneously, the sirens lure you into dangerous waters as fiery Mars trines deceptive Neptune. Tread carefully, for your ideas can be so grandiose that you get lost. The Sun opposes Uranus on **September 9**, increasing the tension prior to the dynamic Solar Eclipse and Virgo New Moon on **September 11**. The lightning strikes and feelings break out into the open. Although it may be unpleasant at first, the air is cleared, creating space for thrilling new adventures.

SEPTEMBER 13 ★ *keep it real*

Bold gestures communicate your big ideas as the Moon and Mercury sextile powerful Jupiter. Even if you start out small, by the time you are finished, you will have turned a short e-mail into a philosophical treatise. Let your thinking expand to reflect your comprehensive vision, but reduce your plan to a manageable size or you will have little to show for your efforts.

SEPTEMBER 17-21 ★ *count to ten*

This can be a rough few days as the Sun activates a difficult Mars-Pluto opposition. Relationship issues are tricky as extreme positions are taken. Even if you know what you want, you will be sorry if you push too hard. Ultimately, the only way to move through this difficult emotional terrain is by discussing the different points of view. If you can restrain your negative emotions, the sweet Venus-Neptune opposition on **September 21** can soothe the frazzled nerves of everyone involved.

SEPTEMBER 28 ★ *quiet times*

You can take yourself quite seriously as Mars swims into self-protective Cancer— and this can be quite a challenge. You are most often fun-loving and even cavalier, so you might surprise others and yourself when you become more introspective. Don't shy away from discord; the good times will return more quickly than if you avoid the less comfortable feelings.

SAGITTARIUS

OCTOBER

DECLARATION OF INDEPENDENCE

A repetitive theme for the year comes to a conclusion when your key planet, Jupiter, stresses unpredictable Uranus for the third and final time on **October 9**. This square may remind you of your experiences during the first two occurrences on **January 22** and **May 10**, but the current circumstances can be quite different. If you have been even partially successful in capturing the growth potential of the previous squares, this one may not be so dramatic. But if you resist, fearful of upsetting the status quo, your restlessness may push you right to the very edge as you seek excitement to revitalize your life. Your rebelliousness isn't mean-spirited, though; it's strictly about being free from the responsibilities and social systems that bind you.

The lovely Libra New Moon in your 11th House of Dreams and Wishes on **October 11** fully supports your current desire for fulfillment, yet it also tempers your expressions. You are more in touch with your own personal vision and can take extra time and energy to make certain that your friends understand what you want. But you will need patience, for Mercury turns retrograde the very same day, marching backward for the rest of the month and requiring you to retrace your mental steps over previously covered ground. Don't let your frustration destroy what you have already started. A series of harmonious aspects from **October 16 to 20** can give you some breathing room at work. Remember that you should be concentrating on long-term goals rather than short-term gratification. You may know exactly what you want to do with the determined Taurus Full Moon in your 6th House of Work on **October 26**, but a Venus-Uranus opposition could surprise you with unexpected alternatives.

> **KEEP IN MIND THIS MONTH**
>
> *It may feel as if you're missing an opportunity to leave on a great journey, but actually you're already on your way.*

KEY DATES

OCTOBER 1–3 ★ *lighten up*

You are more serious than usual as Mercury sextiles stern Saturn on **October 1**, and you may even be obsessed with trying to organize everything you know into a grand master plan. But as much as you want to make progress, your obsessions slip into sensual scenarios as Venus harmonizes with compelling Pluto on **October 3**. Your feelings are driven now by deep instincts that are beyond logic. Don't try to figure it all out. Express your needs as gently as possible; otherwise, your intensity could scare others away.

OCTOBER 8 ★ *big surprise*

Although a Sun-Jupiter sextile blesses you with optimism, you could overlook something very important. You are also feeling discontent from the perspective-widening Jupiter-Uranus square that is exact tomorrow. Be careful about your aspirations, for you may want something or someone that is totally out of reach. Fortunately, self-directed Mars is supported by hardworking Saturn today, giving you the stamina to achieve your goals and deliver on what you promise.

OCTOBER 13 ★ *temporary isolation*

As loving Venus joins austere Saturn, you may feel isolated from those you love. In fact, you may even push up against the edges of your own comfort zones now as you withdraw from others. If you aren't emotionally free and easy, remember that your current state of seriousness won't last. Don't try to change your feelings; just observe what makes you lonely, and learn from your experience.

OCTOBER 16–20 ★ *emotional building blocks*

You are back in the groove now as prevailing planetary currents smoothly carry you along in your preferred direction. With supportive sextiles among Mercury, Venus, and Mars, you are able to express your feelings in a simple and casual way. But you travel right into the core of your own volcano as intense Pluto enters the picture on **October 20**. Bring your passion to the surface, where it can add substance to the emotional structures you are creating.

SUPER NOVA DAY
OCTOBER 29 ★ *for your mind only*

Sweet Venus squares indulgent Jupiter, encouraging you to overdo it on every front. Also, Jupiter hooks up with dreamy Neptune, diffusing the boundaries that normally remind you of your limits. Giving yourself permission to feel is commendable. It's even okay to meander around inside your own imagination, for no one knows what you are conjuring up within the privacy of your own mind. But your fantasies are quite strong now, as are your desires, so it may be best to share them only on a need-to-know basis. Today, enjoy your vivid dreams without the need to make them real.

NOVEMBER

FEEL YOUR WAY

Currents that have held you in place for the past few weeks now free you to move forward again as mental Mercury turns direct on **November 1**. It's time to put your updated plans into action and progress toward your revised goals. You feel even better about where you are heading when Venus the Attractor enters pleasant Libra in your 11th House of Friends, Hopes, and Wishes on **November 8**, making the future appear even more desirable to you. Meanwhile, there is a powerful emotional undertow gaining intensity; the passionate Scorpio New Moon in your 12th House of Imagination on **November 9** can send you tumbling down the rabbit hole into a world where your inner life is more significant than outer events.

Your spiritual quest deepens as forceful Mars in self-protective Cancer turns retrograde on **November 15**. This normally assertive planet doesn't express itself easily now, and you could repress negative feelings, possibly making you passive-aggressive. It is essential to stay physically active during this period, which lasts through the end of the year. Bottled-up energy can increase your potential for minor accidents and unnecessary arguments over unimportant issues.

The Sun begins its yearly trek through your sign on **November 22**, which astrologically marks the beginning of the holiday season. Your spirit is carried aloft by both high ideals and visionary thinking. By **November 24**, the wandering Gemini Full Moon has you looking forward to huge changes that may be coming, punctuated by the great conjunction of giant Jupiter and transformational Pluto next month. If you consciously decide to look into the mirror of your own soul, the potential for personal growth—and even metamorphosis—is indeed great.

> **KEEP IN MIND THIS MONTH**
>
> *Although you aren't usually at ease with deep feelings, you have an opportunity to increase your emotional IQ by setting logic aside and trusting your intuition.*

KEY DATES

NOVEMBER 4-7 ★ *transformation at your door*

The Sun forms harmonious trines with energetic Mars on **November 4** and erratic Uranus on **November 7**. You might be inclined to take on extra projects now, but since all three planets are in emotional water signs, it could be challenging to turn your inclinations into action. It may be easier to withdraw, but you won't be as effective by yourself. Involving others can help materialize the exciting break-through you seek. Additionally, loving Venus dynamically squares powerful Pluto on **November 7**, arousing your deepest feelings. You may not be able to hide the intensity of your desires. You have incredible support from the Sun's trines, so breathe deeply and jump into the fire. You will be transformed for the better, but only if you allow it to happen.

NOVEMBER 11 ★ *bad judgment*
Everything is a bit muddled as the Sun squares elusive Neptune. And with the Moon back in your sign for its monthly visit, your optimism outweighs the facts. You are eager to take on a challenge that could take more effort than you expect, yet you might not realize it until too late. If you have any doubts at all, just say no.

NOVEMBER 18–19 ★ *patience required*
Socially adept Venus forms a magical quintile with joyful Jupiter on **November 18**, gracing you with the power to attract and create beauty. Additionally, lovely Venus tensely squares feisty Mars on **November 19**, exciting your senses and making you quite impulsive. Remain self-vigilant to avoid making advances that you will later regret. You can benefit greatly by developing and practicing patience.

SUPER NOVA DAYS
NOVEMBER 24–26 ★ *beyond words*
The energy-scattering Gemini Full Moon in your 7th House of Partnerships on **November 24** can confuse you with overwhelming amounts of information shared by other people. Perhaps the Thanksgiving weekend is more hectic than you wish. And with Mercury squaring diffusive Neptune, you may not be very clear as you try to explain your feelings. You cannot capture your ideas in the written or spoken word. Consider, however, that it may be time to move beyond the limitations of language and into the realm of direct experience.

NOVEMBER 30 ★ *stop struggling*
As the Sun forms its semiannual square to restrictive Saturn, you may feel as if an authority figure is working against you. If you are driven to accomplish a specific task today, take a long, hard look at what your real motivations are for doing it now. It may make more sense to pull back as you regain your footing, and prepare to try again in a few days.

DECEMBER

FROM CATERPILLAR TO BUTTERFLY

This holiday season may be bittersweet for you as your key planet, Jupiter, swells with great power and then leaves your sign, not to return for another twelve years. You may have grown accustomed to the joyful presence of expansive Jupiter. Perhaps you have already widened your horizons by pursuing new opportunities. However, it's just as likely to take years to develop an accurate perspective on this period. Jupiter inches closer to intense Pluto, reaching a once-every-thirteen-years conjunction on **December 11**. With Mercury and the Sun also in Sagittarius, there is no room for small-minded thinking. The sky truly is the limit, and the time for your metamorphosis is now. Your life as a caterpillar is transforming into that of a butterfly. However, your dreams won't materialize without hard work, for you must struggle and fight your way out of the cocoon. On **December 18**, your friend Jupiter says goodbye and enters conservative Capricorn in your 2nd House of Possessions. Although you may miss the presence of your buoyant planetary friend, your life is surely enriched by its visit.

The optimistic Sagittarius New Moon on **December 9** may be overwhelming as it precedes the Jupiter-Pluto conjunction. Self-restraint may seem out of the question, for you are ready to rock and roll. Still, exercising small amounts of moderation can increase the positive potential throughout the rest of the month. The emotional Cancer Full Moon in your 8th House of Shared Resources on **December 23** can reflect your desire for a traditional holiday gathering with friends and family. You may feel different now as the Sun illuminates a more reserved Jupiter in steady Capricorn. A wiser and more mature version of you is beginning to emerge.

KEEP IN MIND THIS MONTH

Sometimes the effects from a great conjunction are less noticeable and more like planting a garden. Don't be discouraged if your life is quiet, as it takes time for seeds to germinate.

KEY DATES

DECEMBER 1–3 ★ *as good as it gets*
Communicator Mercury turns philosophical as it enters Sagittarius on **December 1**, where it joins Pluto, Jupiter, and the Sun, making for a highly spirited party in your 1st House of Personality. You could be riding your own optimistic thoughts right into the land of pleasure, for sensual Venus forms a supportive sextile with

opulent Jupiter on **December 1** and passionate Pluto on **December 3**. What begins as a playful weekend may change into something even better as sweet love enters the scene. Even without romance, you can still have a lovely time with your friends.

SUPER NOVA DAYS
DECEMBER 7–11 ★ *it's show time!*
Dynamic squares to surprising Uranus from the Sun and Mercury are bookends to this period. You must deal with crazy energy now—crazy even by your liberal standards. But as nuts as someone's idea may be, it could very well work. You can see a perfect gem in every rock but aren't lost in fantasy. You have instead realized ultimate potential and find it everywhere you look. The thrill-seeking Sagittarius New Moon on **December 9**, along with the Jupiter-Pluto conjunction on **December 11**, makes these days quite significant and unforgettable. Express your intentions clearly, don't overextend yourself, and slow down for the curves.

DECEMBER 17 ★ *anything can happen*
Lovely Venus harmonizes with out-of-the-box Uranus and tenses up to boundless Jupiter. If you can manage your excesses, you can enjoy the fruits of your labor. Or perhaps you share someone else's fruits, as intimate relationships are activated at this time. This is a great ride, so fasten your safety belt and start the countdown.

DECEMBER 20–23 ★ *humble pie*
Mercury enters traditional Capricorn and conjuncts joyful Jupiter on **December 20**, with the Sun following on **December 21**. This hectic time intensifies right through the family-oriented Cancer Full Moon, charged by feisty Mars on **December 23**. It's tough to maintain a healthy perspective as you get carried away by the powerful emotional currents. Even if everything seems great, blind faith can also land you in trouble. You may be on a roll, but you must practice humility in order to succeed.

DECEMBER 26 ★ *reaching too far*
An opposition between assertive Mars and opinionated Jupiter has you aspiring for even greater knowledge and more adventure. You have your arrows aimed toward the heavens, and you are quite tempted to set aside your responsibilities so that you can head out on the greatest journey of your life. Go ahead and dream of the possibilities, but don't get discouraged if the potential isn't fully realized.

♑

CAPRICORN
DECEMBER 22–JANUARY 19

CAPRICORN OVERVIEW

You are a take-charge, run-your-own-show kind of a person who is generally comfortable with responsibility squarely on your shoulders. However, **learning to share the load is your gift and your challenge this year**. Support is available to you from several sources, but that means having to give up some control. It's natural to resist; after all, you've been self-reliant in so many ways for most of your life. Trusting that someone else will do things exactly as you would is probably not easy. The lesson, though, is in learning that there are many effective ways to get a job done. Accepting this fact opens the door wide to a more rewarding year ahead.

Expansive Jupiter in Sagittarius almost all year is lighting up your 12th House of Spirituality, where dreams are born and the possibility of making them real spurs your imagination. **The greatest opportunities come to you in ways that may not be seen by others.** Inner growth, both in the realm of your desires and in your connection to the divine, is a private activity with rich rewards that don't require external recognition. You are soothing your soul and preparing the soil for future growth with behind-the-scenes activities. Take plenty of time for this contemplative work, even if it makes you less visible socially or professionally. This is a rare chance to advance your spiritual knowledge, a once-every-twelve-years magical retreat, when you recharge your batteries and quest for higher meaning.

Saturn, your ruling planet, starts the year in Leo and enters Virgo on September 2, moving from your 8th House of Regeneration to your 9th House of Higher Learning. Saturn is associated with duty, necessity, and hard, cold reality. Its passage through your 8th House, which began in July 2005, is a time of testing relationships, as issues of trust, control, and power are likely to arise. You may be tempted to pull away from a tough negotiation since neither side is willing to compromise. But Saturn rewards you for persistence; if you value the contribution this individual can make, hanging in there will build a powerful alliance. **Respect the strength of others, and make sure that your value is being recognized by them as well.** When Saturn enters Virgo, the focus will shift from the complexities of partnership to concerns about education, religion, politics, and philosophy. Additional schooling to advance yourself professionally is a good investment of your resources. Expressing your beliefs in practical ways turns theory into reality.

Eclipses in March, late August, and September occurring in your 3rd House of Communication and 9th House of Big Ideas provide new facts that alter your beliefs and future plans. Don't allow stubborn pride to keep you from taking in this information, even though it rocks your boat. Emotions can distort data so that you misread the signs. Take a breath when you react strongly to an unfamiliar idea. Rely on your logic to assess what you hear in a less defensive manner so that you can objectively measure its usefulness.

FACE THE TRUTH

Relationships come to a critical point with responsible Saturn in your 8th House of Intimacy. Dissatisfaction within a partnership or as a single person requires a serious reassessment of your goals and expectations. Facing the hard truths of what you want and don't want works best with a combination of compassion and honesty. Be real, but without being mean or accepting abuse in return. It takes courage to keep your heart open when trust has been shaken, yet that is exactly what it takes to get what you need. Initiate meaningful dialogue so that you can bring up delicate matters with your mate, rather than being quiet and tolerating an unfulfilling situation. Saturn works best when direct action is taken, while denial undermines your prospects for long-term contentment. If you are on your own, step up and take risks to connect with others. This isn't a one-time deal. It's about making an ongoing and dedicated effort to find the affection you deserve and desire. Persistence pays off, because each time you try, you learn something valuable that increases your odds of future success.

AIM FOR THE TOP

Creative trines from lucky Jupiter to your key planet, Saturn, in mid-March and early May should broaden your professional perspective. These giant planets, though, are in risk-taking fire signs that work best when matched with bold action and confidence. Instead of trying to dig a foundation, aim your mind toward the sky. The more inspired you are by your career vision, the better chance you have of turning it into reality. Hook up with powerful individuals who encourage you to go beyond boundaries to forge a more exciting work life. Accept the challenge of dealing with those whose egos can be problematic but whose success you admire. This is a good year to begin an entrepreneurial venture or expand your existing business through merger or acquisition.

 ## BANK ON INSPIRATION

Idealistic and imaginative Neptune continues to illuminate your 2nd House of Money this year but is opposed by your planet, Saturn, in late February and late June. These are key times of clarity about your financial situation. If you've been unrealistic, Saturn will put an end to illusions. However, if your dream is aligned with your true purpose, you will receive validation. Material support from others assures you that you're on the right track. Inspiration will increase your income when matched with practicality, patience, and persistence.

 ## TREAT YOURSELF RIGHT

It's tempting to ignore self-care when it comes to your health this year. Unless a medical problem demands your attention, you can be so busy with other concerns that maintaining your physical well-being becomes your lowest priority. Prevention works best, especially with Neptune opposing your ruling planet, Saturn, which can easily deplete your energy. Fatigue can set in so slowly that you don't notice it at first. Diagnosis can be difficult, so make sure that you get plenty of rest before you're exhausted. Take vitamins daily, eat fresh fruits and vegetables, and, above all, avoid worrying about things you can't change.

 ## COST CONTROL

There's nothing better than having a kind and generous heart, but you must balance compassion with discipline this year. When you extend yourself for a family member, do it on the condition that this person picks up his or her share of the load. Additional responsibilities can fall on you if you aren't careful. The same caution should apply to any major home-improvement project. Plans can go awry, costing more than anticipated. Keep it simple by making incremental changes that let you maintain control of your time, resources, and energy.

TRAVEL TURBULENCE

Two eclipses in your 9th House of Travel should make for unusual experiences on the road this year. The Lunar Eclipse on March 3 squares overwhelming Jupiter, marking a period when you may try to squeeze too much activity into your schedule. Surprising Uranus's presence during the eclipse also suggests a possible last-minute change of plans. This volatile planet is active again during the Solar Eclipse on September 11, which is likely to be destabilizing. An adaptable attitude and schedule can help you make needed adjustments to the rapidly changing conditions.

 INNER WISDOM

Jupiter, the planet of knowledge, blesses you with inner guidance as it occupies your 12th House of Spirituality this year. An innate understanding of your place in the cosmos can bring you peace even when facing challenging circumstances in the world. You will find answers to your philosophical questions, but not in words or abstract ideas. This awareness comes from the direct experience of your connection with the universe. It is so comforting because it is totally real for you. This isn't a matter of faith, but a truth you feel in every bone of your body. You may find yourself with a little smile on your face, because life finally makes sense to you without the need to prove anything to anyone else.

RICK & JEFF'S TIP FOR THE YEAR:
Right Place, Right Time

Hard work and dedication are great qualities, but you need something else to make this the year you desire. The magic ingredient is faith, but not just in yourself or in a higher power. It is the belief that your life has a purpose even if you don't know what it is yet. This is a recognition that you belong on this planet at this time in history. That's all you need. Church attendance, meditation practice, and volunteering at the soup kitchen are admirable, but none of these is required. If you should lose sight of this sense of belonging, just listen to the beat of your heart; it's the metronome of existence that marks your time on Earth.

JANUARY

LEAP INTO THE NEW YEAR

You start your year very productively by finishing off old business before taking on new obligations. Active Mars joins cathartic Pluto in your 12th House of Odds and Ends on **January 13**, which is ideal for clearing your desk, cleaning out closets, and dealing with nagging personal issues. Intense emotions are best used to make changes, rather than battling to hold on to your old position. If you channel these feelings constructively, you will be able to overcome obstacles that may have seemed insurmountable in the past. You may have the sense that you're being attacked, but the greatest challenge is inside you, one that you're perfectly well equipped to meet. Change yourself and you can change your world.

Mars kicks into industrious Capricorn on **January 16**, filling your tank with fuel just before the New Moon in your sign on **January 18**. This one-two punch awakens your adventurous side as caution slips into the background. If you're not exercising, start moving your body. A newfound sense of physical vitality supplies you with a sense of initiative to take the lead in relationships as well as in your professional life. You don't have to plan every step to take the crucial first one now.

Ever-expanding Jupiter forms the first of three tense squares with radical Uranus on **January 22**. You may surprise yourself with an unexpected shift of values or goals. Resist the temptation to make a sudden move, because this aspect returns in May and October, when your perspective is likely to change again. Open your mind to fresh ideas and unusual concepts. Experiment with new and fascinating subjects, and trust your intuition more than you have in the past.

> **KEEP IN MIND THIS MONTH**
>
> *You don't need all of the facts to get started. Once you're in motion, you'll find whatever's necessary to reach your goal.*

KEY DATES

JANUARY 2–3 ★ *less words, more feeling*

A touchy semisquare between communicative Mercury and silencing Saturn can limit conversation on **January 2**. Don't talk unless you feel like it, and when you do, keep it simple. Sharing more information than needed will only slow you down. The Full Moon in watery Cancer on **January 3**, though, is a chance to open up emotionally, especially about relationships. You might be uncharacteristically sentimental and soft, but that could break the ice with someone.

JANUARY 6-8 ★ *safe at any speed*

A Sun-Mercury conjunction on **January 6** aligns purpose with intellect, allowing you to express yourself more clearly. Your sharp vision permits you to cut to the chase when dealing with serious matters or exhibit your dry humor in social situations. Assertive Mars forms a fertile trine with result-oriented Saturn on **January 8**, a great aspect for productivity. Your ability to prioritize tasks is excellent now, as is your ability to accurately assess risk. What might seem like a gamble to most people can almost be a sure thing in your steady hands.

SUPER NOVA DAYS
JANUARY 16-18 ★ *starting over again*

A Sun-Jupiter semisquare on **January 16** is associated with overreaching, but Mars's entry into Capricorn on the same day gives you the self-control to take a mighty leap and land on your feet. Be ambitious and express your honest opinions, as long as you're willing to follow up with commitment and hard work. The annual New Moon in your sign is on **January 18**, which sparks a fresh cycle of activity in your life. But it is so close to the end of Capricorn that your inspiration is likely to come from the past. Enthusiasm for an old dream reawakens and motivates you to take on an old challenge that you are now ready to tackle.

JANUARY 22 ★ *not quite enough*

Venus in your 2nd House of Resources opposes stern Saturn, which can place a limit on your spending. Stick to buying low-cost essentials if you must go shopping now. You may feel underappreciated, which can put a damper on relationships. Encourage and love yourself first before expecting satisfaction from someone else.

JANUARY 27-28 ★ *just the facts*

A tough Mars-Saturn semisquare increases friction on **January 27** and can make an easy job harder than usual. Don't be shy about asking for help with sympathetic Venus entering compassionate Pisces—someone will be more than happy to lend a hand. An opposition between mental Mercury and stoic Saturn on **January 28** serves serious conversations better than light ones. Facts are more convincing than feelings now, so stick closely to the subject to make your point.

FEBRUARY

EMOTIONS ON DISPLAY

The Full Moon in demonstrative Leo on **February 2** falls in your 8th House of Intimacy and Shared Resources. Relationship issues are dramatized by strong feelings that can no longer remain hidden. If you or your partner overreacts, at least it will make you conscious of where the two of you stand. Your need for approval may increase, but that conflicts with a dislike for showing dependency. You might, in fact, compensate by being extra generous rather than speaking openly about your desires. But real unselfishness has to do with sharing your truth, even if it's not what the other person wants to hear.

Mercury, the information planet, turns retrograde in dreamy Pisces on **February 13**. Its backward cycle starts in your 3rd House of Communication and finishes on **March 7** in your 2nd House of Resources. Be vigilant about details and data during this period, since facts can turn slippery and conversations confusing. This can, though, be a positive time for developing your imagination by learning to be less literal in your thinking. Studying symbol systems like astrology or tarot is a good way to cultivate your intuition. The Aquarian New Moon in your 2nd House of Income on **February 17** could initiate innovative moneymaking ideas.

Structured Saturn opposes nebulous Neptune on **February 28** for the second time. Their first opposition, which occurred late last August, began a process of ending old illusions to make way for future dreams. The current transit is a time to reflect on what you started then, so make necessary adjustments to stay on your productive course. The third opposition, in late June, is when the last outmoded ties are broken and the path to greater inspiration, income, or intimacy is fully open to you.

> **KEEP IN MIND THIS MONTH**
>
> *Expect the best for yourself in relationships. Proclaim your dream, and then take the next step to make it real.*

KEY DATES

FEBRUARY 7 ★ *practical magic*
Decisive Mars in Capricorn weaves practical magic with a creative biquintile to Saturn. This ingenious connection between the planets of methods and results increases productivity with an original approach to problem solving. A Venus-Uranus conjunction at the same time brings surprises, thrills, and a fresh take on relationships and money.

FEBRUARY 10 ★ *stand up to pressure*
An opposition between the willful Sun and demanding Saturn can attract stubborn individuals. You may feel like you have something to prove to a skeptical person who lacks faith in you and your vision. You could have logic on your side, but it's going to take enthusiasm to make your point. Wherever you meet rejection, respond by demonstrating confidence and persistence. Compromise will probably be seen as a sign of weakness, so stand your ground until others acquiesce.

FEBRUARY 14 ★ *opening the heart*
This may be a somewhat awkward Valentine's Day as the lovers, Venus and Mars, career off Saturn with a pair of clunky quincunxes. These off-balance aspects may confound plans with crossed messages, especially since the information expert, Mercury, turned retrograde the previous day. A loving gesture may be interpreted as an insult or an act of kindness misconstrued as aggression. Fortunately, romance doesn't always have to flow smoothly to bring two people closer together. Celebrate your uncertainty by sharing your vulnerability rather than denying it. There's something very touching about how we humans dance around one another trying to find the ideal way to connect when all it takes is an open heart.

SUPER NOVA DAYS
FEBRUARY 18-21 ★ *honest relationships*
A Venus-Saturn biquintile on **February 18** can turn an enemy into an ally. Your sweet self can melt an icy adversary to gain his or her support. Then relationships get tense with Venus square to Pluto on **February 19**, followed by Venus's flight into independent Aries on **February 21**. It's going to take conscious intent to move through distrust, power struggles, or a lack of resources without pushing the panic button. If you feel disrespected, don't let resentment cook into a toxic brew. Deal with it directly, even if it creates conflict. Accepting temporary tension can save a long-term relationship.

FEBRUARY 25 ★ *define your desires*
Venus and Saturn hook up in a stressful sesquisquare, a 135-degree angle that places obstacles in the way of pleasure now. You may feel like you have to attend a social obligation that's likely to be less than rewarding. The key, though, is that you have a choice. You're not required to put on a happy front while ignoring your own needs. Be clear about what you're giving and what you wish to receive in return.

MARCH

CLIMB THE HIGHEST MOUNTAIN

Eclipses on the informational axis of the 3rd and 9th Houses of your chart can turn your thinking around now. Changing your mind and altering your perspectives also blends with the mental planet, Mercury, turning direct on **March 7**. This occurs in experimental Aquarius in your 2nd House of Resources, which can give you a fresh slant on earning money. Starting a conversation regarding your salary is timely, but you'll have a stronger case when it's linked to an upgrade of your skills. Improve your professional skill set with additional training to advance or even change your career.

Thinking on a grand scale is appropriate now with planetary giants Jupiter and Saturn forming a helpful trine with each other on **March 16**. This is the first of a series of constructive connections between the planets of expansion and contraction, a process that won't end until late next year. But now is the time to lay a foundation for long-range goals by meshing your high hopes for the future (Jupiter) with a plan to make it real (Saturn). Optimistic Jupiter assists you in overcoming doubt and pessimism. You can feel uplifted by invisible forces that guide you toward a more fulfilling life. If you feel resistance within yourself, uncover the source so that you can devise ways to overcome it.

> **KEEP IN MIND THIS MONTH**
>
> *Concentrate on the big prizes of success and happiness so that the petty frustrations of daily life won't distract you from your work.*

On **March 17**, loving Venus waltzes into sensual Taurus in your romantic 5th House of Love and Creativity. Immediate and eternal bliss are not guaranteed, but a door to pleasure is opening wide. A calm demeanor and positive self-esteem can attract more people to you. Pleasing your senses with art and music will make you that much more alluring to others.

KEY DATES

MARCH 3–5 ★ *free your mind*

An explosive Lunar Eclipse in Virgo on **March 3** can shake up long-range plans and upset your basic beliefs about life. Restless Uranus and Jupiter aspect this Full Moon to provoke original thinking and rebellion. This is a chance to release yourself from overly cautious patterns of perception and self-expression. There's more to be gained by trusting your emotions and taking some chances than by sticking strictly to logic now. Brilliant breakthroughs occur when you least expect them and cast current circumstances in a totally new light. The Sun's exact conjunction with Uranus on **March 5** in your 3rd House of Communication puts a buzz in your brain that makes routine tasks boring but stimulates your interest in learning.

MARCH 8-10 ★ *mixing business with pleasure*
Vivacious Venus forms juicy trines with Jupiter and Saturn on **March 8 and 9**, respectively, that effectively blend business and pleasure. Venus-Jupiter opens the heart and encourages social activity, while Venus-Saturn adds stability and common sense when it comes to love and money. But a Sun-Jupiter square on **March 9** may lead to careless words. Fuzzy facts or inconvenient truths could pop out of your mouth. The Sun and Saturn form a cranky quincunx on **March 10**; if you feel disrespected, address the matter when it occurs instead of ignoring it.

SUPER NOVA DAYS
MARCH 15-18 ★ *profound shift of perceptions*
A clever biquintile between the Sun and Saturn on **March 15** shows you how to work through issues of authority and control in an effective manner. With macho Mars conjunct wounded Chiron, insecurities are close to the surface, increasing the need for trust. Jupiter and Saturn form their trine on **March 16**, a major astrological event that may not be immediately obvious. You can shape the future by making careful choices rather than taking giant steps. Enjoy playful opportunities with romantic Venus entering your 5th House of Fun on **March 17**. A Solar Eclipse in your 3rd House of Communication on **March 18** squares provocative Pluto, stirring deep questions about life and how to express them.

MARCH 22-25 ★ *alternating moods*
A tense Mars-Saturn opposition on **March 22** could spark conflict about resources and intimacy. Locking into an adversarial relationship is all too easy. Fortunately, passionate Mars forms a harmonious aspect with generous Jupiter on **March 23** to show healthier ways of releasing tension. A Sun-Saturn sesquisquare on **March 24** cranks up the pressure again, but there's no need to struggle for clarity or control with Mars conjuncting nebulous Neptune on **March 25**. Relax and realize that the spirit in which you act is more important than the results you achieve.

APRIL

There's a planetary changing of the guard this month as outgoing Jupiter turns retrograde on **April 5** and restrained Saturn turns direct on **April 19**. The backward turn of the planet of optimism, which lasts until **August 6**, is a time to reevaluate long-range plans and seek the truth within rather than from external sources. Opportunities to progress continue, of course, but they work best when you digest them slowly rather than taking on too much too quickly. The forward motion of your key planet, Saturn, is great for making a commitment or laying a foundation, especially in relationships. You're on more solid ground, able to get traction and reliably advance with others. If you've got unfinished partnership business, it's time to address it once and for all.

The agreeable Libra Full Moon on **April 2** falls in your 10th House of Career, giving you a professional boost with the help of a colleague or with some skillful diplomacy on your part. The New Moon in impatient Aries on **April 17** can set off fireworks on the home front. It excites your 4th House of Family with powerful trines from Pluto and Jupiter that are very useful for burning off resentment and finally resolving a long-standing problem. Truth is the medicine that heals old wounds. On **April 20**, the Sun moves into your fellow Earth sign Taurus, warming matters of the heart. The Bull's straightforward nature irons out some complicated wrinkles in self-expression so that you can be more direct with your feelings. A newfound sense of innocence brings fun back to romance and reveals your inner artist. Play is not a waste of time now, Capricorn, but a healthy activity for your body, mind, and spirit.

> **KEEP IN MIND THIS MONTH**
>
> *Simplifying your life may be smart now. Leave room to relax instead of filling every minute with planned activities.*

KEY DATES

SUPER NOVA DAYS
APRIL 1–2 ★ *slow down and get serious*
Normally sociable Venus may be less friendly with a square to stern Saturn on **April 1** when you're not in the mood to be anyone's fool. A desire for solitude is possible, as is a feeling of being underappreciated. Be gracious, though, since pouting won't improve the situation. A serious discussion of relationship

matters, though perhaps uncomfortable for you, should be constructive now. On **April 2**, communicative Mercury is sidetracked by a quincunx from Saturn. Conversations slip off course with misunderstandings or misstatements of fact. Patience and precision are required to express yourself effectively.

APRIL 6-8 ★ *clever and competent*
A super-creative biquintile between Mercury and Saturn on **April 6** allows you to skillfully untangle a complicated situation. Your intuition guides you to know which strings to pull and which buttons to push. Friends or colleagues who have been at odds with one another can find a solution with your help. A smooth Sun-Saturn trine on **April 8** should make for a very satisfying Sunday. The harmonious aspect between these planets gives you a natural sense of authority that is excellent for getting your way without being bossy. Confidence is the key to managing even fast-moving situations with calm competence.

APRIL 12 ★ *check the facts*
An edgy little semisquare between thoughtful Mercury and somber Saturn can bring out your skeptical side. It is appropriate to show some mental caution at a time like this, but avoid slipping from doubt to cynicism. If you don't trust what someone's saying, politely ask for clarification rather than starting an argument.

APRIL 20 ★ *high-speed stability*
A strong trine between intelligent Mercury and solid Saturn helps you operate at a higher level of efficiency. Even though the mental planet is zipping through fiery Aries, which can throw you off balance, you're able to think quickly without losing track of important details. You have the ability to adapt to changing conditions with confidence as your creative talent blends easily with practical considerations now.

APRIL 27-29 ★ *all shook up*
Expect an unusual weekend beginning with a sextile between loving Venus and responsible Saturn on **April 27** that grounds relationships with security. Your stellar judgment and sense of style are beneficial for shopping, business, and socializing. On **April 28**, though, impetuous Mars joins explosive Uranus to send shock waves through your life. A sudden impulse to try something new or an unexpected outburst of anger can shake your world but also thrill you with excitement. A Mars-Saturn quincunx on **April 29** could require an apology or a shift of course. Don't resist; find a way to make a minor but necessary change.

MAY

CLARITY AND CHAOS

Gigantic Jupiter forms two contrasting major aspects this month: a trine with Saturn on **May 5** and a square with Uranus on **May 10**. The former offers you stability and a good sense of proportion that is perfect for choosing solid opportunities for your future. The latter, however, throws a monkey wrench of unexpected information that requires fast thinking and flexibility on your part. This alternating pattern of clarity and chaos may destabilize you professionally, but blesses you with spiritual insights that are well worth the price. The third and final Jupiter-Uranus square in October can reward you with an unexpected awakening and a new sense of freedom.

Another unusual occurrence is that this month has two Full Moons. The first one, on **May 2** in extreme Scorpio, adds pressure to your 11th House of Groups and Friends, which can force you to choose between opposing sides. Your ruling planet, Saturn, is in the picture, so base your decision on practical considerations, even if it's not the most popular choice. The Taurus New Moon on **May 16** plants a seed of potentiality in your 5th House of Romance, Children, and Creativity. It's watered by a square from Neptune that can drown it in illusion or inspire you to indulge your pursuit of pleasure. Rule maker Saturn's square to this sensual New Moon carries a mixed message: "safety first" is this planet's motto, but its occupancy of risk-taking Leo demands that you trust your heart. The second Full Moon, on **May 31** in adventurous Sagittarius, teases your mind with visions of worlds beyond this one and provokes restlessness. Take some time off to let your thoughts wander. The inspiration you gain will make it a wise journey.

> **KEEP IN MIND THIS MONTH**
>
> *This is a fortunate time to validate your future goals. Be just as ambitious about play as you are about work.*

KEY DATES

SUPER NOVA DAYS
MAY 5-7 ★ *big-picture view*
The small stuff can stress you now with a Mercury-Saturn square that clogs communication on **May 5**. But the Jupiter-Saturn trine the same day helps you step back and take a big-picture view, rather than getting bogged down

with petty details. Your vision is wide open, but you may have to take small, careful steps toward making it real. On **May 7**, a biquintile between impatient Mars and slow-moving Saturn shows you creative steps for overcoming obstacles and operating at higher levels of efficiency. Lovely Venus enters your 7th House of Partnerships on the same day, warming your life with caring companionship and an easier flow of mutual empathy and affection.

MAY 9 ★ *conquer fear to move mountains*
A sharp Sun-Saturn square can snag you into a power struggle. Your creative urges may be stifled by a fearful or conservative partner. The real work, though, is internal, because overcoming self-doubt is the greatest challenge. Remembering your previous accomplishments will strengthen your commitment and bolster your resolve to continue forward in spite of any obstacles you encounter.

MAY 14 ★ *on-the-job training*
A clever quintile between mentally agile Mercury and result-oriented Saturn helps you navigate choppy professional waters. You may feel thrust into a position of responsibility without sufficient support or preparation. Don't be afraid to dive in make it up as you go along. You'll quickly see the unfolding patterns that let you develop a strategy and manage the project with your usual high level of competence.

MAY 20-21 ★ *mental order under chaos*
If you feel like more is coming at you than you can handle, ask for help. Mercury opposes expansive Jupiter and squares wild and crazy Uranus on **May 20**, which can overwhelm you with information. Mars semisquares Saturn on the same day, so handling all of this data adds complexity as you attempt to control a potentially chaotic situation. Fortunately, a supportive sextile between Mercury and Saturn on **May 21** brings a semblance of order to your world. Even if the external conditions haven't changed, you'll see the situation clearly enough to be more at ease with it.

MAY 28 ★ *natural-born leader*
A brilliant Sun-Saturn quintile blesses you with wisdom beyond your years or experience level. Your natural ability to lead works so seamlessly because you don't even appear to be in charge, as if you're driving the bus from the passenger seat. Communicative Mercury's entry into your 7th House of Partnerships also favors tender conversation in which feelings are shared without shame in an atmosphere of mutual support and trust.

JUNE

REMEMBER YOUR DREAMS

On **June 25**, your ruling planet, Saturn, makes its third and final opposition to inspirational Neptune, a pattern that began late last August. This is a major transit that could shape the course of your dreams for years to come. It might arrive not as a dramatic event, but as a deep inner sense of purpose. Saturn, the planet of form and structure, facing idealistic Neptune is a time to finally end old illusions that drain your energy and to commit to manifesting your deepest desires into reality. Even if you feel despair due to a loss, turn your thinking into creative action that will serve your highest aspirations.

On **June 14**, an intense Gemini New Moon in your 6th House of Work can make for changes on the job. Discontentment is possible with grumpy Pluto opposing this Sun-Moon conjunction. Issues simmering below the surface may come to a boil. On the plus side, though, you'll have plenty of motivation to let go of bad habits and regenerate your energy with a healthier and more efficient lifestyle. Mercury turns retrograde on **June 15** in your 7th House of Partnerships. The communication planet's backward cycle will last until **July 9**, marking a period when extra care with details and messages of all kinds is necessary to avoid snafus. Reconnecting with a former partner or stirring up an old issue with your current one can be expected during this time. Conversations grow more complex and perhaps more emotionally charged, yet relationship repairs are attainable where mutual respect is present. On **June 30**, the Full Moon occurring in disciplined Capricorn illuminates your 1st House of Personality, urging you to get in shape and consider updating your look or even your attitude.

> **KEEP IN MIND THIS MONTH**
>
> *How you speak to others is as important as the words you say. A warm and gentle tone can be essential to getting your message across.*

KEY DATES

JUNE 2 ★ *serious thinking*

A tense semisquare between Mercury and Saturn can make for a cranky Saturday. Feelings of frustration may be caused by worries, delays, and doubts involving others. But don't isolate yourself, because talking about your concerns can lift your spirits, provide intimacy, and rebuild trust. Being able to analyze the situation without placing blame is an excellent way to turn your day around.

JUNE 21 ★ *trust your tender side*

The Sun enters nurturing Cancer and fills your 7th House of Partnerships with new force. Your confidence can rise, allowing you to reveal your softer side without feeling weak about it. The sensitivity of this water sign will help you seem more approachable to others by tempering your desire for achievement with a greater capacity to listen. This accessibility attracts loyal allies and supporters. If you're a competitive or secretive person, the challenge is to lower your guard to allow someone in. There's some risk, of course, but the greater risk is to keep a closed mind and heart that will only underscore your feelings of isolation.

JUNE 24-25 ★ *the task is to play*

Passionate Mars in sensual Taurus enters your 5th House of Love and Creativity to spice up your life. Taking time to play is a must now, especially if it includes activities that make you feel like a kid. Both Mars and Taurus are simple and direct, which can help you be more straightforward about your desires. Pleasing yourself is job number one, and there can be innocence in the pursuit of pleasure, even of the adult variety. Relax and let your heart lead the way.

JUNE 27-28 ★ *say it again*

On **June 27**, retrograde Mercury backs up to the same semisquare it formed with Saturn in the beginning of the month, which can lead you right back to any unfinished business that began then. Precise communication will help you finally complete the job. On **June 28**, the Sun conjuncts Mercury and forms a semisquare with Saturn. Be patient when dealing with a stubborn person who's not quite getting your message.

JULY

SPEEDING MIND, SLOWING HEART

The inner planets, Mercury and Venus, are changing directions this month, stirring a shift in the mental and social winds in your life. Communicator Mercury ends its retrograde cycle on **July 9** and begins slowly moving forward again in your 7th House of Partnerships. Messages stuck in the cosmic time machine for the previous three weeks finally start flowing again. The Venus retrograde, which is less common than Mercury's, starts on **July 27** in your 9th House of Faraway Places and may complicate or delay travel plans. Political and religious beliefs, also ruled by the 9th House, are currently ripe for reexamination. Romantic Venus's role in the story could require some readjustments in relationships as well. Its station (turning point) closely conjunct the Moon's chronically challenged South Node in Virgo warns against being overly picky or analytical. The wisdom of an open mind will prove helpful while Venus is in reverse through **September 8**.

The New Moon in sympathetic Cancer on **July 14** in your 7th House spurs new perspectives on partnerships, both personal and professional. Its visionary trine with inventive Uranus is likely to enlarge your vision of collaboration. You may attract unique people who help you find ways to cooperate with more freedom but without losing control. However, a tricky quincunx from hard-to-read Neptune might raise some unrealistic expectations, so be aware of promises made with sincerity but not backed up with substance. Significant financial investments should be avoided. The Full Moon in intelligent Aquarius on **July 29** in your 2nd House of Self-Worth is a reminder to explore less conventional ways to express your talents. Upgrade your computer or your skill set to boost your confidence.

> **KEEP IN MIND THIS MONTH**
>
> *There are exciting partnership possibilities, but you may need to do more research before putting a plan into action.*

KEY DATES

JULY 1 ★ *work at having fun*

A conjunction between joyful Venus and no-nonsense Saturn adds a somber tone to the day. You might feel underappreciated or displeased by someone's sense of self-importance. If you're feeling blue, allow yourself to be cajoled into having some fun. It may take a while to overcome negative judgment about wasting time on frivolity. Once you understand the game that's being played, you're likely to enjoy it.

JULY 9–10 ★ *aim carefully*

Mercury's direct turn in your 7th House of Partnerships on **July 9** opens channels of communication that have been clogged. But an overly enthusiastic Mars-Jupiter quincunx on **July 10** may engender misjudgment that puts you in an awkward position. Certainly, it is appropriate to take chances in showing off your artistic skills, playing sports, or expressing your feelings for someone. Yet a tad of caution can ensure that you achieve the desired results without being embarrassed or overshooting the mark.

SUPER NOVA DAY
JULY 14 ★ *a fresh view*

Today's New Moon has the power to change the shape of your relationships. It occurs in caring, sensitive Cancer, which sometimes incites withdrawal to protect your delicate feelings. However, revolutionary Uranus's harmonious hookup to the lunation keeps you moving toward new connections and brings original ideas to an ongoing partnership. It's rare to combine a sense of excitement with the security that you crave, but both are possible now. Venus, the love planet, also enters Virgo, a supportive sister Earth sign. Venus will turn retrograde in less than two weeks, but this shift will, at least temporarily, put you on more solid ground emotionally.

JULY 22–24 ★ *wise skepticism*

Your skeptical thinking can put a damper on someone else's optimism as a stern Mercury-Saturn semisquare greets the Sun's entry into fiery Leo on **July 22**. Perhaps such a measured response is appropriate, though, with an unrealistic Mars square to nebulous Neptune on **July 24**. Imagination and play are perfect, as long as you don't lose sight of practical considerations and get yourself into a situation that costs you much more than it gives back in return.

JULY 31 ★ *one careful step at a time*

A square between mobile Mars and stable Saturn can put the brakes on a plan or severely slow you down today. Tension can be high as you battle obstacles that may be highly resistant to your efforts to move them. A slow approach, on the other hand, may be frustrating but can earn long-term trust and build a enduring foundation. Focus and finesse are much more useful than brute force now.

CAPRICORN

AUGUST

A RISING TIDE OF SPIRIT

Big, jolly Jupiter, shifts into forward gear on **August 6**, ending its retrograde cycle that began four months ago. This direct movement of the giant planet stirs inspiring thoughts from the depths of your mystical 12th House of Destiny. Hopes are raised, even without concrete reasons to support them. But faith is a good thing, Capricorn, because opening your mind to a grander vision of your future is a critical first step toward making it real.

Planets start piling up in your 8th House of Intimacy this month: Saturn's been there for more than two years; the Sun moved in last month; Mercury joins the party on **August 4**; Venus returns on **August 8**; and the Moon meets up with the Sun for the Leo New Moon on **August 12**. All of this activity can enliven and complicate relationships. The fun comes from warmhearted and generous people who enter your orbit. But the challenges include living in an emotionally charged environment where courage is greater than logic. Mistakes may be made, yet the potential gains in love, money, or friendship are worth the risks.

The Full Moon in compassionate Pisces on **August 28** is a total Lunar Eclipse.

KEEP IN MIND THIS MONTH

Everything you need to know is already present in your universe. Move beyond doubt, and truth will shine through when you need it.

The close alignment of the Sun, Moon, and Earth is a powerful force for awakening. But first, it's time to let go of any remnants of victimhood. Whatever pain you have experienced is not to be forgotten, but to be put through the spiritual wash to get out the stains of failure and loss. There are no "wrong" moves, only lessons to be learned. Forgiving yourself and others now is a major leap forward on your spiritual path.

KEY DATES

AUGUST 1-2 ★ *step back from the brink*

Conversations are complex, and perhaps cantankerous, with chatty Mercury making an illogical sesquisquare to Jupiter on **August 1**, urging you to bluntly speak your mind. A quincunx from feisty Mars to unyielding Pluto adds fuel to the conversational fire on the same day and is exacerbated by a cranky quincunx that Mercury forms with Pluto on **August 2**. Questions feel like accusations, and your reactions to others can be quite extreme. Fortunately, a generous trine between the Sun and Jupiter, also on **August 2**, helps you step back from confrontation to view the situation in a larger context, allowing your instinct for strategy to temper an inclination for fierce verbal counterattacks.

AUGUST 6 ★ *claim your power*

Jupiter turns direct and Saturn trines Pluto, two major astrological patterns that are more likely to play out slowly over several days than to appear as immediate events. The constructive alignment between planetary heavies Saturn and Pluto gives you a deep inner resolve, as well as the knowledge that when you are guided by conviction, there are no limits to the power you have to transform your life.

AUGUST 13-15 ★ *light shining through the mist*

Joy and responsibility are combined with a Venus-Saturn conjunction on **August 13**. This could let the air out of a romance as reality leaks into the world of love. Pressure to renew a commitment or change direction is likely. But with the Sun opposing diffusive Neptune on **August 13** and with magnanimous Mercury doing the same on **August 14**, sympathy can overcome common sense. On **August 15**, however, Venus trine Pluto sharpens your desires, and a Sun-Mercury conjunction focuses your mind to cut through the fog and see exactly what you want from someone.

SUPER NOVA DAYS
AUGUST 18-21 ★ *strong leadership*

You're on high alert with vigilant Mercury joining Saturn on **August 18** and entering meticulous Virgo on **August 19**, followed by the Sun's conjunction with authoritative Saturn on **August 21**. You may feel obligated to handle someone else's unmanageable situation. Don't take the job. However, you can be highly efficient and productive, even with reluctant partners, when you set the agenda. Your patient, persistent power forges unbreakable bonds that build a formidable team.

AUGUST 23-25 ★ *busy as a bee*

This is a potentially hyperactive period with impulsive Mars opposing wide-ranging Jupiter on **August 23** and busy Mercury squaring both planets over the next two days. Spreading yourself too thin is a common consequence, yet there is a counterbalancing force with the conscious Sun's entry into practical Virgo on **August 23**. Taking on a big project makes sense, as long as you have a clear plan of attack that allows you to break it down to one detail at a time.

SEPTEMBER

DOWN-TO-EARTH EDUCATION

This month starts with a major shift as Saturn, your ruling planet, moves into efficient Virgo on **September 2** for a two-year stay. Your life may become more comfortable with the planet of reality and responsibility leaving the intense 8th House of Intimacy for your 9th House of Travel and Higher Education. Virgo is an Earth sign like Capricorn, which allows you to learn Saturn's lessons more easily now. Focusing on subject matter with direct application to your life will be more rewarding to you than abstract material. Philosophical ideas are interesting, but being able to use them in tangible ways is where you gain the most satisfaction. On **September 8**, sociable Venus turns direct after almost six weeks of retrograde motion, lagging in your 8th House for about a month. You may have unfinished partnership issues involving money, possessions, or legal matters to complete during this time.

The New Moon on **September 11** is a partial Solar Eclipse in Virgo. This careful sign usually doesn't kick up much dust, but this event is a notable exception. Assertive Mars and excessive Jupiter form tense squares to the New Moon, while erratic Uranus opposes it. Unexpected challenges to your belief system, sudden changes in travel plans, and an overload of new information can occur. Setting priorities and eliminating extraneous activities are ways to reduce the excess of sensory input you're likely to receive. The impetuous Aries Full Moon in your 4th House of Security on **September 26** may trigger a crisis at home that can alter your perspective on deeply rooted family patterns. You may feel torn between public obligations and personal needs, but creative thinking could show you a way to address both.

> **KEEP IN MIND THIS MONTH**
>
> A *long-term commitment to learning—no matter what your circumstances—will reward you now and for years to come.*

KEY DATES

SEPTEMBER 2–3 ★ *cool head needed*

Stable Saturn's entry into critical Virgo on **September 2** may be temporarily shadowed by intense words and explosive communication. Talkative Mercury's stressful square with deep, dark Pluto can engender mistrust. Secrets withheld or revealed can bring an issue to a boil with Mars and Uranus building up to an incendiary square on **September 3**. That same day, a Sun-Jupiter square feeds the flames of disagreement with overstatement and outsized egos. Yet there is hope for a peaceful settlement, thanks to a gentle sextile between Venus and Mars that offers a possible path to compromise.

SUPER NOVA DAYS
SEPTEMBER 9-11 ★ *wake-up call*
An electric Sun-Uranus opposition shocks your mental houses on **September 9**, leading to the high-intensity Solar Eclipse on **September 11**. Your normally well-grounded mind can be flipped into indecision by rapidly changing circumstances and sudden shifts of mood. On the plus side, this can be excellent for clearing out the cobwebs and awakening you to new ways of seeing and thinking. And if you've grown bored lately, unexpected news is bound to thrill you. Delve into a fascinating new area of study to occupy your time.

SEPTEMBER 16-17 ★ *navigate conflict*
A Mercury-Saturn semisquare can have you biting your tongue on **September 16**, but don't keep silent on an important subject. Address your concerns clearly and calmly, if you can. There's a fiery Sun-Mars clash coming on **September 17** that favors conflict over accommodation, so it's best to defuse a tense situation and apply your resolve to moving forward rather than battling over the past.

SEPTEMBER 21 ★ *complex pleasure*
Increasing levels of passion and tenderness make for an emotionally charged day. A Mars-Pluto opposition compels you to fulfill your desires by overpowering all obstacles. However, Venus opposes Neptune, a sensitive, romantic counterpoint that complicates relationships. Still, if you can skillfully adapt to shifting moods and the contradictions of control and surrender, your potential for delight is high.

SEPTEMBER 28 ★ *tender advances*
Active, aggressive, and often impulsive Mars's moods are tempered by its entry into hesitant Cancer. While this might signal withdrawal for most people, this passionate planet is moving into your 7th House of Partnerships and is, therefore, likely to enliven your personal life. Overly sensitive individuals can pull back into defensive postures if you come on too strong, and you may be more susceptible to others' influence as well. Nevertheless, cautious steps taken with tenderness can now bring you closer to those you love.

OCTOBER

MIND EXPANSION

You may feel somewhat hyper this month as Jupiter, the planet that knows no limits, makes two major aspects. On **October 9**, it forms the third and last of a series of squares to chaotic Uranus that began in late January. Images burst from your unconscious, opening you to a higher level of awareness that alters your view of life. There are no boundaries in this thought dimension where spirit overcomes the restrictions of matter. Inspiration blossoms, but restlessness can have you pushing against the restraints of your daily routine. Take time to integrate your discoveries and to apply your newfound wisdom in practical ways. On **October 29**, Jupiter sextiles Neptune, which may overwhelm you with faith and imagination. Neptune's direct turn on **October 31** in your 2nd House of Possessions develops your spiritual reserves and could even show you a more creative approach for earning money.

The New Moon in peacemaker Libra on **October 11** has favorable aspects from Jupiter and Neptune. This enlightens your 10th House of Career with an understanding of the higher purpose of your work, while the easygoing Taurus Full Moon on **October 26** warms your 5th House of Romance, Children, and Creativity.

Mercury, the planet of facts, is opposite Jupiter, the planet of philosophy, on the intellectual spectrum. Mercury's retrograde cycle, which starts on **October 11**, pushes details farther into the background during Jupiter's conceptual tidal wave this month. Enthusiasm for big concepts may be disconnected from actual data, making it difficult for you to distinguish hope from reality. The Winged Messenger's backward turn in your 11th House of Groups and Friends muddles communication with pals and colleagues. The standard Mercury retrograde advice to double-check details, itineraries, and documents is in effect through **November 1**.

> **KEEP IN MIND THIS MONTH**
>
> *Take a break from your routine. Think outside the box to access the wealth of wisdom that's available.*

KEY DATES

OCTOBER 1 ★ *clear talk*

An intelligent sextile between Mercury and Saturn provides you with clear and insightful thinking today. This is especially helpful if you're in a leadership position, because you have a very good sense of how to motivate people with the right words and manner of expression. With Mercury turning retrograde in less than two weeks, get your messages across now before communication channels get fuzzy.

SUPER NOVA DAYS
OCTOBER 8-11 ★ *flexibility under fire*
Dynamic Mars and stabilizing Saturn hook up on **October 8** in a healthy sextile that helps you take care of business efficiently. This orderly aspect is the exception in these wobbly days leading up to the ambiguous Libra New Moon on **October 11**. A messy quincunx between the Sun and rambunctious Uranus on **October 8**, followed by the fireworks of Jupiter square Uranus on **October 9**, can make for some crazy days. Stay light on your feet so that you're able to move quickly under these rapidly changing conditions.

OCTOBER 13 ★ *rebuild trust*
Call this "suspicious Saturday" with the Moon in mysterious Scorpio and tough aspects from both the Sun and Venus to Saturn. Trust issues can arise, especially when you are underappreciated. A friend might even let you down or feel that you haven't been supportive. Either way, there's value in discussing what you want from a relationship rather than accepting less than you deserve. Go slowly to make progress, because patience works wonders when you're trying to reestablish trust.

OCTOBER 19-20 ★ *tough conversation*
The second Mercury-Saturn sextile of the month on **October 19** is excellent for tackling a difficult issue that won't go away on its own. A money matter with a friend could be a cause of consternation and is so delicate that you hate to bring it up. Yet Saturn brings wisdom and maturity, so you're able to wade through muddy emotional waters without making a mess. A Sun-Pluto sextile on **October 20** also makes it safe to deal with forbidden subjects. Concentration will get you through the hard parts without losing your way or your self-control.

OCTOBER 29 ★ *capture the magic*
A sturdy Sun-Saturn sextile provides you with self-confidence and dependability. Even if conditions around you are chaotic, you know your responsibilities and how to fulfill them. This grounding influence helps you assimilate the expansive vision of the inspirational Jupiter-Neptune sextile and eventually turn it into something real, rather than having it pass through your mind like an idea soon forgotten.

NOVEMBER

A CHANGING OF THE GUARD

The planets are twirling forward and backward this month with talkative Mercury turning direct on **November 1**, spark plug Mars going retrograde on **November 15**, and wild Uranus turning direct on **November 24**. Mercury's shift occurring in your 10th House of Career helps you pick up the thread of a work-related conversation that was sidetracked during the past few weeks. If you've been waiting for information from your boss or a response about a job application, the answer is likely to pop up very soon. Energetic Mars is the most forward-moving of planets, but it's been slowed by its stay in cautious Cancer. The retrograde turn in your 7th House of Partnerships on **November 15** can signal retreat in relationships and possible delays in launching any public project. Passive-aggressive behavior is more likely now, but if blame is set aside in the interest of problem solving, constructive course corrections can rebuild trust with others. Rebellious Uranus's change of direction brings its principles of originality and freedom into the foreground. Strange ideas that have been rattling around in your head might come out of your mouth, shocking some but delighting others.

On **November 9**, the New Moon in secretive Scorpio raises the temperature in your 11th House of Groups and Friends, which can instigate a crisis in a team or with a pal. Putting all of the issues on the table may feel risky, but once the truth is out in the open, trust will start to be restored. The Full Moon in busy Gemini on **November 24** illuminates your 6th House of Work and Service. Tough squares from Saturn and the Moon's Nodes may force you to cut back on your responsibilities to bring down your level of stress.

> **KEEP IN MIND THIS MONTH**
>
> *Carrying the load yourself gives you total control but could wear you down. Accept the support you receive from others to make your life easier.*

KEY DATES

NOVEMBER 4–5 ★ *emotional angst*
Call on a competent, dependable friend or ally to give you a hand on **November 4** as a Sun-Mars trine increases productivity when you're part of a team. However, a Sun-Pluto semisquare on the same day could spur a power struggle. Social Venus's square to Pluto on **November 5** might also sow seeds of distrust. Uncomfortable issues can surface, and emotional wounds may demand attention.

Facing your fears is tough, but it can help you finally put an end to an issue that stands in the way of intimacy.

NOVEMBER 10–11 ★ *original thought*
Provocative Mercury makes an agitated semisquare with nervous Uranus just before returning to passionate Scorpio on **November 10**. Impulsive speech can produce brilliant ideas or trigger unexpected reactions. But all should be forgiven quickly when the Sun crosses paths with compassionate Neptune and weaves an intelligent quintile with Saturn on **November 11**. Inspiration can find an outlet as you invent a way to turn a dream into reality for at least one day.

NOVEMBER 16 ★ *contrasting perspectives*
Communicative Mercury makes a logical sextile with serious Saturn and a sloppy semisquare with jovial Jupiter, reflecting two very different kinds of thinking. Expect reliable information when it comes to reality, but long-range plans and promises for the future may be shaky on the details. You can't extrapolate from current data to predict what will happen down the road. Separate certainty from fantasy so that you won't get crossed up by the wide gap between them now.

NOVEMBER 24 ★ *an emotional buzz*
This high-energy Saturday starts off with a hyper Gemini Full Moon that may scatter your attention. Eccentric Uranus turning direct adds another layer of uncertainty, while a Mercury-Neptune square suggests that what you see isn't necessarily what you're going to get. It's easy to become excited, with emotions running strong in one direction before switching to another. Stay flexible to adapt to unexpected changes. Don't rely on the precision of what you say or hear, since Mercury-Neptune reveals more about subjective feelings than concrete facts.

SUPER NOVA DAYS
NOVEMBER 29–30 ★ *take the slow road*
An angular Venus-Saturn semisquare on **November 29** and a formidable square between the Sun and Saturn on **November 30** end the month on a somewhat serious note. Responsibilities may weigh heavily, but you're likely to be your own toughest critic. Give yourself some respect by recognizing what you've already accomplished instead of focusing on where you haven't yet achieved your goals. The patient pursuit of love will be more satisfying than a quick response designed to achieve immediate gratification.

DECEMBER

PLANETARY OVERLOAD

This very busy month is highlighted by benevolent Jupiter's entry into your sign on **December 18**. Expect more opportunities for personal and professional growth in the year ahead, especially when you're willing to sell yourself with greater enthusiasm. Reach for more instead of playing it safe to make the most of the giant planet's powerful push forward. You might feel its energy coming in advance, thanks to the fiery New Moon in Sagittarius on **December 9** and a transformative conjunction between Jupiter and Pluto on **December 11**. These powerful events occur in your 12th House of Spirituality and Dreams and stir forces in the depths of your unconscious. Great waves of fear and desire arise that can sweep reason away. Passions provoke philosophical debates in which differences of opinions can reach dangerous extremes. Beliefs are being tested, so prepare to have yours challenged and changed.

Your ruling planet, Saturn, turns retrograde on **December 19**, but its backward turn will not slow down the planetary blitz heading your way. Mercury and the Sun conjunct Pluto and Jupiter and enter Capricorn between **December 19 and 21** to intensify the holidays with more verbal jousting. The moody Cancer Full Moon on **December 23** is conjunct Mars in your 7th House of Partnerships, where it opposes Pluto, Jupiter, the Sun, and Mercury. Partnerships can be stressed as simple statements may trigger endless discussion. Avoid getting caught in word-by-word dissections of conversations to defend your position or disprove someone else's. The emotionally charged holiday season is better used to deepen your connections through the intimate exchange of ideas shared without judgment or competition. Barriers to closeness can fall when your sharp mind is tempered by a tender spirit.

> **KEEP IN MIND THIS MONTH**
>
> *If a person doesn't get your point quickly, don't force it. A light touch and healthy sense of humor can ease tensions.*

KEY DATES

DECEMBER 6-8 ★ *use words wisely*

A testy square between Mercury and Saturn on **December 6** can complicate communication. Think twice before speaking, since the impact of words tends to last longer now. A klutzy quincunx between Mercury and Mars on the same day also signals the need for verbal caution to avoid conflict. The Sun squares easily excitable Uranus on **December 7**, an edgy pair that can hinder compromise and cooperation. But on **December 8**, Mars and Saturn link up in a sensible sextile that helps you regain control and direct your energies more efficiently.

DECEMBER 12 ★ *astute appraisal*

A sextile between sociable Venus and practical Saturn should put relationships on more solid footing. You have a realistic sense of self-worth and an ability to assess others' talents that favor productive teamwork. Personal matters are attended to in a mature manner, and your instinct for value makes you an excellent shopper.

SUPER NOVA DAYS
DECEMBER 18-22 ★ *managed chaos*

Pre-holiday busyness can reach epic heights this year. Jupiter entering Capricorn on **December 18** brings great promise for the future but could be overwhelming. Mars's slippery sesquisquare with Neptune the same day can bring distractions from unreliable individuals. Verbal Mercury's conjunction with no-nonsense Pluto on **December 19** could diffuse confusion, but conversations may be charged with unresolved emotional issues. On **December 20,** Mercury's entry into Capricorn scores a point for reason, but the Sun's conjunction with Pluto continues to churn the waters of distrust about power and control. The Sun moves into your sign on **December 21** and joins jolly Jupiter on **December 22.** Your administrative skills may be strong, but Venus's hard aspects to Mars and Neptune on **December 21 and 22,** respectively, increase social insecurities.

DECEMBER 24-26 ★ *a rowdy crowd*

Mars's oppositions to the Sun on **December 24** and Jupiter on **December 26** can raise hell. Raucous laughter, competitive games, and fierce disagreement make for loud and lively times. Fortunately, a Mercury-Saturn trine on **December 25** supplies common sense that may temper some of the extreme feelings activated.

DECEMBER 30-31 ★ *magic powers*

The Sun trines Saturn on **December 30**, a positive alignment that can bring a sense of order to the end of your year. You trust yourself, as should others. Yet Venus enters your 12th House of Secrets on **December 30**, and Mars enters your 6th House of Adjustments on **December 31**, which can leave you feeling a bit like Cinderella before the ball. Be your own fairy godmother by making your own magic.

AQUARIUS
JANUARY 20–FEBRUARY 18

AQUARIUS OVERVIEW

Your two key planets are rule-bound Saturn and rebellious Uranus. This year, as fast as Saturn can place obstacles in your path, Uranus comes to the rescue with sudden breakthroughs that allow you to move your life in a successful direction. When Saturn was in your sign, from 1991 through 1993, you undertook the task of putting your life on track. Now, half a Saturn cycle later, you can **look back at the choices you made in the early 1990s to reevaluate your current accomplishments and defeats**. The garden you planted has grown, but you must work hard during the harvest just to keep up with all the chores.

Chiron the Wounded Healer continues to move through your sign this year. Although Chiron can remind you of your physical mortality, raise a variety of health issues, and stir memories of an emotional trauma, it also provides a tremendous potential for healing the body, mind, and spirit. In particular when fortunate Jupiter sextiles Chiron on May 30 and September 7, **you have the wisdom to make changes in your life that can bring you closer to happiness.** You can also be an important mentor to someone who needs your guidance.

Perhaps the most important astrological event this year is the long-lasting opposition between serious Saturn, now moving through your 7th House of Partnerships, and dreamy Neptune, halfway through its fourteen-year journey through your sign. This sometimes enlightening and sometimes discouraging opposition began last summer as tensions surfaced between your fantasies and the realities of your everyday life. And although Jupiter's trine to Saturn throughout the year can add stability to your individual relationships and your interactions with the community, Neptune's dissipating action thwarts Saturn's attempt to crystallize your dreams, especially around February 28 and June 25. **You struggle to understand what is important versus what is not while Neptune puts a confusing soft focus on your lens of life.** Your most concrete goals remain just out of reach until July, when this aspect begins to wane. Instead of setting yourself up for disappointment by building your foundation on shaky ground, perhaps wait until later in the year to make the most significant decisions.

Meanwhile, unpredictable Uranus in your 2nd House of Self-Worth forms three squares—on January 22, May 10, and October 9—with optimistic Jupiter, now in your 11th House of Friends, Hopes, and Wishes. **These squares can surprise**

you with good news as well as bad with respect to your bank account and also relative to your own core values. The socially oriented 11th House is the home base of your chart; Jupiter's presence here throughout 2007 expands your connection to your com- munity while increasing the benefits you receive from being part of a larger group. Hopeful Jupiter's squares with brilliant Uranus elevate your spirit, increase your self-confidence, and show you ways to overcome the sometimes repressive heaviness of Saturn.

MAKE LOVE REAL

Others become more demanding now, requiring commitments, with Saturn moving through your 7th House of Partnerships. You may have to decide whether a relationship is worth the extra effort or if it's time to move on. And as romantic Venus runs quickly around your chart, it activates karmic Saturn several times. Venus is in your 5th House of Love from April 11 through May 7, and in mid-April it forms a harmonious trine with Saturn, possibly deepening a current relationship if you're willing to settle down. You must take full responsibility for issues of the heart when lovely Venus contacts restrictive Saturn in your 7th House on July 1, August 13, and October 13. Whether single or attached, you may feel Saturn's weight standing between you and love. As Saturn enters your 8th House of Intimacy on September 2, expect practical concerns to transform into deeper issues of vulnerability and sexuality as you move closer to someone you love.

HOME STRETCH

Take a hard look at your professional dreams to separate worthwhile ones from those that could be left behind. This isn't just about elimination; with Pluto involved, it's about transformation. You have strength of purpose as Jupiter in your 11th House of Goals forms supportive trines with calculating Saturn, espe- cially around mid-March and early May. Pluto and Mars rule your 10th House of Career. Power-hungry Pluto is in its final year of a long journey through the 11th House. Your career aspirations could be in the last stages of metamorphosis. With Jupiter moving toward a conjunction with Pluto on December 11, visionary planning reaches a culmination that puts far-reaching changes into effect.

SAVE FOR A RAINY DAY

Uranus is full of surprises as it continues to move through your 2nd House of Money and Resources. Erratic Uranus entered your 2nd House in March 2003 and remains there for another three years. But this year, Uranus is activated by a square to optimistic Jupiter, giving you great hope for sudden change. You are more willing to speculate in order to make gains, but overeagerness can encourage you to take risks that may not pay off the way you wish. Therefore, caution is the key to your success. Eclipses in your money houses—on March 3, March 18, August 28, and September 11—reemphasize the overall instability of your financial situation. To achieve positive results, stash money aside when you have it, and resist the temptation to take any shortcuts.

 DISCOVER ALTERNATIVE THERAPIES

Chiron the Wounded Healer in innovative Aquarius encourages you to improve your overall health by learning more about the mind/body connection. One of your key planets, unconventional Uranus, squares open-minded Jupiter; you stand to gain much from trying alternative types of therapies, such as acupuncture and homeopathy. Your other key planet, Saturn, receives strong support from Jupiter, giving you the necessary perseverance to adhere to better health practices. Utilize energetic Mars's extra-long stay in your 6th House of Habits—from September 28 through the end of the year—by revving up your exercise program or even participating in a competitive sport.

 INTERTWINE DREAMS WITH REALITY

As much as you may seek freedom in your life, you will also need equilibrium on the home front. The oppositions between dreamy Neptune and realistic Saturn throughout the first half of the year require that you find a healthy balance between your fantasies and the hard truths you must face at home. Venus, the ruler of your 4th House of Home and Family, activates this sector of your chart from March 17 through April 11, bringing much sweetness to your family life. Also, Venus's retrograde from July 27 through September 8 can have you reconsidering decisions that you've made about your living space. What begins as buying new curtains can easily turn into a major reno-vation, so be wary of any unexpected expenses.

UP, UP, AND AWAY

Jupiter rules long-distance voyages, while Mercury represents shorter trips. Jupiter's ongoing squares to maverick Uranus may have you boarding an airplane without a lot of advance planning. You may suddenly decide to take a vacation or even be required to take an abrupt business trip to an exotic location. In fact, with opportunistic Jupiter's ongoing trine to no-nonsense Saturn in your 7th House, you might travel with a business partner. Make a few quick trips for work or pleasure while sociable Mercury is in your 9th House of Travel in September and October. When Venus transits your 9th House from November 8 through December 5, you might finally be able to splurge on that long-awaited adventure you so deserve.

LESSONS FOR THE SOUL

The year begins with lovely Venus moving toward a conjunction with idealistic Neptune in Aquarius, adding unrealistic expectations to your dreams about the future. Saturn the Taskmaster opposes Neptune on February 28 and June 25, creating roadblocks to your metaphysical development. Discouragement can become overwhelming unless you recognize and appreciate Saturn as your teacher, thereby giving you the spiritual fortitude to overcome obstacles through disciplined practice. Additionally, knowledge-hungry Jupiter hands Neptune strong support this year, especially around October 29, when you may choose to become more involved in a particular religion or course of study. Look ahead in your life as far as possible, understanding that the choices you make now will take years to fully unfold.

RICK & JEFF'S TIP FOR THE YEAR:
Finish Old Business First

You must follow through on what you have already started, or your years of sincere effort could be for naught. You are in the final stages of your work, but it could take time to fully understand how best to use what you now harvest. Finish up old business in all areas of your life before you start anything new. However, if something is not working out, let it go. Do not look at this as a failure; instead, think of it as a learning experience along the way as you create your new future.

JANUARY

WEIRD, WONDERFUL YOU

This month starts with an emotional Full Moon in Cancer in your 6th House of Health and Work on **January 3**. Although you may seek ways to complete practical tasks, you aren't necessarily following the same old way of operating. This Full Moon forms a harmonious trine to your key planet Uranus in the 2nd House of Self-Worth. Finding original solutions to old problems can build your confidence, but you may worry needlessly about unimportant details along the way. Sweet Venus enters Aquarius on **January 3**, allowing you to express your unorthodox desires. On **January 15**, clever Mercury enters your sign, propelling your mind into new directions as you begin to think even further outside the box, if at all possible.

Assertive Mars enters ambitious Capricorn on **January 16**, staying there until **February 25**, giving you endurance along with a solid foundation from which to move forward. The spiritually grounded Capricorn New Moon in your 12th House of Imagination on **January 18** provides you with the chance to stop and pause, to look back once more before taking an exciting quantum leap into your future. The Moon and the Sun join the Aquarian pack of planets on **January 19 and 20**, respectively, charging you with great energy and giving you a strong sense of individuality.

KEEP IN MIND THIS MONTH

You can be even more unconventional than ever. Celebrate your individuality, for it is essential now to be uniquely you as possible.

The key to this month, however, is the first of three squares—the others are in May and October—between fortunate Jupiter and eccentric Uranus. It is exact on **January 22** but impacts the entire year. Your awareness is heightened, your mind opened, your horizons widened. A powerful restlessness pervades your everyday activities as you seek opportunities to make new friends and revitalize your life.

KEY DATES

JANUARY 8 ★ *take charge*
Ambitious Saturn in your 7th House of Partnerships forms an efficient trine with energetic Mars, granting you keen organization skills, strong determination, and the ability to work well with others. Whatever you do now carries the power of your intentions, so apply well-considered ideas to your master plan. You have the tasks set out for yourself and will let nothing prevent you from accomplishing your goals. Do not waste today's potential; follow your ambitions with bold and decisive action.

JANUARY 13 ★ *express your passion*

The impulsive fire of Mars aligns with powerful Pluto today in your 11th House of Groups, creating a volcanic intensity that can release repressed energy with great force. You may have more impact now on your team of coworkers or your friends than you realize. Even lighthearted activities arouse a full spectrum of emotions. You cannot help but play for keeps as survival issues rise from the depths of your subconscious. Don't try to suppress the wave; instead, find healthy outlets to express your physical energy and buried feelings—especially anger—or the potential benefits can elude you.

SUPER NOVA DAY
JANUARY 18 ★ *no escape*

The effects of the conservative Capricorn New Moon may not be apparent, as it is hidden in your secretive 12th House. This is a transitional day that signals a move from fantasy to reality in the weeks ahead. An exact conjunction between lovely Venus and magical Neptune lures you into a world of artistic beauty, infatuation, and flights of fancy. Avoid negative escapist behaviors, including overindulgence with sex, drugs, or alcohol. Instead, seek a balance between your spiritual practices—drumming, meditating, praying, whatever—and the chores you must complete in the real world.

JANUARY 22 ★ *denied pleasure*

Today's opposition of lovely Venus to restrictive Saturn may not allow you to have much fun until you consider the consequences of your desires. Self-restraint is rewarded, and if you forget about your obligations, something might happen to remind you of what you must do. If an authority figure stands between you and enjoyment, don't argue. Listen to the voice of reason, and remember that you can always play later.

JANUARY 28 ★ *strengthen your ideas*

Even though you may be a loner at times, you usually work well with others. Now, however, someone may rain on your parade as somber Saturn is opposed today by the messenger planet, Mercury, creating blockages in the normal flow of your thoughts. This can be frustrating, but the key to success is to use the current restrictions to tighten your thinking and to refine your communication skills.

FEBRUARY

RELATIONSHIP REALISM

Personal fulfillment in the context of relationships is your top priority with the expressive Leo Full Moon in your 7th House on **February 2**. The Moon is close to the ongoing opposition between restrictive Saturn and inspiring Neptune and can highlight issues relating to a larger crisis of confidence that you may experience in the months ahead. Your concern now is how to balance your need for individual freedom with the responsibilities you accepted by entering into a particular personal or business partnership.

Mental Mercury convinces you to set logic aside for a while as it slides into spiritual Pisces on **February 2**. Uncharacteristically, you would rather talk about your dreams than about a new scientific discovery. But you are less certain of yourself; your thoughts become more difficult to share as the Winged Messenger turns retrograde on **February 13**, remaining in backward motion until **March 7**. Use this time to rethink your assumptions, revise your plans, and reinvent your future. The intelligent Aquarius New Moon on **February 17** is a jumping-off point, bringing a sudden flash of awareness that helps you resolve a nagging feeling that something isn't quite right. The Sun moves into responsive Pisces on **February 18**, and sexy Venus races ahead into impulsive Aries on **February 21**, firing up your desires. Still, you remain anchored in the present with assertive Mars just entering your sign on **February 25**.

Realistic Saturn, moving through your 7th House of Relationships, reaches exact opposition with elusive Neptune in your sign on **February 28**. This slow-moving aspect began to dissolve foundational structures and concrete assumptions last summer. Even though you may revisit the possible discouragement of confronting your failures, there are still many things for you to learn, as the spiritual lessons are more significant than any disappointment.

KEEP IN MIND THIS MONTH

Although you often use facts as a way of feeling secure, more data won't necessarily validate your emotions. Rationalization is not as important as experience when it comes to the heart.

KEY DATES

FEBRUARY 3 ★ *superhero powers*

The Sun receives buoyant support from jovial Jupiter, so you feel like you can do anything. Also, unpredictable Uranus is being fired up by self-directed Mars. You are eager to respond to any situation in a creative and spontaneous way, but your optimism can cause trouble. Temper your enthusiasm with a touch of realism.

FEBRUARY 7–10 ★ *sparks fly*
The lightning of love might strike as romantic Venus conjuncts shocking Uranus on **February 7**. The Sun joins imaginative Neptune on **February 8**, so it may be nearly impossible to be practical. By **February 9**, Venus squares Jupiter, encouraging you to overindulge. But the Sun opposes karmic Saturn on **February 10**, giving you a reality check. If you have let responsibilities slip, the party may now be over.

FEBRUARY 13–14 ★ *postpone pleasure*
Venus and Mars happily support each other, teasing you with the possibility of true love, heightened creativity, and enjoyable social activities. But they each form irritating quincunx aspects with dutiful Saturn in your 7th House of Partnerships, suggesting difficulty in balancing your desires with the needs of others. You could get pretty grouchy, for although you want to play, someone else wants to put you to work. Accept that you may have to postpone enjoyment for a while.

FEBRUARY 19 ★ *open your heart*
Alluring Venus forms a tense square with dark Pluto, arousing sexual tensions that can agitate intimate relationships. Power struggles over love or money may demand your attention. Confronting new, deep feelings can be frightening. Since you can be so comfortable in the detached world of intellect, this may be disconcerting, but don't let that stop you. Whatever conflicts arise, gifts await you in the nonverbal world of emotions, where analysis is less important than actual experience.

SUPER NOVA DAY
FEBRUARY 28 ★ *be vulnerable*
Turning your dreams into reality is a slow, ongoing process that is activated by today's Saturn-Neptune opposition as you revisit relationship issues that were stirred last August. You may need to accept big changes beyond your control, yet letting go of something or someone can be a healthy choice. Mercury the Communicator forms a supportive sextile today with psychologically intense Pluto. Dig deeply into your subconscious, and bring the real issues to the surface. Your willingness to talk about fears that normally are hidden from others can help the process and make everyone feel better about what is happening.

MARCH

WATCH YOUR BOTTOM LINE

Watch your finances, for two pivotal eclipses turn your resource houses topsy-turvy. First, a Virgo Full Moon Eclipse in your 8th House of Shared Resources on **March 3** is opposite the Sun and Uranus in your 2nd House of Personal Resources, requiring you to spend your money on jointly held property. Surprise repairs can make this month somewhat hazardous to your checkbook. Second, a perplexing Pisces New Moon Eclipse in your 2nd House on **March 18** is square Pluto, so you may have power struggles with an associate who disagrees with your spending decisions. Someone may try to change your viewpoint by questioning your core beliefs. Although the effects of these eclipses may be felt for weeks or even months, their potency and urgency are heightened around these exact dates.

Counterbalancing the uncertainty of the eclipses is the first of two stabilizing trines between the cosmic regulators, expansive Jupiter and contractive Saturn, on **March 16**. The month has a feeling of equilibrium, even if hectic circumstances have you around in circles. With reliable Saturn in your 7th House of Partnerships and Jupiter in your 11th House of Friends, other people may help you out of a difficult situation. Don't pretend that everything is fine when it's not. Let yourself be vulnerable and accept the support of those around you, especially as the Sun moves through compassionate Pisces until **March 20**.

Assertive Mars in Aquarius gives you energy, but beware of burning the candle at both ends, or you will be left depleted by the end of the month. Mars reactivates the **February 28** Saturn-Neptune opposition, which reminds you of the work you must do to heal your own personal disappointments.

> ### KEEP IN MIND THIS MONTH
>
> *You don't always need to have all of the answers. Listen to the wisdom of others, even if it's hard to admit uncertainty.*

KEY DATES

MARCH 3-5 ★ *sudden shift*

The Virgo Full Moon Eclipse on **March 3** makes the conjunction between Uranus and the Sun on **March 5** more unpredictable. You may feel the stress financially, emotionally, or both. Regardless, it's critical to stretch your awareness, rather than hiding from the truth. If your life feels out of balance and circumstances are fraught with tension, your flexibility and sense of humor can be great allies.

SUPER NOVA DAYS

MARCH 8-9 ★ *window of opportunity*

Venus, now moving through fiery Aries, forms a grand trine with Saturn and Jupiter on **March 8 to 9**, creating a moment when your world appears to be in balance. But you could be lazy, expecting wonderful opportunities to come your way. It's crucial, however, to act now, even if it feels like you have plenty of time. The Sun moves into a dynamic square with powerful Jupiter on **March 9**, charging your system with an overabundance of enthusiasm and making you feel like you can accomplish anything you desire. Overextending yourself will not necessarily bring you happiness. Highly focused small steps are much more productive than scattered giant steps.

MARCH 16-17 ★ *share your heart*

The harmonious trine between optimistic Jupiter and realistic Saturn on **March 16** blesses you with excellent judgment that can overcome almost any self-doubt. Romantic Venus forms a harmonious trine with passionate Pluto, strengthening your desires. This is amplified by clever Mercury in intelligent Aquarius creating harmonious sextiles with both Venus and Pluto, allowing you to communicate intense feelings that are outside the realm of your usual language. Take time to decide what you wish to experience and how you hope to grow, and then discuss your personal goals in depth with a lover or close friend.

MARCH 22 ★ *detour in the road*

Frustrations grow as assertive Mars opposes stern Saturn, and expressing your pent-up emotions only makes matters worse. Unfortunately, suppression isn't an option either, for your annoyance can turn to resentment if you withdraw from others. Don't try to just force your way through; instead, slow down, carefully share your perspective, and then continue on your way.

MARCH 25 ★ *let it be*

Mars meets up with foggy Neptune today, softening your demeanor and perhaps taking the wind out of your sails. You may not feel as driven and could be confused as to your next move. Instead of attempting to conquer your uncertainties, just relax and let your faith gently steer you where you need to go. This is a perfect day for a spiritual retreat, quiet meditation, or simply passing the time with friends.

APRIL

HOLD ON FOR GROWTH

Deep tidal currents this month can be disconcerting as buoyant Jupiter turns retrograde on **April 5** and ambitious Saturn turns direct on **April 19**. These two planetary giants are still harmonized with each other as they move toward a **May 5** trine that repeats the stabilizing patterns they set up on **March 16**. The pleasant Libra Full Moon in your 9th House of Big Ideas on **April 2** draws you toward Jupiter's inflationary side of the equation as you balance the needs of others with your own. Meanwhile, Saturn's restrictive side is activated by sensual Venus now in stubborn Taurus, demanding that you become aware of what you must sacrifice to achieve your long-term dream.

Although you may feel let down on **April 6** as Mars leaves your innovative sign to enter the more intuitive realm of Pisces, the Sun illuminates the continuing Jupiter-Saturn trine, blessing nearly anything you do with great potential for success. All is not easy, however, for Mercury's square to power-hungry Pluto on **April 9** encourages you to fight for survival, even if you are not in as much danger as you think.

Find time to play with Venus in restless and flirty Gemini in your 5th House of Romance from **April 11 to May 7**. The Aries New Moon in your 3rd House of Communication on **April 17** is trine to compelling Pluto, adding intensity to your words and actions. Although every New Moon can initiate something, this one has the power of lasting endurance, especially as Mercury in creative Aries trines both Jupiter and Saturn on **April 20 and 21**, respectively, once again encouraging this deep wave of steady growth.

> **KEEP IN MIND THIS MONTH**
>
> *Don't act impulsively. This is an ideal time to make plans to accomplish your heart's desire over the months ahead.*

KEY DATES

APRIL 1-2 ★ *elusive equilibrium*

Mental Mercury can bring confusion as it moves through daydreaming Pisces, but its conjunction with brilliant Uranus in your 2nd House of Finances on **April 1** stimulates clear communication about money matters. Venus's square to nay-saying Saturn gives you the feeling that you don't have enough nice things in your life, including both money and love. The harmony-seeking Libra Full Moon on **April 2** offers you what it takes to put your life back in balance.

SUPER NOVA DAYS
APRIL 8-9 ★ *well-deserved confidence*
A coherent sense of your goals offers real possibilities for success. The Sun creates easy trines with both joyful Jupiter on **April 8** and serious Saturn on **April 9**, allowing you to play both ends of the spectrum quite effectively. Although Jupiter and Saturn are opposites, you can brilliantly balance these principles of expansion and contraction and assume a graceful posture that gets you exactly what you need. Work toward building structures that will endure, for Saturn's law now suggests you will get what you earn, while Jupiter won't bring rewards without your full participation.

APRIL 12-14 ★ *admit your vulnerability*
Thoughtful Mercury now in aggressive Aries forms tense aspects with crystallizing Saturn on **April 12** and with dissolving Neptune on **April 14**. You may not be feeling as positive about recent choices, but your forceful communication style can hide your insecurities. Avoid the temptation to cover weakness with an image of strength. Instead, be open to critical feedback, and revise your plans as needed before continuing on your way.

APRIL 20-21 ★ *dress rehearsal*
Enthusiastic Mercury in impetuous Aries wires your thoughts by activating the same harmonious Jupiter-Saturn trine that the Sun touched earlier this month, making this a perfect time to finalize your plans. You have been plotting and scheming long enough; much can happen in the next few weeks, and the decisions you make now will help to actualize your dreams. Find a balance between the blind optimism of Jupiter and the rigid pessimism of Saturn to make the best decisions.

APRIL 28 ★ *minor lifequake*
You are all hyped up now as feisty Mars catches up with one of your key planets—shocking, erratic Uranus. This can set your world aflame with chaos if you are fearful, or it could vitalize you with thrills if you are up for change. It is more challenging to contain the energy than to roll with the waves. If you feel like you are constrained, your grievances may be very real. Work with the issues on a deep level, for this isn't going to be solved by a quick emotional outburst.

MAY

RESTLESS YEARNINGS

Retrograde Jupiter provides you with an opportunity to gain momentum this month and put your intelligence to practical use. Benevolent Jupiter harmonized in a long-term trine with Saturn on **March 16**, creating potential for you to establish a firm footing. This trine was activated several times since, and as it gains maximum power on **May 5**, you must take action again to stabilize your future. You barely have a chance to relax, as the second of Jupiter's dynamic squares to Uranus, on **May 10**, returns the restlessness you might have first encountered on **January 22**. This is not necessarily a setback, but it does demonstrate that there are many options you haven't considered and that there is still plenty of room for growth.

The intense Scorpio Full Moon in your 10th House of Career on **May 2** opposes both the Sun and Mercury in your 4th House of Roots and kindles the desire to balance your professional work with more personal experiences. The sensible Taurus New Moon in your 4th House on **May 16** grounds you with a strong base of operations from which you can make necessary changes. With a square to spiritual Neptune in your 1st House of Personality, others may perceive you as unrealistic, even dreamy. It doesn't matter what people think; rely on your instincts, for they will not steer you wrong now. An unusual second Full Moon this month on **May 31** offers another round of opportunities as you visualize your future. This inspirational Sagittarian Full Moon in your 11th House of Dreams receives a boost of energy from gutsy Mars, which supports you with the initiative and drive to manifest your thoughts into actions.

> **KEEP IN MIND THIS MONTH**
>
> *Powerful forces are at work—some supportive, some disruptive—but it's up to you to take charge of your life and make the most of the major changes at hand.*

KEY DATES

SUPER NOVA DAYS
MAY 5–7 ★ *maintain hope*
The long-lasting wave of the Jupiter-Saturn trine is exact on **May 5**, offering opportunities to increase your standard of living, which can build a foundation for what is yet to come. Mental Mercury in practical Taurus squares Saturn,

planting obstacles that can feel impassable, but this short-lived transit will not negatively impact your overall plans. Still, you might have to adjust your thinking so that your own rigidity does not get in the way. Sweet Venus opposes manipulative Pluto on **May 6**, possibly making you feel that others are taking unfair advantage of you. And once Mercury squares doubtful Neptune on **May 7**, your confidence could waver as you feel uncertain about your future.

MAY 9-10 ★ *follow your dream*
You are tantalized with unlimited possibilities when you look out at the distant horizon regardless of the burdens you presently carry. Jupiter's square to Uranus on **May 10** refreshes your dreams, while a restrictive square between the Sun and Saturn creates an air of heavy responsibility. Although you may be cautioned not to take the more exciting path, don't settle for anything less. Look back to remember the choices you made at the end of January. Don't make similar mistakes again, or you will be facing the same dilemma for a third and final time when these planets meet up again on **October 9**.

MAY 20 ★ *high anxiety*
Mercury is a bit scattered now in its home sign of flighty Gemini. Today, the Winged Messenger opposes big-thinking Jupiter and squares unorthodox Uranus. Everything is moving so fast that it may be difficult to tell whether your thoughts are coming, going, or meeting one another in between. This is an erratic, electric, and eccentric day that has you rocking and rolling—even before you take your first sip of coffee. Anything that helps soothe your nerves is highly recommended now, for you could spin your wheels all day without having anything to show for it later. On the other hand, if you can slow yourself down to a steady pace, you stand to gain from the brilliant ideas that flash across your mind.

MAY 27 ★ *deep dive*
Mercury the Communicator stands in opposition to compelling Pluto, and although it might appear that fast-talking Mercury has met its match, you are gifted with clever verbal tricks up your sleeve. This stimulates your 5th House of Love, and you have the mixed blessing to be transformed by emotional discussions without being burned by the intensity. Be fearless, and you just may learn something very profound about yourself and your partner.

JUNE

DREAMS COME AND GO

Saturn opposes nebulous Neptune for the third and final time on **June 25**. This realignment began last August, came back into focus around **February 28**, and now colors the entire month as the hard, cold reality of Saturn precipitates the boundless ideals of Neptune into everyday life. You may feel discouraged and that your world is an unfriendly place as you face your unfulfilled dreams. With Saturn in your 7th House of Partnerships, you may look to others for something you can hold on to as stable foundations dissolve beneath your feet. Rest assured, however, that this month is not all gloomy. The Sun and Mars fill your dreams with optimism through the first half of the month. Mars forms an enthusiastic trine with confident Jupiter on **June 4**. And sweet Venus happily prances into playful Leo in your 7th House on **June 5**, triggering your generosity and sense of drama in relationships.

The hyperactive Gemini New Moon on **June 14** fills you with wonder and a desire to live life more fully. Its close trine to Neptune suggests that meditation or any spiritual pursuit will be beneficial at this time. But its close opposition to Pluto indicates that someone may stand between you and happiness. However, if you can prove your integrity and your commitment, you still may get what you want. There are delays, though, for Mercury's retrograde phase starts on **June 15**, requiring you to revisit old ground, rethink thoughts, and revise plans. Progress is slow until thinking Mercury turns direct on **July 9**. The conservative Capricorn Full Moon in your 12th House of Divinity on **June 30** poses an interesting dilemma as you rely on both traditional spiritual practices and your sound judgment to help reclaim your faith.

> **KEEP IN MIND THIS MONTH**
>
> *You may be overwhelmed by the everyday demands. Relinquishing some control allows you to develop an intuitive strategy, refresh your spirit, and re-create your goals.*

KEY DATES

SUPER NOVA DAYS
JUNE 4–5 ★ *not so fast*
These uplifting days can elevate your spirit so much that your overconfidence may land you in trouble. The Sun and energetic Mars are traveling along in a high-energy sextile that lasts throughout the middle of the month. Meanwhile,

Mars harmoniously trines larger-than-life Jupiter on **June 4**, boldly assuring you that you can climb mountains or swim the English Channel without preparation or training. Vivacious Venus's entrance into proud Leo on **June 5** gives you just the push you need to flaunt your stuff. Needless to say, self-restraint and common sense are critical.

JUNE 11 ★ *hard work is easy*
Assertive Mars forms a harmonious trine with conservative Saturn, granting you a sharper-than-usual organizational sense, along with the physical stamina to accomplish your goals. But these are not last week's inflated dreams, for practicality now drives your actions. Just remember that you may be suffering from the aftereffects of your recent visit to fantasy land, so don't let your attention wander. Apply yourself in the real world, and real rewards will follow.

JUNE 18–21 ★ *vanquish fear*
Strong survival instincts are aroused as passionate Pluto is touched by a tense opposition from the Sun on **June 18** and then by a harmonious trine from fearless Mars in combative Aries on **June 21**. Although these aspects could provoke deep fears or even paranoia, you have the willpower to conquer your demons and face the healing truth. Turn your words into action even if you meet resistance. Lovely Venus makes an easy trine with joyful Jupiter on **June 19**, encouraging you with love and support from friends, partners, or coworkers.

JUNE 25 ★ *don't give up*
Though the big planetary news is the weighty opposition between somber Saturn and elusive Neptune, its effects can last weeks or even months. Still, relationship issues may have you comparing your current circumstances to your ideals and wondering why they don't match up. You may wish to withdraw from intimacy as Venus quincunxes freedom-loving Uranus. Hang in there, for the skies are about to clear.

JUNE 30 ★ *responsible dreaming*
The steady Capricorn Full Moon in your 12th House of Inner Peace may find you nostalgically longing for the safety and security you crave. Additionally, loving Venus opposes dreamy Neptune and then bumps into stern Saturn on **July 1**. Your conscience keeps you in touch with the consequences of your actions, leaving you little leeway to drift into the outer reaches of the spiritual 12th House. Pleasure may be yours, but you must accept your obligations and fulfill your responsibilities.

JULY

DELAYED GRATIFICATION

This month opens on a difficult note as pleasure-seeking Venus in Leo meets up with somber Saturn on **July 1** in your 7th House of Partnerships. Although the effects of this serious aspect usually last for only a couple of days, this time—because of Venus's slowing speed —the impact lasts for several months. It may be tough for you to enjoy the fruits of your labor, to experience the pleasures of sensuality, or to find the love you seek. Venus backs up over Saturn again on **August 13** and conjuncts Saturn for the third and final time on **October 13**. But all is not bleak, as this is also a chance to create enduring love with integrity and commitment. It's time to stabilize both your heart and your finances. Additionally, if you concentrate on long-term goals rather than immediate gratification, your efforts will be rewarded at work as well as in love.

Mercury turns direct in sensitive Cancer on **July 9**, instructing you to take one last look back before finalizing your plans. Review time is over, though the Cancer New Moon on **July 14** in your 6th House of Daily Routines may have you wondering what you have left undone. Venus's entrance into detail-oriented Virgo on the same day contributes to your heightened enjoyment as you focus your attention on the little things. But satisfaction becomes more elusive as Venus turns retrograde on **July 27**. The overstimulating Aquarius Full Moon on **July 29** in your 1st House of Personality draws your emotions very close to the surface. Others can see past your apparent detachment. Your discomfort in dealing with your feelings could turn frustration to anger as hot Mars squares cold Saturn on **July 31**.

> **KEEP IN MIND THIS MONTH**
>
> *Some pleasures may be postponed, but there is room for relaxation and enjoyment as long as you don't have unrealistic expectations.*

KEY DATES

SUPER NOVA DAY
JULY 1 ★ *behind closed doors*
It's not a lighthearted day as Venus, the planet of desires, aligns with Saturn, the planet of resistance, emphasizing serious issues about love and money. If your unrestrained emotions have been flying all over the place, the party ends abruptly as your pleasures are delayed. Although your feelings are strong,

they may hit a wall that holds back a flood of heartfelt expression. Don't push it; the more you seek now, the less you will find.

JULY 8 ★ *express buried feelings*

Loving Venus forms the first of three harmonious trines with deeply passionate Pluto. You may feel quite vulnerable, and your drive for intensity could arouse issues that connect sex with power as you obsess over the object of your love. Addressing your fears can be therapeutic, especially if you are able to bring your most secret desires into the open. Your efforts to transform negativity will ease the impact of the next occurrences of this transit on **August 15** and **October 3**.

JULY 20 ★ *naturally brilliant*

Brazen Mars forms a smart sextile with crazy Uranus today, bestowing sudden courage upon you. This erratic planetary combination can also add pizzazz to an otherwise unexciting weekend. You can be brilliant without saying a word, for your message is contained within your actions. Don't try so hard to be different. You'll be more readily accepted by your friends and family if you explore common ground.

JULY 24 ★ *loss of direction*

Red-hot Mars cools off a bit as it forms a dynamic but confusing square with slippery Neptune. Although you knew where you were going as you got ready, now that you are all dressed, you may not be so sure. It's as if your power circuits are being drained without reason, creating a lack of resolve and maybe even uncertainty. It's easy to fall into a whirlpool of fantasy or just sloppy thinking, so don't jump to conclusions until you are positive you know the truth.

JULY 31 ★ *against the grain*

Work obligations may keep you from enjoying yourself as your boss loads you up with new tasks. Someone may even be purposefully antagonizing you now, as if they were trying to ruin your day. You might be tempted to fight back, but it's apparent that outright conflict will not settle anything and will certainly not help you achieve your goals. Find a way to express your anger without taking it out on the wrong person. Laying low for a while before making another push forward may be your best strategy at this time.

AQUARIUS

AUGUST

INEVITABLE EVOLUTION

The underlying theme of this month is sounded by a harmonious trine between your traditional ruler, Saturn, and the slowest planet, Pluto, on **August 6**. It is rare for these two planetary heavyweights to be working so easily together, yet loyal Saturn in your 7th House of Partnerships is compelled to transform by intense Pluto. Great changes are necessary, and you may need to draw upon the deep energy reserves now available to you. The dramatic Leo New Moon on **August 12**, with five planets in your 7th House, turns up the heat on your relationships; with elusive Neptune involved, you can have trouble uncovering the truth as illusions surround you. The paradox is that Venus conjuncts Saturn on **August 13**, so you won't be able to escape the harsh realities of the present circumstances.

Relationship issues stick with you, for on the days following the New Moon, both Mercury and the Sun form conjunctions with Venus and Saturn. You have the willpower now to confront difficult issues as the Leo planets harmoniously trine formidable Pluto one at a time on **August 15, 17, and 19**. Your optimism can prevail over the most challenging problems as action hero Mars opposes lucky Jupiter on **August 23**, followed by Mercury's hardworking square to both Mars and Jupiter.

But it's all too easy to lose your perspective and overlook even the most obvious warning signs. Venus's opposition to Neptune increases your current escapist tendencies. A Full Moon Eclipse in intuitive Pisces in your material 2nd House of Possessions on **August 28** can signal a shift in the cosmic weather, combining imagination with practicality.

> **KEEP IN MIND THIS MONTH**
>
> *Face the truth about what you are willing to sacrifice to save a relationship. Make essential changes to strengthen the bonds and increase intimacy.*

KEY DATES

AUGUST 2 ★ *good day, sunshine*
The glorious Sun in outgoing Leo harmonizes with broad-minded Jupiter today, prompting you to feel great about your life. Even if your confidence isn't based entirely on reality, it can still ease the fear of the unknown. Express your opinions judiciously, and don't blindly step over others in your bold enthusiasm. Remember that time is on your side; if an opportunity is real, then it will last.

AUGUST 12–13 ★ *you can't always get what you want*

The extra needy Leo New Moon has Mercury, Venus, and Saturn joining the Sun and Moon in your 7th House of Relationships on **August 12**. Dream as you may, perfect love may seem very far away. Rich Venus conjuncts austere Saturn on **August 13** as responsibility takes precedence over pleasure and gratification is again delayed. Real gains can be made if you isolate what you require for your own happiness, in or out of a relationship.

AUGUST 15–17 ★ *resistance is futile*

Strong emotional undercurrents take you on an intense journey as retrograde Venus harmoniously hooks up with tenacious Pluto on **August 15**. But you may be pleasantly surprised if you express your current dissatisfaction as Mercury the Communicator makes a similar trine to Pluto on **August 17**. Don't waste energy trying to suppress the darker side of your attractions, for bringing them into the open can diffuse the power they hold over you. Remember that flexibility is your friend; rigidity can create a rough ride.

AUGUST 23–25 ★ *no limits*

Fiery Mars in your 5th House of Play forms a stressful opposition with bigger-than-life Jupiter in your 11th House of Friends on **August 23**, yet the tension can provide you with a whole lot of fun as long as you don't overdo it. An opposition between sweet Venus and illusory Neptune on **August 25** may have you fantasizing about perfect love. However, in your enthusiastic zest for life, you may not realize your limits until you have surpassed them. No matter how far out your imagination takes you, bring your inflationary thinking back to earth before you become your own unsuspecting victim.

SUPER NOVA DAY
AUGUST 28 ★ *wake-up call*

Although today's Lunar Eclipse in psychic Pisces is a harbinger of changes that will continue to unfold for months, the immediate action originates from mental Mercury's tense opposition to electric Uranus. Ideas strike like lightning bolts, creating moments of great awareness. Your words, too, carry a sudden snap of originality and a sizzle of shock, stimulating conversations about unusual topics. Seek out other like-minded explorers to travel with you to the edges of the universe.

AQUARIUS

SEPTEMBER

A WHOLE NEW BALLGAME

Your traditional ruling planet, Saturn the Tester, enters efficient Virgo in your 8th House of Regeneration on **September 2**, bringing two years of relationship lessons to the next level. While Saturn is in Virgo—until **October 29, 2009**—you will be required to fine-tune the transformations that have begun. If you experienced the demise of an intimate relationship while Saturn was in "me first" Leo, now you may seek new and improved ways of expressing your love so that you don't repeat your mistakes of the past. If, however, you strengthened a partnership, you must embrace your vulnerability and commit to deep emotional change. Since the 8th House also pertains to other people's shared resources, pay particular attention to jointly owned property, taxes, and even legal issues over an inheritance.

Active Mars continues to move through restless Gemini, squaring shocking Uranus on **September 3**, urging you to do something original, perhaps even risky, in your search for excitement. Venus turns direct on **September 8** and opposes imaginative Neptune on **September 21**, re-creating dreams of ideal love and spiritual perfection that may have first surfaced on **June 30** and **August 25**. Additionally, Mars opposes Pluto on **September 21**, compelling you to fight for your beliefs; surrender is not an option.

The analytical Virgo New Moon Eclipse in your 8th House of Transformation on **September 11** opposes erratic Uranus. The 8th House and 2nd House are related to finances, so expect a surprise or two concerning money. The impulsive Aries Full Moon on **September 26** overwhelms your communication houses. Think before you speak; a sense of urgency pervades your life, but you have time enough to get it right.

KEEP IN MIND THIS MONTH

It feels as if things are really moving, but don't rush the process. Methodical progress creates more lasting results than a sprint to the finish.

KEY DATES

SEPTEMBER 3 ★ *circus act*
Energetic Mars squares off today with high-strung Uranus, creating an electrified environment where impulse rules, tempers may flare, and people can do crazy things. Hidden tensions suddenly explode into view. Your attraction to thrills is

surpassed only by your need for freedom. And with the Sun's dynamic square to optimistic Jupiter, you might not see the pitfalls of your desires. Suppression doesn't work, for the energy must release, so express it gradually and moderately, rather than waiting for something big to happen.

SUPER NOVA DAYS
SEPTEMBER 8-11 ★ *big surprises*
The days leading up to the dynamic New Moon Eclipse in perfectionist Virgo on **September 11** are filled with unexpected twists and turns. Loving Venus forms an irritable quincunx to nonconformist Uranus on **September 8**, creating an irresolvable tension that just won't go away. Unfortunately, you might not even be able to locate the source of your discomfort, so resolution is unlikely. Your energy is further confused by Mars's trine to nebulous Neptune. You wish to escape uneasiness and take a day of rest, for you don't have a solution at hand—and it exhausts you to think about it. But even if you believe that the script has already been written, the Sun-Uranus opposition on **September 9** sets the stage for surprise endings. The eclipse is an exclamation point on this crazy phase, showing you the truth exactly as you need to see it. Make changes now, for they will have lasting significance.

SEPTEMBER 17-21 ★ *intense pressure*
Another series of powerful waves forces you to stand up for yourself as feisty Mars squares the Sun on **September 17** and then opposes passionate Pluto on **September 21**, increasing the potential for ego skirmishes. This complex mix can signify power struggles in relationships, but it can also symbolize the power of positive change. The pressure intensifies; you are like a volcano ready to erupt, and you may not consider the consequences of your actions. It may be challenging to be nice to those around you unless you can find a healthy outlet for your excess physical energy.

SEPTEMBER 26-28 ★ *logic prevails*
The Aries Full Moon in your 3rd House of Communication on **September 26** is opposite the relationship-oriented Libra Sun, prodding you to maintain your individuality even when involved with someone else. Messenger Mercury's trine to insistent Mars helps you make your point, but Mercury enters enigmatic Scorpio on **September 27** and Mars enters sensitive Cancer on **September 28**, luring you into a less rational world where feelings are more important than thoughts.

OCTOBER

HURRY UP AND WAIT

The third and final square between ever-expanding Jupiter and unorthodox Uranus on **October 9** sets an edgy yet upbeat tone now. You may have felt incoming waves of anticipation from unexpected quarters and even far-off galaxies as these two giants of unpredictable growth squared each other, first on **January 22** and then again on **May 10**. It's time to take advantage of what you experienced throughout the year and to boldly step into the next phase of your adventure. You have become a character in your own *Star Wars* saga. You wrote the script; now you get to play a part. However, life isn't moving quite as quickly as it was last month now that Mars is reducing speed in hesitant Cancer, preparing to turn retrograde on **November 15**. You aren't quick and eager to swing into action, although Mars's supportive sextile with efficient Saturn on **October 8** can sharpen your organizational skills so that you are ready for the opportunities coming your way.

You may be dreaming of going back to school or taking an exotic vacation as the lovely Libra New Moon in your 9th House of Travel and Higher Education on **October 11** harmoniously trines fantasy-driven Neptune. But inquisitive Mercury stands in your way as it turns retrograde in passionate Scorpio on the same day. Untangle emotional issues before starting anything new. Reevaluate your feelings about your career and your future plans, but don't put anything into action until mental Mercury goes direct on **November 1**. The steady Taurus Full Moon in your 4th House of Home and Family on **October 26** may remind you of household obligations, while a Venus-Uranus opposition on the same day lures you into doing something totally outrageous just for fun.

> ### KEEP IN MIND THIS MONTH
>
> *Let circumstances set your pace so that you don't drive yourself so hard. Patience is the key to the personal growth and life changes you desire.*

KEY DATES

OCTOBER 1-3 ★ *open your heart*

You may be nudged into unfamiliar waters of emotional intensity as you obsess over secret desires that are aroused by sensual Venus's easy trine to intense Pluto on **October 3**. The residual effects from probing Mercury's supportive sextile to "make it real" Saturn on **October 1** allow you to express your thoughts clearly.

Don't close off the possibility of having a life-altering experience, even if you don't think you are prepared to enjoy this irrational journey. Keep the communication channels wide open, and the complexity will get simpler in the days ahead.

OCTOBER 8 ★ *lead by example*
You can easily express your opinions today in an inspiring manner, for the Sun-Jupiter sextile activates your higher understanding of life while giving you a chance to actualize what you already know. Additionally, a sextile between "take charge" Mars and authoritative Saturn bestows an air of certainty on everything you say. Your leadership skills are keen now, but nothing will come to you without effort on your part. Don't let your overconfidence lull you into slacking off. You'll need to reach for the golden ring if you really want a shot at success.

OCTOBER 13 ★ *no satisfaction*
Warmhearted Venus conjuncts cold Saturn for the third and final time, reminding you of what you yearn for but do not possess. If you are in a relationship, romance and sweetness may temporarily recede or even disappear. If you are unattached, feelings of inadequacy or sadness may surface. Venus also symbolizes material wealth, so money may now be in short supply. If you have overextended yourself recently, it's time to take a hard look at your finances, deal with an unpleasant situation, and conserve your resources for later on.

OCTOBER 16–20 ★ *effective communication*
You can make steady progress without even trying too hard as retrograde Mercury conspires with assertive Mars to involve Saturn the Boss in your schemes. Trust your logic; your words carry authority, and others at work will listen to what you say. Remember, however, that your goal now is not to get anywhere special; rather, it's to be more effective right where you are.

SUPER NOVA DAYS
OCTOBER 25–26 ★ *love without strings*
The down-to-earth Taurus Full Moon on **October 26** reflects your need for physical love and emotional stability, but beautiful Venus's tense opposition to rebellious Uranus highlights a core dilemma. You are attracted to the niceties of romance and the pleasures of the senses. But Uranus shocks you out of your delicious reveries if you are too dependent on anyone or anything. You want closeness and distance and are satisfied with neither. Ride this one out without making any lasting choices.

NOVEMBER

HIGH EMOTIONAL IQ

This can be a highly emotional month as the planets link up in sensitive water signs—Cancer, Scorpio, and Pisces. Mercury turns direct on **November 1**, picks up steam, and makes communication more intense by its entry into passionate Scorpio on **November 10**. The driven Scorpio New Moon on **November 9** squares meditative Neptune, pitting your lust for power or sexual satisfaction against more spiritual considerations. On **November 15**, Mars the Warrior in self-protective Cancer begins its retrograde phase, which lasts through the end of the year. As much as mental Mercury, now moving direct again, collects your thoughts and propels you forward on a search into Scorpio's shadows, Mars cautions you not to take any risks. From **November 19 to 21**, intellectual Mercury activates a Grand Water Trine with Mars and Uranus, bolstering your confidence and giving you a healthy respect for your feelings. It may, however, be challenging to turn your intuitive awareness into action as the tentative expression of retrograde Mars in supersensitive Cancer encourages you to keep your eccentric dreams to yourself.

The Sun moves into fun-loving Sagittarius on **November 22**, shining its light in your 11th House of Friends, Hopes, and Wishes just in time for the holiday weekend. The flirty Gemini Full Moon in your 5th House of Romance and Children on **November 24** is the perfect addition to an already socially active phase. Enjoyment is yours for the asking, but be careful about scattering your energy and trying to do too much at once. You could escape into a comfortable fantasy around **November 26**, when sweet Venus harmonizes with dreamy Neptune, but as the end of the month nears, you are drawn back to reality by hard aspects to Saturn. There is work to be completed before heading into the holidays ahead.

> **KEEP IN MIND THIS MONTH**
>
> *You are most comfortable with abstract thinking, but now you can learn much about yourself and others by traveling through uncharted emotional territory.*

KEY DATES

NOVEMBER 4–7 ★ *emotional warrior*

The Sun forms harmonious trines with feisty Mars and electric Uranus on **November 4 and 7**, respectively, charging your nervous system and encouraging you to act with brilliant originality. Also, sensual Venus squares passionate Pluto on **November 5,** intensifying your physical urges and pushing deep problems into the light where solutions can be found. Don't succumb to fear and deny your emotions; fight for your inner truth. The more honest you are, the better the outcome.

SUPER NOVA DAYS
NOVEMBER 9–11 ★ *powerful dreams*
A magnetic Scorpio New Moon in your 10th House of Public Status on **November 9** attracts power to you without much apparent effort at work and in the community. The Sun tensely squares faith-based Neptune on **November 11,** creating stress between your spiritual path and your materialistic goals. A bit of disorientation is to be expected. If you cannot relax, you'll be opening the door to unnecessary frustration and might miss a chance to travel into the unknown. However, if you can let go of the details, this can be a meaningful time for you that is rich with magical experiences.

NOVEMBER 19–21 ★ *walk your talk*
You may not be saying as much these days with communicator Mercury in secretive Scorpio, but as it harmoniously trines Mars on **November 19** and unorthodox Uranus on **November 21,** you have the impetus to initiate a significant discussion. You have a deep connection between your thoughts and actions, so make your intentions known if you are willing to walk your talk. What appears to be impulsive behavior to others is actually the result of deep consideration on your part. You know what needs to be done; you can feel it in every nerve of your body.

NOVEMBER 26 ★ *sweet buzz*
Lovely Venus forms an easy trine with diffusive Neptune, blending reality with fantasy. This aspect can be spiritually enlightening, romantically beautiful, or just plain confusing. Make sure you know when you are wearing your rose-colored glasses today and when you should take them off.

NOVEMBER 30 ★ *constructive improvement*
Your long-term plans may run into resistance from someone who doubts your wisdom. The Sun, in your 11th House of Friends, crosses intellectual swords with authoritative Saturn—a battle in which truth will prevail over power. Obstacles appear, not as reasons for you to give up, but as reminders of what needs work. Don't be discouraged, even if your most ardent supporter thwarts your best efforts. Instead, listen carefully to the criticism, and make your plan even better.

DECEMBER

CELEBRATE TRANSFORMATION

You truly feel as if you have stepped into an exciting new world as this month begins with big-thinking Mercury flying into Sagittarius and joining the Sun, Jupiter, and Pluto, which are already in your 11th House of Friends and Wishes. Your spirits are lifted as cerebral Mercury leaves the watery world of Scorpio for more comfortable philosophical realms. It could feel as if your goals are coming to fruition—and maybe they are. The joyful Sagittarius New Moon on **December 9** confirms what you probably know: this is going to be an amazing, high-intensity season, although you may feel great pressure to make these the best holidays ever. The most significant planetary event this month occurs when far-reaching Jupiter joins transformative Pluto on **December 11** in a once-every-thirteen-years alignment. Acknowledge your deep urges for success, for the stars are within reach. You must, however, apply all of your wisdom and maturity to the present moment to make your dreams come true.

The next great shift occurs when adventurous Jupiter says goodbye to its yearlong stay in Sagittarius to visit ambitious Capricorn in your 12th House of Imagination, where it remains throughout 2008. Then, as stern Saturn turns retrograde on **December 19**, the harsh reality becomes clear. And although you know there's a lot of work waiting for you, you may be able put it off until the new year.

On **December 20**, Mercury joins Jupiter in dutiful Capricorn, followed by the Sun marking the Winter Solstice on **December 21**. Join in the familiar noise of holiday traditions as you entertain and socialize with close friends and family. The power-packed Cancer Full Moon on **December 23** conjuncts fiery Mars and opposes Mercury, heating the long nights with spirited conversations.

> **KEEP IN MIND THIS MONTH**
>
> *Although you are inclined to drive yourself too hard, it's crucial for your well-being to stay in touch with your emotions and your spiritual path.*

KEY DATES

DECEMBER 1 ★ *positive spin*
A supportive sextile between charming Venus and upbeat Jupiter may encourage you to have fun, but Mercury enters philosophical Sagittarius today, aiming your words toward loftier goals than just sensual fulfillment. Start holiday planning, but don't go overboard with optimism, or others may assume you are overcompensating.

SUPER NOVA DAYS
DECEMBER 7-11 ★ *adrenaline rush*
You are driven to accomplish something great as jumbo Jupiter conjuncts compelling Pluto on **December 11.** This long-lasting alignment is brought into exact focus as the Sun and Mercury each tensely square Uranus on **December 7 and 11,** respectively, opening your mind and bringing forth unexpected solutions to problems you didn't know you had. Events may be moving too quickly, making it difficult to turn off your thoughts. Even if you would rather be distracted by the light show within your brain, a supportive sextile between active Mars and practical Saturn motivates you to turn your edgy ideas into workable realities.

DECEMBER 17-18 ★ *surprising treat*
A harmonious trine from sweet Venus to crazy Uranus on **December 17** spices up your life with a few thrills. You are given planetary permission to express your normally inexpressible desires and actually have a chance to get what you want. Electricity is in the air, sparking relationships with unexpected newness. Even though jolly Jupiter begins a long stay in reserved Capricorn on **December 18,** you may not even notice until next year when you're at work.

DECEMBER 22 ★ *over the top*
You are pushed and pulled in so many directions today that it's tough to know where to begin. It may feel as if you have lost your footing yet willingly slip into your fantasies, eager to have the time of your life. As Jupiter conjuncts the Sun, it's hard to know whether your daydream has any possibility of becoming real. You are on to something big but cannot quite put all the pieces together. Too much of a good thing can be problematic, and with feisty Mars opposing wordy Mercury, you need to watch your tendency to be overly aggressive.

DECEMBER 25-26 ★ *best of intentions*
Although you may not know your limits until you've gone too far, common sense will keep your enthusiasm in check. Mercury trines conscientious Saturn on **December 25,** giving you great mental discipline, but an exaggerated Mars-Jupiter opposition on **December 26** can paint a very rosy picture. The overblown optimism plays well for holiday celebrations but can present problems when you come back down to earth over the days ahead.

PISCES

FEBRUARY 19–MARCH 20

PISCES OVERVIEW

Opportunities abound for makeovers of your image, personal relationships, and career this year. Eclipses of the Sun on March 18 and the Moon on August 28, both in your sign, give you a fresh perspective on yourself that can stimulate a change in appearance and will almost certainly provoke a shift of attitude, hopefully toward a bolder, more spirited you. **Let go of overly self-protective patterns, and express your power, individuality, and desires more freely now.** Meet fear and contraction with daring action by expanding your bubble of thoughts. No matter how grave the situation, there are always options. Naturally, your relationships will be affected by your transformation, opening up opportunities to deepen a current connection or to discover a new one. Since you're not standing still, it's likely that you will expect anyone you're with to be growing, too. Eclipses of the Moon on March 3 and the Sun on September 11 in your 7th House of Partnerships underscore the need to reexamine the agreements, spoken and unspoken, that you have with others, to either update the arrangements or put them out to pasture.

Confident Jupiter in Sagittarius is spurring you on to greater heights in your professional and public life by transiting your 10th House of Career. The potential for advancing your position is considerable, but your challenge is to be more assertive in going after the brass ring of success. **Fiery Sagittarius is a sign of salesmanship that will reward you when you're willing to open your mouth and speak up for yourself.** If it is difficult for you to promote your own skills and accomplishments and honor the work that you are doing. Think of your good intentions and the service you provide to others. Jupiter makes high-energy squares with electric Uranus on January 22, May 10, and October 9, stirring restlessness that might shake up your job situation. Impulsive reactions may cause you to quit, lash out at the boss, or finally start a business of your own. Sometimes it takes a shock to get moving, which is fine, but keep your wits about you to avoid jumping from the frying pan into the fire.

Serious Saturn is spending much of the year in your 6th House of Health, Work, and Daily Routines, a transit that calls for more discipline and maturity in these areas. Yet Saturn in expressive Leo until September 2 instructs you to add more creativity to your life on a regular basis. Hobbies or interests that enable you to stretch your artistic talents should be highly rewarding. Be patient in developing these gifts, however, since beginner's frustration will be conquered with experience. Saturn opposes your ruling planet Neptune on February 28 and June 25 to complete a process that began late last August. These can be periods in which you lose sight of your boundaries and wear yourself out emotionally or physically. Take private time to relax, recuperate, and pamper yourself. **Treating yourself with tender, loving care is an admirable act, not a selfish one.** Respecting your own vulnerabilities and acknowledging your needs honor your heart and your soul.

 ## BOUND TO CHANGE

Two eclipses in your 7th House of Partnerships and the love planet, Venus, turning retrograde in this part of your chart are likely to radically change the shape of your relationships this year. The strong presence of independent Uranus during the March 18 and September 11 eclipses signals shake-ups that alter the way you connect with a loved one. If you're bored, you won't be able to hide it; if your significant other is feeling itchy, you'll find out. But if you're single and available, opportunities to meet someone exciting and unusual can pop up anywhere. Just prepare to adjust your expectations, since Uranus almost always brings surprises with a twist. Additionally, this means that you can break free of your relationship past this year. Whatever wounds or disappointments you previously experienced won't be forgotten, but the scars can heal so rapidly that you feel like a new person when it comes to love. Venus, the planet that specializes in matters of the heart, does a backward turn in analytical Virgo on July 27 that can trigger memories of an earlier liaison in your life or stir up an old issue with your current mate. Don't despair if you feel like the situation is regressing; sometimes you have to take one step back to make a major leap forward.

 ## OPPORTUNITY KNOCKS

Expansive Jupiter in your 10th House of Career and Community is bound to raise your public profile this year. Advancement can come quickly, along with unexpected duties and, perhaps, even a totally new profession. Jupiter forms dynamic squares with revolutionary Uranus on January 22, May 10, and October 9 that can turn your work life upside down. Be bold now; reach for what inspires you most and where you can make a greater contribution to the world. A position that allows you more independence is especially attractive. If one doesn't exist where you're currently employed, go ahead and explore alternative professional outlets for your creative talents.

 ## REVENUE INNOVATION

A steady paycheck to cover the bills is nice, but you could earn additional money on an irregular basis. Sudden infusions of cash from a commission job, the sale of property, or a side business can tip the financial scales in your favor. Use your imagination to create your own opportunities, rather than limiting yourself to just what you earn from a job. Greed, of course, doesn't motivate someone as altruistic as you, but when you apply your intuition to increasing your revenue, you might find yourself successfully inspired.

 ## ALTERNATING CURRENTS

Your energy can fluctuate considerably this year with unpredictable Uranus in your sign. Be prepared to alter your diet and level of physical activity to adjust to these changing conditions. You might crave hamburgers one month and swear off meat the next, but it's better to follow your instincts than strive for a consistency that doesn't correspond with your feelings. Uranus tends to push more electricity through the body, which can overstimulate your nervous system. A flexible attitude helps keep you calm when the increased input of thoughts seems to set you on edge. Allow yourself to break away from the noise to seek peace where and when you can find it. Meditation and yoga help, as do the tranquilizing effects of nature.

 ## TEND TO YOUR NEST

Preoccupation with your public life can lead you to overlook important issues at home this year. Your job, community service, and social life may have you spending so much time out of the house that family members feel ignored and even household chores fall behind schedule. Clearly, extra attention and effort are required, especially during Mercury's three-week retrogrades beginning

February 13, June 15, and October 11. These are great times to catch up on practical and emotional matters that need your input. And while the eclipses in March, late August, and September could have you itching to move, avoid impulsive changes of locale that won't make you feel more secure.

BELIEFS GONE WILD

You're unlikely to be laid-back about your beliefs this year. A rising tempo of engagement in religious, political, or social causes may demand more time and energy than ever. When you feel your philosophical temperature reaching the boiling point, back off and cool down to avoid an explosive conflict. Your patience for conventional learning and thinking may be short, too. A radical shift of interests could open your mind to an unconventional subject to which you can apply intuition and empathy. Travel tends to be mentally stimulating rather than relaxing, so hit the road to expand your mind, but stay home to rest your body.

PUT YOUR FAITH INTO PRACTICE

The ongoing opposition from serious Saturn to idealistic Neptune makes this a pivotal time spiritually. The challenge to commit your faith to a more serious level of practice began in late August and repeats this February 28 and June 25. If you feel that you're falling short of your expectations, self-punishment won't help. Instead, take a few simple steps to act on your principles with prayer, charity work, or quiet contemplation, which can salve your soul and reinforce your connection with the divine.

RICK & JEFF'S TIP FOR THE YEAR:
Follow Your Dreams

Logic and reason are desirable, but don't let them take precedence this year. Intuition is one of your greatest gifts, and the planets are raising it to even higher levels now. Not every vision you might have is realistic, but it's still appropriate to expand the boundaries of your expectations and reach for more than you have. At least one dream among the many you create has a real chance to come true. Let your heart choose where to invest your greatest hopes; combine deep commitment, hard work, and intelligence, and you have a recipe for success.

JANUARY

ALONE IN A CROWD

Your energy is pulled in several directions this month. The purposeful Sun, lovely Venus, communicative Mercury, and passionate Mars spend time in ambitious Capricorn in your 11th House of Groups and Friends. Pressure as part of a team may restrict your free time with demands for a very high level of performance. Stick to the job at hand, avoiding office or organizational politics as much as possible. Proving that you can take care of business, whether at work or with a friend in need, earns you respect and can raise your status. Still, the call of romance is not drowned out by less personal issues. The Full Moon in sensitive Cancer on **January 3** falls in your 5th House of Romance, Children, and Creativity. Emotions may be intense in these areas, possibly triggering a crisis but hopefully leading to a breakthrough in awareness and understanding. The New Moon in dutiful Capricorn on **January 18** swings the pendulum from individual concerns to collective issues, continuing the theme of individual desires versus group needs.

Mercury and the Sun enter thoughtful Aquarius on **January 15 and 20**, respectively, turning your mind away from outer events as you seek more time for private activities and spiritual practice. Your mind may wander while busy colleagues or pals are buzzing around. The quiet moments become more valuable to you, so take them when you can. On **January 22**, far-reaching Jupiter makes the first of three squares to explosive Uranus, popping your mind open with surprises that can change the shape of your reality. If you're shocked, breathe deeply and slow down. Whatever's been shaken is unlikely to settle until the last of the series on **October 9**, when what currently seems like an inconvenient disruption will make perfect sense.

> **KEEP IN MIND THIS MONTH**
>
> *Don't lose sight of your needs regardless of how much others ask of you. Self-preservation isn't selfish; it's a necessity.*

KEY DATES

JANUARY 2–3 ★ *open the floodgates*

The brave Sun forms an intelligent sextile with Uranus on **January 2** that helps you speak to a person in power. Get your facts straight; a tough sesquisquare between informative Mercury and strict Saturn will not tolerate imprecise communication. The Cancer Full Moon on **January 3** triggers a release of pent-up feelings. You definitely can use an emotional outlet, so make sure you have a safe way to vent.

JANUARY 12–13 ★ *clarity equals strength*

You're not usually the aggressive type, but if someone pushes you now, you may push back even harder. A delightful sextile between sociable Venus and outgoing Jupiter on **January 12** suggests harmony and fun, but nitpicking Mercury's semisquare to Jupiter could cause verbal sparring. The conjunction of pugnacious Mars and impenetrable Pluto on **January 13** can make the atmosphere heavy with power struggles and control issues. When you're clear about your motives, you're stronger inside and have less need to demonstrate your force to others.

SUPER NOVA DAYS
JANUARY 16–18 ★ *hard work and sweet compensation*

Mars enters disciplined Capricorn on **January 16**, as the Sun semisquares Jupiter on the same day and then Uranus on **January 17**, threatening to disrupt order at work. Control what you must, but accept that innovation can grow out of chaos. Besides, the **January 18** New Moon in Capricorn is an opportune time to put an up-to-date system in place. Still, your urge for accomplishment is countered by a desire for delight, thanks to a romantic Venus-Neptune conjunction. Your judgment may not be precise about love or money, but an entertaining escape from reality could be worth the price.

JANUARY 21–22 ★ *brilliant connection*

Overcome your inner critic and give yourself some slack on **January 21**, since trying harder is likely to put you farther off course. An easygoing attitude on **January 22** will also allow you to find useful answers within the information explosion of the Jupiter-Uranus square. Mental Mercury's fortunate sextile to strategic Jupiter sharpens your intuition and your communication skills.

JANUARY 26–28 ★ *from fantasy to reality*

Mercury's conjunction with nebulous Neptune on **January 26** is better for fiction than fact. Take what you hear with a grain of salt, and let others know when you're kidding with a wink or a smile. Alluring Venus enters your sign on **January 27**, opening the door to a socially appetizing weekend. Just don't permit your overly warm heart to make an agreement your head will regret when rational Mercury opposes serious Saturn on **January 28** and reality returns with a vengeance.

FEBRUARY

February may be short on days, but it's long on activity and emotional intensity. Communicator Mercury floats into your sign on **February 2**, only to turn retrograde on **February 13**, and falls back into quirky Aquarius on **February 27**. This mental turnabout can lead to more than the usual amount of information mix-ups of Mercury's three-times-a-year retrograde cycle. Leave yourself room to change your mind, especially when a brilliant idea enters your head and you present it before doing your homework. Additional attention to details is a requirement to avoid confusion, conflict, or chaos when the messenger planet turns tail. The Full Moon in enterprising Leo on **February 2** offers big promise for your job, perhaps motivating you with greater recognition or more creative tasks. However, it's best not to accept additional responsibilities until you're sure that you have a committed team to support your dedicated effort. The New Moon in progressive Aquarius on **February 17** rouses your community spirit and encourages idealistic endeavors. It opposes restrictive Saturn, but is assisted with a sextile from powerful Pluto that shows you a way to reduce the burden of your daily chores to allow you more time for inspiration.

The month ends with one of the most important planetary events of the year: a Saturn-Neptune opposition. This is the second in a series of three that began late last August and ends on **June 25** of this year. The 180-degree angle between the planets of reality and illusion, of form and formlessness, puts an end to old illusions and punishes frauds. But it also rewards dreamers who are willing to do the work necessary to bring their fantasies to life and committed idealists intent on transforming their spiritual values into reality.

> **KEEP IN MIND THIS MONTH**
>
> *Reduce grand schemes to their basics, and start working from the ground up to build your castle in the sky.*

KEY DATES

FEBRUARY 2–3 ★ *panoramic perspective*

The Full Moon in Leo and Mercury's entry into visionary Pisces on **February 2** spark your imagination. This can be of great value when applied with a purpose, but could just stir up emotional drama without a project as an outlet. Whatever you are feeling or thinking may seem larger than life. If you enjoy the show, have fun, but lower the volume on your feelings if it's breaking your heart. Fortunately, a Sun-Jupiter sextile on **February 3** expands your vision and increases your wisdom.

SUPER NOVA DAYS
FEBRUARY 8-10 ★ *heights and depths*
The life-giving Sun conjuncts dreamy Neptune on **February 8** and puts a slow-moving opposition with Saturn into motion on **February 10**. A quick trip from fantasy to reality can darken moods and create melancholic moments if your aspirations seem out of reach. However, a Venus-Jupiter square on **February 9** prefers excessive play now to worrying about what tomorrow may bring. Moments of pleasure can provide a needed break and enliven your spirits. But overindulgence can be a temporary physical fix for a long-term malaise of the soul if deeper needs are not addressed.

FEBRUARY 17-18 ★ *happy birthday*
The Aquarius New Moon on **February 17** is accompanied by a brilliant Sun-Jupiter quintile. This magical aspect connects the solar heart to Jupiter's expansive vision, weaving sense into a senseless world and producing a workable plan to support your ideals. The Sun enters intuitive Pisces on **February 18**, marking the annual renewal of your life force and the reaffirmation of your soul's unique purpose.

FEBRUARY 22 ★ *into the mystic*
Retrograde Mercury joins the Sun, aligning identity and intellect to enrich your self-awareness. But the backward turn of the communication planet in your dreamy sign implies that what you're discovering may not be easily explained. This is a private journey, an inner voyage of revelation that needs no external approval. Allow yourself to delight in your own mind without the obligation of trying to translate the transcendental into words that can only hint at what you're experiencing.

FEBRUARY 27-28 ★ *seek the truth within*
Mercury backs into cerebral Aquarius and forms a clever quintile with Jupiter on **February 27**. This blends original thinking with gentle power, a good combination for broaching a delicate subject. On **February 28**, Saturn opposes Neptune, and the big gears of life slowly engage at the depth of your being. If you're encountering external resistance, don't attempt to justify yourself. This is a test of faith that you can pass within yourself instead of trying to prove anything to anyone.

PISCES

MARCH

A FRESH NEW IMAGE

A pair of eclipses could make this month a significant turning point in your personal life. A Lunar Eclipse on **March 3** creates waves of change to your 7th House of Partnerships. Sudden ups and downs with others may alter your outlook on relationships. An exciting person can kick down the doors of your resistance and open the way to a connection like none you've ever had. But you're also charged with a need for absolute truth that won't allow you to settle for less than total honesty now. If you feel trapped in a relationship or conversely can't stand to be alone another day, it's time to break old habits and experiment with a new look and a fresh approach to others. A Solar Eclipse in your sign on **March 18** prompts a thorough self-examination. Be kind if you don't like everything you see, because facing the negative can be the first step to turning your life in a positive direction. You are not likely to be in the mood to compromise, which can trigger power struggles where you might not be your usually gracious self. But style points don't count when you're dealing with such substantial matters like self-respect and a search for deeper meaning in your life.

Intellectual Mercury turns direct in your 12th House of Secrets on **March 7**, awakening your mind to a broader understanding of your spirituality and even your subconscious self and prompting intimate conversations with trusted friends or with counselors. The Spring Equinox on **March 20**, when the Sun enters Aries in your 2nd House of Self-Worth, begins a new astrological year. Turn the fiery force of this dynamic sign into action by seeking money-making opportunities, developing your unique talents, and improving your overall health.

> **KEEP IN MIND THIS MONTH**
>
> *A flood of new and wild ideas is thrilling yet can be overwhelming. Pick one thought, and try it on for size before exploring the next.*

KEY DATES

MARCH 1–3 ★ *relationship shift*
Aggressive Mars prods overconfident Jupiter with an impatient semisquare on **March 1** that could turn a small disagreement into a major argument. Apply your excess energy positively at the gym or on the job, rather than provoking conflict. The Virgo Full Moon Eclipse on **March 3** is a high-frequency event that pushes your nervous system to its limit. An unexpected move by someone you rely on

may catch you off guard; flexibility is your best protection against an emotional meltdown. Put on your explorer's hat, and venture forth in a new approach to relationships to create the kind of surprises you want.

MARCH 8-9 ★ *appropriate indulgences*

Spoil yourself with a gift of beauty, a special meal, or a romantic tryst on **March 8** to celebrate the trine between sensual Venus and generous Jupiter. Venus forms favorable aspects with Saturn and imaginative Neptune on **March 9**, connecting dreams with the means to make them real. A Sun-Jupiter square on the same day may earn you more recognition at work, but beware of exaggeration and conceit.

SUPER NOVA DAYS
MARCH 16-18 ★ *spring cleaning*

A cooperative trine between open-minded Jupiter and responsible Saturn on **March 16** is the first in a series that ends late next year and is excellent for strategic vision and long-range planning. Curious Mercury enters your sign on **March 17**, which opens your eyes to a more magical view of reality and stirs your creative impulses. Venus also enters earthy Taurus, providing good sense to apply and absorb the new information. A Solar Eclipse in psychic Pisces on **March 18** could show you where it's appropriate to put an end to an unsatisfying situation. Mourn the loss if you must, but a complete cleanup is necessary to make way for a more fulfilling future.

MARCH 21-23 ★ *reasonable risks*

Strong impulses to start and stop flow through you with a Venus-Jupiter contact that encourages risk on **March 21**, followed by a hard Mars-Saturn opposition on **March 22** that resists taking chances. But don't let anyone else's fears hold you back. Pioneering Mars sextiles outgoing Jupiter on **March 23**, lifting your confidence and giving you the wisdom to explore the unknown safely.

MARCH 25-26 ★ *compassionate action*

Your ruling planet Neptune is joined by Mars on **March 25** and aspected by the Sun on **March 26**. Acting on blind faith can lead you astray unless your innate intuition is very finely tuned. Avoid forcing a situation or committing to projects likely to exhaust your energy. Acts of creativity and charity, though, can be inspiring, so invest in doing what touches your heart, and you'll find the motivation to carry you.

APRIL

MOTIVATION FROM MARS

The month starts off with a bang as verbal Mercury conjuncts electric Uranus in your sign on **April 1**. Lightning bolts in the brain trigger original ideas, and you blurt out words without slowing down to consider their consequences. Brilliant insights are possible, but take some time to digest new concepts before jumping to conclusions. The giant planets Jupiter and Saturn are changing directions this month, which can shift your big-picture view of the future. Opinionated Jupiter, the traditional ruler of your sign, turns retrograde on **April 5** and will continue moving backward through the zodiac until **August 6**. Revisions of beliefs and philosophies are possible as you reconsider previously held positions. Find guidance within, rather than relying on external events or authorities to drive your decisions. Saturn the Taskmaster, on the other hand, turns direct on **April 19** in your 6th House of Health, Work, and Daily Routines. This can enable you to gain traction in these areas and make slow and steady progress in small but meaningful ways. Focus on one task at a time to reap the benefits of Saturn's concentrated power.

Macho Mars moves into your sign on **April 6** to give you some extra motivation for the next six weeks. This is an excellent time to move your body, take on new challenges, and assert your independence. Excess energy builds up inside if you don't use it now, so if you're feeling cranky or defensive, transfer those emotions into activities that will do you some good. The Sun enters calm Taurus in your 3rd House of Information on **April 20**, giving stability to your ideas and allowing you to express them in simple, trustworthy terms.

> **KEEP IN MIND THIS MONTH**
>
> *There's no need to hurry when you're in the groove. You're on the right track when you glide forward rather than go against the grain.*

KEY DATES

APRIL 3–4 ★ *gentle touch needed*

Your good intentions may be misinterpreted on **April 3** with awkward aspects from Mercury and Venus to Jupiter. Approach others gently, and don't overload them with more information than they can handle. A supportive sextile between initiating Mars and relentless Pluto on **April 4** shows more finesse as you're able to weave your way through tight spots and apply just the right amount of pressure to achieve your objectives.

APRIL 9–11 ★ *public and private advancement*
A joyous Sun-Jupiter trine on **April 9** grants you a chance to shine as long as you choose your words carefully to avoid ruffling feathers. Mental Mercury zooms into Aries on **April 10**, instigating fresh ideas for earning money or improving valuable skills. A sweet sextile between the willful Sun and flexible Neptune on **April 11** gives you faith in yourself and provides inspiration to others. Additionally, lovely Venus enters your 4th House of Home and Family, fostering an especially creative period that's perfect for turning your environment into a more harmonious and beautiful place.

APRIL 14 ★ *out of focus*
Intelligent Mercury thinks and speaks very quickly now in fiery Aries. But its clunky semisquare with fuzzy Neptune can produce unclear communication and chaos. Speak slowly to be understood, and don't assume that you're getting what someone else is saying, either. Details are hazy or simply made up, so double-check everything to avoid errors or confusion.

APRIL 21–22 ★ *a point of wisdom*
Your intuition is right on the mark when Mercury trines Jupiter on **April 21**. This healthy alignment of detail and meaning makes for wise decisions and intelligent conversation. On **April 22**, the communication planet forms a productive sextile with spiritual Neptune, encouraging you to find the right words to express difficult concepts. You are capable of reading between the lines to gain understanding even when the message is poorly sent. However, a tight Venus-Mars square sends mixed signals when it comes to romantic matters.

SUPER NOVA DAYS
APRIL 28–30 ★ *extreme measures*
Tension grows with a Venus-Jupiter opposition on **April 28** that magnifies your expectations in relationships while you overestimate the value of people and things. This excessive but good-natured aspect occurs at the same time as an explosive Mars-Uranus conjunction that can be a volatile cocktail of thrills and impulsiveness. Enjoy the excitement, but temper the highs to avoid sudden disappointment. A Mars-Saturn quincunx on **April 29** can attract an uncooperative or stingy individual. Assertive Mars packs a punch with an aggressive square to strident Jupiter on **April 30**. Happily, a forgiving Venus-Neptune trine on the same day will sweetly soothe any acrimonious feelings.

MAY

DARE TO LEAP

This month is so packed with planetary events that it even has two Full Moons. The first occurs on **May 2** in penetrating Scorpio, a compatible water sign that helps you express your feelings more passionately. Disputes caused by conflicting belief systems can be stressful, especially in your workplace, so avoid a showdown over differences of opinion unless it's worth the battle. The New Moon in stubborn Taurus on **May 16** is an odd mix of surefootedness and foolishness. This earthy sign occupies your 3rd House of Data Collection, giving you fresh impetus to learn and to connect with others. However, nebulous Neptune forms a challenging square to this Sun-Moon conjunction, which may confound facts with fiction. Positively, it works in favor of serious conversations softened by compassion or of turning your imaginative ideas into practical form. The Full Moon in fearless Sagittarius on **May 31** illuminates your professional goals and opens a window of opportunity for more meaningful work. Optimistic Jupiter conjuncts the Full Moon while active Mars supports it with a trine, making this a time when risk-taking can be very rewarding.

Jupiter makes two contrasting aspects within a matter of days—a harmonious trine with stable Saturn on **May 5** and a tense square with wild Uranus on **May 10**. The former balances expansive vision with practical judgment, which is excellent for anchoring a realistic strategy to reach long-term goals. The latter, though, tends toward impulsive and instinctive actions unbound by law or logic. A healthy application of these seemingly opposing forces is to blend the wisdom of the Jupiter-Saturn trine with the revolutionary ideas and unconventional initiatives of the Jupiter-Uranus square. If the formula is right, you can establish a solid base from which to launch your rocket of dreams.

> **KEEP IN MIND THIS MONTH**
>
> *When it comes to your job and public image, nothing ventured, nothing gained. Be aggressive about getting ahead.*

KEY DATES

MAY 5 ★ *a minor slip*
A quirky quincunx between speedy Mercury and ponderous Jupiter may knock conversations out of sync and cross communication signals. Major time spent on a minor chore could distract you from more productive activities. The slow-moving Jupiter-Saturn trine is likely to keep you from sliding very far off track.

MAY 7–10 ★ *over the top*

A Mercury-Neptune square on **May 7** suggests that even a reliable individual can give you faulty information. If it sounds too good to be true, it probably is. Delightful Venus dances into your 5th House of Romance on the same day, which can pave the way to a more joyous heart during the next four weeks. Have a love affair with life by taking time to play, create, and celebrate whenever you can. The Sun quincunxes Jupiter on **May 8**, blurring reason with excess, followed by a Sun-Saturn square on **May 9** that is sure to put a stop to any foolish expectations. But the Jupiter-Uranus square on **May 10** has little respect for the laws of reality, as the will to be free can lead to sudden actions against your own best interests.

MAY 12–14 ★ *play it safe*

The Sun squares squishy Neptune on **May 12** and Venus sesquisquares Neptune on **May 14**, creating elusive fantasies that can prove costly if you invest too much of yourself in them. A square between tough guys Mars and Pluto separates these two planetary softies on **May 13**, making a three-day sandwich that's sweet on the outside but bitter inside. Moderate your moods to avoid emotional indigestion.

SUPER NOVA DAYS
MAY 20–23 ★ *higher intelligence*

Eyes open wide with a mind-expanding Mercury-Jupiter opposition and a Mercury-Uranus square on **May 20**. Incredible insights can soar into your head, but the mental buzz may be overwhelming at times. The Sun moves into cerebral Gemini on **May 21**, adding more smarts to the equation, while Mercury's stabilizing sextile to Saturn calms your nerves. Mercury then trines Neptune on **May 23**, carrying a wave of soft words and spiritual insights. Still, a Venus-Jupiter quincunx may bring an unreasonable cry for love or recognition. Asking for what you want is fine, as long as you're not too needy about it.

MAY 28 ★ *a last-minute win*

Romantic Venus gets tangled up with illusory Neptune, which can be about looking for love or approval in all the wrong places. However, an embarrassing moment could lead to a sweet connection or unexpected delight. If you're disappointed or deceived, don't give up too quickly, because you can right your ship of joy in a most surprising way.

JUNE

DESTINY IS WAITING

This month's Gemini New Moon in your 10th House of Career on **June 14** triggers new connections, ideas, and opportunities, reinvigorating your interest with variety. But a tense square from eccentric Uranus to the New Moon can really shake up your position. A boss may act inconsistently, or you could be struck by a sudden case of restlessness. Embrace an original approach or attitude to free yourself of the old routine so that you can discharge this energy in a nondisruptive manner. Transformative Pluto also participates with an opposition to the Sun-Moon conjunction that engenders distrust or power struggles. A small disagreement may expand into a serious blow-up, but if you're ready to move on, this could provide the necessary impetus. Mercury the Communicator turns retrograde on **June 15** and will continue backpedaling in your 5th House of Love and Creativity until **July 9**. Revisiting unfinished business in these areas is quite possible as feelings you thought settled stir again, giving you another chance to reconsider recent relationship decisions.

The Summer Solstice marking the Sun's entry into determined Cancer on **June 21** brings courage and a quiet confidence to advance your personal agenda in an assertive but nonthreatening manner. On **June 25**, Saturn opposes Neptune for the third and last time in a series that began late last August, to finally end crumbling illusions and build a framework for new dreams. The Full Moon in rational Capricorn on **June 30** forces an objective look at your relationship to friends and groups. A supportive trine from active Mars in easygoing Taurus, though, provides practical solutions for almost every interpersonal issue. Focus on finding answers rather than adding confusion to the situation.

> **KEEP IN MIND THIS MONTH**
>
> *If you're ready for big change, go for it. But if you seek only minor adjustments, stick to basics to avoid complications.*

KEY DATES

JUNE 4–5 ★ *a big appetite*

An energetic Mars-Jupiter trine on **June 4** might bring out your competitive side. It's certainly healthy to be active, mentally or physically, and to use this force in an enterprising way. Enthusiasm grows on **June 5** with an overblown Sun-Jupiter opposition and Venus's entry into showy Leo. Have fun, but avoid overindulgence in food, drink, or shopping to save yourself from the consequences of excess.

JUNE 9-13 ★ *master of your fate*
A Sun-Uranus square on **June 9** sparks rebellion, leading to a newfound sense of freedom or a battle with authority. But **June 11** is a very constructive time, with positive aspects connecting the Sun with Mars and Saturn while these two hardworking planets are trine each other. The Sun then trines Neptune on **June 12**, followed by Mars's trine to the spiritual planet on **June 13**. Your determined sense of purpose can grab on to the upcoming Saturn-Neptune opposition and blend lofty aspirations with earthbound competence to make dreams come true.

JUNE 19-21 ★ *pleasure principle*
Passion and pleasure dominate with a high-calorie Venus-Jupiter trine on **June 19**, followed by a sexy Mars-Pluto trine on **June 21** just as the Sun enters your 5th House of Romance. Going overboard is possible, perhaps even inevitable, but sometimes you have to go too far to wind up where you want to be. Don't let a fussy or critical individual dampen your desires with his or her fears. Whatever you do in a goodhearted way will bring joy to others as well as yourself, even if it is a bit self-indulgent.

JUNE 25 ★ *honor your spirit*
The exact opposition of Saturn and Neptune may not manifest itself as a major event today, but it is still a watershed point in your life. If you don't have a dream to inspire you, a dark cloud can hover overhead. If you do have a special wish, an inner feeling of certitude can guide you toward it. Either way, take a moment to meditate or reflect upon the majesty of your existence and to gratefully acknowledge the preciousness of your life.

JUNE 28-30 ★ *unclear reflection*
A Sun-Mercury conjunction aligns identity and intellect on **June 28**, but both of these planets sesquisquare Neptune to blur any clear picture you might want to present. Forgive yourself for not being able to speak perfectly or rationalize your actions to others. When Venus opposes yearning Neptune on **June 30**, love grows even more delicate, wavering between divine desire and disillusionment. The Capricorn Full Moon in your 11th House of Friends and Wishes on the same day, though, points to a reliable buddy who helps you address romantic issues logically.

PISCES

JULY

FOLLOW YOUR HEART

Mercury turns direct in your 5th House of Fun on **July 9**, starting communication flowing more freely again, especially related to romance, creativity, and children. But unabashed frankness in heart-related matters is challenged by the slowing down of Venus, which will turn retrograde on **July 27**. In an unusual little dance, Venus enters orderly Virgo and your 7th House of Partnerships on **July 14**. This would appear to open the door to new connections or the refinement of an existing liaison. However, the love planet's backward turn less than two weeks later suggests that steps in partnership will be retraced until Venus turns direct on **September 8**. The bottom line is that all hookups—personal or professional, perfect or perplexing—will be subject to reevaluation, so be sure to advance with care during this time.

Still, the heart is ever hopeful with an initiating New Moon in Cancer in your 5th House of Romance on **July 14**—the same day Venus enters your relationship house. Impulsive feelings can propel you toward an object of desire that's quite different from your usual attractions. Original Uranus trine the New Moon blazes alternative routes to pleasure that can lead to experimentation in novel forms of fun. This can work well as long as you're into discovery and not into controlling the end results. It's tough to be that emotionally involved without expectations of something more to follow, but stay as cool and open-minded as possible. On **July 29**, the Full Moon in quirky Aquarius falls in your mysterious 12th House of Secrets and drags one of yours out into the light. Embarrassment is possible, but the upside is in finally releasing the need to suppress anything and, thereby, freeing your spirit.

> **KEEP IN MIND THIS MONTH**
>
> *Approach relationships like a mountain climber who is well secured by a rope and always has an escape route nearby if needed.*

KEY DATES

JULY 2–3 ★ *escape artist*
A brilliant biquintile between dynamic Mars and strategic Jupiter on **July 2** turns you into Houdini. There's no trap you can't evade, no puzzle you can't solve. Such talents could come in handy on **July 3**, when a Sun-Jupiter quincunx can lead to overcommitment or poor judgment in personal matters. Trying new experiences is healthy as long as you balance excessive optimism with common sense.

JULY 9-10 ★ *wise and foolish*

Another crossing of intelligence and foolishness arises with a smart Sun-Jupiter biquintile on **July 9** followed by a foolhardy quincunx between Mars and Jupiter on **July 10**. This story could start with a brilliant move that encourages being overconfident and taking on more than you can handle. The Mars-Jupiter aspect sparks misdirected anger, but there is yet another planetary source of insight to help regain your balance. The Sun trines inventive Uranus, which is especially good at coming to the rescue with unconventional solutions.

JULY 18 ★ *no need to quarrel*

The Sun and Mercury form challenging sesquisquares with overinflated Jupiter that can blow a small difference of opinion out of proportion. A misinterpretation of what's been said could trigger a response that only adds more fuel to the fire. You're being tested to see if you can maintain your focus as more and more information comes pouring into your mind. Think quickly, but speak slowly to avoid giving answers that precipitate frustrating arguments.

SUPER NOVA DAYS
JULY 24-27 ★ *gentle magic*

A complex Mars-Neptune square on **July 24** requires a delicate touch, since your actions can generate surprisingly sensitive responses from others. Practice the art of gentle persuasion and let instinct guide your behavior, because your inner sense probably works better than so-called common sense. Feel your way through situations to move forward gently rather than with force. Talkative Mercury creates clever biquintiles with Neptune on **July 26** and Jupiter on **July 27**, a sign that intuition is an ally that can inspire you with great answers, even if you barely understand the questions.

JULY 30-31 ★ *mixed messages*

A klutzy quincunx between precise Mercury and impressionistic Neptune on **July 30** can make for some slippery thinking and sloppy communication. This is wonderful, though, for poetic speech and imaginative expression. However, when facts are important, do your research and stick to the script, since winging it may drive you to make inaccurate statements. A stressful square between Mars, the planet of go, and Saturn, the planet of stop, on **July 31** can make even simple chores exhausting. Tackle one vital task with concentration, rather than scattering your forces.

AUGUST

IN THE RIGHT DIRECTION

On **August 6**, your ruling planet Jupiter turns direct after four months of backward movement. This forward shift in your 10th House of Career and Community is likely to expand your understanding of your role in society and even lead to new professional opportunities. Plans that were bubbling under the surface during the retrograde cycle can be expected to emerge in the days and weeks ahead. A powerful Saturn-Pluto trine exact on the same day is a slow-acting transit that provides a sense of purpose that taps into your deep desire to be of service to humanity. Invest in developing your talents to reach the highest level of potential that's available to you now. Energetic Mars's entry into your 4th House of Home and Family, also on **August 6**, may stimulate plenty of discussion that can change the ways you connect with those around you. Moving furniture and rearranging rooms can make your living space more functional and add vitality to your life.

The Leo New Moon on **August 12** sparks exciting ideas that add creativity to your daily routine. Imagination abounds with limitless Neptune opposing the Sun-Moon conjunction, but this compassionate planet could also inspire you to make sacrifices that wind up costing more than you anticipate. Acts of kindness are, of course, encouraged, but avoid making an open-ended commitment that could prove draining in the long run. The Full Moon on **August 28** is a total Lunar Eclipse in your sign, provoking strong emotional reactions. Its message is to trust yourself, for even so-called experts can't be relied upon to know what's best for you. You discover more by following your own instincts—though they may lead you astray at times—than by allowing others to influence you too strongly.

> **KEEP IN MIND THIS MONTH**
>
> *Your inspiration is worth more than all the facts in the world. When you feel it inside, you're closer to making it real.*

KEY DATES

AUGUST 1-2 ★ *hungry mind*

Your enthusiasm could lead you to overstate your case on **August 1**, when a Mercury-Jupiter sesquisquare favors salesmanship over facts. Still, your hunger to learn more and speak openly is admirable, activated by an expansive Sun-Jupiter trine exact on **August 2**. Your zeal should make you persuasive, although it can expose your gullibility. Be sure you're dealing with trustworthy individuals before buying into any schemes.

AUGUST 9 ★ *encouraging words*

A cooperative trine between fact-based Mercury and faith-driven Jupiter enriches your communication skills and your ability to grasp bold new concepts, making you a captivated student and a fascinating teacher. Your mind is very sharp and notices where details are needed to turn a promise into reality. This is excellent for motivating a team, since you back up your plan with the steps required to execute it.

AUGUST 13-14 ★ *fantasies conquer facts*

August 13 has planet waves rippling in several directions, including a Mercury-Uranus quincunx that tightens the nervous system with pressure to explain your unusual ideas. Loving Venus joins limiting Saturn—a sign of social insecurity that could have you underestimating your worth. Yet the Sun opposes your key planet Neptune as you seek spiritual refuge from life's demands. An escape into fantasy, especially of the romantic kind, is a less effective route to travel. On **August 14**, Mercury opposes Neptune, sensitizing communication so that each word is loaded with emotion. While this is wonderful for creative expression and compassionate conversation, it tends to fuzz facts in favor of dreams.

SUPER NOVA DAYS
AUGUST 23-25 ★ *sharp mind, tender heart*

The Sun enters your 7th House of Partnerships on **August 23** while a hyperactive Mars-Jupiter opposition can urge you to leap with nowhere to land. Measure your circumstances carefully before you launch yourself into action. Mental Mercury's squares to Mars and dogmatic Jupiter on **August 24 and 25**, respectively, spur debates that add more heat than light. A Venus-Neptune opposition on **August 25** is supersensitive, which is sweet for romance and pleasure but not helpful for forming objective assessments of the intrinsic value of objects or relationships.

AUGUST 28-30 ★ *the wisdom of emotion*

Feelings may overflow with the Lunar Eclipse in compassionate Pisces on **August 28**. Yet even if they seem overly dramatic, these strong emotions can wash away old needs for approval from someone who doesn't give you the respect you deserve. It's better to back off than try to justify yourself to such individuals. A Mercury-Neptune quincunx on **August 30** may bring unreliable information from a usually reliable source. Seek a second opinion if you have any doubts.

SEPTEMBER

RELATIONSHIP SHIFT

Saturn, the reality planet, steps into discerning Virgo and your 7th House of Partnerships on **September 2** for a stay of two-plus years. It's time to take a hard look at where you stand in personal and professional relationships and begin the serious work of improving them. The urgency for change can be especially intense with a partial Solar Eclipse, also in the 7th House, on **September 11**. This is a supercharged event with electric Uranus opposing the New Moon Eclipse, which is also squared by expanding Jupiter, penetrating Pluto, and punchy Mars. There's a tremendous amount of planetary action that's bound to make change a strong theme in your connections with others. Whether you're going public to get deserved attention, rebelling against a controlling mate, or jumping into a new social arena, it's wiser to take the initiative than to wait and react to unexpected events. This seems difficult if your emotions are all over the place, but the magic is in your heart, not what logic dictates. Just be gentle with yourself by recognizing that there are no mistakes—only experiences that help you learn as you go.

The Full Moon in go-getter Aries on **September 26** puts a jolt into your 2nd House of Money and Resources, moving you to maximize your assets. Advance your skills with training, launch a business plan, or get in better shape to increase your self-worth. Clever Mercury enters Scorpio on **September 27**, channeling diffuse feelings into a narrow focus and empowering you to go the distance in your thinking and communicating. Impassioned Mars in watery Cancer swims into your 5th House of Love on **September 28**, nurturing your personal life. Open your heart to romance and play by stretching your creativity and connecting with your inner child.

> **KEEP IN MIND THIS MONTH**
>
> *Don't hold on tightly or judge yourself while the wheels are still spinning, especially if you're vacillating between confidence and self-doubt.*

KEY DATES

SEPTEMBER 3-4 ★ *overdoing it*

A big, fat Sun-Jupiter square on **September 3** urges you to aim for more in your personal or professional life. Jupiter squares are about raising expectations, yet with a tendency to go too far that requires a bit of restraint to hit the mark. A brilliant Mercury-Jupiter quintile on **September 4**, though, can save the day with an innovative idea and a compelling argument.

SEPTEMBER 8-9 ★ *graceful moves*

Sweet Venus turns direct on **September 8**, permitting love and pleasure to begin flowing more freely in the weeks ahead. A sesquisquare from Mercury and a trine from Mars, both to Neptune, could make you careless on details but slick on execution. Information may be unclear, but your smooth moves and intuition carry you through the most awkward situations. You can lead others with such subtlety that they think they're leading themselves. This gentle touch can be critical on **September 9**, when an electric Sun-Uranus opposition incites uncooperative behavior but, hopefully, also awakens a breakthrough in consciousness.

SUPER NOVA DAYS
SEPTEMBER 11-13 ★ *riders on the storm*

The Solar Eclipse on **September 11** sends lightning bolts through your life, surprising you with exciting discoveries, sudden losses, and unexpected changes of attitude. Temporarily lower your standards of order and control to survive the storm. A Sun-Neptune quincunx on **September 12** springs a leak of emotion that may not make sense while it's happening, but will relieve some internal pressure. Happily, little Mercury and giant Jupiter align in a constructive sextile on **September 13** that makes it possible to patch up a misunderstanding. The knowledge planets send you merrily on your way by revealing a road map to carry you safely toward your next grand adventure.

SEPTEMBER 18-19 ★ *intuitive insights*

On **September 18**, your intuition could be off the chart and working at a very keen level, especially on your job. A Sun-Neptune biquintile and a Mercury-Neptune trine weave reality and imagination together in an intelligent way to show you patterns that others can't see. Share your insights discreetly, though, as a Sun-Pluto square on **September 19** can provoke the ire of a person in power. You have the right to assert yourself, but do it carefully to avoid instigating a conflict.

SEPTEMBER 21 ★ *being human*

A soft Venus-Neptune opposition and a hard Mars-Pluto opposition fill the day with complexity. Feelings of insecurity could prompt personal attacks or a plunge into despair. If either happens, ask for the support of a friend, as you don't need to go through this alone. But if you are willing to explore an emotional transformation, it's likely that your experience will be one of passion and exhilaration.

OCTOBER

FREEDOM AND FAITH

Your traditional ruling planet, Jupiter, brings rumbles of change with two major aspects this month. On **October 9**, it forms the last of three tense squares with revolutionary Uranus, a mind-blowing event that activates exciting visions of more freedom in your future. Restlessness can be expected; make sure to invest it in creating something new rather than digging up dirt from the past. Whatever's been brewing inside since the first transit in late January is finally ready to pop. Jupiter's supportive sextile with Neptune on **October 29** has a very different flavor. This is a soft and subtle opening of your spiritual awareness and artistic abilities. A sense of peace operates in the background in spite of any disturbances in your day-to-day life. Faith in yourself and the universe grows in moments of meditation, prayer, or quiet time in nature. Music, art, dance, and poetry soothe your soul and can inspire creativity in all areas of your life.

The New Moon in diplomatic Libra on **October 10** in your 8th House of Intimacy reshuffles your agreements with others. Generous Jupiter's assistance makes this a time for getting better deals in all of your exchanges. Mercury turns retrograde on **October 11**, beginning three weeks of review and revision. Travel and education are two areas likely to require extra attention to every detail. The Taurus Full Moon on **October 26** in your 3rd House of Communication is strengthened by a trine from solid Saturn that stabilizes your thoughts and adds authority to your words. On **October 31**, Neptune, your sign's modern ruler, turns direct after five months in reverse. Neptune's change in direction arrives right on the heels of its sextile with hopeful Jupiter, allowing psychic forces, spiritual impulses, and vivid fantasies to flow more freely.

> **KEEP IN MIND THIS MONTH**
>
> *Seek out a calm and caring person who can help you find your way back to a more peaceful state, especially if your mind is buzzing with anxious thoughts.*

KEY DATES

OCTOBER 1 ★ *nerves of brilliance*
The Moon in Gemini triggers the upcoming Jupiter-Uranus square with hard aspects to both planets, releasing a great deal of nervous energy. You could feel scattered with a sudden confrontation at home destabilizing your day. However, slowing Mercury forms a sextile with Saturn that adds a safety net of reason and

maturity that should keep chaos from getting out of hand and, ideally, turn high-frequency emotions into constructive ideas.

SUPER NOVA DAYS
OCTOBER 7-9 ★ *sudden delight*
Venus, the pleasure planet, enters your 7th House of Partnerships on **October 7**, producing opportunities for sharing life's joys. You could, though, attract a picky person, so respect his or her ways if you want to take this connection to the next level. The Sun sextiles Jupiter on **October 8** while Mars sextiles Saturn. This pair of positive aspects combines an ambitious idea with the means to make it real. **October 9** brings the Jupiter-Uranus square as Mars makes a disorderly sesquisquare with Neptune, a combination of great enthusiasm but possibly sloppy execution. Walk, don't run, toward your dream.

OCTOBER 12-13 ★ *restrained pleasures*
A lovely Sun-Neptune trine on **October 12** could make for a dreamy Friday night as imagination and hope shine. But reality comes calling on **October 13** as Venus conjoins no-nonsense Saturn. A good time is still possible, but in a responsible, contained way that stays within a budget financially and under control emotionally.

OCTOBER 21 ★ *circular arguments*
Retrograde Mercury backs into an edgy semisquare with opinionated Jupiter, which can jar judgment and blur details. Overstating positives and underestimating risks are possible. However, this can also be a day for a wide-ranging conversation that fills in gaps in your knowledge. You may discover something that could alter long-term plans, but it's better to know about it now. Philosophical differences may spin in circular arguments in which neither side really hears what the other is saying. If good humor is fading, cool down the rhetoric to avoid a verbal battle.

OCTOBER 27-29 ★ *keep it real*
Standing up for your beliefs makes sense with a proud Sun-Jupiter semisquare on **October 27**, but don't waste your breath on a person too close-minded to hear what you're saying. Venus aligns with a difficult square to Jupiter and a quincunx to Neptune on **October 29**. Your feelings can be easily bruised when others don't respond to your desires. You may be asking for too much, so if you wish to create intimacy, reduce your expectations to come closer to what someone is able to give.

NOVEMBER

LEAD WITH DISCRETION

The Scorpio New Moon on **November 9** is squared by metaphysical Neptune and trined by physical Mars, continuing the powerful spiritual activity started late last month. Studying with a master or mentor and sharing your own wisdom with others are healthy ways to experience this enlightening energy. Mars turns retrograde on **November 15** in your 5th House of Love and Creativity. Retracing your steps in these heartfelt areas is likely through late January, when Mars begins moving forward again. A desire to retreat can keep you from expressing yourself fully, but just be cautious rather than clamming up completely. On **November 22**, the Sun enters dauntless Sagittarius, the sign that occupies the top of your chart and represents your public life. There are more exciting opportunities for recognition at work or as a community leader—another reason not to allow retrograde Mars to pull you back into the shadows.

The Gemini Full Moon on **November 24** is usually a high-spirited event. This year, it stretches across your most public and private houses, which can create tension as you're pulled between your inner life and the outer world. However, stern Saturn makes a hard square to the Full Moon that reduces its tendency to overdose on activity. There's a clear message for you to set your priorities and stick to them. Focus your attention on the most important task, and you can make slow but steady progress. One solid step forward to lasting accomplishment is worth more than several delightful dances that are quickly forgotten. Revolutionary Uranus turns direct on the day of the Full Moon, opening your wings so that you can begin your flight to freedom.

> **KEEP IN MIND THIS MONTH**
>
> *Self-doubt is not a reason to avoid responsibility, but a note of caution reminding you to be a thoughtful leader.*

KEY DATES

NOVEMBER 4-5 ★ *heal the past*

Powerful Pluto is aroused by a semisquare from the willful Sun on **November 4** and a square from approval-seeking Venus on **November 5**. These aspects can result in power struggles rooted in distrust. Don't bury your feelings just because you disagree with someone; discuss issues kindly to demonstrate your goodwill. Old wounds can reopen with Venus-Pluto aspects, evoking painful feelings when no harm is intended. Being vulnerable with a willing partner can deepen a relationship.

NOVEMBER 10-12 ★ *follow a fantasy*

Communicative Mercury, moving forward since **November 1**, reenters secretive Scorpio on **November 10**, where it's not likely to be especially chatty. Your mind runs toward the mysterious, and you prefer research and depth over trivialities. The Sun's square with nebulous Neptune on **November 11** brings out the pied piper instinct that could have you foolishly following a fraud or leading a group astray. But if the point is to escape from reality, you're on the right track. A Venus-Neptune sesquisquare on **November 12** foments tender feelings that could confuse compassion with love.

NOVEMBER 16-18 ★ *the heart is wiser than the head*

Perceptions could be off when nearsighted Mercury makes a tense semisquare with farsighted Jupiter on **November 16**. Words are easily misinterpreted as your mind is challenged to stretch itself to handle the contrast between high hopes and critical comments. On **November 18**, a magical quintile between astrology's darlings, Venus and Jupiter, pulls delight out of difficult situations and shows you answers to daunting questions about intimacy, love, and self-worth.

SUPER NOVA DAYS

NOVEMBER 24-26 ★ *a steady path to fulfillment*

The noisy Gemini Full Moon, wild Uranus turning direct, and a mentally hazy Mercury-Neptune square on **November 24** make for a very complex day. Resist the impulse to leap into action, which can put you in an even more perilous position. You radiate confidence and increase your likelihood of success with a surefooted approach rather than a leap into the unknown. Breathe deeply to gather yourself, because precise aim is required to hit your target. A forgiving trine between Venus and Neptune on **November 26** brings joy with little effort on your part. Life can be sweet, even without a lover or a bankroll, as pleasure unfolds for you naturally now.

NOVEMBER 29-30 ★ *just rewards*

A slick Sun-Neptune quintile on **November 29** shows you a shortcut at work or a creative way to do your job. But cold Saturn's square to the Sun on **November 30** demands that you prove your worth by doubling your efforts or handling additional responsibilities. Don't give in without asking for fair compensation for your work.

PISCES

DECEMBER

PLANETARY FIREWORKS

This is one of the wildest Decembers in recent memory. Philosophical Jupiter makes a once-every-thirteen-years conjunction with transformational Pluto on **December 11**, creating deep tremors of change that may eventually alter your career. A profound reexamination of your beliefs can leave you doubting what you knew to be true in the past, but whatever is left standing will be clearer and more powerful than ever. Teaching, preaching, and telling it like it is are likely once the dust settles. On **December 18**, Jupiter enters Capricorn in your 11th House of Groups, which should make you a more organized team member and a more effective leader in the year ahead. From **December 19 to 22**, Mercury and the Sun conjunct Pluto, enter Capricorn, and conjunct Jupiter, which can bring the effects of the two outer planets' potent union to the surface. Buried feelings and family secrets are uncovered and intensify the holidays. Stress levels could be high, which is why keeping a cool head is so important. Revealing long-hidden truths can be healing but could also be a pretty upsetting operation.

The Sagittarius New Moon on **December 9** is hemmed between tense squares from rigid Saturn and explosive Uranus that can ramp up workplace pressure. Be inventive and fast on your feet to adapt to sudden changes, exceptional demands, and unreasonable administrators. If you've ever considered venturing into a new field or starting your own business, those desires are activated now. On **December 23**, the Full Moon joins assertive Mars in sensitive Cancer while opposing the Sun, Mercury, and Jupiter. This can fill the holiday table with angry opinions derived from wounded feelings. Speak the truth without self-pity if real communication is your goal.

> **KEEP IN MIND THIS MONTH**
>
> *There's more going on than can be explained or assimilated, so bite off a little bit at a time to avoid emotional indigestion.*

KEY DATES

DECEMBER 1 ★ *immune to criticism*

Mental Mercury leaps into Sagittarius, where blunt honesty overcomes discretion. Fortunately, a savvy sextile between loving Venus and outgoing Jupiter tends to keep disagreements from turning ugly and, in fact, favors delight with others over fighting with them. Even the most critical individuals are unlikely to shake your good humor, so you can enjoy playing with anyone.

DECEMBER 5-7 ★ *independent spirit*
Accommodating Venus squares individualistic Uranus before sashaying into persevering Scorpio on **December 5**. Don't settle for anything less than you think you deserve. But if you hit a brick wall with someone on **December 6**, you won't need to knock it down with logic when you can come up with a clever way to work around the resistance. On **December 7**, the Sun squares Uranus, giving you the spunk to fight back against anyone who tries to control you.

DECEMBER 11-13 ★ *riding the big one*
Jupiter joins Pluto on **December 11**, which can jolt your reality. But this influence will roll out over a period of weeks, while two fast-moving aspects bring more comforting news now. A socially skillful Venus-Mars trine on **December 11** brings pleasure to ordinary activities and helps you prod others in a gentle and inoffensive manner. A steadying Venus-Saturn sextile on **December 12** enables you to earn trust and show reliability as a friend or colleague. On **December 13**, intelligent Mercury sextiles Neptune, giving voice to your imagination and enlightening you with a sincere and compassionate message.

SUPER NOVA DAYS
DECEMBER 20-22 ★ *intensity rising*
On **December 20**, Mercury joins Jupiter while the Sun joins Pluto, an intense combination that could make you more opinionated or find you facing a verbal bully. If you're looking for a philosophical tussle, then speak up, especially if you have an ally who supports your position. The Sun's entry into Capricorn on **December 21**, the Winter Solstice, usually provides stability, but an extremely sensitive Venus-Neptune square on **December 22** touches your sentimental side. A Sun-Jupiter conjunction on the same day tends toward exaggeration, so small slights can feel like major insults. Still, your generosity and idealism shine through as you demonstrate the true spirit of the holiday season.

DECEMBER 26 ★ *holiday indulgence*
Mars opposes Jupiter today, a high-energy aspect that stirs your rarely seen competitive side. This can also increase your libido and a need to play, whether in serious adult games or in a more innocent and childlike manner. An ill-fitting sesquisquare between the confident Sun and fanciful Neptune can be exhilarating but may also produce unrealistic expectations and extravagant promises.